CHAOS IN THE NOVEL

THE NOVEL IN CHAOS

CHAOS IN THE NOVEL
THE NOVEL IN CHAOS

ALVIN J. SELTZER

SCHOCKEN BOOKS • NEW YORK

Library of Congress Cataloging in Publication Data

Seltzer, Alvin J   1939–
    Chaos in the novel, the novel in chaos.

    Includes bibliographical references.
    1. Fiction—History and criticism. I. Title.
PN3491.S4   809.3′3   73-91347

TO MADELINE

"the sweet'st companion that e'er man
bred his hopes out of."

Acknowledgments

I'd like to thank Professors Paul West, Philip Young, and Morton Levitt for their sensitive readings of the original manuscript, their helpful comments and advice. I'm especially indebted to Professor David H. Webster and Professor Robert Frank for their painstakingly close, conscientious reading of the manuscript, their extremely perceptive and useful comments and suggestions, general counsel, and encouragement. I owe as much to these two men as to their minds; their great, inspiring humanity, compassion, and concern have helped both me and this book out of chaos many times. I'm eternally grateful to them.

I'd also like to thank my brother, Professor Leon F. Seltzer, for his valuable advice on style and presentation, his broad scholarly background which helped me fill in many vital gaps, and a series (still running) of stimulating, exciting, provocative discussions on chaotic vision and chaotic art which did much to germinate and nurture this project.

I was most fortunate to be able to work with John Thornton, an editor whose understanding of what I was doing and what else needed to be done helped considerably in getting this into its final form.

For general but crucial contributions to the thinking which led to this book, I owe deep thanks to Professors Mabel P. Worthington, Deborah Austin, and Elmer Borklund; Philip and Elaine Terranova, Sandra Suino, Samuel Sandweiss, Marian Pehowski, Rebecca P. Guth, Sheldon Berkowitz, Jane Smith, Lynn Fasten, Joshua Gold, Celeste Cheyney, and Lenore Snyder. And for equally valuable support, encouragement, and infinite patience with me as I worked on this, I'm profoundly grateful to Jane Liebman, Kenneth Schaefer, Sue Ellen Holbrook, Paul Shallers, Vickie Poulakis, Frank and Geraldine Burd, Barry Morgenstern, Gerald Croce, and Joseph Friedman. I must also include thanks here for many of my students at Temple University who have added much to my knowledge and understanding of experimental fiction. So many of my ideas on the novel were crystallized in front of them and in response *to* them.

Finally, for their love, I want to thank my parents, Rose and Joseph Seltzer, and my daughter, Lara.

A permanent resident of chaos myself, I would have taken far fewer sidetrips to sanity without the constant love, understanding, support, and encouragement of a most wonderful wife who, with truly extraordinary patience and good temper, worked with me on this book literally page by page and phrase by phrase. She helped bring to fruition and expression every idea in this book, and from moment to moment, kept me somehow on top of the clutter in my own mind which did everything possible to keep it from ever coming to completion. To my wife, Madeline, I owe not only eternal thanks, but the book itself, for I honestly cannot imagine its (or my own) existence without her.

Elkins Park, Pennsylvania
January 1974

Contents

CONTENTS

PART II: THE NOVEL IN CHAOS

PART III: CONCLUSION

CHAOS IN THE NOVEL

THE NOVEL IN CHAOS

Introduction

Like any literary form, the novel can be used for many purposes, but those we consider its greatest writers have guided it toward significant ends—that is, toward saying something important about man's existence, something basic and quintessential to what his life is all about. Often their principal preoccupation has been to define the quality, worth, and meaning of life; to investigate values and ideas, and to pattern complexities into some coherent form which eventually yields explanations. "If the world were clear," said Camus, "art would not exist." And so such a novel attempts to *clarify* our universe, defeating mystery where it can, and bringing that mystery into sharper focus where it cannot penetrate it altogether. To enter such realms is necessarily to confront darkness and dilemma on every level, but the serious novelist is willing to grapple with whatever drives him forward in his search for meaning, aids in his exploration of human problems.

The key word here is *meaning,* and it is this toward which most major novels are directed, for it is in the form itself that meaning is discovered or apprehended, that complexities finally coalesce into some form of workable knowledge which contributes to our lucidity. By shaping experience as only it can, the novel becomes itself one of our most essential experiences because it provides the insight, intelligence, and coherence which life alone never offers. Man therefore uses the novel to learn more about his own life—and this is true whether he's writing one or reading one.

Truth, however, is out of fashion these days, and the search for meaning seems increasingly futile, if not absurd, to the existential man who perceives his universe as unfathomable, phenomenological, and utterly alien to the human mind. Most contemporary novelists (whether they delight in or despair of their view) see life as quintessentially chaotic—an interesting but ultimately meaningless jumble of phenomena which simultaneously tempt and thwart our efforts to structure impressions into meaningful patterns. In the face of apparent chaos (beyond which seems to lie not a deeper reality of truth or order, but only a deeper level of chaos), man seems finally to have admitted defeat, to have abandoned his quest. But now the question remains: Is the novel to be abandoned too? Has its original function become outmoded?

Of course, man will continue to write novels—a habit tends to endure long after the need for it has waned—but that is not the important point. The real questions are whether the novel is *worth* writing anymore, whether its creation can still seem a noble endeavor rather than a tired ritual or trivial pastime. Can the novel still purport to examine life, or must this aim finally be disregarded as presumptuous? If not, then what can the novel do that it has not already done by now; and if so, can it be used for any other purpose worth achieving? Finally, how far can the form be stretched for survival before it undoes itself entirely and becomes another mode of experience?

It is, of course, the philosophically oriented novelist who is most likely to exploit his form as an escavating tool in his search for truth, meaning, and values; but any author who probes deeply enough into the most critical aspects of human existence eventually finds himself confronting the problem of chaos at some level. Basically, there are five levels on which an examination of life can lead toward a significant thematic statement embodying chaos:

1. *Inner conflict:* man's battle with his own soul to discover his essence and identity—a Kurtz-like dive into his inner heart of darkness. *Lord Jim, The Sound and the Fury,* and *Molloy* depict struggles of this type.

2. *Conscious conflict:* man's attempt to arrive at a satisfactory value system; to create meaning, order, and beauty in his life; to grapple with his dreams; to understand his limitations and potentials by direct confrontation with the qualities that make him unique. *Hamlet* is the paragon of this type of creation, but novels

such as *To the Lighthouse, Lord Jim,* and *Miracle of the Rose* also find their focus here.

3. *Social conflict:* man's struggle with other men in a broad but clearly defined context: usually societal or political. The emphasis here is on an examination of external reality leading to a definition of basic needs. The primary conflict is often between good and evil, tradition and revolution, or incompatible ethical codes. At bottom, such a work always presents a clash of visions: one mode of perception collides with others, thereby disrupting successful, constructive intercourse between one mind, sensibility, or imagination and another. *Tristram Shandy, As I Lay Dying, Light in August, The Hamlet,* and *Naked Lunch* would represent variations of this type.

4. *Human conflict:* man's struggle with *man* in a narrow context. Love and hate become important subjects here, as well as the difficulty involved in achieving meaningful communication in our most crucial relationships. The inability to get close enough to another person; the impossibility of ever knowing or understanding another fully; the deceptiveness of appearances when one seeks to fathom the reality of his fellow human beings; and the problem of sustaining valuable relationships founded upon temporal feelings and passions—all these frustrations lie at the core of such novels as *To the Lighthouse, The Sound and the Fury, As I Lay Dying, Light in August, Absalom, Absalom!, Molloy,* and *Jealousy.*

5. *Spiritual conflict:* man's confrontation with the universe— all the mysteries which shake, uproot, or undermine his own ideas about himself. Time, death, God, chaos, art, suffering, etc., are all prominent subjects as man searches desperately and often self-destructively for meaning. Man here reaches beyond morality into mystery; and on this level, good and evil become meaningless, arbitrary distinctions based on absurdly relative systems, while only suffering seems verifiably real. Values here tend to be weak at best and therefore based more on the quality of the struggle itself than on what is ultimately attained or even recognized. *The Trial, The Confidence-Man, The Sound and the Fury, Malone Dies, The Unnamable,* and *In the Labyrinth* are all expressions of chaos on this level.

Several kinds of conflicts can of course operate in a single literary work, and indeed, the greatest masterpieces touch on all of them. We can see, though, that each of the five basic conflicts dealt with by most serious writers sweeps us into an area swarming with complications. The fact that a writer decides to treat any one area does not, however, necessarily predispose him to rendering a chaotic situation or statement. Here, perhaps, we can distinguish between apparent confusion and genuine chaos: whereas confusion represents a general state of disorder or complexity ultimately resolved within or by its form, chaos occurs when things do not fit, when the author is content to rest upon his negative capability, feeling no obligation to synthesize. He refuses to resolve contradictions into paradox, observations into explanation, hypotheses into knowledge, endings into conclusions. *Tom Jones*, then, may be full of confusions, but it is not a work of chaos, for the confusion is successfully contained within a structure that leads to a vision of order embracing a positive moral statement.

The obvious temptation for the novelist is to allow his form to frame its substance to the point where his matter becomes impregnated with meaning: the conclusion to *Wings of the Dove*, for example, presents a resounding curtain-line that rounds off the story by revealing a pattern of morality in human behavior and values which leads to inevitable consequences. Kate loses, Millie wins, Merton learns—and the point has been made. The general disorder in human affairs, which has throughout the novel veered perilously close to chaos, now seems less frightening because the final page makes a kind of moral sense that satisfies us in a way in which we all want to be satisfied: it brings meaning to one jumbled area of life by implying a universal law beyond human control which regulates morality and dispenses justice.

But how valid a law is this? Does it really seem consistent with our experiences and observations, or is it a false, if convenient frame of the intellect, methodically contrived to impose meaning where none exists? The novel form itself, in short, tends to give structure, pattern, and meaning to chaos, thereby transforming it into order—things suddenly *do* start fitting because the novel's structure and conventions have forced them to fit. As with a jigsaw puzzle, the pieces have been cut in advance and the final picture predetermined all along, no matter how much confusion has been thrown in along the way.

The compensatory novel, by imposing meaning upon its material, has no validity as a work of chaos—worthy as it may be in all other respects. While a list of such works would surely include some of the greatest and most powerful novels in our literature (besides *Wings of the Dove*, a sample selection might contain such masterpieces as *Crime and Punishment, The Brothers Karamazov, Huckleberry Finn, Moby-Dick, The Mill on the Floss, A Farewell to Arms*, and *Ulysses*), all seem finally to have made some compromise in their vision for the sake of their art. Such novels seem the product of an aesthetic temperament which, because it is unwilling or unable to concede the inevitable conclusion of its chaotic intimations, uses the novel form to supply motivations, meanings, answers, conclusions, resolutions, or higher laws of reason which the universe itself never truly implies. Novelists of this temperament tend to exploit the therapeutic benefits of art, using their form to remedy rather than simply reflect their frustration. One suspects that in such books as *Huckleberry Finn, Moby-Dick*, or *The Brothers Karamazov*, the authors were simply too disturbed by the pain implicit to their vision to pursue it all the way to despair. Perhaps negative capability proved too much of a threat to these writers' psychological well-being; at any rate, their works provide such tension, that one senses desperation in their novels' swerve toward formal resolution. Certainly it is the powerful portrayal of chaos that constitutes the real force of these books and seems much more authentic, compelling, and memorable than their conventional conclusions, which attempt to push that chaos away. Nevertheless, such creations allow us our chaos and our comfort, too—and the combination is indeed so pleasing for both writer and reader, that this type of work has long constituted the novel's greatest tradition.

On the other hand, though, the writer who deals with chaos and is content to *end* his novel without *concluding* it shows a kind of aesthetic (as well as psychological) courage which we are too apt to mistake for artistic irresponsibility or just plain slovenliness. We are annoyed at his dismissal of conventional structure just as Ben Jonson was offended by Shakespeare's disregard for the Greek unities. Many critics have, as a result, assumed that the form was breaking down when it was actually being expanded. Still, exhilaration with expansion inevitably leads sooner or later to a bursting point, and we do seem now to be in an era when the novel's very survival as a viable form has been quite legitimately called into question. Maximum freedom is, ultimately, another name for a vacuum; and the artist who opens his form too widely eventually eradicates its identity, its potency, and its usefulness.

Chaos is reality not chiseled, focused, or framed by form—and this is exactly the kind of experience offered by many contemporary writers who purposely and adamantly dismiss the intelligence which orders otherwise unselected life. These avant-garde novelists scorn the artificiality, contrivance, and outdated value systems built into the traditional novel, and attempt to rescue their form from obsolescence by experimenting with new techniques more suitable to a new sense of reality. The result is a work of multiplicity, fragmentation, and arbitrariness in place of the unity, wholeness, and cohesiveness previously achieved through conscious artistic control. And lest the form itself should imply control, most of these novels are set up to self-destruct on contact.

In all fairness, we must concede to the experimentalists the best motivations: if their creations are often destructive, so too are their destructions frequently creative. They are, after all, trying to salvage their form by reshaping it to serve the contemporary author and his audience. In the long run, it may well be those writers continuing to turn out conventional novels who will be seen to have impeded their form's potential development, for if the novel is to stay with us, it most probably will have to make the necessary evolutionary adjustments for survival in a new philosophical–psychological atmosphere, while losing none of its power as an art form. Contemporary attitudes certainly demand, at the least, that the novel be able to absorb existential vision and refract it through the varying depths and dimensions of our subconscious existence. It must manage, in short, to convey an impression of life contrary to the novel's very identity as form, as an ordering principle making structural sense (philosophically, psychologically, and aesthetically) by moving toward clarity, finality, resolution, and meaning.

But chaotic vision is so totally at odds with all sense of form that the two can hardly be true to each other without being unfaithful to themselves. Thus, while the compensatory novel finally provides more meaning than can be accommodated by a genuinely chaotic vision, the opposite danger becomes the pervasion of more chaos than can be accommodated by the form. Whereas form has too often seemed to shackle chaotic vision, that vision seems now to have shattered form, so that many experimental works, rather than impressing us as a different *kind* of novel, seem simply to be *less* of a novel. Like acid seeping deeply into the novel's texture, chaos burns so many holes through its form that any distinction between the life outside and inside its boundaries soon evaporates altogether. As a result, the novel loses its identity and, dissolving into the general disintegration of chaotic experience, becomes another form of raw life rather than a conscious, reflective representation of that life.

One can see why. Both consciousness and reflection reveal implicit faith in the efficacy and importance of our rational powers, but because experimental writers see our deepest identities as submerged somewhere in the subconscious, they necessarily regard reason and all its by-products as irrelevant and outmoded perceptual instruments. It's no wonder, then, that old notions of character (as complete, consistent, closed human beings) give way, along with other remnants of a world view resting on rationality; plot, theme, and structure, too, must disappear from the novel predicated on the proposition of chaos and dedicated to the principle of formlessness.

It is at this point, however, that certain things do become clear: the writer who chooses to express himself within a certain form must respect it enough to accept its limitations, for an excursion outside of the form usually becomes an entrance into a different type of experience which the reader must confront on different terms. If the novel form fails to satisfy the writer's purpose, he should by all means abandon it, but any attempt to stay within it while rebelling against the very bases of its identity (*as* artifice, for example, or conscious, controlled creation) is doomed to fail *as* a novel—even if it succeeds as another kind of experience. We must finally label irresponsible the novel which, in its determination to depict faithfully the full chaos of life, abdicates self-consciously any aesthetic criteria or obligations to the form's components. As an artist, the author must have the aesthetic power of his philosophical convictions, for in that alone lies his claim to our attention.

Between the compensatory novel (which reduces chaos to structured confusion) and the irresponsible novel (which sacrifices art to reproduce rather than represent true chaos) lies the genuinely chaotic novel which betrays neither its art nor its vision, but carefully camouflages structure or technique with disorienting effects to insure the impression that no meaning has been found in the area explored. The chaotic novel we may define as one that manages to incorporate its vision into its formal components: plot, structure, characterization, language, narrative technique, point of view, etc. Such a novel will express a sense of chaos *through* its components rather than achieve actual chaos from their abandonment. And just as when one sense is lost, the others tend to become sharpened, the artist of chaos can block out or handle eccentrically any one of the means through which the novel expresses itself without blurring at the same time the reader's perception of his ideas. The responsible novelist will, though, compensate *aesthetically* for anything he takes away by heightening or tightening one of the other aspects of his form so that the bewildered reader will at least have something stable to guide him through the confusion. There is, of course, no one component that is absolutely indispensable, and so the writer can do away with whichever one hinders his purpose, and strengthen whichever other one seems most appropriate. Beyond this, the amazing flexibility of the form enables subtle nuances to seep through that characterize the author's vision in all its individuality. What such novelists have in common, however, is the capability to explore some phase of life where things seem not to fit, only to conclude that they do indeed seem not to fit at all.

Because the novel's form tends to falsify chaotic vision by unifying experience in a meaningful way, it presents common aesthetic problems for those writers who regard the universe as basically impenetrable, mysterious, and meaningless. First of all, the novel must seem to explore rather than assert its apprehension of chaos; otherwise, it tends to become an existential tract. Second, its exploration must be as frenetic as it is futile. Typically, the novel reflects the intensely tormented state of its creator through an organic tension between his characters' drive for comprehension, and the resistance of a silent, inscrutable, impassive world. And finally, just as the cosmos blocks the writer's craving for clarity, so the writer, in turn, blocks the reader's expectations for elucidation—thus duplicating his own struggle and failure to capture in form what he cannot capture in life. The essential point here is that while the form's philosophical failure signifies fidelity to its vision, it still salvages an aesthetic triumph by remaining true to the demands of artistic creation.

The art of chaotic creation is characterized by the constant maintenance of a delicate but desperate tension between formal fulfillment and formlessness. The instant the mind controls chaos too tidily or tightly, the work becomes too ordered to reflect its vision faithfully; the novel begins to offer more meanings and make more sense than the world does, and so reverts to its traditional role of compensating for our own unsuccessful relations with reality. Aesthetically, then, the novel's components need to be completely realized, but to remain ambiguous or inconclusive in meaning. Thus, we're likely to have a fully drawn character who remains enigmatic, a carefully worked-out plot which results in obscurity and uncertainty, a perfectly balanced aesthetic structure which offers no philosophical correspondence for the harmony of its formal achievement (as distinguished from a Jane Austen novel, say, in which moral, thematic, and structural resolution all coincide).

Although the work itself must satisfy as an aesthetic whole, it is obvious that the writer must keep his novel in hand by forever letting it seem to get out of hand, for chaotic vision can be captured only through the form's failure to account for all it finds. The tension between freedom and form must not be permitted to go slack at any point. Indeed, it is crucial for the integrity of a work built on chaotic vision that it manage always to lead us on, while simultaneously leading us nowhere; we are drawn into a struggle that perpetually energizes, but never finalizes the work. Like the world itself, the chaotic novel is endlessly intriguing and evocative, but ultimately elusive and inconclusive.

To realize such a chaotic creation, in short, the writer must be willing to surrender a good deal of intellectual control while simultaneously tightening the reins on his aesthetic control. While the world may be outside of his authority, the aesthetics of his form are not. Unlike the world outside, *his* creation is manmade, and can therefore be *meaningfully* meaningless because it is conscious. Man's most valid compensation in a meaningless universe is aesthetic, not philosophical; and the one achievement should not imply victory on another level. Once it does, the result is a compensatory novel.[1]

1. Joyce and Proust, surely two of the greatest literary giants and innovators of our century, still used their art in a traditional way: to round off reality through a structure sufficiently complex to contain its own vast scope, account for all it caught within its sphere, and ultimately to affirm its own power as a perceptual agent. Joyce's *Ulysses*, for example, while providing chaotic texture, actually offers us a world dominated by reason. Meanings are hidden or submerged, perhaps, but they are lurking like nuggets throughout the work. Every word, pun, image, and allusion is purposeful, telling, and revealing; every chapter, every

Using this relationship between form and vision as our basic criterion, we can now distinguish at least five types of novels:

1. The *conventional novel* (represented by such works as *Tom Jones* and *Pride and Prejudice*) which uses form to reflect an ordered vision of reality.

2. The *compensatory novel* (represented by such works as *Moby-Dick, The Brothers Karamazov,* and *The Mill on the Floss*) which uses its form to control chaos, thereby exploiting its aesthetic power to compensate for its philosophical impotence.

3. The *inconclusive novel* (represented by such works as *The Mysterious Stranger, Great Expectations,* and *Steppenwolf*) which finds more chaos than its form can successfully accommodate through traditional structural resolution. The result is a work which *seems* conventional or compensatory for the most part, but which, while it cannot seem to conclude itself in a conventional way, has failed to set up a structure that would make inconclusiveness an *aesthetic* as well as a philosophical necessity. What such a novel gains in vision, it loses in art; the work is weakened by sudden structural collapse.

4. The *genuinely chaotic novel* (represented by such works as *Lord Jim, The Confidence-Man, The Trial, To the Lighthouse, The Sound and the Fury,* and *As I Lay Dying*) which exploits form to express chaotic vision: such works are philosophically inconclusive, but aesthetically whole. Both novel and vision retain their identity because, while man's ability to order, unify, and draw *relative* meanings from his experience helps to relieve him psychologically, it does not alter his painful existential condition. The author's artistic power is used only to convey, rather than to compensate for the anguish of philosophical impotence.

---

character, every literary, mythological, and historical reference is meaningful, fruitful, and relevant. The world of *Ulysses seems* chaotic, but is lucid at its core. One struggles to unlock the mysteries, but once the proper key is used, they *can* finally be interpreted, understood, absorbed. The chaotic presentation has no philosophical overtones or conceptual repercussions. The characters, for example, are all knowable, consistent, conventional creations; our impressions of Leopold, Molly, and Stephen are not substantially altered by different points of view or even the dazzling virtuosity of Joyce's narrative techniques. Likewise, the chaotic form only disguises but does not undermine a basically conventional structure which resolves the experience it frames while engendering clear themes. This, then, is compensatory rather than chaotic art. The latter will rarely present an appearance at odds with its reality, for it cannot conceive of reality as anything but another appearance.

5. The *irresponsible novel* (represented by such works as *How It Is* and *The Soft Machine*) which purposely abdicates the artificiality of the novel's components to render chaos more accurately. But chaos, of course, cannot render *any*thing—including itself—and so such works, while frequently exciting, lose the advantage of aesthetic controls which permit chaos to be experienced, appreciated, enjoyed, and remembered as artistic creation.

Whereas the inconclusive novel is a mutation of the conventional and compensatory novels, the irresponsible novel is a mutation of the genuinely chaotic novel, and reveals a form in supreme distress—unwilling to falsify its vision through form, yet unable to stop using that form as a means to express and end its struggle. But as his form continues to perpetuate meaning, the novelist ends by fighting that form until he has knocked out those components which constitute its vital organs. Chaotic vision is thus achieved at the expense of the form's survival, and the inevitable result is that successful operation in which the patient dies.

The greatest threat to the novel *as* a form has been the psychological–philosophical shift from a world view asserting ultimate order to one maintaining chaos to be the deepest level of reality. But this tension between form and a vision which upsets its basic principles (consistency of character, clarity of motivation, aptness of chronological narrative and one-dimensional point of view, proper integration of plot, structure, and theme; the value and validity of language and logic as agents of lucidity, etc.) is hardly new; it begins even in the eighteenth century to modify the way the novel delivers experience. Thus, right in the company of such figures as Moll Flanders, Clarissa Harlow, Tom Jones, and Elizabeth Bennett, we find Tristram Shandy, Gentleman— not so much a character as a mind, a sensibility, a point of chaotic perspective. His narrative, structured on the principles of Locke's theory of association, is deliberately distorted, splintered, fragmented. While there are a number of "stories" going on simultaneously, they are structured not according to concepts of order, but according to the dictates of *dis*order: the associative tracks in the mind by which one image, incident, or idea stimulates another not necessarily related in time, logic, or consequence. Chronological narrative is replaced by stream of consciousness, and plot itself is little more than the *story* of different streams of consciousnesses converging and colliding. Theme, in turn, is not only conditioned by chaotic vision, but revels in that chaos as a new, more fruitful and truthful approach to the realities which form our lives. The life of Tristram Shandy is less important than his opinions, and what this means, simply, is that existence is now defined by perception rather than the other way around. How the mind takes in experience becomes more important than the experience itself, and this new conception of our minds gives us ultimately a new conception of ourselves. Sterne not only incorporated this new awareness into the framework of his form, but he also exploited it for new kinds of comic, dramatic, and psychological effects that signify a major growth spurt in the evolution of the novel.

In the nineteenth century, Conrad and Melville struggled against but finally capitulated to the notion that the cosmos itself was chaotic at the core. Both *Lord Jim* and *The Confidence-Man* focus on the enigmatic human character, but as the implications grow, the nature of reality is itself called into question. Chaos is seen no longer as the product of deficient human perception, but as the sum of supreme lucidity. The reader is confronted with a world so baffling in its inscrutability, that he is forced eventually to surrender any sense of authority and adopt, instead, the author's own suspicion (quickly freezing into a conviction) that truth is unknowable in a universe so utterly alien to our minds. Man's previous psychological disorientation now becomes a philosophical dislocation as well, and man is ultimately as much estranged from a strange world as he is from a strange self.

In our century, the tradition of chaos has been carried forward by such writers as Faulkner, Woolf, and Kafka—all of whom allow chaotic notions to sink deeper and deeper into their novels' texture, conditioning treatment of style, character, narrative technique, structure, theme, and point of view. All external experience becomes suspect and subservient to individual perception (although subjectivity does not, at this point, necessarily imply solipsism) as the novel begins to shift from a direct representation of life to cubistic delineation of a private, relative, multi-faceted reality, apprehended through the mind but generated from a subconscious, irrational, unknowable part of ourselves. Any kind of conscious meaning is fraudulent because as our belief in the subconscious grows, the importance of logic subsides, and with it all its now disreputable constructs: language, reason, morality, philosophy, and even, perhaps, the novel itself.

So long as we can discuss a life which *seems* meaningless, we remain in the midst of our struggle and well within bounds of the system we are questioning. We still use our rational faculties to validate skepticism and project our struggle into the ordered realm of the novel. The chaotic novelists are dissenters, agnostics, skeptics, perhaps—but they are not atheists or nihilists. Once *that* step is taken, we *do* withdraw from the system entirely and begin to work on new assumptions which ultimately create a new life (and a new art) for ourselves. As new values are adopted, they become incorporated into the important elements of our lives—one of which is art itself.

In *The Myth of Sisyphus*, Camus points to the primary problem for the contemporary novelist (he who's writing in the calm *after* the storm rather than in the eye of it) by wondering whether the absurd work of fiction can retain its integrity when the form itself tempts explanations, interpretations, and conclusions at every turn. All principles, values, and conventions are built on assumptions about the meaning and purpose of our lives—and when the foundations for these assumptions begin to falter, we can hardly expect the rest of the system to remain standing. Camus' philosophical notions are very much to the point here, for his existential premises undermine some of the most basic tenets which have helped shape the novel since the eighteenth century. The assumption of absurdity in defining man's relations with his universe has repercussions which have shaken the novel so considerably, that we may well wonder whether it can survive as a viable form in our existential age.

As soon as we move from the fear that life may be meaningless to the conviction that it *is* meaningless, we have erased the most fundamental *raison d'être* for the novel that searches for meanings. All such investigation is irrelevant, even foolish now. There remains, in fact, not a single valid purpose for art beyond its very gratuitousness, and so we have little choice but to embrace this absence of deep purpose as itself a meaningful gesture of our free choice: a sign of self-definition through defiance. According to Camus, we need have no reason to create art beyond our desire to do so; we create because we enjoy the process of multiplying what we cannot unify. We like to project the tones, moods, and feelings of our existences onto as many different images as our imaginations can create and our minds contemplate. We want to feel our realities filtered through new forms which reflect the various facets of our lives. While these forms do not reveal meanings, they do offer interesting surfaces which in their richness, variety, and vitality, help ultimately to make us more intimate with our own existences and our own selves.

In his section on Absurd Creation, Camus, with admirable eloquence and thoroughness, lays down the new assumptions for an art which is no longer out to challenge chaos, but having already acknowledged it, proceeds to erect a thing of beauty on a foundation of meaninglessness.[2] What emerges is a new kind of manifesto for the novel,which describes the assumptions built into a great deal of serious contemporary fiction. The writer's intensity, one of the grand values in traditional works—and especially the cha-

2. Some sample passages follow: "the constant tension that keeps man face to face with the world, the ordered delirium that urges him to be receptive to everything leaves him another fever. In this universe the work of art is then the sole chance of keeping his consciousness and of fixing its adventures. Creating is living doubly. At the same time, it has no more significance than the continual and imperceptible creation in which the actor, the conqueror, and all absurd men indulge every day of their lives. All try their hands at miming, at repeating, and at re-creating the reality that is theirs. . . . For the absurd man it is not a matter of explaining and solving, but of experiencing and describing. Everything begins with lucid indifference. . . . the emotion delighting us when we see the world's aspects comes to us not from its depth but from their diversity. Explanation is useless, but the sensation remains, and, with it, the constant attractions of a universe inexhaustible in quantity. The place of the work of art can be understood at this point. . . . It marks both the death of an experience and its multiplication. . . . It does not offer an escape from the intellectual ailment. Rather, it is one of the symptoms of that ailment which reflects it throughout a man's whole thought. . . . For an absurd work of art to be possible, thought in its most lucid form must be involved in it. But at the same time thought must not be apparent except as the regulating intelligence. . . . The work of art is born of the intelligence's refusal to reason the concrete. . . . It will not yield to the temptation of adding to what is described a deeper meaning that it knows to be illegitimate. . . . The absurd work requires an artist conscious of these limitations and an art in which the concrete signifies nothing more than itself. It cannot be the end, the meaning, and the consolation of a life. Creating or not creating changes nothing. . . .

"Thus, I ask of absurd creation what I required from thought—revolt, freedom, and diversity. . . . In that daily effort in which intelligence and passion mingle and delight each other, the absurd man discovers a discipline that will make up the greatest of his strengths. The required diligence, the doggedness and lucidity thus resemble the conqueror's attitude. To create is likewise to give a shape to one's fate. . . .

"Let me repeat. None of this has any real meaning." (Albert Camus, *The Myth of Sisyphus*, New York: Random House, 1955 [pp. 69–86 *passim*].)

otic novel—is now as outdated as the old value of authorial sincerity, and is replaced by lucid indifference. As absurd creator, the novelist can at last afford to be indifferent (not to his art, of course, but to the meaning of his life)—to ignore the fruitless struggle for meaning, and to free himself and his form from any obligation to rationalize the world he presents to the reader. The imagination need work now for nothing beyond its own exercise, enjoyment, and enlightenment without reference to any ethical, philosophical, intellectual, or representational systems. Recognizing his art's gratuitousness, the writer can still use it to expand his consciousness of chaos, to live it more intensely, know it more intimately. No longer need he work toward clarity, cohesiveness, and conclusiveness, for he is not to be held accountable for the world he depicts; his sole responsibility is to his art.

Yet this new freedom of vision does not imply freedom *from* form, but only freedom *within* form. Camus admires the diligence, doggedness, and discipline by which the author shapes his fate and controls his form; it is in this determination and perseverance that he resembles the conqueror. The artist exploits his form to capture consciousness, and by so doing intensifies the experience of living out his meaningless life. Irrationality is no longer feared, but treasured as our sole relief in a universe that yields no meaning beyond what we create for ourselves. Now that the struggle for truth has ended in man's defeat, he can at last begin to assert his one valid claim to mastery: rather than despair in his nihilism, he can now rejoice in the existential freedom which allows him to determine his own meanings (whose only test of legitimacy is their existence in his imagination). In this new kind of art, as in life itself, we live from minute to minute, changing our interpretations along with our perspectives, always insecure and uncomfortable as our search for meaning becomes the product, as well as the process of this existential concept of fiction. But our discomfort and insecurity are actually welcomed as proof that we are perpetually "becoming" the selves we choose to create; it is we who define our realities, and life itself is no more than such constant consciousness of our changing conditions. The value of life is no longer to be determined by the truths we find, but only by the truths we create; life *is* process and awareness, neither of which has anything to do with ultimate answers. And our art is to *reflect* our lives rather than to *reconstruct* them into more meaningful, palatable forms.

What we experience in existential fiction, finally, is our protean impressions of a kaleidoscopic world of shifting points of view, cubistic spatial and temporal relationships, impenetrable objects, inconsistent, unfathomable, but infinitely mysterious characters, shadowy surfaces, and evocative images. And all this spins around in a void, the vacuum underpinning everything—the empty core of a cosmos totally incompatible with our deepest spiritual needs. But although all appearances are insubstantial and arbitrary, we are to realize too that the images we project onto nothingness become our defense, our expression of defiance, and our ultimate triumph over a meaningless universe. By filling with images and meanings the vacuum our natures abhor, we make life bearable, and finally do salvage something from the emptiness. Our whole lives are spent in efforts to fill in the cavities that challenge us, but as we fill them, we create the substance that defines us. We are gods, creating ourselves from nothing.

As philosophical exploration gives way to aesthetic intensification, the novel shifts its emphasis from probing to playing. Both writer and reader now play with forms not to master them, but simply to *know* them as facets of our lives. One life may be as chaotic as another, but there are an infinite variety of forms that chaos can take—and so the reader is treated to a protean performance in which the imagination seeks an assortment of guises to present the changing contours of its life. The progression of forms is not a meaningful sequence, but an arbitrary one: like a kaleidoscope, it reflects, refracts, splinters, gathers, breaks, grows, bursts, joins, erupts, dissipates, clusters, scatters, collects, shatters, amasses, explodes, fuses in a series of constantly changing patterns which generate the texture of an experience. By refusing to reason the concrete, art accepts a new position of humility: it seeks no longer to illuminate, but only to describe the reality it renders.

Such a theory seems reasonably compatible with the kind of experience the novel is able to provide; freedom, revolt, and diversity can certainly be projected (and *have* been by the chaotic novelists already mentioned) with the kind of artistic impact peculiar to the novel. Character, incident, tension, plot, and structure still seem valid ingredients for this type of work. Why, then, are we said to have a dead or decaying form on our hands? The answer lies, apparently, not in the theory, but in the novels themselves.

We can get some sense of what has happened by considering where four major contemporary novelists have taken us and their form. Beckett, Burroughs, Robbe-Grillet, and Genet are all great artists and influential innovators who have reshaped the novel radically to accommodate their chaotic visions, but who seem at the same time to be driving their form to extinction. Each represents a different theoretical approach to the form which promises regeneration, but seems to deliver death. In each case, too, the problem seems to be an increasing intolerance for the falsity of form itself; the traditional novel, it is felt, cannot deliver a satisfactory sense of chaos when its very components insinuate unity and cohesiveness. Since order as a means always figures as a misleading influence in the end, the novel that tries to transmit chaos through artifice will lose its vision to the form. The very conception of language, for example, is a way *out* of chaotic experience, so how can language be used as a way *into* it? One after another, the novel's components are seen to hamper, negate, and falsify chaotic vision—and so, one after another, they are purged, pried out, or severely deformed by the avant-garde writer.

Obviously, the fact that much of our lives is utterly chaotic and meaningless is no recent discovery: the novel has dealt with this brutal truth all along and seems somehow to have survived it. Yet it is ironic that the novel, which has so often been used to convey chaos, seems now to be caught up in that same chaos; no longer content to portray the disintegration of our lives, the novel has now become an active participant and, in its unrelenting search for truthful experience, may finally have annihilated itself.

This study will seek to determine just how much of the damage done to the novel's form in recent years is essential for its survival, and how much is, on the other hand, unnecessarily harmful. Because such an examination can, I think, be misleading unless placed in its proper context, I have considered first the tradition of the chaotic novel through six novelists who did have the aesthetic power of their philosophical convictions: Sterne, Melville, Conrad, Faulkner, Woolf, and Kafka. In each case, I have concentrated upon the chaotic area being investigated to determine why it forces one or more of the conventional elements of the form to be largely ignored or reconceived to bring the chaotic area into focus, while emphasizing the futility of the reader's attempt to synthesize or satisfactorily resolve the chaotic situation confronting him. Finally, I have tried to evaluate the novelist's success in expressing vision through the novel's form. Success here would mean the author's ability to find techniques which defeat the form's tendency to falsify chaotic vision by unifying experience in a meaningful way. Since these authors have been innovative and brilliantly successful in resisting the novel's predisposition toward meaning, a study of their methods will enable us to see more clearly and evaluate more fairly the startling new directions taken by their successors.

Because we find in Beckett the most radical departure from the traditional novel, his works provide a useful place to begin an investigation of the experimental novel. Beckett's novels are characterized by a reductive principle which ultimately extricates itself completely from the world of appearances in order to plummet to the lowest common denominators of experience. While *Murphy* and *Watt* do some strange things with the novel's components, they remain basically conventional in their depiction of chaotic theme through character, plot, structure, setting, and situation. In the remarkable trilogy which follows, however, Beckett's reductive and elliptical procedures eventually eclipse every component through which the novel has traditionally expressed itself. Plunging deeper and deeper to get at those lowest common denominators, we gradually discover that all characters are essentially the same person, all settings are similar, all stories, situations, and styles look alike. As the movement toward silence and nothingness becomes increasingly successful, chaos begins to dictate artistic techniques while simultaneously rendering them absurd. Molloy continues on his travels "like one dying of cancer obliged to consult his dentist"; and it is he, too, who knowing that one lost in a forest thinks he is going forward in a straight line when he is actually going in a circle, does his best to go in a circle, hoping in this way to go in a straight line. Lost in the illogical logicality of it all, the reader wanders through the novel as if in a maze, never knowing when his straying may lead somewhere, but finally concluding that there is nowhere to go *but* astray.

In *Molloy* and *Malone Dies*, we find a progressive loss of the novel's ability to formalize, and along with this, technique becomes more subversive and substance more ineffable as the mind loses its hold on chaos, even though art manages to salvage some minimal control. That control quickly buckles, however, in *The Unnamable*, which gradually squeezes out all those components

which had previously characterized the novel's particular way of representing reality. Taken together, the trilogy represents in microcosm the process of decomposition which announces nothingness as its ultimate objective. Since nothing really matters (and this is a positive as well as a negative statement: the concept of nothingness is all that matters), any sign of *some*thing signifies failure. Beckett's gain can best be measured by the reader's loss. Thus, in *Molloy,* we have only the barest framework of a plot, and structure collapses, too, as we find ourselves unable to integrate the two main parts of the work. Still, there is movement, there are quests, there is conflict—a few pathetic remnants of the traditional novel. *Malone* puts us at a point of stasis; there is a physical paralysis which eliminates all but mental action—which is itself in a comatose state. The novel contains a succession of stories which all become the same story and which all fall apart before long anyway. The reader has no meaning to carry away with him, but he does at least retain a vivid memory of Malone, for whom he's come to feel an affection which keeps him engrossed in his story and concerned for his welfare. While chaos is rampant in this book, there *are* characters, plots, and a structural scheme (albeit fragmented, disjointed, and inconclusive) which keeps the chaos contained within the novel's components. But while the first two books of the trilogy recount the dissolution of all the central characters into chaos, the third book, *The Unnamable,* slips itself into the chaos, and the novel is gradually submerged beyond saving. There is no real structure (though there *is* a rather primitive rhythmic pattern: "You must go on, I can't go on, you must go on, I'll go on. . . . You must go on, I can't go on, I'll go on," etc.), no characters, no identifiable plot, not even an identifiable narrator. While the book is not without some dazzlingly brilliant artistic effects—it is, in truth, a solipsistic masterpiece—these effects seem more poetic than novelistic. Only in length does *The Unnamable* resemble a novel, but we now begin to wonder whether an extended prose passage such as this can qualify as a novel when its form has so little in common with the rest of the species.

How It Is goes even further than *The Unnamable* by breakin down not only the structure of the novel but the very structure language itself. A collection of fragments, *How It Is* will pro infuriatingly inaccessible to most readers. As presentation of ch otic vision, it is quite impressive, but as (or, as Beckett would s *qua*) novel, it is nothing but so much quaqua. Chaos has by n

completely engulfed, devoured, and chewed up into little splinters the form we once labeled the novel. As Beckett continues to flatten out his form, the vitality of his earlier works is snuffed out, and the novel now begins to seem capable of expressing little more than its own suicide.

For contrast alone, Genet would seem a natural choice to examine next, for his novels concentrate on idiosyncratic experience—that very diversity which Beckett's reductive procedures seek to erase. Genet inflates, expands, and amplifies the novel for self-aggrandizement: he wants to allow full play to an omnipotent, self-autonomous imagination which disdains feats of representation, preferring to create and then live within its own system. The novel, for Genet, is a gratuitous act executed in defiance of a world so dulled by safe, conventional systems, that it has not yet learned to exult in the freedom offered by an existential vacuum. *Miracle of the Rose* and *Our Lady of the Flowers* are both brilliant, powerful, and provocative combinations of autobiography and fantasy with exclusive emphasis on subjective experience—especially the expression through dream of subconscious life. Because he uses the novel as a form of wish-fulfillment, Genet structures his works on his own whims: he keeps us continually conscious of his own heavy hand pushing his characters around wherever it pleases him at the moment—changing their sex, their names, their roles with all the smugness, belligerence, and pugnacity of the bully who has just discovered his power to be virtually unlimited. And so story, setting, and style (ranging from the sublime to the obscene) are all shoved around mercilessly and put through protean transformations for no reason other than the author's self-gratification, which may necessitate the most drastic changes from one moment to the next. In a perfect representation of "freedom, revolt, and diversity," Genet turns the novel into a highly personal expression which rejoices in the absurd because it leaves him free to fill the void as he pleases. Genet's novels, like our own dreams, *do* have plots, characters, and structural designs—all familiar features of the traditional novel—but each is controlled by chaotic technique, an aesthetic reversal that puts the novel at the disposal of chaos. Again, vision molds the novel, rather than the other way around. Genet's works are lawless, anarchistic, and arbitrary; they are novels rebelling against not only the world, but themselves as well. His very success seems alarming, though, because controls of every sort have been

abandoned, and the novelist has chosen to embrace chaos much as Mann's Aschenbach embraced the Venetian plague: as a compatible companion in recklessness, formlessness, and destruction. Total freedom leads straight to hedonism; and the novel, as means, revels in its chaos as a testament to that freedom, thereby abetting its traditional enemy. Reality exists to be transcended, transmogrified, or exploited; in itself, it is too petty to even warrant our interest.

Robbe-Grillet does not want to ignore reality, but he does discard all the traditional methods and assumptions by which writers have always chosen to approach it. Unlike Genet, he seeks supreme objectivity—and in his abandonment of traditional forms, concepts, and modes of expression, he offers yet another direction for a novel so resigned to chaotic perception that it becomes not the chief problem, but only the basic assumption of his work. Both in theory and technique, Robbe-Grillet is radical enough to divorce his novels from any representational, philosophical, spiritual, or humanistic traditions. In his writings, the mind surrenders all claim to knowledge, and the imagination works for nothing beyond its own exercise and self-awareness. Not reality, but reality refracted through the imagination, dipped into the subconscious, and apprehended as a process of creativity replaces the traditional notion of a reality grasped as objective truth. The New Novel, claims Robbe-Grillet, does not express—it *explores;* and what it explores is itself. The New Novel, then, no longer purports to *represent* our world, but to *replace* it. It becomes its *own* world—elusive, irreducible, provocative, contradictory, irresolvable, endlessly intriguing us with infinite possibilities as it drifts around in time and space, simultaneously inviting and invalidating interpretations, all valid but none ultimate. Determined to resist the traditional view that man and his universe can relate to each other in a meaningful way, Robbe-Grillet throws metaphor out of his work entirely, along with any other stylistic features that might imply man's comprehension of his world to be anything but presumptuous and illusory. Instead, the "noninterpretative" novel—otherwise known as the New Novel—seeks to know only the *form* of experience. The novel creates not to know life, but only to know itself. Even while we may now admit life to lack order, meaning, or stability, we can still take pleasure in tracing the contours of chaos, living and reliving an experience until we feel its insinuating form, recognize its surfaces, and touch its life. There is absolutely no philosophical dimension to all this; it is a solely aesthetic experience apprehended through the imagination. We study it from multiple temporal and spatial vantage points, rejoicing rather than despairing in the relativity which keeps it eternally new, infinitely interesting, continually mysterious. *The Voyeur, Jealousy,* and *In the Labyrinth* are typical novels of this type, offering us worlds without depth, but with unique textures, subtle tones, and strong moods. We watch a work in continual evolution and revolution. The result is an experience which perpetually intrigues and eludes: rotating now swiftly, now slowly, it constantly defies analysis, contradicts and revolts against itself, and persistently destroys itself in order to start all over again. Gratuitous, arbitrary, self-contained, and self-negating, it expresses nothing beyond its own irreducibility. It does not, in short, attempt to *represent* chaos—it *is* chaos: chaos caught in the act of eluding forms, chaos captured as vital experience, chaos captivated by itself. Rather than seeking to control chaos, such a novel willingly capitulates to it, for it asserts that since chaos is the only reality of our lives, then we might as well live and know *it* as fully as possible. We begin humbly enough by confronting appearances *as* appearances, trying to see them more clearly and objectively rather than trying to see *through* them more ingeniously. This means stripping language of its anthropomorphic qualities which only provide a false sense of security in a world where nothing can be known, but only imagined. Every vestige of humanization is siphoned off, so it is not really surprising to find man himself slipping out of the novel, for he, too, is only appearance now—another object among objects. Robbe-Grillet's worlds can be lived in, but we are apt to feel lonely after a while; we will find no companions in them, no correspondences to the moral spheres or spiritual dimensions of our own lives. Our souls no longer flounder in the chaos: they simply dissolve.

Burroughs illustrates another revolutionary means of dealing with chaos by eagerly surrendering the measured self-discipline and aesthetic goals of a Robbe-Grillet. In the Introduction to his extraordinary novel *Naked Lunch,* Burroughs disclaims the traditional role of the author when he makes the following fantastic statement: "I have no precise memory of writing the notes which have now been published under the title *Naked Lunch."* The effects in that book are, however, so superbly controlled that the form does manage to corral its chaos for maximum impact. Perhaps buoyed by his success here as an unconscious creator, Burroughs turns his amnesiac artistry into a conscious literary approach. The random novels which follow (such as *The Soft Machine, The Ticket That Exploded,* and *Nova Express*) attempt to project experience onto many levels simultaneously in order to reproduce more accurately the way the human mind and nervous system actually absorb reality. Not that reality is so easily come by: we are much too imprisoned by conventional associative tracks to see even our own lives clearly. We *think* ourselves out of existence, numbing feeling, misdirecting our energies into cancerous control systems, and deadening the senses until our antennae no longer pick up the vital signals of the reality surrounding us. The control systems must be sabotaged so that we can live again, see again, feel again. Accident, then, is the only answer: the artist himself sets the example by yielding his artistic control in order to give reality a chance to emerge as itself, rather than as a series of straitjacketed systems sagging under the intellectual overload of western civilization's various attempts to confine reality's dimensions to our own limited minds. Set adrift in chaos, the random novel surrenders all claims to conventional controls and attempts instead to absorb accidentally and arbitrarily whatever combinations of chaotic reality happen to wash up within its frame. Burroughs' use of cutup insures an artistic integrity now defined by the extent to which it is willing to forgo all authority, and cater to the chaotic world. Like Beckett, he wants to render language useless except as it can be exploited for its own annihilation. Burroughs wants to vandalize the novel, rip from its frame the machinery he feels has enslaved us so that he can free us from forms that block perception and kill life. While the intentions are certainly noble, the novel, in order to serve them, must become an Exercise-for-Freedom book at best, a piece of propaganda at worst.

As the balance shifts from chaos in the novel to the novel in chaos, we find the character of the novel form caught in a degenerative process that does indeed resemble a moribund condition. Rebelling against the validity of its own components, the novel can no longer contain the vision which works to contradict its every premise. But the problem is less the dead state of the novel as it is this new state of the deadly novel. Beckett, Genet, Robbe-Grillet, and Burroughs are all serious, dedicated, exceptionally talented writers, and major voices in the contemporary chaotic novel, yet each, too, is helping to put his form in an untenable position where only a Pyrrhic victory becomes possible; the novel built to self-destruct can engender no tradition, but only insure its own extinction. *Malone Dies, Our Lady of the Flowers, In the Labyrinth,* and *Naked Lunch* are all devastatingly brilliant works, innovative but also powerful artistic creations which kindle our imaginations and stir up our emotions in new ways. But each of these works is followed by a weaker one which involves the reader less and less and leaves a larger and larger part of his sensibility outside of the novel. Each theory finally pushes the novel into a cul-de-sac where, cut off from so many of its traditional sources of energy, it can only repeat the same limited experience with lessening novelty and effect until the reader finally turns away from it in frustration. As a result, so much of the novel's identity has been tampered with, so much of its richness lost and its vitality drained away, so much of its human and emotional appeal sacrificed that the novel ceases to be a viable, valuable form with a legitimate claim to our attention.

This study does not pretend to be inclusive, but only indicative of the dominant trends in the novel today. The four experimental novelists dealt with are representative, I think, of the major directions taken by contemporary authors to keep their form from becoming obsolete. Now that the traditional novel has been discarded in order to reflect chaos more accurately, we must determine how much of the damage can actually be turned into exciting new possibilities for the novel's future, and how much has been needless, masochistic, and self-defeating. But such radically different works cannot be satisfactorily evaluated by the old standards; we need new critical assumptions and apparatus if we are to make fair judgments. On the other hand, we have a right to impatience, too; we should not be so intimidated by the innovative artist, that we forget to demand an experience which will make itself accessible to us by engaging our minds and arousing our emotions. Otherwise, we are in the same dangerous position as the customers of Chez Robert in Burroughs' *Naked Lunch* who, unaware that the management has been taken over by the owner's brother who has emerged "from retirement in a local nut house," and too intimidated by the restaurant's reputation to protest, permit themselves to be served with "literal garbage."

I don't think any of the writers discussed here are offering us garbage or anything close to it, but they are certainly providing enough problems to upset both reader and critic alike. In the concluding chapter of this book, therefore, I have tried to sift out the most salient problems and, finally, to offer thoughts toward a critical theory equipped and willing to cope with them.

Where, then, can the line be drawn between the novel that controls chaos and the one that capitulates to it; the novel that creates chaos and the one that caters to it? Although it would be unreasonable to expect a simple answer, the question asserts itself strongly enough to warrant investigation, if only to throw some shadows to one side and some to the other. My object is to determine whether the novel form has indeed become obsolete, or whether it can still be made to serve the contemporary artist and his audience. What is at stake here is not simply a literary form, but the pertinence of a particular kind of experience engendered by the novel which has so often enriched our lives by seeming to bring them closer to us than we could ever have managed to get by ourselves.

Part I

Chaos in the Novel

1

A Thousand Splinters

The Deliberately Distorted Narrative
of Tristram Shandy

*T*ristram Shandy provides us with an excellent example of a work that teeters on chaos without ever falling into it. By considering Sterne's artistic devices here along with his vision—which bears some striking resemblances to that of such modern writers as Samuel Beckett—we may find hope for the novel's future, and a way *into* chaos which also leaves a way *out* of it. Sterne seems to me to have falsified neither his art nor his vision, and the successful integration and assimilation of the two can provide some important lessons for the modern practitioners of the novel. Certainly, Sterne's narrative technique seems so confused as to belie any conscious aesthetic control, yet the reader's experience of confusion has been so carefully manipulated and shaped toward Sterne's specific goals, that we find his freedom to have been an illusion all along. The freedom created by and disciplined through art may still be the most effective kind for transmitting a sense of disorder. Whereas many writers today feel impelled to dismiss their artistic control, Sterne found it sufficient simply to disguise it, and the disguise is brilliant indeed: chaos and control have rarely been so beautifully united.

No sooner had the novel acquired conventional techniques to arouse and fulfill the reader's expectations in a certain way than Laurence Sterne took it upon himself to upset as many of them as possible. Knowing how quickly the human mind adapts itself to consistent patterns of response—a novelty surprises us for such a short time before we adjust to it, expect it, and then demand it—Sterne was able to keep his readers constantly surprised and delighted by playing upon their expectations for a carefully structured work. Since only a few precedents are needed to establish a tradition, the novel had by this time developed a set of procedures which seemed so logical and effective that they were already in danger of becoming rigid conventions. Thus, while Richardson had told tragic stories and Fielding comic ones, both were still storytellers who followed a chronological narrative which, by duplicating the progressive pattern of a man's life (or part of his life), seemed the most sensible way of moving from the beginning to the end. The novel's impact was cumulative, and carefully planned for by the author on a dramatic line of suspense, complication, climax, and denouement which carried the reader along in a clear and consistent direction. Even when the author himself was present as a voice in the novel, his primary function was to interpret the action of his story and direct the reader's response to it. He was, in short, helpful, and his role, though subsidiary to the action, was consistent with it—that is, to tell a story centered around a main character, and enable the reader to learn from the experiences of this character's interaction with the world.

But while *Clarissa* is about Clarissa, and *Tom Jones* about Tom, who would say that *The Life and Opinions of Tristram Shandy, Gentleman,* is about Tristram or even a segment of his life? Clearly, Sterne was up to something quite different from anything his predecessors had attempted, and as a result, he found traditional techniques of storytelling confining and inadequate to his purposes. Nowhere is this clearer than in Sterne's deliberate distortion of narrative technique, which seems utterly chaotic and fanciful until we understand how well it suited his purposes. An examination of his method will, I think, reveal how he has enlarged the scope and potential of the novel to depict the chaotic mental life of man while at the same time achieving a purposeful and aesthetic consistency that brings his chaos into the framework of his form. The artist who expands the form's capability to project experience and vision without compromising either form or vision must be seen as a crucial figure in the development of the novel. As James Work says in his Introduction to *Tristram Shandy*, Sterne "loosened the English novel in structure and in style and in content, damaging its form perhaps but liberating its spirit and potentialities, and preparing the way for the psychological novelists, his spiritual and aesthetic descendents, of our own day."[1] To what extent Sterne "damaged" the novel's form is questionable, but loosen and play with it he certainly did, until he had shaped it anew to conform perfectly to his intentions.

In his title page to the first London edition of Volumes I and II of *Tristram Shandy*, Sterne uses as his epigraph a motto from Epictetus which can help us to recognize his intentions: "It is not actions, but opinions concerning actions, which disturb men" (p. 1). Since, as we have said, those novelists writing before Sterne had emphasized action as the main concern of the novel and the means through which vision and theme were to be communicated to the reader, it seems obvious that their narrative techniques will not suffice for the psychologically oriented novelist. Our lives, for example, may be composed of a series of chronological events, but it is also true that our interpretation of these events is often changed radically by later knowledge. The past is continually being reshaped by the present, and so can never be totally detached from it. A strictly chronological method, therefore, cannot be psychologically satisfying; the narrative must be flexible enough to jump, drift, and boomerang through time if it is to delineate man's mental make-up.

But *Tristram Shandy* is not simply a psychological novel—it is above all a comic one, and it will be seen that Sterne breaks the traditional narrative pattern for a whimsical effect, too, if it aids his comic intent. The important thing to remember here, however, is that Sterne's comic purpose coincides with his psychological statement. When the reader laughs, his laughter is always to the psychological point which Sterne wants to emphasize. In this way, he is able to give us a carefully if unconventionally structured narrative disguised by chaos, modeled on chaos, even paraded *as* chaos, but never serving chaos.

---

1. Laurence Sterne, *The Life and Opinions of Tristram Shandy, Gentleman*, ed. James Aiken Work (New York: The Odyssey Press, 1940), p. lxiii. All future page references, cited in parentheses, are to this edition.

In one of his typical asides to the reader, Sterne remarks early in Volume VIII that his method of beginning a book is surely one of the most religious ever practiced by a writer—"for I begin with writing the first sentence—and trusting to Almighty God for the second" (p. 540). He adds that in so doing, he has no doubt often intercepted a thought intended for another man, but this possibility certainly does not bother him unduly. The statement is a marvelously succinct justification for Sterne's capricious narrative technique—one that drifts aimlessly through time, upsets incidents in the very act of being formed, and plays upon every reasonable expectation of the reader. We cannot, of course, take it seriously, but we have to admit that the effect of Sterne's chaotic narrative makes this cause seem quite plausible.

Sterne's narrative devices are to a great extent the result of his love for frustrating the reader; he delights in surprising us, teasing us, throwing us completely off guard on the basis of those false assumptions he has so carefully led us to accept. Yet he is honest: he says very early in *Tristram* that he intends to follow none of the rules of Horace, or of any other man. In another passage he promises to pay the reader the extreme compliment of keeping his imagination as busy as the author's own by "amicably" leaving out half of his material (p. 109); the understanding reader will fill in the rest with ease and a good amount of enjoyment. Finally, Sterne admits that he intends to provoke the reader's natural propensity (a "vicious taste," he calls it) for rushing forward through a story, perpetually waiting for action to resolve itself, rather than enjoying the knowledge and erudition along the way. "The mind," he insists, "should be accustomed to make wise reflections, and draw curious conclusions as it goes along" (p. 56).

We have, then, been warned, and Sterne refuses to apologize for the mad ride on which he has taken the reader. When, at one point, he charts his narrative movement for the reader thus:

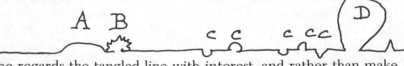

he regards the tangled line with interest, and rather than make an effort to justify it, simply observes with some pride that he *is*, after all, making a certain kind of progress and has hardly gone a yard out of his way (p. 474). Obviously, his "way" has little to do with any logical development of a story line, but it has much to do with his primary interest in that story, which is reflected in the narrative itself.

We could generalize and say that the basic principle behind Sterne's narrative technique is the Lockean theory of association—and this is certainly true; like Mrs. Shandy's question about the winding of the clock the night of Tristram's conception, Sterne seems to shift from his point the moment it reminds him of something else. But while the theory of association points to a logical method, it does not describe an aesthetic one. Sterne himself distinguishes the two when he says that "writing, when properly managed (as you may be sure I think mine is), is but a different name for conversation" (p. 108). The qualifying phrase here is significant, for it reminds us that Sterne, even while free-associating to give us the *impression* of conversation, is most purposefully controlling his chaos so that his form is not nearly so formless as real-life conversation would be. His digressions are so natural and lengthy that we tend to forget that eventually he always does get back to his main topic (even while creating several new main topics in the process) and by the end of the book has dealt at some length with every subject referred to in the early chapters.

If we remember that Sterne's main concern is not with the actions of man, but with the impact and influence of these actions on his mind, we can easily see why he found it desirable to structure his narrative in such a way as to duplicate the process by which we take in external experience. He believes that "our minds shine not through the body, but are wrapt up here in a dark covering of uncrystalized flesh and blood; so that if we would come to the specifick characters of them, we must go some other way to work" (p. 75). That way, he implies, is of necessity roundabout, and this is why his digressions form an integral part of his narrative technique. Sterne, in fact, makes quite sure that the reader recognizes his achievement:

when a thing is executed in a masterly kind of fashion, which thing is not likely to be found out;—I think it is . . . abominable, that a man should lose the honour of it, and go out of the world with the conceit of it rotting in his head.

This is precisely my situation.

For in this long digression which I was accidentally led into, as in all my digressions (one only excepted) there is a master-stroke of digressive skill, the merit of which has all along, I fear, been overlooked by my reader,—not for want of penetration to him,—but because 'tis an excellence seldom looked for, or expected indeed, in a digression;—and that is this: That tho' my digressions are all fair, as you observe,—and that I fly off from what I am about, as far and as often too as any writer in *Great-Britain;* yet I constantly take care to order affairs so, that my main business does not stand still in my absence. . . . .

By this contrivance the machinery of my work is of a species by itself; two contrary motions are introduced into it, and reconciled, which were thought to be at variance with each other. In a word, my work is digressive, and it is progressive too,—and at the same time. (Pp. 72–73)

In the above passage, Sterne has been referring to the subtlety with which he was drawing in for us the character of his Uncle Toby while the unsuspecting reader was conscious only of a lapse in the narrative, but this digressive (or seemingly digressive) technique not only constitutes his primary method of characterization, but is used in his narration of events as well. It is the means by which he wants his reader to assimilate his story; he demands that the reader take an active, creative role in learning about the life and opinions of Tristram by scrambling for his information wherever and whenever he can find it. This is Sterne's "way" of telling his story, so that any bumps in the narrative line cannot be said to have taken him off his course in the slightest. Our mistake is in our limited conception of a narrative *as* a line when it can just as easily and validly take some other form.

Because Sterne prefers circles to lines, traditional narrative patterns are uninteresting to him. Why not add delight to knowledge by producing it always with the element of surprise? Even Artistotle saw that man not only *needs* to learn, but *delights* in learning through the surprise of recognition. What Sterne does is to heighten this surprise by intentionally arousing in the reader expectations of one kind of knowledge, and then confronting him with another. The baffled reader then has to work for his knowledge (the author, remember, has promised to keep our imaginations humming, actively engaged in piecing bits and scraps of information together for our edification) and when it finally comes, his gratification and sense of satisfaction is that much greater. Here is where the circle comes in. Life and learning are more dynamic than traditional narrative would suggest; we do, perhaps, learn by degrees, but those degrees can never be struck off in a straight line—charted, as it were, by expectation and accuracy. If our learning process were linear, then even though we might not be able to predict the knowledge waiting for us at the end of the line, we would at least have by now an idea of the *form* and so be able to presume what the future will be like. Thus, if we start here:

--------------and are here, we can guess that we will end here-----------

rather than at the corner of the page. On the other hand, a circle can be trickier: you see an arc here, an arc there, but you are not at first sure of what the final form will be like. You do, of course, eventually surmise it—and long before the circle has been completed

—but the knowledge comes in assorted scraps that must embody or contain a certain amount of space before its final form can be predicted. Now what Sterne does is to confuse you more and more as you wait for the form to be outlined, and then force you to discover it just a split second before he has completed it for you. It is as if you were facing forward waiting for someone, eyes alert and watchful, when you suddenly feel a hand from behind tapping your shoulder. Surprise! You have been caught off guard even while you were taking such pains to find what you were waiting for before it found you.

Getting back to the novel, we can try to fit the analogy into Sterne's narrative technique. It is typical of him, for example, to begin a story in the middle—he almost always does this—and then leave it hanging while dashing on to something else. After a short while, you begin to enjoy the something else, get absorbed in it, completely forgetting about the original incident which sparked the digression when with a shock it suddenly dawns on you that this supposedly new story is really the beginning of the story the author started in the middle and then dropped. And always you see this just an instant before Sterne makes the connection explicit for you.

The same thing is true with Sterne's handling of irrelevancies: he pulls you into an irrelevant discourse, and you start enjoying it for its own sake when suddenly you sense its relevance; it was really a part of the same story all along. In the very first chapter of the book, Sterne instigates what is to be his method throughout. Why Mrs. Shandy should ask her husband if he has not forgotten to wind up the clock perplexes us not only in itself, but in relation to what the narrator has started to tell us—that is, his certainty in arriving at the very date of his conception. A few pages intervene before we begin to understand why the question was asked, by which point the matter of the date of Tristram's conception has begun to recede, when the relationship between them suddenly steals on us. From this time on, Sterne surrounds us with arcs until we have segments of each event buried somewhere in our memories, waiting for the proper moment to rise to the surface and form a complete circle. More than twenty-five pages elapse between the first mention of the noise attending Tristram's difficult birth and Sterne's resumption of that event; Walter Shandy, distraught after learning about the unfortunate damage to his son's nose during delivery, falls onto his bed where Sterne leaves him for eighty pages while the narrator's Preface is finally written, numerous discourses on noses are delivered, and other arcs drawn before we finally see Walter Shandy begin to play upon the floor with his toes; and close to 150 pages have gone by from the time we learn about Walter Shandy's detestation of the name "Tristram" and his determination to provide his son with a truly inspirational name ("When this story is compared with the title-page,—Will not the gentle reader pity my father from his soul?" [p. 55]) and the narrator's final explanation of this puzzling paradox.

But let us look at a smaller arc to see how Sterne gets a part of his story told: the episode of the sash. The reader first learns about this incident in Chapter XVII of Volume V when Tristram tells us that " 'Twas nothing—I did not lose two drops of blood by it—'twas not worth calling in a surgeon, had he lived next door to us—thousands suffer by choice, what I did by accident.—Doctor Slop made ten times more of it, than there was occasion . . ." (p. 376). The reader, of course, has not the faintest idea of what Tristram is referring to, and since the story comes on him so suddenly, he has not been equipped with any previous information to help him cope with it; he can do nothing but allow the narrator to take him by the leash and lead him onward, if not forward. So the reader then leaves the house with Susannah, and in the next chapter, watches the blood withdraw from Trim's cheeks as he listens to her story. But what has either of them to do with whatever has happened to Tristram? We know that Susannah had accidentally caused the sash to fall down upon the child, but what was she referring to when she cried, "Nothing is left—nothing is left—but for me to run my country—"?

The next chapter begins with Uncle Toby addressing Trim, regretting the lack of a couple of field pieces to mount in the gorge of that new redoubt and requesting Trim to "get me a couple cast." And now the facts start falling together: Trim must have carried out the orders by taking the two leaden weights and sash pulleys from the nursery window, which accounts for its having fallen off as soon as Susannah's hand touched it. In the next chapter, our suspicion is confirmed when Uncle Toby decides that he must take the blame for his servant for having issued the orders that led to the theft of the sash rods. After a discussion with Yorick (with whom Toby had been talking when told of the affair), Toby decides to stand by Trim, and so the whole group, led by Toby and Yorick, marches back to Shandy Hall. As they walk (in the next chapter), Trim sadly reflects on his mistake, and says he wishes he had cut off the church spout instead of the sash weights, to which Yorick replies: "You have cut off spouts enouw." If the reader had not yet gotten the point, he has it now: the various images tumble together in a sequence that reveals the story of Tristram's circumcision a few lines before Sterne makes it explicit. Now all the hints (such as Susannah's cry that "Nothing is left") become strikingly obvious and hilarious, and the arcs fall into a perfect circle. Then, and only then, does Sterne go back to the middle of his story and fill in the gaps from where Susannah had left the house. Thus, we see that Sterne's narration of the episode started at the end, then flew back to the exposition, then resumed where he had left off, and finally filled in the middle—or just enough of it to enable us to surmise and interpret the whole action. Yet Sterne uses no transitional devices to help us distinguish past from present events. The reader himself must sort out the elements and add some inferences of his own before he has a clear picture of what has happened: that Toby had issued a command, that Trim fulfilled it in such a way as to render the sash useless, that Susannah, while lifting Tristram onto the window sill, had caused the sash to fall upon him and circumcise him in a stroke. A funny tale—but how much more amusing when the reader is left to his own devices to find the double-entendres and paste together cause and effect.

The fragmented, disjointed narration of this episode demonstrates Sterne's technique of always sneaking up on the reader, and evoking that sense of delight that comes with pleasant surprises. He does this by swimming through time so that the form of his story remains hidden as long as possible (and is found just as you thought you had turned away from it) and by tricking your imagination until it ceases to function in a helpful (traditional) way. As a result, the reader, forced to fill in his own outlines, helps write the story himself (as was the author's expressed intention) and gains added pleasure from the involvement of his own mind.

My point is that Sterne's narrative technique *is* a technique—quite a bit more than capricious self-indulgence. It is a technique brilliantly calculated for supreme comic effect based on the elements of surprise and discovery. It *is* free association, but free association molded into *form,* as distinguished, for example, from Twain's story of "Jim Blaine and His Grandfather's Old Ram"—in which the narrator free-associates himself right off the precipice of his main point and becomes forever lost in parentheses. Sterne is a comic artist, not just a humorist.

The apparent formlessness of Sterne's narrative is, we have found, a successful comic device for one of the funniest novels in our literature, but it has also a serious purpose which we have so far ignored. While Sterne has insured our delight in learning what he has to offer us, what he *does* have to offer for our edification is much more than a story or moral; it is a psychological study of ourselves based on the Lockean principle of the association of ideas. Sterne himself refers to Locke's *Essay Concerning Human Understanding* as a history book "of what passes in a man's own mind" (p. 85), and in many ways, *Tristram Shandy* can be seen as the fictional embodiment of Locke's most fundamental principles. In his *Essay,* Locke almost prophesies the appearance of Sterne's novel when he notes that

this wrong connexion in our minds of ideas, in themselves loose and independent of one another, has such an influence, and is of so great force to set us awry in our actions, as well moral as natural, passions, reasonings, and notions themselves, that perhaps there is not any one thing that deserves more to be looked after. (P. 9)

It is the utter privacy of each mind's association of ideas that accounts for most of the humor, conflict, and purpose of the novel, and Sterne has taken great care to reproduce the chaos of communication among his characters in his own relationship to the reader; in this way, the narrative is carefully calculated to duplicate in the telling the very matter which is being demonstrated through the story. It is impossible, therefore, for the reader to keep his traditional position of detachment from the novel because he himself is subject to all the frustration and confusion he sees reflected in Sterne's characters.

The relationship between Walter and Toby Shandy is marked by their inability to communicate in meaningful terms through words and logical structures; in both cases, the peculiar uniqueness of their associations of ideas shuts them out of the other's inner life. At the same time, though, their failure to communicate successfully is never depressing because their attachment is so strong that their hearts are always meeting, even when their minds are not. Walter Shandy, always the victim of his obsession for hypotheses, has a one-track mind, while that of his brother often seems altogether derailed. Until we understand the basis of their association of ideas, their responses puzzle us completely, but once their hobby-horses are known, the reader has no difficulty in accepting the built-in logic of their respective positions. Still, lest the reader begin to feel a bit self-assured when he has figured out what makes each man tick, Sterne makes sure that no matter how familiar we become with them, we never stop being surprised at their unexpected consistency. The reader's expectations are based on his own sense of logical sequence and consequence, and when these are thwarted, the astonishment causes laughter. Time and time again we are greeted with the unexpected, yet we never become immune to Sterne's surprises—and this reminds us that our minds are as helplessly limited as those of the characters we are laughing at. Look, for example, at the following interchanges:

We'll go, brother *Toby*, said my father, whilst dinner is coddling—to the abby of Saint *Germain*, if it be only to see these bodies, of which monsieur *Seguier* has given such a recommendation.—I'll go see any body; quoth my uncle *Toby*; for he was all compliance thro' every step of the journey—Defend me! said my father—they are all mummies—Then one need not shave; quoth my uncle *Toby*—. (P. 513)

. . . my mother broke silence.—

"——My brother *Toby,* quoth she, is going to be married to Mrs. *Wadman.*"
——Then he will never, quoth my father, be able to lie diagonally in his bed again as long as he lives. (P.472)

——My nephew [Bobby], said my uncle Toby . . . .
——he is dead . . .
——Without being ill? cried my father. . . . (P. 350)

And later:

"If my son could not have died, it had been matter of wonder—not that he is dead."
"Monarchs and princes dance in the same ring with us." (P. 353)

In each case, a piece of surprising information is responded to in an hilariously illogical way—but wherein lies the illogic, really? Actually, nothing could be more logical than Uncle Toby's remark that since they will be visiting dead people, the necessity for shaving is obviated; that Walter Shandy, lying in bed with his wife, should see his position there as the most striking consequence of his brother's decision to marry; or that Walter's greatest surprise on hearing of his son's death is that there had been no previous illness to point to such an end? What accounts for our laughter here is not the illogicality of responses, but the utter consistency of each man's logic at times when logic itself seems totally out of place. When we meet with information that logic has not prepared us for (such as the news of a sudden death or unexpected marriage), it is our emotions that respond while our minds are numbed or simply kept too busy trying to cope with and assimilate a strange fact. The thing we least expect is that such news will be taken in perfect stride as if it were trivial or expected (that the response, "Well, I'll have tea, then" to the statement, "We're out of coffee" will recur when the statement is changed to "The coffee is poisoned!"). Our conception of logic carries with it a sense of its limitations and inappropriateness which is never catered to in this novel. No matter how familiar we become with Walter Shandy's fondness for hypotheses, we still would never dream that even the sudden death of his son could provide him with an opportunity to work toward another one. The more we consider it, the less surprising it seems, but Sterne always gets the benefit of the initial shock because *our* logic at such times has been completely overturned by an association of ideas so foreign to our own that no amount of previous experience with it can prepare us for the next time it occurs. But is not this the exact position of Walter Shandy himself throughout the novel when his most precious hypotheses go tumbling as soon as he tries to make mental contact with his brother or his wife? In this way, Sterne has made our experiences as reader to parallel with the exasperating experiences of his characters.

How, for example, can we feel superior to Walter Shandy's desperate clutchings at reasonable hypotheses when we ourselves are so often made victim of the same madness? Consider this illustration: when Obadiah has been sent for Dr. Slop to assist at Tristram's delivery, Sterne allows his narrative to drift for a while, and then takes out a chapter to discuss the legitimacy of his dramatic use of time. Though he confesses it to be only an hour and a half's reading time from the moment Obadiah has left until Dr. Slop is announced, Sterne justifies his adherence to the poetic rules of time rather than to any realistic use by discoursing on what the reader has learned while Obadiah has been away. Certainly he draws up an impressive list of assorted knowledge which has taken the reader through four years and across several countries. Why, then, should the reader object if the actual time elapsing has been but two minutes and thirteen seconds rather than the apparent hour and a half? After all, he reminds us, "the idea of duration and of its simple modes, is got merely from the train and succession of our ideas—and is the true scholastic pendulum," and certainly the only one by which the author has a right to be judged. But now that he has us on solid logical ground, out comes the surprise, and the reader goes spilling. For now Sterne informs us that if the real truth of the matter must be known, the hour and a half's journey to Dr. Slop's house happened not to be necessary in this case, because Obadiah had not got above three yards from the stable-yard before he met with Dr. Slop (pp. 103–4). Typical of Sterne: after exhaustive justification of dramatic time lapse as a valid aesthetic device, he in one stroke overturns his whole argument (and the reader's new line of logic) by the addition of one new fact which renders totally irrelevant and absurd all the hypotheses he has foisted upon us and gotten us to accept. He has constructed a logical trap for his readers that we fall into immediately, and as soon as the strings are pulled, the door snaps shut behind us, and we are caught in as ludicrous a position as Walter Shandy has ever been put in by the non sequiturs of his brother.

And this is true throughout the book: whenever Sterne has set our minds moving in a certain direction only to throw us off the track of *his* logic, we, like Walter Shandy, suddenly find that we have been hypothesizing irrelevantly and must pay for the presumption by having our thunder stolen at just the moment it is bound to make us look most ridiculous. In the book, Toby is most frequently the means by which Tristram mocks his father's propensity for building speculations into hypothetical towers that can be whisked away with a word, but we must remember that what Toby does to Walter is paralleled all along by what Sterne has been doing with us. Thus, on the basis of our having been tricked by the author's argument for his "poetic" use of time, we can only share (never feel superior to) Walter Shandy's frustration as a fellow victim when we read that

though my father said *"he knew not how it happen'd,"* [that while only two hours and ten minutes had transpired since Dr. Slop had arrived at the house to attend Tristram's birth, it seemed to his imagination almost an age],

—yet he knew very well, how it happen'd;—and at the instant he spoke it, was pre-determined in his mind, to give my uncle *Toby* a clear account of the matter by a metaphysical dissertation upon the subject of *duration and its simple modes*, in order to shew my uncle *Toby*, by what mechanism and mensurations in the brain it came to pass, that the rapid succession of their ideas, and the eternal scampering of discourse from one thing to another, since Dr. *Slop* had come into the room, had lengthened out so short a period, to so inconceivable an extent.—"I know not how it happens,—cried by father;—but it seems an age."

—'Tis owing, entirely, quoth my uncle *Toby*, to the succession of our ideas. . . . .

. . .Do you understand the theory of that affair? replied my father.

Not I, quoth my uncle.

——But you have some ideas, said my father, of what you talk about.— No more than my horse, replied my uncle *Toby*.

Gracious heaven! cried my father, looking upwards, and clasping his two hands together . . . . (Pp. 188–89)

Or consider Walter's exasperation here:

When I reflect, brother *Toby*, upon MAN; and take a view of that dark side of him which represents his life as open to so many causes of trouble—when I consider, brother *Toby*, how oft we eat the bread of affliction, and that we are born to it, as to the portion of our inheritance . . . I say, *Toby*, when one runs over the catalogue of all the cross reckonings and sorrowful *items* with which the heart of man is overcharged, 'tis wonderful by what hidden resources the mind is enabled to stand it out, and bear itself up, as it does against the impositions laid upon our nature.—'Tis by the assistance of Almighty God, cried my uncle *Toby*, looking up, and pressing the palms of his hands close together . . . .

——That is cutting the knot, said my father, instead of untying it. (Pp. 277–78)

In both passages, Tristram is having the same kind of fun at his father's expense that Sterne has been having with the reader at *his* expense. The use of logical method in this book or *with* this book is doomed to boomerang on whoever attempts it, turning him into the helpless victim of his own hypotheses. Logic ties up nothing here except the person trying to utilize it; whereas we may hope to untangle things with it, we succeed only in entangling ourselves *within* it.

Thus, the constant element of surprise in Sterne's narrative technique forces the reader to be victimized over and over again by his own narrow sense of logical sequence—and it is obvious that Sterne sees this as no less than his duty. He warns us at the end of Volume I that "if I thought you was able to form the least judgment of probable conjecture to yourself, of what was to come in the next page,—I would tear it out of my book" (p. 80). The ultimatum constitutes a serious part of Sterne's purpose, for by confronting us with the mystery of another mind (Tristram's) running nonchalantly on its own track, the narrator re-creates for us in the most intimate way the basic condition of his characters and the chaos confronting all men who, at the mercy of their limited minds, can only stumble in darkness in their desperate efforts to communicate with the people they love.

But just as Toby's defiance of his brother's brilliant logical theories is always innocent and mitigated by his constant goodwill, so Sterne's defiance of his reader's logical expectations is never disdainful or irritating. Rather, he enjoys a peculiar and quite special relationship to the reader marked by honesty on his part, and trust on the reader's. It is true, as I have said, that he tricks and teases the reader by leading him down familiar paths of logic until the reader feels he can begin to make it on his own, and then by shoving him abruptly into unknown territory, and deserting him. But Sterne refuses to alienate his readers—he demands only that we recognize who is in charge here and acquiesce to his judgment. "I would go fifty miles on foot," he says, "for I have not a horse worth riding on, to kiss the hand of that man whose generous heart will give up the reins of his imagination into his author's hands,—be pleased he knows not why, and cares not wherefore" (p. 182). The narrator bears full responsibility, then, for the telling of his story, and Sterne makes every attempt to capitalize on that power. When, toward the end of his last volume, he skips Chapters XVIII and XIX only to include them later within Chapter XXV, he makes no apology for such irregularities, but only hopes "that it may be a lesson to the world, *'to let people tell their stories their own way'* " (p. 633).

On the other hand, Sterne is constantly assuring us that his manipulation of the narrative is always purposeful, never arbitrary or merely capricious. He *is* determined to tell his story in his own way, but this is more than sheer willfulness on his part; it is his aesthetic responsibility both to his material and his reader. This responsibility he takes quite seriously by frequently explaining his handling of the action. Even when he suddenly decides to drop the story of his uncle's affair with the Widow Wadman toward which he confesses his entire narrative has been directed and which he has foreseen as the choicest morsel of his novel, he faces the reader squarely in lamenting his want of powers to tell the story properly, and even explains his deficiency as a possible result of a loss of much blood during a fever he suffered at the beginning of the chapter (p. 627). Nowhere is the intimacy of his relationship to the reader more clearly and poignantly suggested than here.

Most of the time, however, Sterne prefers to justify rather than excuse himself, and his justifications are nearly always aesthetic ones which remind the reader that the author's apparently confused narrative is skillfully designed for artistic (as well as comic and psychological) effects. Thus:

I have dropp'd the curtain over this scene for a minute,—to remind you of one thing,—and to inform you of another.

What I have to inform you, comes, I own, a little out of its due course;—for it should have been told a hundred and fifty pages ago, but that I foresaw then 'twould come in pat hereafter, and be of more advantage here than elsewhere.—Writers had need look before them to keep up the spirit and connection of what they have in hand. (P. 144)

According to this passage, therefore, the careful writer will place facts and events not necessarily where they belong chronologically or even psychologically, but where he feels they will have the maximum effect dramatically. In this way, too, Sterne justifies his sometimes graceless leaps through time. He contends that so long as he jumps forward and backward in time with absolute freedom, he creates his own kind of unity. His seemingly random jumps in narration are justifiable artistic devices, he insists, and this is important because it explains his sense of an order beyond the psychological explanation of association of ideas. No matter how chaotic his material seems to become at any given point, Sterne's respect for his craft, his sense of obligation as literary artist, and his responsibility to the reader are never left in doubt because he has so often taken the trouble to articulate his credo of aesthetic control.

Still, Sterne delights in verging on chaos whenever possible, and his wanderings in this direction have often a strikingly modern tone to them. In him, perhaps, we see the glimmerings of a Beckett or Robbe-Grillet with one crucial distinction—and that is Sterne's steadfast self-confidence. Chaos in his work is almost always finally decipherable; the author can play with it or plow through it at will. Whether he decides to deliver it immediately, or hold it back for a while, or tantalize us before presenting it, the narrator here always holds that extra bit of knowledge which, when furnished, will explain any disparities, reconcile any contradictions, or make the unknowable known.

He plays, for example, with the possibility (which in our century has become so widespread) of the narrator's inability to know *everything* about the materials in his own story when he conjectures on whether his father had written before or after the incident of the sash took place "that remarkable chapter in the *Tristrapaedia*, which to me is the most original and entertaining one in the whole book;—and that is the chapter upon *sash-windows*, with a bitter *Philippick* at the end of it, upon the forgetfulness of chambermaids." He has us on one plane of logical thought, then—whether Walter Shandy wrote the chapter before or after the event—when the matter is taken care of thus:

. . . I have but two reasons for thinking otherwise [that the chapter was written before the incident].

First, had the matter been taken into consideration, before the event happened, my father certainly would have nailed up the sash-window for good an' all;—which, considering with what difficulty he composed books,—he might have done with ten times less trouble, than he could have wrote the chapter, even after the event; but 'tis obviated under the second reason, which I have the honour to offer to the world in support of my opinion, that my father did not write the chapter upon sash-windows and chamberpots, at the time supposed,—and it is this.

——That, in order to render the *Tristrapaedia* complete,—I wrote the chapter myself. (Pp. 383–84)

Once again, Sterne has set our minds to weaving complex logical patterns only to throw us off *his* logical track, which was headed in an altogether different direction. We have been trapped, duped, fooled, surprised—and the pleasure is all ours. But the passage is interesting too, as a contrast to the many modern writers who refuse to be accountable for the very material they are presenting. No one, they argue, can possibly know enough to offer the final word on anything; the author himself can only speculate on what the truth *might* have been or else present several varying interpretations of what happened. Sterne here comes so close to this view that the modern reader may well be amazed at how easily Tristram overcomes the problem, how quickly the ambiguity evaporates.

We have already seen how poorly speculation comes out in this book (witness the passage in which Walter considers the sad plight of men's lives and wonders how it is borne by so many, only to have Toby blurt out faith in God as the answer), and there can be little doubt that Sterne enjoys poking fun at any philosophical explanation of the mysteries of man's existence. Although he recognizes the chaos of much of our lives, he is obviously comfortable with that chaos, for he sees no necessity for trying to resolve it in a way that will appease man's yearnings for logic, order, and purposefulness. He differs from so many modern writers not so much in perception as in assumptions—in his apparent belief, for example, that our inability to penetrate the mystery of things has no effect whatever on the basic value and enjoyment of our lives. The following passage, for example, might well have come from Beckett's *Watt*, except for the total lack of consequential philosophic implications stemming from man's contest with the unknowable:

Whether *Susannah*, by taking her hand too suddenly from off the corporal's shoulder, (by the whisking about of her passion)—broke a little the chain of his reflections——

Or whether the corporal began to be suspicious, he had got into the doctor's quarters, and was talking more like the chaplain than himself—

Or whether—— —— —— —— —— —— —— —— —— —— ——

Or whether——for in all such cases a man of invention and parts may with pleasure fill a couple of pages with suppositions—which of all these was the cause, let the curious physiologist, or the curious any body determine——'tis certain, at least, the corporal went on thus with his harangue. (Pp. 364–65)

This is a rare instance in which Sterne, as narrator, simply gives up trying to find convincing causes for his effects. The implication seems to be that it simply does not matter why Trim continued with his speech—that the *why*, in fact, of *anything* is irrelevant to the matter of living. In order to profit from experience, one must allow the experience to take shape as it will, without having to account for the reasons it worked out as it did. As narrator, Sterne makes sure to insist upon his omniscient powers, but he is quite willing at the same time to acknowledge his limitations as a man trying to discover the fundamental mystery at the heart of all human beings and life itself.

Again, if we drop the last reassuring statement which enables a man to live comfortably with the unknowable, we can see how contemporary Sterne really is:

—But mark, madam, we live amongst riddles and mysteries—the most obvious things, which come in our way, have dark sides, which the quickest sight cannot penetrate into; and even the clearest and most exalted understandings amongst us find ourselves puzzled and at a loss in almost every cranny of nature's works; so that this, like a thousand other things, falls out for us in a way, which tho' we cannot reason upon it,—yet we find the good of it, may it please your reverences and your worships— and that's enough for us. (P. 293)

Tristram Shandy, of course, reflects the essentially cheerful attitude of its author, and so no skirmish with chaos is apt to be fatal. If the universe refuses to supply explanations beyond a certain point, Sterne is quite willing to meet that universe on its own terms with no hard feelings involved. Indeed, anyone who tries to penetrate the impenetrable is seen as an essentially comic figure whose efforts reveal only the utter absurdity and futility of human reasoning when it becomes too ambitious for its own good. We can best cope with chaos simply by letting it sit there in the middle of our lives, and doing all we can to leave it undisturbed while we go about our business, using our minds for more fruitful endeavors. I would not call this a philosophical statement as it appears in Sterne's narrative, but it is, I think, an important psychological precept—the one means (that of avoidance) which permits us to live with some amount of sanity and grace.

It is Walter Shandy who plays the Overreacher in *Tristram Shandy*, and whenever his mind seems about to catapult him into dangerous areas, Sterne always makes him the butt of his joke on the mind's presumption in tackling matters it cannot hope to decipher. When, for example, Walter sets forth his plans for the infant Tristram, Toby's innocent retort just about demolishes the validity of his stand:

Tristram, said he [my father], shall be made to conjugate every word in the dictionary, backwards and forwards the same way;——every work, *Yorick*, by this means, you see, is converted into a thesis or an hypothesis;——every thesis and hypothesis have an offspring of propositions;—— and each proposition has its own consequences and conclusions; every one of which leads the mind on again, into fresh tracks of enquiries and doubtings.——The force of this engine, added my father, is incredible, in opening a child's head.——'Tis enough, brother *Shandy*, cried my uncle *Toby*, to burst it into a thousand splinters.——(P. 409)

Toby's comment is indeed prophetic of so many modern novelists who have thrown their conjectures into the progression of the novel itself, and so have perhaps splintered their art form. But whereas they find a state of chaos insupportable, Sterne seems to have found it quite tolerable; while he never defeats it, neither does he ever allow it to defeat *him*. He is content to call a truce in a battle he knows can never be won, and accept his compromise in perfect good humor.

But if Sterne found it easy to satirize Walter Shandy's preoccupation with the possibilities of language and logic, there are indications throughout the novel that he himself, as narrator, was frequently frustrated in the struggle of the artist to depict the full chaos of life without falling victim to it—that is, the artist's responsibility as he saw it, was to subdue the chaotic elements of his world in order to bring them into clear focus through a well-ordered work. That he also saw and understood the temptations of giving way to the forces which splinter a man's mind and thus his creative efforts, seems obvious from the two passages which will conclude this discussion. In the first, Sterne is talking not about himself, but about John de la Casse, the lord archbishop of Benevento who, according to Sterne, spent forty years working on his *Galateo*, the result of which was but a slender volume seemingly belying the great effort put into it. Sterne, however, admires the man for his lucidity, conscientiousness, and artistic integrity:

I own had *John de la Casse*, the archbishop of Benevento, for whose memory (notwithstanding his *Galateo*) I retain the highest veneration,— had he been, Sir, a slender clerk—of dull wit—slow parts—costive head, and so forth,—he and his *Galateo* might have jogged on together to the age of *Methusalah* for me,——the phenomenon had not been worth a parenthesis.——

But the reverse of this was the truth: *John de la Casse* was a genius of fine parts and fertile fancy; and yet with all those great advantages of nature, which should have pricked him forwards with his *Galateo*, he lay under an impuissance at the same time of advancing above a line and a half in the compass of a whole summer's day: this disability in his Grace arose from an opinion he was afflicted with,—which opinion was this,— viz. that whenever a Christian was writing a book (not for his private amusement, but) where his intent and purpose was bona fide, to print and publish it to the world, his first thoughts were always the temptations of the evil one.——This was the state of ordinary writers: but when a personage of venerable character and high station, either in church or state, once turned author,—he maintained, that from the very moment he took pen in hand—all the devils in hell broke out of their holes to cajole him.—'Twas Termtime with them,—every thought, first and last, was captious,—how specious and good soever,—'twas all one;—in whatever form or colour it presented itself to the imagination,—'twas still a stroke of one or other of 'em levelled at him, and was to be fenced off.—So that the life of a writer, whatever he may fancy to the contrary, was not so much a state of composition, as a state of warfare; and his probation in it, precisely that of any other man militant upon earth,— both demanding alike, not half so much upon the degrees of his WIT—as his RESISTANCE. (Pp. 373–74)

I do not mean necessarily to equate de la Casse's experience of writing with Sterne's, but the image is a striking one, and quite in accord with Sterne's conception of the artist in a constant struggle against the chaos of creation. The creator's role is to resist as fully as possible those invisible forces which seem at times to lift the work out of his own hands altogether, and throw it into the general stream of disordered life. The metaphor here is very similar to the position of Beckett's narrator in *The Unnamable:* the writer, beset on all sides by forces or (when he attempts to define them) figures which undermine his work by distracting his attention and acting like higher authorities ready to lead him onto a new level of lucidity. What do they have to tell him, what can they offer him, where can they take him? Beckett never has more than a fleeting glimpse of them—they sometimes resemble characters he himself has created to help him in his pursuit of some kind of viable knowledge—yet they disturb the peace he has found in total acceptance of nothingness. If they are merely splinters—conjectures of his own reeling mind—as he suspects, then whatever they might have to say is worthless because he has already followed them without finding the results he was looking for. This artist has admittedly lost control over both his life and his art; chaos has seeped into the mind that was his only recourse for managing it.

Sterne is obviously a very different kind of artist: it is he who is in control throughout. Yet the narrator of *Tristram Shandy* is not immune to the exasperation of trying to incorporate a basically chaotic narrative into an adhesive, coherent (even if chaotically coherent) framework. In one of his few confessions of fallibility, Sterne as Tristram wonders how he will ever get through the telling of his story, and finds himself at such a stalemate that he is forced to call on higher powers to come to his aid:

O ye POWERS! (for powers ye are, and great ones too)—which enable mortal man to tell a story worth the hearing—that kindly shew him, where he is to begin it,—and where he is to end it,—what he is to put into it,—and what he is to leave out,—how much of it he is to cast into shade,—and whereabouts he is to throw his light!—Ye, who preside over this vast empire of biographical freebooters, and see how many scrapes and plunges your subjects hourly fall into;—will you do one thing?

I beg and beseech you, (in case you will do nothing better for us) that wherever, in any part of your dominions it so falls out, that three several roads meet in one point, as they have done just here,—that at least you set up a guide-post, in the center of them, in mere charity to direct an uncertain devil, which of the three he is to take. (P. 207)

A passage worthy, indeed, of Robbe-Grillet, with the difference that one of *his* novels might very well end on such a note, whereas Sterne then recoups his powers, recovers, and goes on to finish Volume III and six more volumes of his work after that. Even when seen in all its complexity, then, the act of creation is never beyond Sterne. His craft requires discipline—and this he fully realizes—but it never, never, requires abdication.

We have seen that Sterne's narrative in *Tristram Shandy* is marked by such radical characteristics as frequent shifts in chronological sequence; abrupt halts of the action in the most unlikely places; endless series of digressions; absolute wrenching of his form (as when he waits until he has written nearly a hundred pages to begin his Preface, or when he skips two chapters in the last volume, only to include them in a later chapter); series of false suppositions which are then either overturned or ignored, and intimate confessions to the reader of the difficulty in organizing his material. Yet all of these characteristics are ultimately justified as legitimate techniques to help him achieve his purposes in the novel: whether they be to reinforce his principle of the workings of man's mind by trapping the reader in his own logic; whether it be to enhance his comic effects, heighten his dramatic effects, satirize his own profession or form; play purposeful havoc with the reader's imagination as part of his special relationship to him, or simply to reproduce in a realistic way the dynamic, erratic process by which man learns things in this world. Since actions are subservient to opinions concerning them, it is the formation of those opinions rather than the action itself which Sterne is out to make us experience. His wrenching of traditional narrative form constitutes, then, a purposeful, effective, and highly structured aesthetic technique (toward comic, psychological, dramatic, and tonal ends) which loosens the form only to enlarge the kind of experience it can project.

It is fitting that Sterne ends his novel with a mixture of self-satire and self-congratulations, for while his sense of the comic provides the impetus for the book, his remarkable success in finding the proper artistic methods to relate it surely accounts for its impression as one of the most ingratiating, delightful, spirited, and memorable novels in our literature:

L—d! said my mother, what is all this story about?—A COCK and a BULL, said Yorick—And one of the best of its kind, I ever heard. (P. 647)

To which the reader can only add his warmest applause and heartiest congratulations.

2

The Whiteness
of the Whale
Turned into Ice

Melville's Slippery Confidence-Man

"And some significance lurks in all things, else
all things are little worth, and the round world
itself but an empty cipher, except to sell by the
cartload, as they do hills about Boston, to fill up
some morass in the Milky Way."
—*Moby Dick*

In this passage, the narrator of *Moby-Dick* reveals an awareness of the catastrophic consequences of a nihilism which the novel itself manages ultimately to resist. It is clear that for Ishmael, the loss of cosmic meaning would signal a simultaneous deathblow to morality; and as a result, much of the book represents his struggle to overcome the horrifying implications of "whiteness"—the threat of a spiritual vacuum which, by annihilating the significance lurking in all things, would cause the world to collapse into vast acres of material substances hiding no values beyond their immediate monetary worth. The earth now becomes worth only what you can get from it or *for* it: sell it by the cartload, and if you make a profit, sell some more. In a universe lacking spiritual dimension,   knowledge and morality become as irrelevant to man as they are for the whale who destroys lives out of necessity and is worth only the sum total of oil he contains.

If we carry this idea over to *The Confidence-Man*, we find that Melville's suspicions have now hardened into convictions: the

Confidence Man himself is the supreme exploiter, one who "sells" the spiritually deflated materials of the world—whether it be natural herbs or working boys—to men valued only for what he can extract from them. Here the "whiteness of the whale" has become realized—and the result is a cosmic darkness rendering all men blind and helpless. Perhaps Melville's changed vision is comprehensible only after we have seen how his earlier novel managed to refute it; it would then become clear that although he has used his genius to create two entirely different works, each is carefully executed with the full artistic integrity found only in novels of the first rank. Through the recognized greatness of *Moby-Dick*, we might be able to discover the unrecognized greatness of *The Confidence-Man*.

Whenever Ishmael talks about the world, he assumes a basic unity and pattern to all things. The materials for our universe were always present, but it was not until God created the world from them that chaos disappeared, the earth became an integral part of a greater entity, and man was placed in a moral and spiritual atmosphere. Ishmael's fear of man's mind undoing the supposed creation of God and thereby throwing himself into chaos once more supplies a great deal of *Moby-Dick's* imaginative energy. In his desperate attempt to find value in life, meaning and significance in the various destinies of men, Ishmael constantly "reads" Nature in all its forms and then applies his new knowledge to particular situations or relationships aboard the Pequod. Everything is at stake in his search for meaning because a failure to discover some rationale beneath the surface of things would automatically justify the nihilistic perspective he is trying so hard to discredit.

Although the epigraph is taken from "The Doubloon" chapter (in the latter half of the book, when we really seem to be hearing Melville's voice, rather than his narrator's), the substance of it has already played a large part in the novel, beginning perhaps with Ishmael's reflections on the whiteness of the whale. But the possibility of a meaningless universe is finally defeated artistically as well as thematically; apart from what he may conclude on the basis of Ahab's quest and destruction about the worth, meaning, and potential stature of a man's life, the reader ends by finding significance in everything. Even if we see Ahab's annihilation as the result of a mad delusion which drove him to grapple with forces better left alone, we could never feel the Pequod's voyage to be senseless, for it has revealed a great deal about human nature consistent with the consequences of behavior and attitude. And even if we acknowledge the ambiguity at the core of Melville's vision, we see that it leads to complexity, rather than to hopeless confusion. In short, the world of *Moby-Dick* is saturated with artistic meaning and controlled by it. With a few exceptions, such as Bulkington, we feel that the author has fully worked out the import of his subject. The fact that Ahab's venture ends by destroying his crew as well as himself may seem cruel and unjust, but it *is* fully justified by the artistic context and so leads directly to a moral meaning. Like the end of a Shakespearean tragedy, the hero's fall has brought down many innocents, but still the right person survives to tell the story, and perhaps to restore order to a drowned world. Indeed, the very writing of the book is Ishmael's attempt to do just this.

As he reconstructs the fate of the Pequod, Ishmael simultaneously constructs its meaning for himself and for us. When the Pequod goes down, for example, it takes a "living part of heaven along with her" in the form of a sky-hawk, and this enables Ishmael to compare Ahab's plight with the fall of the proud, overreaching, yet vital angel, Satan. The symbol forces us to feel the reverberation of a fall from Heaven to Hell. Also, the fact that Ishmael alone is saved helps to focus the moral meaning of the Pequod's disastrous outcome. His rescue by the "devious-cruising Rachel, that in her retracing search after her missing children, only found another orphan" is artistically satisfying and, as Gertrude Stein might say, completely completing. Everything in the book fits, then, into a formal whole as the result of Melville's artistry, and it is clear that the author is paying more attention to his aesthetic goals than to his representation of reality. It is always the latter that is sacrificed to the symbolic scheme of the novel, with the result that such characters as Fedallah and such incidents as the sky-hawk's being pinioned to the flag of the sinking Pequod seem contrived and unconvincing, even if they do have their proper meaning in terms of the book's overall plan.

According to Alfred Kazin, it is Ishmael's (or as we soon come to feel, Melville's) mind that actually lies at the center of the book, providing its direction, its imaginative power, its spiritual intensity. And it is true that we feel the presence of a mastermind working behind the scenes, creating order from chaos and instilling every object with maximum significance. The principal proof of this would be the great whale himself, whose meaning transcends his material worth. No matter how we interpret him, it is clear that he functions as no "cartload of earth" to be regarded solely as a profitable oil supply. Ahab, Ishmael, and Starbuck all attribute some human or divine qualities to him, and view him as the embodiment of certain moral, intellectual, and spiritual forces—and the reader also interprets his importance on these levels.

This does not imply that the meaning of the book's characters, symbols, and incidents is always clear—rather, it is almost always highly complex and ambiguous—but that everything *does* signify and intensify, we are certain.

We are thrust into quite a different imaginative world in *The Confidence-Man*. In this last novel of Melville to be published during his lifetime, we no longer feel the presence of a mind operating behind the scenes, and we are no longer certain that there is a "meaning" to all that is going on, or even an artistic justification for the ambiguities. What we feel instead is an artist who has not lost his control so much as surrendered it. If we are to discover his meaning, then, we must do so exactly as we are forced to in real life—with strong reservations about the validity of our conclusions, along with a constant gnawing suspicion that what we seek is finally unknowable, and therefore any "discovery" the sure sign either of a hoax or of a rash subjective interpretation mistaken for objective fact.

Until the last fifteen years or so, *The Confidence-Man* has puzzled critics to the point where most of them have debunked it as a failure just because its meaning *is* so hazy, its form so uncertain, its intentions so unclear. But in recent years, the book has begun to make its way up through the ranks of Melville's most successful writings as various critics have started to point out that the very qualities hitherto depicted as the book's weaknesses are actually its strengths, that the form is entirely justified by the writer's intentions, and that the meaning is, in turn, fully consistent with the form.

It seems to me perfectly obvious that *The Confidence-Man* has at last been vindicated by the critics *from* the critics: it is clear that Melville has here set out to prove nothing, but to question everything, to assert nothing, but to suspect everything; and that he succeeded brilliantly in adapting his new vision to his art form. Far from having lost his artistic genius, Melville has in fact gained control of it to the point where he can actually construct a new kind of novel which utilizes all the traditional techniques of the novelist for the paradoxical purpose of creating disorder. He has now broken away from the tradition of providing meaning through the art form (as he had done in *Moby-Dick*); instead, he has very consciously used his form to *destroy* meaning, to perpetuate chaos—and that is what makes this such a strange and often baffling work. Here is the representation of a universe broken down to its original state and reduced to its essential materialistic value—that view which Ishmael so feared, that view which would apparently justify any act of exploitation because it signaled a world in which no significance lurked in things. Here is the Confidence Man who sees all value in monetary terms, who sells his cartloads of philosophical goods for a profit, and upon whom no judgment is made (whereas Ahab fails, *he* triumphs). And so like a god working in reverse, Melville hollows out his creation carefully until it fills up with darkness, hurls us into it, and leaves us stranded there.

But again, this represents no diminishing of Melville's powers as a novelist; rather, I think it indicates a fuller development of his artistry, for Melville, in order to convey his vision of life, had to sacrifice some of his favorite devices for getting a story told. If Ishmael's presence in *Moby-Dick* provided a base of solidity for the reader and acted, in addition, as a fountainhead for meaning, then such a presence would be entirely inappropriate for *The Confidence-Man*. As a result, the narrator has been stamped out so completely in *The Confidence-Man* (except for three crucial chapters of authorial intrusion), that we hardly recognize the writer who was always so sure to guide us personally through his story.

Another feature of Melville's earlier works was the constant juxtaposition (rather than fusion) of realistic fact and artistic fantasy. It is apparent that Melville always felt guilty about the discrepancy between art and reality, and since he was not yet able to blend them, he gave us both separately: in *Moby-Dick, Typee, Redburn, Benito Cereno,* and later, *Billy Budd,* his realistic documentations were almost always explicit apologies from one whose craft necessitated artificiality. But now Melville seems to have found a way to incorporate realism within the framework of symbolic fiction, and one peculiar but purposeful result of this is that new meanings now subtract from, rather than add to, those formerly established in the work. If the author of *Moby-Dick* manages finally to saturate his universe with meaning, we can say that the author of *The Confidence-Man* has successfully *drained* his of meaning.

In the first of his three chapters of authorial intrusion, Melville reveals the new assumptions on which he is working, and we can infer immediately that such a work as *Moby-Dick*, which often sacrifices a sense of reality to a sense of artistic validity, is no longer possible for him:

Upon the whole, it might rather be thought, that he, who, in view of its inconsistencies, says of human nature the same that, in view of its contracts, is said of the divine nature, that it is past finding out, thereby evinces a better appreciation of it than he, who, by always representing it in a clear light, leaves it to be inferred that he clearly knows all about it.[1]

Such an artist would never attempt to take us into the minds of his characters; the writer who reproduced Ahab's thoughts in trying to account for his motivations must now regard it as illegal to trespass beyond appearance. Even while he is quite aware of the fact that the reader, accustomed to being led on a leash by the author, will resent his refusal to make things clear and sensible (as the book's long-time unpopularity well attests to), Melville now refuses to compromise reality as he sees it for the end of art. If art must falsify to give us a consistent view of human nature, if it must contrive in order to drench the universe with meaning and significance, then the old conception of art as an ordering principle must be set aside for one truer to reality. For this reason, the Confidence Man himself must remain a complete enigma to us; we cannot evaluate him because we cannot be quite sure of his motivations. We can, of course, take them at face value, but that means falling into the class of his victims. Because we know the danger of accepting someone for what he *appears* to be, and because Melville refuses to give us anything *beyond* appearance, we hesitate to make any judgments at all.

Of course, our very confusion is an intrinsic part of Melville's purpose; we would be greatly mistaken to think that he himself was confused about what he was doing. Rather, we are dealing

---

1. Herman Melville, *The Confidence-Man: His Masquerade*, ed. Hennig Cohen (New York: Holt, Rinehart and Winston, 1964), p. 73. All future page references to this edition will be noted parenthetically in the text.

now with an artist who considers it misleading to provide his audience with clues to motives that life itself normally withholds. In this way, Melville veers closely to purely dramatic representation, and he is quite aware of this. It is no coincidence that Shakespeare is mentioned so frequently:

" ' This Shakespeare is a queer man.' At times seeming irresponsible, he does not always seem reliable. There appears to be a certain—what shall I call it?—hidden sun, say about him, at once enlightening and mystifying." (P. 187)

The meaning is clear: "Shakespeare himself is to be adored, not arraigned," as the cosmopolitan says a little later, "but so we do it with humility, we may a little canvass his characters" (p. 187). Although the characters may be analyzed on their own terms, it is not the author's responsibility to help us. Shakespeare *is* enlightening in his depiction of people, but ultimately mystifying in his failure to explain to us how we are to interpret and evaluate them.

Melville's intention is, then, to delineate reality, not to decipher it; since his basic point is that the truth about anything is unknowable, to explain would be automatically to falsify. The complexity of reality often leads us to a stalemate in judgment just at those times that we have the most lucidity—we are suddenly aware of many perspectives and evaluative approaches, none of which seems necessarily more valid than the others—and by bringing us to such a stalemate where judgment becomes almost impossible, Melville is able to convey his vision of reality by making us feel it ourselves.

It is therefore essential to his effect that the author refuse to furnish for the reader anything more than life itself offers him in the way of conclusive evidence. Man's inability to know anything certain—whether about himself, all human nature, or the universe—is by now an axiom of Melville's, and the one to which this book is dedicated:

"What are you? What am I? Nobody knows who anybody is. The data which life furnishes, towards forming a true estimate of any being, are as insufficient to that end as in geometry one side given would be to determine the triangle." (P. 209)

It is true that these words are spoken by the Emersonian-type stranger who finally emerges as a cold, unlikable character, but no statement in the book expresses so well the principle which alone unifies it and explains why so much appears to be murky or missing.

Now that we have Melville's purpose established, we can see that our voyage on the Fidèle will complicate and confuse our impression of reality in exactly the way that our journey on the Pequod clarified it. The important point here is that the means are the same, and only the ends different—which is to say that Melville's artistry will be every bit as evident as it was in *Moby-Dick*. We must be careful not to confuse the final vision of chaos with fuzziness of artistic technique—and that is what many critics have done at Melville's expense. What is needed, in short, is an aesthetic justification of Melville's method here to prove that this work deserves far more attention and acclaim than it has been receiving. This entails a study of character, symbol, action, and idea that goes just far enough to show how each is used to bring chaos into focus.

If we examine the various means through which the characters aboard the Fidèle approach reality, we find that they can be pretty well reduced to three alternatives: pragmatic, theological, or philosophical. The first arrives at truth through common sense based on factual evidence, the second through revelation based on faith, and the third through a reasoning process based on logic. Melville examines each one, but eventually finds them all inadequate to make the crucial distinctions between what is real and what is not.

Melville's ingenuity in finding symbolic expression for his skepticism can best be illustrated perhaps by the clever device of the counterfeit detector, a seemingly infallible means of verification. Given as a gift to the old man by the young peddler who has already profited from his lack of confidence, the detector leaves him hopelessly confused in his attempt to distinguish the good bill from the false one. As a practical guide to truth, it contains so many exceptions and qualifications that it can only puzzle one the more he studies it. Reality, we must conclude, is too complex for pragmatism to work efficiently.

While speaking to the sick man on board, the Confidence Man, disguised now as an herb doctor, says, "A sick philosopher is incurable" (p. 84), and the implication is that in our weakest state, we need a staff of faith to lean upon; faith is the only source of hope for man, and as long as we refuse to surrender our reason to it, our sickness will continue. Yet as soon as the sick man comes around to the Confidence Man's point of view and purchases his medicine, we know that he has been duped, victimized, played for a "sucker." Faith now seems foolish because it is always impossible to know when the object of one's faith is a false god. And yet we have seen, too, that the perfect reasonableness of the counterfeit detector led us to the same blind end. As long as nothing is knowable, neither approach can be more valid than the other.

One is tempted here to reach a conclusion: true, we might say, the sick philosopher is incurable, but he is nevertheless superior to the man of faith because he remains in touch with reality. We know that the sick man cannot be cured by the quack medicine of the herb doctor; we know that his case *is* hopeless. Therefore, although both the philosopher and the believer have incurable illnesses, the philosopher, by at least *knowing* his case to be incurable, is not deluded.

But the book defeats any such simplified solution. First of all, we cannot deny that the Confidence Man *does* usually leave behind some marked improvement in the mental and psychological state of his victim. The bitter cripple who requires the utmost of the Confidence Man's mastery before he is finally persuaded to buy his medicine, shows a typical response:

As the herb doctor withdrew, the cripple gradually subsided from his hard rocking into a gentle oscillation. It expressed, perhaps, the soothed mood of his reverie. (P. 106)

Even if he does not cure, then, the Confidence Man does comfort those who put their trust in him, and perhaps the new hope he has given them may also effect some improvement in their physical condition. Furthermore, the rational man is no less susceptible to the Confidence Man's guile. Pitch refuses to be swayed by the herb doctor's argument for confidence; he is a thinking man who must be convinced by reason before he will believe. As the herb doctor who operates on a man's feelings, the Confidence Man comes off poorly against Pitch's solid arguments, but as soon as he changes his outfit and role to that of a representative from the Philosphical Intelligence Office and directs his appeal to the mind rather than the heart, he dupes Pitch as easily as he has the others, and we cannot ignore the implications of his success here: the Confidence Man cannot get at Pitch through faith, so he gets at him through reason. But Pitch's confidence in reason is really just as arbitrary as any kind of religious faith, since his complete trust in some assumed approach to truth acts as the basis for his actions and decisions. Nor is it any longer pertinent to say that *any* faith is unreasonable, for reason, too, is just another assumption. As an alternative to nihilism and passiveness, we must accept one criterion for judgment, even though we do so on faith; otherwise, human thought and action are rendered useless. But Pitch's reason has led him just as far astray as faith has led the sick man; he has been manipulated by his own logic.

We have seen that any approach to reality must be based on blind trust, a confidence that assumes truth to be discoverable. And we have seen, too, that as long as man operates on that assumption, he is certain to be victimized. We can only conclude that the man who believes he has found truth is a presumptuous fool.

In a manner reminiscent of Lear's fool, Pitch assaults the Confidence Man:

> "Pray, which do you think are most, knaves or fools?"
> "Having met with few or none of either, I hardly think I am competent to answer."
> "I will answer for you. Fools are most."
> "Why do you think so?"
> "For the same reason that I think oats are numerically more than horses. Don't knaves munch up fools just as horses do oats?" (P. 114)

If his victims are fools, then the Confidence Man is apparently the knave who feeds on them. Like the man who sells cartloads of earth in the form of hills about Boston, he profits from *men* who seem to have lost their spiritual significance but have become only material closets of money to be eaten by the more aware animal. As soon as we disregard or disallow a man's spiritual value, the tendency is to reduce him immediately to a concept of worth measured solely in monetary terms—an attitude similar to that exhibited by the Southerners toward Jim in *Huckleberry Finn*.

I have said that for Ishmael, a world suddenly stripped of that significance lurking in all things would instantly signal a nihilistic perspective from which sheer exploitation of natural (or human) resources would become justifiable. Melville, of course, has refused to tell the reader how his Confidence Man should be judged, and so it is finally up to us to evaluate his behavior and determine to what extent he is evil and worthy of our most severe condemnation.

The Confidence Man always extracts a price for his services or goods, but this in itself would not necessarily make him evil. We always have to pay for our faith: every notion of a divinity has its demands for the believer. Could the Confidence Man be, then, a Christ-like figure who exchanges salvation for personal sacrifices? There is, I think, much evidence for this view if we admit that, although the validity of Christ's divinity may never be established, the comfort and meaning he gives to the human condition may be real enough to justify a Kierkegaardian "leap of faith." It is to the weak that the Confidence Man offers his greatest appeal: "Believe me that, like your crutches, confidence and hopefulness will long support a man when his own legs will not," he says to the sardonic cripple. "Stick to confidence and hopefulness, then, since how mad for the cripple to throw his crutches away" (p. 106). Christ is the only means by which man can endure his unhappy, helpless condition on earth, and as such He seems to represent the only alternative to utter cynicism and misanthropy. His necessity for us is a practical one, for men are weak and need something to lean upon.

But what of the strong—those who need no crutch, those who seek truth rather than comfort and have the strength to live with it? Again, we have only suggestion to work with, but it seems clear that those strong enough to live without Christ have no right to deprive the weak of His consolations and offerings of hope. After leading away the old sick man who has been leaning on him, the Confidence Man returns to Pitch and charges him with a lack of heart in attempting to destroy the old man's faith in him, for

granting that his dependence on my medicine is vain, is it kind to deprive him of what, in mere imagination, if nothing more, may help eke out, with hope, his disease? For you, if you have no confidence, and, thanks to your native health, can get along without it, so far, at least, as trusting in my medicine goes; yet how cruel an argument to use, with this afflicted one here. Is it not for all the world as if some brawny pugilist, aglow in December, should rush in and put out a hospital fire, because, forsooth, he feeling no need of artificial heat, the shivering patients shall have none? Put it to your conscience, sir, and you will admit, that, whatever be the nature of this afflicted one's trust, you, in opposing it, evince either an erring head or a heart amiss. (P. 117)

At this point, the Confidence Man is making no attempt to verify his claims for his products, and it now becomes irrelevant whether the hope he sells is true or false; the fact is that it does comfort those who need comforting, gives hope to the despairing, resolution and strength to the trembling and fearful—it offers, in short, the only kind of solace available to man in times of his greatest weakness and suffering. Even operating on the assumption that his products have no innate value, the Confidence Man's practical argument for humanity is strong and can no longer be attacked from a philosophical point of view—that is, one which will commit itself only to what it has resolved to be true.

Pragmatic ethics would resolve the problem here by refusing to condemn those who, in their weakness, must leap to faith in order to save themselves from despair, yet crediting fully other alternatives that reach the same end of providing man with a renewed sense of his significance, hope for the future, and some kind of philosophical or spiritual ballast to add weight and value to his existence. The above passage would imply, therefore, that although Pitch is fully justified in refusing what the Confidence Man offers, he is *not* justified in condemning the sick old man for requiring and accepting such products and services.

All very good. Except, of course, that the novel never does leave us with any such synthesis, but goes on to provide a whole new set of implications which destroys, rather than merges with the former one. Thus, although the Confidence Man acts as a crutch to the crippled, he is a poor crutch, indeed. As the old miser leans on him (in the scene with Pitch), the herb doctor becomes increasingly impatient and fatigued with the weight of his patient:

> "Pray, my venerable friend," said the herb doctor, now trying to straighten himself, "don't lean *quite* so hard; my arm grows numb; abate a little, just a very little."
>
> "Go," said the Missourian, "go lay down in your grave, old man, if you can't stand yourself. It's a hard world for a leaner." (Pp. 118–19)

The facts are now such that Pitch's advice assumes a new validity which all the Confidence Man's best arguments do little to refute. The truth is that the Confidence Man has *not* been able to deliver the strength and security he promised; his support cannot be sustained. Furthermore, it is immediately after the herb doctor has stated his case for the pragmatic value of his confidence that he

and Pitch get into a discussion on abolition in which Pitch definitely comes out ahead—perhaps the only time in the novel
when the Confidence Man comes off second-best and really appears to be a genuine fraud. His sidestepping of Pitch's direct
questions, his slippery evasiveness is no longer a sleight of hand
which impresses us in spite of our cautionary attitude toward
him; it is here the elusiveness of the weak and uncommitted and
fully deserves Pitch's response:

"You are the moderate man, the invaluable understrapper of the wicked
man. You, the moderate man, may be used for wrong, but are useless for
right. . . . Is not that air of yours, so spiritlessly enduring and yielding, the
very air of a slave?" (P. 120)

Really put to the test, then, the Confidence Man's philosophy
emerges as nothing more than bland professions of good will.
Still, this does not necessarily remove the possibility of his being
an essentially Christ-like figure. Like Christ, he professes the noble sentiments of love, virtue, mercy, benevolence without judgment; and also renders his service to the sick in mind, body, and
spirit. But He himself never interferes on the level of action,
never makes His force felt in a direct way in the affairs of men.
His role is primarily to give hope—false hope, perhaps, yet with a
very real value. He offers salvation for the future, rather than
instigating it in the present.

Perhaps this would account for the bewildering first chapter
of the book, in which the Confidence Man enters in his first disguise and, bathed in images of Christ, proceeds to write out his
statements on charity. The reaction of the other passengers is so
obviously hostile that the reader is forced to realize that charity
itself cannot be an effective means of mollifying the suffering of
man, either because the very concept of charity is out of tune
with the times or, as is much more likely, because it is out of tune
with the true nature of man. Therefore, the Confidence Man
must work with trust: only faith will produce charitable acts in
this world; only his belief in some power beyond himself will
prod man's goodness into the open where it can help to relieve
the general lot of humanity. The Confidence Man, as a restorer of
faith, does a service even in his disservice.

Nevertheless, the fact remains, and always remains, that the
Confidence Man *is* a confidence man—a mountebank who appears to be motivated by self-interest—and is therefore an ironic

character in that we must distrust everything he says. No matter what else the passengers' distrust of him may say about the cynicism of modern man, we must remember that their suspicion is entirely justified, and that it would be just as valid to point to their distrust as a sign of their own perspicacity as it would be of their lack of charity and faith in their fellow man.

Melville is so insistent in juxtaposing images of Christ and Satan when describing the Confidence Man, that we are finally forced to admit that we cannot hope to decipher him. In the following passages, for example, the Confidence Man is delineated, through sound, in satanic terms; he is the snake, the vicious charmer who fairly hisses at his approach:

"Pray, now," with a sort of sociable sorrowfulness, slowly sliding along the rail. . . . (P.25)

"I see," slowly spiriting upward a spiral staircase of lazy smoke, "I see; you go in for the lofty." (P. 146)

The force of the language is so striking at such points that we have no alternative but to see the Confidence Man as a clear representative of the devil in his serpentine state (which idea is reinforced by the frequent snake imagery). Yet both these descriptions precede statements which are utterly Christian and could easily be seen as coming directly from the mouth of Christ, since they are His sentiments that are being poured out. Unlike the tempter of Eve, this snake does not try to alienate man from God, to convince him to disobey His commandments, but instead tries to effect just the opposite: he insists on the common fellowship of man and the true Christian attitude of love, mercy, submission, and faith.

What, then, are we to make of him? What can we do with Christ in the shape and sound of a serpent; how synthesize this ambiguous character? I suggest only that it cannot possibly be done, and that Melville has rendered futile any attempt to clarify the enigma. The bewildered mind tries desperately but in vain to draw some final meaning from the total evidence; but again, we can only conclude that reality is too complex and truth too far out of reach for us to know them. The book, like life, fails to resolve its contradictory evidence.

Much recent criticism on *The Confidence-Man* has fixed upon the appearance–reality motif running through the book. But since, as we have seen, Melville's overriding assumption seems to have been that reality is unknowable, a more exact description of the novel's chief concern might be appearance vs. appearance. We are presented with a series of Socratic dialogues which must amount to nothing because Socrates' basic assumption that truth *could* be attained by the wise, rational man is no longer a reasonable hypothesis (and because we have only appearances to work with in the world of *The Confidence-Man,* Plato's intellectual leap into the realm of truth is no more valid than the leap of faith on the part of the sick man). Furthermore, even when the Confidence Man clearly has the more convincing argument, we have only to remember that his motives are not to seek truth, but to delude—and we are thrown right back into chaos and indecision. In the middle of his conversation with Charlie, for example, the cosmopolitan becomes so eloquent in his advocacy of philanthropy, that we automatically begin taking his side, an easy thing to do since his opponent is obviously not to be trusted or respected. But then suddenly the cosmopolitan adds a new insight to his others:

"Now, the genial misanthrope, when, in the process of eras, he shall turn up, will be the converse of this; under an affable air, he will hide a misanthropical heart . . . to so genial a degree, indeed, that it may possibly fall out that the misanthrope of the coming century will be almost as popular as, I am sincerely sorry to say, some philanthropists of the present time would seem not to be . . . ." (P. 193)

We are in the midst of applauding his views and attitudes, his tremendous concern for the human race, when it suddenly strikes us that we ourselves have been duped by him—for this is a perfect description of the Confidence Man himself. Since the idea comes from his own mouth, he becomes the last one we would expect to illustrate it, but the author, by tricking us in this way, has forced us to respond with the same perplexity as the other passengers. We are no more immune to his charm than they, and this awareness makes all judgment extremely difficult.

Is the Confidence Man truly evil? Or can he possibly represent the Second Coming of Christ in a world whose motto has become "No Trust?" If he is evil, we find it still hard to condemn him because we are never given his motives. Also, when he is taking advantage of the greed, gullibility, and hypocrisy of others, we can hardly feel that he is to be blamed more than they. Although he profits from the peculiar vulnerabilities of his victims, it is important that they *are* weaknesses in a shallow society which lacks valid criteria for distinguishing the true from the false. Because there is no one standard shown or implied to be superior to the others, we tend to suspend all judgment.

What makes matters even more confusing is the fact that even if the Confidence Man is indeed nothing more than a scoundrel, he is surely such a shrewd and enormously appealing one that we ourselves are too closely drawn to him to condemn him. Though the possibility of his being analogous to Christ is never completely eliminated, we continue to feel that his first entrance as a deaf mute remains to be explained. Finally, we realize that we cannot possibly come to any conclusion without the help of the author, and so we come with relief to the third and final chapter of direct comment to the reader where Melville at last starts talking about his own creation in his chapter on originals in literature.

Melville defines the true original character as one who implies original instincts, and he gives as examples Hamlet, Don Quixote, and Milton's Satan. Such characters are "like a revolving Drummond light, raying away from itself all around it—everything is lit by it, everything starts up to it" (p. 261). Certainly, the Confidence Man, while a shadowy character himself, *does* throw light on the microcosmic world traveling on the Fidèle, and he also seems a new fictional species, rather than a striking variation on one of the rare originals. It would be tempting, of course, to alight on Melville's mention of Milton's Satan as an indication that we might well take to heart the many demonic qualities represented in our Confidence Man and see him as the original charmer, sneakily coiling and slithering his multi-patterned skin over the boards of the Fidèle. Like Satan, he can assume any form that best suits his immediate purposes and enables him to deceive those who would never be fooled by him in any other guise. But the tempting conclusions in this book always manage to recede just as we are ready to pounce on them, and so we must remember that in the same breath with Milton's Satan, Melville mentions Don Quixote who, as the supreme idealist, optimist, and romanticist would appear to be his very opposite; and Hamlet, who would seem to represent a midway point of ambiguity between these two extremes (whereas the motivations of both Satan and Quixote are quite clear, Hamlet's are obtuse and almost indecipherably complex).

I think we *can* call the Confidence Man a true original because *his* instincts, unlike the others, are completely unknown. He has *both* Satan and Quixote in him, but these remain potentialities rather than clear character traits, and since their antithetical features cannot be reconciled, he can be like neither. And whereas Hamlet's instincts and motivations are complex, those of the Confidence Man must remain utterly unknown. We can add up the clues to Hamlet's character, and though the totality of him may elude us, the clues do not cancel each other out as they do in the Confidence Man.

Yet how explain the fact that the author says he has written this chapter for the express purpose of showing the inappropriateness of the phrase *"Quite an Original,"* as used by the barber's friends in referring to the cosmopolitan? Also, Melville says that original characters in fiction are so rare, that "a grateful reader will, on meeting with one, keep the anniversary of that day" (p. 260). Fine, but the day we meet the Confidence Man is on April 1, All Fool's Day, when no information is to be trusted, when all data must be regarded with suspicion. Again, we must remain hopelessly confused, but again, too, Melville seems perfectly aware of the smoke screen he has created and fully intends to stay hidden behind it:

In the endeavor to show, if possible, the impropriety of the phrase, *Quite an Original,* as applied by the barber's friends, we have, at unawares, been led into a dissertation bordering upon the prosy, perhaps upon the smoky. If so, the best use the smoke can be turned to, will be, by retiring under cover of it, in good trim as may be, to the story. (P. 261)

And indeed, off he then goes into the final chapter of the book, which is undoubtedly the most perplexing of all.

The scene opens with a description of the intense light radiating from the solar lamp, which throws a halo around the old man:

The light of this lamp, after dazzlingly striking on marble, snow-white and round—the slab of a centre-table beneath—on all sides went rippling off with ever-diminishing distinctness, till, like circles from a stone dropped in water, the rays died dimly away in the furthest nook of the place.

Here and there, true to their place, but not to their function, swung other lamps, barren planets, which had either gone out from exhaustion, or been extinguished by such occupants of berths as the light annoyed, or who wanted to sleep, not see. (P. 262)

The significance of the light is thus established very early, and it does seem to represent our world as the only one containing conscious life. It is under this light which, on captain's orders, is required to stay lit until dawn, that the final dialogue takes place. The light itself, which has been left on because of the obvious ill consequences of darkness in such a group of strangers, becomes an ironic presence as the old man and the cosmopolitan affirm their deep trust in the innate goodness of man and further, in the pervading presence of a beneficent God. "From what you say," says the old man, "I see you are something of my way of thinking—you think that to distrust the creature, is a kind of distrusting of the Creator" (p. 266); and so the hypothesis set up within the circle of dazzling light reveals the implications of distrust of one's fellow: it automatically defeats the supposition of a meaningful world created by God.

The old man and the cosmopolitan read selections from the Bible, and it is clear that their faith in a Creator is both real and vital to them. Later, the old man even says,

in all our wanderings through this vale, how pleasant, not less than obligatory, to feel that we need start at no wild alarms, provide for no wild perils; trusting in that Power which is alike able and willing to protect us when we cannot ourselves. (P. 273)

This is a noble sentiment and, from what he has said earlier, we know that it means implicit trust in all men as well, for to doubt the one is necessarily to doubt the other. But, of course, the scene becomes flooded with irony as soon as we realize that this is the same man who has just purchased a traveler's patent lock and a money belt, and had a counterfeit detector thrown into the bargain. When the cosmopolitan asks if he intends to wear the money belt that very night, the old man replies, " 'It's best, ain't it?' with a slight start, 'Never too late to be cautious. "Beware of pickpockets" is all over the boat' " (p. 270). Nor does he trust the companion to whom he has just been expounding his trust in man and God. When the cosmopolitan offers to help him put on the money belt,

"Oh no, no, no!" said the old man, not unperturbed, "no, no, I wouldn't trouble you for the world," then nervously folding up the belt, "and I won't be so impolite to do it for myself, before you, either." (Pp. 270–71)

Because of his earlier remarks, we know that the whole question of God is now at stake, and the Confidence Man senses it, too:

with you, sir, I believe in a Committee of Safety, holding silent sessions over all, in an invisible patrol, most alert when we soundest asleep, and whose beat lies as much through forests as towns, along rivers as streets. In short, I shall never forget the passage of Scripture which says, "Jehovah shall be thy confidence." The traveler who has not this trust, what miserable misgivings must be his; or, what vain, short-sighted care must he take care of himself.

"Even so," said the old man lowly. (Pp. 273–74)

The scene immediately becomes comically pathetic as the old man, looking around for a life-saver to take to bed with him, accepts in all good faith a chamber pot from the Confidence Man. As he checks it closely to make sure it is in good repair, the situation becomes increasingly absurd:

"Sure its *quite* perfect, though?" Then, anxiously putting on his spectacles, he scrutinized it pretty closely—"well-soldered, quite tight?"

"I should say so, sir; though, indeed, as I have said, I never use this sort of thing, myself. Still, I think that in case of wreck, barring sharp-pointed timbers, you could have confidence in that stool of a special providence."

"Then, good-night, good-night; and Providence have both of us in its good keeping."

"Be sure it will," eyeing the old man with sympathy, as for the moment he stood, money-belt in hand, and life-preserver under arm, "be sure it will, sir, since in Providence, as in man, you and I equally put trust. But bless me, we are being left in the dark here. Pah! what a smell, too." (P. 275)

We somehow find it difficult to laugh at the old man: foolish as he is, there is something terribly touching about the sight of him clutching his money-belt and life-saver while being told that he puts trust equally in man and Providence, and never realizing that the two objects he hugs are respective symbols of distrust in each.

It is small wonder that the light starts burning out just at this point: obviously, the radiant light under which they have been holding their "enlightened" conversation has signified a vision which has been obliterated by the conversation itself. It is clear that the old man does *not* dwell in the sphere of a Divine Presence—or at least his purchases and actions during the scene have completely undercut any belief he has ostensibly upheld. Melville has emphasized three aspects of the light during this scene: its spiritual significance (reflecting the presence of a Supreme Being—that is, the dazzling light of Heaven flooding downward to earth); its protective quality (by which one is prevented from being victimized by thieves), and its illuminative powers (which enable one in its sphere to make clear distinctions, to perceive what is going on). It has by this time, then, become a symbol for Divine presence, protection from the evil of man, and philosophical lucidity and insight. In the progression of the scene, however, each one of these qualities has been invalidated by the speech and action of the old man, and so the light's burning out is justified symbolically, as well as realistically. Also, it gives off a bad odor, as if the vision it represented were rotting.

"Ah, my way now," cried the old man, peering before him, "where lies my way to my state-room?"

"I have indifferent eyes, and will show you; but first, for the good of all lungs, let me extinguish this lamp."

The next moment, the waning light expired, and with it the waning flames of the horned altar, and the waning halo round the robed man's brow; while in the darkness which ensued, the cosmopolitan kindly led the old man away. Something further may follow of this masquerade. (P. 275)

The darkness which closes this novel (or perhaps more appropriately, the darkness into which the novel sinks) is alarming on several counts. Aside from its philosophical implications, it leaves us with the uncomfortable feeling that violence may soon take place: the cosmopolitan is almost certainly after the old man's money, and there is no reason to believe he will not get it. And if the money belt cannot save the old man from the threat of human thievery, will the chamber pot be any more effective in saving his life? The old man is entirely helpless and a perfect victim for any criminal. Ironically enough, he *has* put his confidence in man (namely, the boy who sold him the lock and money belt, and the cosmopolitan himself who gave him the life preserver and a promise to lead him back to his cabin), even as a result of his *lack* of confidence in man.

But why should Melville insert the word "kindly" here? Is this simply a gratuitous touch of irony, does it imply that the cosmopolitan is perhaps a philanthropist after all and has no intentions of robbing the old man, or does it imply something altogether different? Perhaps the word becomes most meaningful only when we consider the cosmic consequences of this new state of darkness.

If we go back to the beginning of the chapter, we find that Melville's insistence on the light as a symbol of our own planet is inescapable; and it presents a striking contrast to the other lights (symbolic of other planets) which have by now been snuffed out. We are told, further, that the other lights "had either gone out from exhaustion, or been extinguished by such occupants of berths as the light annoyed, or who wanted to sleep, not see" (p. 262). Because he has emphasized both the solar light's *exhaustion* (it had been dying out, and its rotten smell suggests that it had nearly completed its self-annihilation) *and* its *extinction* by the Confidence Man, Melville clearly intends for us to apply both meanings here. We have already explained the significance of its exhaustion: the scene between the cosmopolitan and the old man indicates that the old vision of a world observed through and protected by the radiating light of Heaven is no longer operable on this planet; it has ceased to function as an active basis for men's dealings. But we are also told that the other lights had been put out by those who wanted to sleep, not see; and it is in these terms that I believe we are meant to interpret the cosmopolitan's final act.

In the world presented here by Melville, perception and lucidity are the remotest of possibilities: rather, man is confronted by a world whose appearances are so confusing that they thwart the best-intentioned efforts to discover "the significance lurking in all things." Man has been rendered so helpless in his attempts to distinguish truth from falsehood (exemplified by the bewildered state of the old man as he tries to use his counterfeit detector), that we infer his only comfort to be in total surrender. His only alternative is the gift of unconsciousness, the one state in which he need no longer be bothered by the overwhelming ambiguity of life. To remove such a man from his condition of helplessness and confusion to one where he could sleep and forget about trying to "see" would seem the merciful thing to do for him; and in this sense, the cosmopolitan's act of leading the old man away into the darkness could be seen as a kindly gesture—an ironic one, to be sure, but still comprehensible.

The planet has now been darkened and rendered as barren of life as the others which have been quenched from the beginning of the chapter. What is to follow? "Something further may follow of this Masquerade" is as far as Melville seems to care to commit himself. Indeed, who could say what would follow nihilism? The word "something" opens up all sorts of possibilities, but our choice can never be more than arbitrary. Perhaps utter disaster and chaos: the Confidence Man may rob and even murder the old man. Perhaps simple nothingness in the form of surrender of consciousness and acceptance of the continuing state of darkness and despair. Perhaps a new beginning: the darkness is, after all, only a transitional state between the previous day and the following dawn—and the new day would perhaps bring us to a new level of meaning, an ordering of the chaos which has preceded. It would, at least, be April 2, a return to some minimal state of normality in which we could begin placing our faith in new things. Any of these is possible, but Melville would be sacrificing his vision of life as unknowable if he were to suggest any one conclusion. Surely, this seems the most satisfactory ending for the book.

In his article on *The Confidence-Man,* Daniel G. Hoffman finally calls the novel an interesting failure. It is

clearly a desperate experiment, whose partial success—the satiric power of individual episodes and characters—was won at the cost of a larger failure.

This is the failure of form. Melville has led himself into a maze of nondramatizable speculation to which none of the traditions he could make use of were fitted to give adequate form. . . . He attempts allegory without a superstructure of belief, and dialectic without the possibility of resolution. . . . A book of brilliant fragments, its method of development is too like a charade in which the clues are perversely half-concealed, or incomplete.[2]

This kind of reserved praise is typical of the great bulk of critical response to Melville's last novel to be published during his lifetime, yet one wonders if Hoffman has really understood the book, for he attacks it without considering Melville's intentions. I have shown again and again that Melville's deception of the reader is purposeful and meaningful—it is the only means by which he can communicate his conviction that truth is undiscoverable for man. If his clues are incomplete, they are not perversely so, but are meant to reflect a world in which clues are never complete and

2. Daniel G. Hoffman, *"The Confidence-Man: His Masquerade," Melville: A Collection of Critical Essays,* ed. Richard Chase (New Jersey, 1962), p. 142.

opposing views often irreconcilable. Their resolution would have given us not only a very different kind of novel, but also a different (and for Melville, false) vision of life. Melville is no longer willing to *invent* the significance lurking in things, as he was in *Moby-Dick;* he makes no attempt to represent through his art what he has not been able to find in reality. When a book purports to express the futility of faith, it seems foolish to criticize its lack of a superstructure of belief. Such a superstructure would have defeated Melville's whole purpose by compromising reality through artistic contrivance.

Later, Hoffman notes that although Melville has satirized many follies in the book, "his viewpoint is less satiric than ironic. And irony is the uncomforted refuge of perception without power."[3] Now this is sheer nonsense: to suggest that irony represents a falling off for the writer who lacks the power of a totally satirical vision is an assumption which cannot possibly be justified outside of one's own prejudices. A writer will hardly strive for satire unless he sees clear distinctions between what he takes to be proper and improper assumptions, beliefs, and modes of behavior.

It is true, as Hoffman says, that Melville had here "led himself into a maze of nondramatizational speculation to which none of the traditions he could make use of were fitted to give adequate form," but the fact is that Melville purposely dispensed with those traditions which by their very nature would interfere with his basic intentions. Nevertheless, he *has* managed to dramatize his philosophical speculations through a series of dialogues based on the automatic tension and opposition of conflicting points of view. Character, incident, and symbol are all used as dramatic embodiments of the abstract philosophical struggle being waged throughout the book, and the fact that they constantly contradict one another as well as contain their own contradictions (as in the depiction of the old man with his money belt, chamber pot, and noble words) only reinforces their effect on both levels.

Hoffman seems to think that Melville's very vision of nihilism precludes a successful "formal" work, but later critics have given much attention to the novel's hidden formal framework and have proved that even if carefully plotted to be elusive, the structure itself has full integrity and control.[4]

3. Hoffman, p. 142.
4. See especially John G. Cawelti's "Some Notes on the Structure of *The Confidence-Man," American Literature,* XXIX (1957), 278–88. Cawelti's basic thesis is

But the real danger in much recent criticism has been to vindicate Melville from such attacks by refusing to acknowledge the nihilistic implications of the book, and thus imposing a new pattern on it which, I believe, evades, rather than justifies its confusions. Thus, Richard Chase, one of the first to assert the novel's prominent position among Melville's works, says of it: "Usually considered a work of chaotic pessimism, it is in fact, one of the subtlest of all satires on the American spirit, a buoyant book despite the cunning with which it examines the national temperament."[5] It *is* true, of course, that the book is brimming with satire of all sorts and that many of Melville's targets can certainly be traced to specific people and theories. But that the work has satirical elements in no way precludes its also being a work of "chaotic pessimism." First of all, no matter how splendid the satire is here, it is really Melville's vision which holds us, which makes the book absorbing, forceful, and important. Satire does not seem the central purpose of the book any more than encyclopedic documentary on whales and whaling seems the heart of *Moby-Dick*. It is something else that attracts us, and that something is just the chaos that Chase denies—our failure to arrive at *any* conclusion that will meaningfully interpret the persons and events presented to us. Second, it is hard to see how anyone could call this a "buoyant" book, except by doing Melville the great injustice of

that Melville's "view of reality as ultimately inscrutable and ambiguous leads to a dynamic search for some way to structure and represent this reality," and therefore the great amount of conflicting evidence in the novel is no sign of Melville's perversity, but rather the structural means by which he is attempting to convey his vision to the reader. Once we see how this principle operates throughout the work, we have found the key to its formal foundations, its structural solidarity.

"That key is what we might call the incomplete reversal: something is presented, a character, an incident, an idea, anything which might give the reader some clue to the interpretation of the represented reality; then a counter incident or idea appears, powerful enough to destroy the usefulness of the first clue, but insufficient to provide a foundation for a new interpretation of what has been presented. We are left in the air with no way of resolving two mutually exclusive possibilities" (pp. 282–83).

After an analysis of Melville's consistent use of this technique, Cawelti concludes that "*The Confidence-Man*, then, is not a random collection of episodes, it is not the bitter polemic of a despairing man; it is not merely a philosophical leg-pull, but a serious, carefully-planned attempt to present one man's vision of reality. As the vision sees ambiguity at the heart of things, so the basic structural principle is one that leaves the reader alone with an enigma. One cannot deny . . . that Melville prepared for this result painstakingly and skillfully" (p. 287).

5. Richard Chase, "Melville's *Confidence-Man*," *Kenyon Review*, XI (1949), 122.

refusing to take him seriously, or simply by confusing buoyancy with vigor. Like *Moby-Dick, The Confidence-Man* is full of humor, yet never seems *essentially* humorous. Also, because the passengers' lack of trust is validated, rather than mocked, by the circumstances, it is difficult to look upon them exclusively as satirical targets, especially when as many are tricked by their own generosity and goodwill as are swindled by their greed. Finally, satire can hardly exist in the absence of some norm by which to evaluate human behavior. If we can find no satisfactory alternative for those people we feel to be acting poorly, then it becomes difficult to adopt a satirical attitude toward them. All this is not to deny the great amount of satire in the book; I am only denying this satirical view to be the organizing principle underlying its structure.

Walter Dubler has tried to exonerate Melville from the attack that he offers no standard for evaluating behavior.[6] According to Dubler, the satirist need not incorporate his standard into his work, since that standard will always be understood, even if in virtue of its very absence. Thus, Dubler concludes that it is the *extremes* of any kind of belief that Melville is attacking, and that the supposed norm (absent from the novel) is a more moderate viewpoint, a sensible one that lies halfway between bitter cynicism and foolish optimism. Like Chase and Hoffman, Dubler works on the assumption that Melville's chief purpose is satirical, but his point is an important one, sensibly argued, that *would* justify the book as a highly successful satire. His argument is just a bit *too* sensible, though: too pat, too reductive to be entirely convincing. It is true, of course, that a writer can attack certain social evils (such as hypocrisy, blind faith, and avarice) without presenting their virtuous counterparts which both he and his readers assume. But Dubler's conclusion that Melville's concept of the good is some kind of intelligent mean between the two extremes of confidence and cynicism seems too easy a solution. First of all, there is no middle ground where faith is concerned: one either believes or suspends belief, one either trusts the Confidence Man or one does not. Since there is no way of knowing for sure whether he is telling the truth, we must commit ourselves to the one possibility or the other. It is not a question of being "on our toes,"

6. Walter Dubler, "Theme and Structure in Melville's *Confidence-Man,*" *American Literature*, XXXIII (1961), 307–19.

because as long as we are suspicious of him, we are not believing; and as soon as we suspend our suspicion, we are, like Pitch, taking a leap of faith, even if that faith is based on a logical structure of reasoning. Second, if Dubler is correct, then this is really quite a simple book and seems unnecessarily complicated. Given his view, exemplary behavior is rather easy to ascertain: we simply take over the whole Aristotelian system of Nicomachean Ethics, and the puzzle is solved, the solutions are crystallized. Virtue consists of pursuing the mean between extremes.

It is not, however, possible for one always to choose the mean and still take an active part in life. The Confidence Man's greatest defeat comes at the hands of Pitch, who loathes his noncommittal attitude toward slavery. Either one is an abolitionist or one is not, and Pitch is quite correct in attacking the Confidence Man as "the moderate man, the invaluable understrapper of the wicked man, [who] may be used for wrong, but [is] useless for right" (p. 120). No, moderation is no solution here; it is only an escape from responsible commitment. Dubler's idea makes a good deal of sense when applied to various incidents in the book, but it does not resolve, except by oversimplification, the basic ambiguity and mystery at the heart of Melville's vision. If anything, the book might be seen as a savage satire on any one philosophy of life, any perspective or attitude which fails to take its opposite into account. Therefore, any attempt on the part of the critics to impose on the book one consistent philosophical pattern cannot hope to succeed, for such a view must necessarily evade the tremendous difficulty in living that Melville has clarified for us here.

Are we forced, then, to conclude that Melville's perspective *is* essentially ironic and nihilistic, and that any attempt to explain the book in other terms is doomed to be invalid? I myself see no way of avoiding this conclusion.[7] In examining various elements of the book, we have often found ourselves on the very brink of some satisfactory conclusion, but always a little more investigation has thrown us back into total obscurity. Now if this is true—if

7. Neither does a more recent critic: in his article, "Camus's Absurd and the World of Melville's *Confidence-Man,*" *PMLA*, LXXXII (March 1967), 14–27, Leon F. Seltzer makes a strong claim for viewing *The Confidence-Man* as an absurdist creation, bearing a remarkable affinity to the qualities outlined by Camus in *The Myth of Sisyphus* as characterizing the art of the Absurd. Seltzer finds striking parallels in the philosophical visions and aesthetic stances of the two writers. He concludes that Melville's novel is a supreme illustration of the aesthetic principles evolving from nihilistic convictions.

pessimistic chaos does lie at the very center of the book, and if each incident is simply revolving around that particular perspective—we have two matters left to consider: first, how to account for the partial success of those critics who have tried to view the book within a perspective of meaning; and second, wherein lies Melville's achievement if the book is as great as I think it is?

I think the one question answers the other. Melville's control here is so complete that he can purposefully deceive the reader into believing that some meaningful pattern to the book does exist. We have found that the critics who seem to have misinterpreted *The Confidence-Man* have done so on the basis of theories which are false only in that they are incomplete. The book's form is so tight that one is encouraged to use it in a search for meaning. Everything seems so carefully worked out that we find it hard to admit that it could lead us only to a conclusion of chaos. Thus, Daniel G. Hoffman, after working out the numerous biblical references in the last chaper, interprets the final sentence as a clear indication that "the consequences of man's traduction aboard the Fidèle will be revealed in Hell on Judgment day,"[8] a conclusion that ignores the other equally valid possibilities and assumes that Melville felt obligated to provide one definite answer to the questions his book has raised.

We have seen, though, that Melville's intention was not to give answers, but to construct an elaborate labyrinth that would most emphatically reveal the futility of expecting *any* answers from the world which refuses to provide even enough clues for an intelligent guess. It is in his particular use of artistic techniques that Melville has scored such a success and deluded so many readers into thinking they can find a way out of the maze.

Perhaps this can best be seen by going back to *Moby-Dick* and noting the real contrast between the two novels. *Moby-Dick* utilizes all the traditional techniques of the novel form to construct a reality whose complexity intensifies rather than obliterates meaning. I have said that Ishmael's mind searches everywhere for meaning and that Melville finds it for him by some artistic contrivances which, though they may be justified artistically, can hardly be convincing in a realistic framework. In *The Confidence-Man*, however, Melville uses these techniques to destroy, rather than create meaning, through the method of amassing

8. Hoffman, p. 142.

complexities which finally crumble into utter perplexities. We have only to contrast the complex Ahab to the ambiguous Confidence Man to see how this works with characterization, but there's hardly *any* feature of the novel that is not undermined by its vision. In *Moby-Dick*, names and dates are consistently meaningful: the Rachael fulfills her function as the mother seeking her lost children, and the Pequod embarks on Christmas Day. But the experience aboard the Fidèle only confuses our conceptions of faith, and the action of the novel takes place on April Fool's Day. The meanings here are not so much ironic as mysterious. Again, in *Moby-Dick*, the doubloon nailed to the mast means different things to different men, while the counterfeit detector in *The Confidence-Man* takes on a complexity which finally defeats any man's attempt to work with it. And finally, the book's form—as a series of Platonic dialogues—becomes itself an ironic reminder of reason's irrelevance and ultimate uselessness, for in a world which mocks our very concept of truth, any inquiries directed toward such an end must be seen as absurd. Whereas Socrates' reasoning represents an impartial quest for truth, the Confidence Man's arguments, based on self-interest and aimed toward deception, only exploit the mind's presumptuous pursuit of wisdom. The dialogues in *Moby-Dick* (among Ahab, Starbuck, Stubb, and Flask) are of course by no means conclusive, but they do represent, at least, sincere attempts to justify an attitude toward life commensurate with the truth as each man sees it. In short, while *Moby-Dick* certainly offers us consistently the possibility of multiple meanings, each meaning tends to enrich our sense of that idea, whereas in *The Confidence-Man*, each possibility undercuts the other to leave us totally confused. The chief difference between *Moby-Dick* and *The Confidence-Man* is, finally, the difference between complexity and confusion.

In *The Confidence-Man*, then, Melville has twisted every artistic tool in such a way as to leave us consistently baffled—and the result is the depiction of a universe whose secrets man cannot hope to penetrate, one that defies his searching at every turn. Yet the novel has complete artistic integrity, and the fact that it has confused its readers to such a point is one indication of its success in delineating the reality Melville perceived and wanted to express. It *is* the slipperiest novel, but even as we flounder over it, we owe it to Melville to observe that it is a beautifully constructed block of ice.

3

The Rescued Fragment

Elusiveness of Truth in Conrad's Lord Jim

*J*oseph Conrad uses the novel to excavate the core of reality buried beneath a familiar surface of people and events, but because that core cannot be cracked by any tool at the author's disposal, the result is a novel which contemplates rather than penetrates experience. Pursuing the truth beneath appearances, yet never getting beyond the appearance of truth itself, Conrad remains fixated on the subject that eludes him and finally forces the reader into the same position. Contemplation becomes, then, both subject and method of his novels: resigning himself to the futility of ever knowing enough to interpret facts—yet scorning the facts alone as worthless—Conrad turns life's mystery into his main theme. In *Heart of Darkness* and *Lord Jim,* Marlow is obsessed with the inscrutability of existence, but it is clear that his superiority as a perceptive agent is the direct result of his ability to fix the limits of human intelligence and to accept the unknowable as the most fundamental part of his knowledge.

As he explains in his Preface to *The Nigger of the "Narcissus,"* Conrad sees as his basic duty the attempt "to snatch in a moment of courage, from the remorseless rush of time, a passing phase of life . . . to hold up unquestioningly, without choice and without fear, the rescued fragment before all eyes in the light of a sincere mood. It is to show its vibration, its colour, its form; and through its movement, its form, and its colour, reveal the substance of its truth—disclose its inspiring secret; the stress and passion within the core of each convincing moment." The chief characteristic of truth is, then, its elusiveness; it can be contemplated only in the totality of events which enclose it. Once detached, it becomes explicit, and once explicit, it immediately becomes false. But while it can never be grasped, it *can* sometimes be apprehended, felt, sensed; and the author's task is to present its ambiance with such clarity and vividness that the truth will emerge as submerged within the texture of the moment—that "moment of vision" which brings meaning to action. "And when it is accomplished," says Conrad, "—behold!—all the truth of life is there," but this is little consolation when we consider that what is sensed is never ascertainable as explicit knowledge, but only as a *presence* of truth which must remain forever beyond man's comprehension. Thus, clarification leads to confusion, and lucidity illuminates only darkness.

Conrad's novels, as a result, often offer inconclusive experiences—they present a battleground on which man struggles against a world which torments him, only to be swallowed up in its immense silence, totally defeated in his efforts to understand the forces driving him to destruction. The physical defeat is unimportant, but the spiritual defeat is shattering, for it precludes any sense of resolution or meaning. We feel truth only as the inexplicable ingredient of our lives, and perspicacity leads to nothing but a confession of utter helplessness in trying to interpret or define the truth embedded in a particular situation. Again and again, Conrad pushes the reader into a stalemate where he is left dangling at the novel's end, but this is an intentional part of his artistic method, which seeks to communicate philosophical assumptions. In short, indirectness of technique and inconclusiveness of theme reflect both the struggle and defeat with which Conrad is preoccupied.

If chaos is defined as a situation in which things do not fit together in meaningful patterns for the human mind, then *Lord Jim* is surely a work focused on chaos so consistently that it finally becomes the central subject of the novel. What is significant about Jim is his inexplicability—and to the very end he remains as mysterious and hidden to himself as he does to Marlow and the reader. We know much about him, yet can explain nothing about him. We study him without ever understanding him, and the more we learn about him, the fewer conclusions we can draw. He is enigmatic not because of any special quality he possesses, but because he is a human being; and if he is an exceptional person, it is only because he is so eager and honest in his attempt to understand himself.

"Truth," says Marlowe, "floats elusive, obscure, half submerged, in the silent, still waters of mystery."[1] How, then, is one to get at it? Conrad begins his novel by charting Jim's background and character from the seemingly authoritative position of an omniscient point of view—a perspective which should enable him to explain his character fully. Yet as Jim submits himself to the questions of the court, trying "to hold up unquestioningly, without choice and without fear, the rescued fragment before all eyes in the light of a sincere mood," the author suddenly finds his point of view inadequate to "reveal the substance of its truth." Why? Because Jim himself is as foreign to his own actions as any outsider could be. He can sense the irrelevance of the questions being thrown at him, yet his inner thoughts are as confused as his answers are hollow. No amount of willingness can provide the insight he so desperately seeks, and his honesty leads him again and again to the mystery of the deepest part within him. How to fathom those depths? Certainly, Jim himself cannot do the job— and that means that the author's omniscience is no help either, because once in Jim's mind, we find ourselves immediately restricted by his own inadequate perception:

He wanted to go on talking for truth's sake, perhaps for his own sake also; and while his utterance was deliberate, his mind positively flew round and round the serried circle of facts that had surged up all about him to cut him off from the rest of his kind: it was like a creature that, finding itself imprisoned within an enclosure of high stakes, dashes round and round, distracted in the night, trying to find a weak spot, a crevice, a place to scale, some opening through which it may squeeze itself and escape. This awful activity of mind made him hesitate at times in his speech. (P. 24)

Nowhere in the book can we find a better statement of Conrad's method in dealing with his subject, for he himself is like the creature darting desperately from one corner to another, trying to find an opening through which he can squeeze out of the world of appearances into the truth beyond. The whole novel, is, I think, an effort on Conrad's part to wriggle his way out of the net

1. Joseph Conrad, *Lord Jim* (Cambridge, Mass.: Houghton Mifflin Co., 1958), p. 155. All future page references, cited in parentheses, are to this edition.

which confines his comprehension of reality—"trying to find a weak spot, a crevice, a place to scale." The novel recounts his failure, and the failure itself is the whole point of the novel.

Conrad's first method is the most obvious, the most direct, and the least successful: he attempts to elucidate Jim's character by taking us inside him. But once thrown into the dark confusion of his soul, we have nothing more than a very good view—a front-row seat, as it were—of that confusion. Perhaps then, just as a brain surgeon cannot dissect his own brain and a psychiatrist cannot work effectively on his own psyche, further detachment is necessary before truth can be scooped out, laid before us, and examined. We do not diagnose cancer by imaginatively placing ourselves within our bodies; we go to a doctor who knows how to recognize and treat it. Facts are useless—they become knowledge only when they are interpreted by a skilled, sensitive mind.

So Conrad hands over his narrative to Marlow—and this offers the reader several advantages: first, we now have the necessary detachment to see Jim objectively; second, we can now have the facts interpreted into helpful knowledge by a man who is no doubt Jim's intellectual superior; and finally, Marlow's identification with Jim as "one of us" insures the universality of Jim's condition. For the author, the advantage of using Marlow is that it offers a new way of looking for the truth; perhaps a new perspective will provide new insights.

As soon as Marlow takes over, however, Jim recedes from the foreground of the novel until he seems as distant and unreachable as the object seen from the wrong end of a telescope. The price we pay for detachment is the loss of intimacy with the major character: Jim seems less a person now than a problem—remote, elusive, abstract. He seems no longer the subject of the novel, but the object of Marlow's scrutiny as the book's direction changes from a story of a character to a study of a character. It is Marlow's sensibility which now becomes the center of the novel; his quest for truth turns Jim into a symbol for the unattainable knowledge that Marlow wants so much to find. Our attention centers less and less on Jim's actions and more and more on Marlow's interpretations of them, just as *Heart of Darkness* depends less on Kurtz's tragedy than on Marlow's edification resulting from that tragedy.

It is not long after Marlow becomes the narrator of *Lord Jim* that we see just where his ability lies as a lucid consciousness. In recounting Captain Brierly's suicide, Marlow mentions the exasperation of those near him in trying to account for an utterly inexplicable act; all their conjectures—whether solid speculations or desperate, unfounded guesses—fail to produce a satisfactory explanation. As Captain Jones confesses to Marlow, "I sit here sometimes thinking, thinking till my head fairly begins to buzz. There must be some reason." And Marlow replies: "You may depend on it, Captain Jones . . . it wasn't anything that would have disturbed much either of us two" (p. 49). Marlow's answer is remarkable in its objectivity because it implicity asserts life to be a wholly different experience for every man. Captain Jones cannot find the reason for Brierly's suicide because he can think only in terms of what might cause *him* to commit that drastic act, but Marlow's statement implies the futility of such reasoning. While reeling out speculations from our own perspectives, we forget to consider that a different emotional and psychological temperament may find cause for suicide in a matter that would not even give *us* cause for concern. We can never know enough about anyone to account for his actions, and indeed, the person himself might be no more expert at furnishing clues to his behavior (as demonstrated in Jim's own case).

Marlow, then, distinguishes himself early as a man with negative capability—he refuses to press conjectures into certainties or even probabilities, but acknowledges, instead, the inconclusiveness of most human experience. Thus, his previous statement on Brierly prepares us well for his later one on Jim:

I don't pretend I understood him. The views he let me have of himself were like those glimpses through the shifting rents in a thick fog—bits of vivid and vanishing detail, giving no connected idea of the general aspect of a country. They fed one's curiosity without satisfying it; they were no good for purposes of orientation. Upon the whole he was misleading. (P. 57)

If we cannot hope, therefore, ever to get at the essence of a man, we can rely only on observation and interpretation of his actions, hoping that these will provide some clues to the character hidden within. Yet the more perceptive the observer, the more uncertain will be his conclusions; Marlow reaches a complete stalemate in trying to decide between alternatives which might explain Jim's manner when he notes that "he talked soberly, with a sort of composed unreserve, and with a quiet bearing that might have been the outcome of manly self-control, of impudence, of callousness, of a colossal unconsciousness, of a gigantic deception. Who can tell!" (p. 58). Marlow at this point is describing not simply his first impression of Jim, but his final impression as well, and it is the reader's inability, too, even upon completion of the novel, to single out the most valid alternative, that accounts for our nebulous impression of the main character, our feeling that we have never gotten close enough to fathom him. His is not so much a character as a container of possibilities—heroic or fraudulent, courageous or deluded, intelligent or foolish, headstrong or humble, idealistic or naive, romantic or sentimental. Is Jim all of these, or just some of these, and if so, in what combinations? Which of his potentials solidify into definite characteristics?

Marlow's search for answers is a failure, but in his failure he discovers the reality of mystery at the core of every human being:

It is when we try to grapple with another man's intimate need that we perceive how incomprehensible, wavering, and misty are the beings that share with us the sight of the stars and the warmth of the sun. It is as if loneliness were a hard and absolute condition of existence; the envelope of flesh and blood on which our eyes are fixed melts before the outstretched hand, and there remains only the capricious, unconsolable, and elusive spirit that no eye can follow, no hand can grasp. (P. 129)

Ironically enough, this unknown factor at the core of Jim's character draws Marlow closer to him than if he had been able to define those forces at work distinguishing him from other men; it is Jim's inability to know enough about himself—despite his willingness, even eagerness to confront that truth fully, no matter what it might be—that makes him "one of us," a fellow searcher for self-knowledge. This is undoubtedly what Marlow means when he later says: "it seemed to me that the less I understood the more I was bound to him in the name of that doubt which is the inseparable part of our knowledge. I did not know so much more about myself" (p. 159). It is this realization and emotional acceptance of it that finally distinguishes Marlow from Jim: while Marlow can rest quietly in the awareness of his helpless position, Jim continues to resist it actively, constantly and vainly asserting his significance and independence. Like that of most tragic figures, his imagination makes him suffer more than most men, and forces him into more extreme actions as he struggles against the destructive elements embedded in all life. As Marlow says: "your imaginative people swing farther in any direction, as if given a

longer scope of cable in the uneasy anchorage of life" (p. 161).
Because their fight is more desperate, their action more extreme,
and their suffering more intense, the active men are the traditional heroes in literature, for their resistance defines most clearly the problem being worked out by the author. But it is no coincidence, either, that they eventually take enough cable to bind
themselves into a helpless position: Jim feels detached from his
will, divorced from his own actions as if he had had nothing to do
with them. This in itself would not be unusual, for as Marlow
implies, all men are subject to laws which they cannot hope to
understand and which they can best leave alone. It is Jim's refusal
to leave things alone, however, which makes him a Romantic—
he insists on believing right up to his death that man can buck the
arbitrary forces of chance by imposing moral laws which make a
man's fate just and meaningful. The vigor, intensity, and willfulness of Jim's fight against chaos makes him a touching and appealing figure, but the falseness of his frame of reference impresses
us, too. Marlow's very presence in the book precludes our idealiz-
ing Jim because, while Jim has the imagination, Marlow has the
intellect and perception to evaluate experience objectively. What
he finally learns that Jim never does is that accident is the only
principle at work in the natural world, and that reality includes
the unknowable—is, in fact, solidly entrenched in it.

The reader himself is forced finally to accept Marlow's view as
he tries in vain to weigh all the subtle implications of Jim's final
decision to sacrifice his life rather than desert his principles. Are
his principles really valid in this particular instance, or do they
represent a misguided extension from a previous situation—one
which contained a different set of standards resulting from different variables? Can values remain static and absolute even as life
continues every day to suggest the heterogeneity of all experience? If Jim's death can be seen as atonement for his desertion of
the pilgrims, does his desertion of the girl who loves him and
depends on him constitute a new mistake which never can be
atoned for? In attempting to determine whether Jim has acted
bravely or stupidly, the reader must consider so many consequences leading to different moral conclusions that his final evaluation must remain hopelessly ambivalent and confused. We begin to think that there is no such thing as a right action because
the complexities of morality render all judgment presumptuous.

Ultimately, therefore, we neither admire nor condemn Jim's behavior; we simply accept it as one man's attempt to pin his vision onto the universe. We feel too detached to cry for him, yet always sufficiently sympathetic to appreciate the quality of his struggle. As I said before, I think we simply "contemplate" him more than anything else; and this is undoubtedly Conrad's intention, for his interest is not so much in Jim's character or struggle, as in their philosophical consequences—all of which finally deny man's ability to penetrate life's mystery. Resigning ourselves to everlasting ignorance seems the only dignified and intelligent response to a chaotic universe.

"There are no words for the sort of things I wanted to say," Jim tells Marlow when recounting his abandonment from ship; and Marlow himself echoes this idea frequently throughout his narrative. Language for Conrad is inadequate because it falsifies certain feelings by rendering them explicit. If life's elusiveness is to be his main theme, then words must be used to suggest that idea without expressing it so directly that we feel the security of knowing truth. Articulation invariably distorts, and so even he who has perceived truth in its silent suggestiveness must resign himself to the inevitable failure of his attempts to communicate it in direct terms. Once the author himself has acknowledged the futility of language, however, he is left in a paradoxical position which must be satisfactorily resolved before he can advance very far—and again, Conrad's solution is a method of indirectness. Although feelings themselves cannot be communicated, the situation giving rise to them, if transmitted in its entirety, *can* reproduce similar feelings in the receiver. Words do, after all, have evocative powers, and so long as they are used to evoke rather than express, they can be used to establish some viable, if minimal, kind of communication. Shadowy thoughts cannot be conveyed, perhaps, but the *sense* of shadows can be projected with enough intensity to settle in another's imagination.

Vision, then, embodies thought, and language, in turn, can be used to project vision. But because truth can never be detached from the terrain in which it grows, but is suggested only through successful visualization of the appearances through which it glows so faintly, Conrad's method of communicating his vision will be as indirect as his manner of telling the story. It is not surprising, therefore, that he uses nature metaphorically, and that his descriptions of nature consistently insinuate his sense of moral and philosophical chaos.

Conrad's chaos is usually quieter and less dramatic than Faulkner's, but both writers typically provide an extremely vivid sense of the atmosphere which renders their vision. While nature in Faulkner's works seems to have an energetic life of its own, Conrad's nature moves slowly and almost indistinctly, quietly slipping in and out of shadows, threatening in its Rousseauesque serenity. Because it tends to reflect philosophical rather than psychological chaos, its movements are slow and sinuous, subtle and ominous, silent and foreboding. On his last day with Jim on Patusan, Marlow watches the dusk descend as if it were about to cut him off from Jim forever:

The sun, whose concentrated glare dwarfs the earth into a restless mote of dust, had sunk behind the forest, and the diffused light from an opal sky seemed to cast upon a world without shadows and without brilliance the illusion of a calm and pensive greatness. I don't know why, listening to him, I should have noted so distinctly the gradual darkening of the river, of the air; the irresistible slow work of the night settling silently on all the visible forms, effacing the outlines, burying the shapes deeper and deeper, like a steady fall of impalpable black dust. (P. 219)

Even if Marlow does not know why the atmosphere at this time should make such an impression on him, it is obvious to the reader that this outer darkness represents an inner one as well—the darkness in the depths of Jim which will keep him always veiled to the most perceptive mind. Again, when Marlow bids Jim goodbye for the last time, his description of the scene becomes a metaphorical statement of the elusiveness of Jim's personality:

He was white from head to foot, and remained persistently visible with the stronghold of the night at his back, the sea at his feet, the opportunity by his side—still veiled. What do you say? Was it still veiled? I don't know. For me that white figure in the stillness of coast and sea seemed to stand at the heart of a vast enigma. The twilight was ebbing fast from the sky above his head, the strip of sand had sunk already under his feet, he himself appared no bigger than a child—then only a speck, a tiny white speck, that seemed to catch all the light left in a darkened world. . . . And, suddenly, I lost him. . . . (P. 242)

And so Conrad has given us a visual embodiment of his philosophical attitude: this tall, white figure gradually becomes immersed in his environment until his distinguishing characteristics are lost in the immensity of a world as dark and mysterious as a man's soul. At this point, Jim's human reality merges with that of the land which absorbs him, engulfs him, obliterates him—and the two realities become one vast enigma that defies comprehension. Seen from this distant vantage, Jim becomes more and more difficult to distinguish visually, just as the detachment in Conrad's narrative method makes it harder for us to decipher him morally and psychologically. The truth evades us on both levels as, taken in perspective with its surroundings, it becomes increasingly lost from view and therefore impossible to know.

On the last day of Jim's life, Marlow again describes the surroundings in a way that becomes immediately metaphorical: "A heavy mist lay very low on the water, making a sort of illusive grey light that showed nothing" (p. 287). Here is a description of physical atmosphere that emphasizes the unreality of our lives. The light itself is faint enough to be illusory, yet it still reveals nothing but the impregnable darkness of the land. *Lord Jim* is crammed with descriptions such as this one that suggest in a most powerful way the impenetrability of our universe; and because the description serves to characterize human beings as well, our understanding of the men we share the sun and stars with must remain every bit as limited as our understanding of the sun and stars themselves.

Acknowledgment of our inability to understand the world—both human and natural—does not, however, justify man's surrender of the struggle to dominate chaos so that he can live within it comfortably. Even if this comfort is illusory, it is no less valid as a psychological necessity. It is in this way that art becomes necessary to our lives, for it helps us to resist the chaos that surrounds us and threatens to annihilate us. Thus, even Marlow, with his negative capability, can respect Jim's efforts to create and live by a code of behavior meaningful to him in direct defiance of the blind, amoral forces which control his life, because he sees reflected in Jim's struggle his own war against the natural state of things. Marlow's weapon is language, and that is why his obsession with talk is motivated by a deeper instinct that his dinner guests surmise. In the very attempt to fathom Jim, Marlow is in effect offering a weak light against the forces of darkness and disorder. While listening to the horrifying story of Jewel's mother's manipulation at the hands of Cornelius, he says,

It had the power to drive me out of my conception of existence, out of that shelter each of us makes for himself to creep under in moments of danger, as a tortoise withdraws within its shell. For a moment I had a view of a world that seems to wear a vast and dismal aspect of disorder, while, in truth, thanks to our unwearied efforts, it is as sunny an argument of small conveniences as the mind of man can conceive. But still—it was only a moment: I went back into my shell directly. One *must*—don't you know?—though I seemed to have lost all my words in the chaos of dark thoughts I had contemplated for a second or two beyond the pale. These came back, too, very soon, for words also belong to the sheltering conception of light and order which is our refuge. (P. 225)

It is this same instinct that saved Marlow from the heart of darkness: whereas Kurtz submitted to the chaotic, destructive forces he came to see as the only reality, Marlow was willing to make a concession to the false order created by man for his own survival by lying to Kurtz's "Intended" and so slipping back under the protective shell of civilized conventions and illusions. So, too, in recounting Jim's story to his dinner guests (just as he had related Kurtz's tale to his fellow sailors in *Heart of Darkness*), Marlow refuses to allow the ultimate meaninglessness of life to preclude man's need to bring meaning to the world he inhabits. "There shall be no message," he tells his listeners, "unless such as each of each you can interpret for himself from the language of facts, that are so often more enigmatic than the craftiest arrangement of words" (p. 244). In a novel which fails to illuminate its main character, the author seems to be justifying himself here by insisting on the utter subjectivity of all our knowledge. The last installment of Jim's story comes in a batch of papers sent from Marlow to one of his more interested listeners, and this new change in Conrad's narrative device reinforces the idea that facts become knowledge only when filtered through a selective consciousness which interprets its own truth. Even Marlow's view can never be definitive, for there is now yet another sensibility involved which will sift the facts for a meaning that is certain to be somewhat different.

Marlow's own interpretation of his story seems to see Jim as the helpless victim of incomprehensible forces, but as a genuine hero in his efforts to impose order and significance on his own life in the face of stronger powers which promise destruction:

There's nothing more; he had seen a broad gulf that neither eye nor voice could span. I can understand this. He was overwhelmed by the inexplicable; he was overwhelmed by his own personality—the gift of that destiny which he had done his best to master. (P. 245)

Whether Jim's fight was hopelessly romantic or not, he does finally emerge as a colorful, charismatic, and even admirable figure, for we cannot help but be impressed by the intensity with which he resisted and challenged the natural chaos of life. Like that creature searching desperately for a crevice in the trap that confines him, Jim never finds a way out of the dark confusion inside him which prevents his knowing himself fully, but his struggle does appeal to *our* imaginations and sympathies, and invites interpretation—which is the reader's challenge in the face of a story with no inherent meaning, yet with strong suggestiveness of truth.

We have seen that Conrad's novel leads us into a chaotic vision which justifies his handling of the story. The title character is seen from a distance so great that we cannot pin him down at all; he eludes our faculties for categorizing, interpreting, and evaluating human behavior, and so remains a mystery as great as the forces against which he struggles. Yet Conrad has constructed his work very carefully toward that end: his narrative flops around like a netted fish seeking the one opening which will return him to the familiar world; his point of view switches frequently and abruptly at crucial points in his tale; his presentation of atmosphere suggests philosophical vision, and the negative capability of his narrator implies the basic intent of his theme. His indirectness almost always results in inconclusiveness and perceptual confusion, but that is the very effect Conrad seems to be reaching for. He forces us to see things as he sees them, but with a mastery that makes great inroads through the chaos he has reproduced for us. Although the world is still "too dark altogether," our despair is mitigated by awareness that some fragment *has* been torn and ultimately rescued from that darkness.

4

"Hold on! For God's Sake Hold on!"

Struggle and Survival in Faulkner's Whirlpool

*W*illiam Faulkner's novels are masterpieces of chaotic vision projected through an atmosphere which drives his characters in certain directions and instigates or inhibits their actions. It is in this context, too, that values are determined, for we cannot assess a man's behavior until we have assessed the world he has to cope with. The more vividly that world is defined for us, the more fairly we can evaluate the man who acts in it, for it is in the relationship between the two that a man's potentials are displayed, his limitations depicted, and his character revealed. Unlike the vision in such a work as *Tristram Shandy*, then, the chaos in Faulkner's world has serious consequences which reverberate through all of men's relationships and are reflected in every facet of the novel itself. Both thematically and structurally, the suggestion of chaos as a permanent condition of the universe takes its toll: actions become further divorced from minds and bodies; values become vaguer; form and style become looser, and technique more radical.

The perfect suitability of Faulkner's artistic methods to his vision accounts for the stunning power of his best works and finally enables him to master that chaos to some degree. Faulkner's novels seem to reel themselves out uncontrollably (in a manner reminiscent of later Beckett), and his characters tend to be as kinetic as his prose. In both cases, the energy of movement carries strong implications of the hysteria which precedes a total breakdown, yet both are finally brought under control within the structure of the novels themselves. The vision of chaos may condition the author's conception of human values, but at least these values, however weak, can still assert themselves in a meaningful way once we understand the characteristics and consequences of Faulkner's chaotic world.

Faulkner's universe is a spinning one: it is as if we were watching the action from a distance so great that we could actually see the globe revolving in its sphere, upsetting all those tiny figures who try to defy natural laws of motion by running wildly in the wrong direction. And because we observe them from a distant vantage point, we see little more than their general outlines: they rarely become highly individualized characters, but tend instead to grow into mythic archetypes, defined by their movements and backgrounds. We are not always at a safe distance, of course, for Faulkner will suddenly telescope in on them until their agony becomes most explicit, and we see their hands flailing, their bodies writhing, their spirits struggling. But even when we are close to them (and to be close means to be right inside them), their figures are so blurred by the incredible speed of the world moving beneath them that their contortions become for us their identities.

These characters do not gyrate in a vacuum, however; the sense of atmospheric substance is strong, and that substance is thick, heavy, oppressive, and powerful—like quicksand, it seeps around the character, immersing him the more he struggles to extricate himself. The earth throbs and pulsates, boils up, palpitatingly alive, and the same can be said for other external atmospheres such as the river and even internal atmospheres such as the memory or the whole mental process. In short, the dynamism of Faulkner's world is so intense and frenetic that it resembles a gigantic whirlpool that swirls around his characters until all sense of order and stability is destroyed. Because the force of movement is so great, there is no one place which can be marked off as the present, and so the threat of complete chaos is always imminent. The past becomes hugely relevant as an integral part of the present, and even the future flows in as the character spins closer and closer to the eye of the vortex. Consciousness heightens as the body is flung to the center, but it is at this point, too, that it is doomed to be engulfed, pushed under, and consumed.

Faulkner's short novel *Old Man* demonstrates graphically the vision which seems to pervade most of his major works. In the mighty, swirling movement of the river, a man fights desperately to steady himself, but the river gives him no opportunity: it holds him, hurls him, tosses him around, pushes him out, sucks him in, forces him to exert every bit of strength, courage, stamina, energy, and determination just to keep his head above the water from one minute to the next. In the following passage, we can see how style, technique, and vision fall together, and if we further consider that the word "It," here referring to the river, could very well refer to the particular movement of Faulkner's style and that the flying debris could easily represent broken or fragmented images from the past, we could have a metaphorical statement, too, of the way vision determines style and technique:

And he was not alarmed now either because there was not time, for although the visibility, for all its clarity, did not extend very far, yet in the next instant to the hearing he was also seeing something such as he had never seen before. This was that the sharp line where the phosphorescent water met the darkness was now about ten feet higher than it had been an instant before and that it was curled forward upon itself like a sheet of dough being rolled out for a pudding. It reared, stooping; the crest of it swirled like the man of a galloping horse and, phosphorescent too, fretted and flickered like fire. . . . He continued to paddle though the skiff had ceased to move forward at all but seemed to be hanging in space while the paddle still reached thrust recovered and reached again; now instead of space the skiff became abruptly surrounded by a welter of fleeting debris—planks, small buildings, the bodies of drowned yet antic animals, entire trees leaping and diving like porpoises above which the skiff seemed to hover in weightless and airy indecision like a bird above a fleeing countryside, undecided where to light or whether to light at all, while the convict squatted in it still going through the motions of paddling, waiting for an opportunity to scream. He never found it. For an instant the skiff seemed to stand erect on its stern and then shoot scrabbling and scrambling up the curling wall of water like a cat, and soared on above the licking crest itself and hung cradled into the high actual air in the limbs of a tree, from which bower of new-leafed boughs and branches the convict, like a bird in its nest and still waiting his chance to scream and still going through the motions of paddling though he no longer even had the paddle now, looked down upon a world turned to furious motion and to incredible retrograde.[1]

What we have here is a Chagallian picture turned into a nightmare: all objects are uprooted and flying in space while man whirls among them feeling himself thrust forward, yet unable to make his own will felt (the convict's attempt to paddle becomes at once touching, pathetic, ludicrous, and wildly inappropriate because it is so utterly futile). His very identity dissolves in a universe where nothing is fixed or stable, where nothing can be grasped, stopped, or held onto. Common objects of the external world have been ripped from their places and come swimming together:

He did not have to paddle now, he just steered . . . while the skiff sped on across that boiling desolation where he had long since begun to not dare believe he could possibly be where he could not doubt he was, trying with his fragmant of splintered plank merely to keep the skiff intact and afloat among the houses and trees and dead animals (the entire towns, stores, residences, parks, and farmyards, which leaped and played about him like fish), not trying to reach any destination, just trying to keep the skiff afloat until he did. (P. 116)

He tried to tell that too—that day while the skiff fled on among the bearded trees while every now and then small quiet tentative exploratory feelers would come up from the wave behind and toy for a moment at the skiff, light and curious, then go on with a faint hissing sighing, almost a chuckling sound, the skiff going on, driving on with nothing to see but trees and water and solitude: until after a while it no longer seemed to him that he was trying to put space and distance behind him or shorten space and distance ahead but that both he and the wave were now hanging suspended simultaneous and unprogressing in pure time, upon a dreamy desolation in which he paddled on not from any hope even to reach anything at all but merely to keep intact what little of distance the length of the skiff provided between himself and the inert and inescapable mass of female meat before him: then night and the skiff rushing on, fast since any speed over anything unknown and invisible is too fast, with nothing before him and behind him the outrageous idea of a volume of moving water toppling forward, its crest frothed and shredded like fangs, and then dawn again (another of those dreamlike alterations day to dark then back to day again with that quality truncated, anachronic and unreal as the waxing and waning of lights in a theater scene) and the skiff emerging now with the woman no longer supine beneath the

1. William Faulkner, "Old Man," *Three Famous Short Novels* (New York: Random House, 1962), pp. 112–13. All future references, cited parenthetically, are to this edition.

shrunken soaked private's coat but sitting bolt upright, gripping the gunwales with both hands, her eyes closed and her lower lip caught between her teeth and he driving the splintered board furiously now, glaring at her out of his wild swollen sleepless face and crying, croaking, "Hold on! For God's sake hold on!" (Pp. 124–25)

The confusion of time and space exhibited here is typical of the chaos produced by the whirlpool on its victim, and Faulkner's earth is hardly a welcome *terra firma* after the upsetting speed of the river. On dry land, his characters suffer in the same way: the sense of helpless, unwilling movement is just as strong. This, then, is man's basic situation in a world that rushes around him so fast that he cannot even find the time to scream. He is completely caught up in the struggle to survive and so tends to respond instinctively rather than thoughtfully to the threat of utter disorder.

Faulkner's vision determines to a great extent both his method of characterization and the gradual evolution of a value system by which these characters may be most fairly judged. Given such a world, what can a man do, how should he act, what will constitute admirable behavior? It is at this point that it becomes difficult to decipher Faulkner because the movement of characters within chaos is of necessity severely limited. Obviously, for the writer defining humanity against such a backdrop, man's ability to affect his world will be so greatly restricted that heroism is apt to be a quiet quality at best. Indeed, it seems that the most a man can do is (in the words of the convict) to hold on, for God's sake, hold on!

When I think of certain Faulknerian characters, I tend to remember them in certain positions or modes of movement: Dilsey stands, Quentin moves impetuously, Lena walks slowly, Joe Christmas runs, Ratliff and Hightower sit, etc. Now obviously it is not a question in Faulkner of sifting the good people to one side and the evil to the other, but perhaps we can arrive at some conclusion of the value system at work here by examining the implications of these different postures and considering to what extent they are related to our final evaluation of how this character behaves, and what kind of behavior constitutes, in Faulkner, the best means of coping in a world that is always throwing one off balance.

Most of the more likable people in Faulkner tend to be slow-moving or sedentary, while most of the least likable are fast-moving. In *The Sound and the Fury*, we have the contrast between Dilsey's slow, deliberate movements and Jason's frantic ones; in *The Hamlet*, we have the impetuous rashness of Henry Armstid set against the calm, easy-going movements of Ratliff and even Ike Snopes; in *Light in August*, we have the serene movements of Lena contrasted to the frenzied running of Joe Christmas. Slow movement in such cases seems to indicate a clearness of purpose and solidarity of character: in the whirlpool, these people manage to tread water, to hold on to the most important things without upsetting their equilibrium. What is more important, however, is that they do not destroy anyone else's either.

We can see right away that the slow-moving people are not always admirable: most of the Snopeses, for example, are so phlegmatic that they move with no more will or direction than a cow in a pasture. We *can* say, though, that the slow movers in Faulkner are, on the whole, less dangerous than the swift movers. Another generalization applies: even the most admirable of the slow movers are hardly very aware individuals; they are perhaps the least troubled people because they are the least complicated, the least self-conscious. Again, this would explain their ability to survive, while the destructive people almost always end by annihilating themselves along with their victims.

By far the most interesting group of Faulknerian characters are the runners—those who seem to be approaching the vacuum at the center of the whirlpool where consciousness heightens, danger is imminent, and the indivdual feels himself controlled by some outside force—a current so strong that he's simply swept along by it. I have mentioned this effect in *Old Man*—when the convict's movements are determined by the force and direction of the whirling river, rather than by his own mind and will—and the outcome is the same on earth: as soon as the person starts running, all earthly elements are dislodged and start eddying toward the center, swarming around the runner until chaos becomes complete. Instead of the dead mules, rats, chickens, snakes, and houses that gyrated around the convict, the earthly runner is every bit as insecure on the trembling, fluid earth among such dislodged objects as trees, stars, cows, horses, and barns, all intermixed with the pounding of blood and breath; the smell of honeysuckle, jasmine, and manure; the scorching glow of fire, and the choking mustiness of smoke. As the hard land squishes into mud, earth becomes equivalent to water as a metaphor for the uprooting and liquefaction of previously stable forms.

But to what extent is the chaotic atmosphere an objective reality? Unlike Melville's chaos, which exists wholly outside of the human mind, Faulkner's chaos often seems to be *caused* by that mind. It is obvious that the road Lena walks down is very different from the one Joe Christmas runs down; that the river in *As I Lay Dying* becomes more chaotic after the Bundrens and their burden tumble into it; that *The Hamlet* is a calm place for living before the Snopeses introduce wild horses and burning barns. The chaos, then, is composed of the totality of those elements inside and outside of man which seem to be conspiring for his destruction. Thus, nature in Faulkner's world includes not only the land and the sea, but the mysterious powers which impel them into destructive activity. Ultimately, it seems clear that these powers in Faulkner are psychological as well as metaphysical; it is the disoriented mind which helps to disintegrate, decompose, and dissolve the natural world into a chaotic universe. The runner compounds the confusion through his unwitting externalization of the disorder lodging in his excited mind. Thus, the mind that perceives chaos almost immediately begins also to reflect it.

Perhaps this explains why the whole earth seems to be revolving with incredible speed as the runner hurls himself through time and space. And just as he cannot be oriented in space, so has he run outside of man's structured circle of time as well. As he runs along a road, the past, present, and future converge, toppling upon one another and spilling around him: as the road flies up to him, the future rushes into the present, the present instantly becomes past, and the past, which is simply the steady unreeling of the future, remains a permanent extension and condition of the present. At such a time, the present cannot possibly be isolated or even distinguished, for the world is moving too rapidly.

Joe Christmas, for example, is the typical runner who immediately loses his sense of time and space as he flees first from his stepfather, then from the town, and finally from the posse led by Grimm. When he finally leaves the house recently deserted by Bobbi, Max, and the blond woman, "he enters the street which was to run for fifteen years."

The whiskey died away in time and was renewed and died again, but the street ran on. From that night, the thousand streets ran as one street, with imperceptible corners and changes of scene. . . . The street ran into Oklahoma and Missouri and as far south as Mexico and then back north to Chicago and Detroit and then back south again and at last to Mississippi. It was fifteen years long: it ran between the savage and spurious board fronts of oil towns. . . . It ran through yellow wheat fields. . . . And always, sooner or later, the street ran through cities, through an identical and well-nigh interchangeable section of cities without remembered names. . . .

He thought that it was the loneliness which he was trying to escape and not himself. But the street ran on: catlike, one place was the same as another to him. But in none of them could he be quiet. But the street ran on in its moods and phases, always empty: he might have been himself as in numberless avatars, in silence, doomed with motion, driven by the courage of flagged and spurred despair, by the despair of courage whose opportunities had to be flagged and spurred.[2]

The expression of his despair, Joe's running is desperate, compulsive, obsessive—a trait common to all of Faulkner's runners, who fall through ordered patterns of space into a chaos created and nourished by their own minds.

After having killed Joanna, Joe flees again, and now he becomes disoriented in time as well as space:

When he thinks about time, it seems to him now that for thirty years he has lived inside an orderly parade of named and numbered days like fence pickets, and that one night he went to sleep and when he waked up he was outside of them. . . . He felt no surprise. Time, the spaces of light and dark, had long since lost orderliness. (Pp. 290–92)

Of course, such a flight can get a man nowhere in this Faulknerian world; he is doomed to end up just where he began: "though during the last seven days he has had no paved street, yet he has travelled farther than in all the thirty years before. And yet he is still inside the circle" (p. 296). Joe's plight here is very similar to Joseph K.'s in Kafka's novel *The Trial*. It does seem that once a man exits from the normal pattern of life, he can never again find his way back in and so must do the rest of his living in a new context.

It is at this point, too, that the runner seems to lose not only his sense of time-and-space dimensions, but the consciousness of his own will as well; he is now driven by outside forces which

---

2. William Faulkner, *Light in August* (New York: Random House, 1950), pp. 195–97. All future page references, cited in parentheses, are to this edition.

hurtle him forward without or even against his own desire. In his flight from Percy Grimm, Joe "was moving again almost before he had stopped, with that lean, swift, blind obedience to whatever Player moved him on the Board" (p. 405).

Of course we could say that such sluggish characters as Lena seem hardly to move of their own volition either, but I think it will be found that the slow-moving characters (and Ike Snopes is a perfect, if extreme example) lack the awareness to perceive and so feel their own helplessness. Chaos, then, would seem to emanate from a character's consciousness, the product of a disordered and frenzied sensibility nourished in isolation. And since their motion is dictated to a great extent by their perception, Faulkner's people are frequently characterized for us as we watch them move.

Quentin Compson is another desperate character, whose potential for love has been perverted by an obsolete, parochial code of honor which affirms meaning only while negating life. Rejecting his father's nihilism, Quentin persists in imposing a strict set of principles onto a world too chaotic to accommodate them. As his need for order becomes increasingly compulsive, his inflexible nature finally settles into a rigid resistance to time, which perpetually gnaws away at those fixed values he cherishes above life itself. Death becomes ultimately his only means of escaping a world of time and thus preserving his beliefs. On the day of his suicide, he journeys through Cambridge and its outlying districts, wandering outside of time and space:

and then I could hear my watch and the train dying away, as though it were running through another month or another summer somewhere, rushing away under the poised gull and all things rushing.[3]

and then as I turned into the quad the chimes did begin and I went on while the notes came up like ripples on a pool and passed me and went on, saying Quarter to what? All right. Quarter to what?

The symptoms here are certainly those of the runner, though it is not Quentin's body that moves with such rapidity but his mind, which reflects disorientation to the present, because it refuses to allow the past to pass. Spinning restlessly and obsessively through time, certain images, scenes, and sensory perceptions keep

3. William Faulkner, *The Sound and the Fury* (New York: Random House, 1946), p. 212. All future page references, cited in parentheses, are to this edition.

bouncing off the flywheel of Quentin's mind, until past and present become indistinguishable, and Quentin is engulfed and finally drowned by the workings of his own mind. This becomes literal, too, when that mind dictates the drowning of his body.

That the chaos swirling around the runner seems to have psychological origins may be seen quite clearly with Jason Compson. Unlike Quentin, Jason exercises complete control in reality: his coldness allows him to penetrate the outside world and manipulate other people from his omnipotent position as head of the family. He is consciously cruel to everyone and gets deep sadistic joy out of victimizing them—as when he burns the carnival tickets that Luster wants so badly. His very callousness seems to insure his control over others, for as long as he lacks the warmth necessary to feel pity for those he mistreats and tortures, he himself is immune to pain. But finally, Jason himself is victimized, and at this point, his compulsion for revenge becomes so overpowering that it dooms him to the vacuum of the whirlpool. From the moment Jason discovers that his money has been stolen, his nature becomes passionate, and he loses his grip on the outside world to the inner obsession which dominates him. As he rushes out of the house to meet the sheriff, he enters our ranks of runners, and now that we have seen the pattern, we know that he will travel fast and far and end up at the beginning; we know that his own mind will trick him, possess his body and send it fruitlessly spinning. And that, of course, is what does happen: he develops a severe headache and feels his blood pulsing heavily and rushing to his temples as he becomes more and more excited by the chase. His movements become increasingly frenetic as his paranoia grows:

From time to time, he passed churches, unpainted frame buildings with sheet iron steeples, surrounded by tethered teams and shabby motorcars, and it seemed to him that each of them was a picketpost where the rear guards of Circumstance peeped fleetingly back at him. "And damn You, too," he said. "See if You can stop me," thinking of himself, his file of soldiers with the manacled sheriff in the rear, dragging Omnipotence down from His throne, if necessary; of the embattled legions of both hell and heaven through which he tore his way and put his hands at last on his fleeting niece. (P. 382)

Jason's imagination has by now become psychotic—he is at this point a genuine megalomaniac—and this is reflected in the new, uncontrollable frenzy of his movements.

The transformation of Jason into a desperate runner is even more sharply emphasized by the descriptions of Dilsey in the same section, as she walks slowly uphill to church or quietly and laboriously mounts the stairs to bring Mrs. Compson her hot-water bottle: "Dilsey said nothing. She turned slowly and descended, lowering her body from step to step, as a small child does, her hand against the wall" (p. 339). The runner, then, is destined for self-destruction, while the slow person moves with quiet authority and resolution. Even Benjy really dooms himself when he rushes out of the gate and grabs the schoolgirl he so desperately wants to be Caddy. Again, the fast mover seems always to be bucking reality. The lethargic movers are, on the whole, a bit sluggish-*minded*, too, though this is by no means a hard-set rule. Lena and Ike Snopes seem in harmony with nature, but so do Dilsey, Ratliff, and even Old Varner. The important point is that the slow movers are in control (compare Flem Snopes to any of the runners), while the runners seem only to be living out their psychic hysteria. Like men caught in quicksand or an undertow, they are sucked beneath by forces which seem to thrive on human panic.

Another example of the dispassionate man turned obsessive is Mink Snopes of *The Hamlet*, who kills a man in a premeditated act but finally loses the power to manage his destiny when he becomes a runner:

The night was moonless. He descended through the dry and invisible corn, keeping his bearing on a star until he reached the trees, against the black solidity of which fireflies winked and drifted and from beyond which came the booming and grunting of frogs and the howling of the dog. But once among them, he could not even see the sky anymore, though he realized then what he should have before: that the hound's voice would guide him. So he followed it, slipping and plunging in the mud and tripping and thrashing among the briers and tangled undergrowth and blundering among invisible tree trunks, his arm crooked to shield his face, sweating, while the steady cries of the dog drew nearer and nearer and broke abruptly off in mid-howl. He believed for an instant that he actually saw the phosphorescent glints of eyes although he had no light to reflect them, and suddenly and without knowing that he was going to do it, he ran toward where he had seen the eyes. He struck the next tree a shocking blow with his shoulder; he was hurled sideways but caught balance again, still plunging forward, his hands extended. He was falling now. If there's a tree in front of me now, he thought, it will be all. He actually touched the dog. He felt its breath and heard the click of its teeth as it slashed at him, springing away, leaving him on his hands and knees in the mud while the noise of its invisible flight crashed and ceased.[4]

The adjective "invisible" is used three times in this passage, and the repetition does more than simply reinforce the description of a moonless night. The most threatening sights and sounds speed by the runner, but his inability to define them clearly leaves him in a most helpless state, since dangers cannot be fought before they have been found. As a result, he has no choice but to continue:

Now he began to run, or as fast as he dared, that is. He could not help himself. I got to find the road now, he thought. If I try to go back and start over, it will be daylight before I get out of the bottom. So he hurried on, stumbling and thrashing among the briers and undergrowth, one arm extended to fend himself from the trees, voiceless, panting, blind, the muscles about his eyelids strained and aching against the flat impenetrable face of the darkness, until suddenly there was no earth under his feet; he made another stride, running upon nothing, then he was falling and then he was on his back, panting. He was in the road. But he did not know where. (P. 255)

Runners must finally stop, if only just long enough to die. The faster one runs, the faster the earth spins, and the dizzier the runner becomes, until he must break down physically and/or, like Quentin, mentally. It is as if, once in the vacuum of the whirlpool, the body (rather than the man) is thrown about in an increasingly narrow spiral until it reaches the eye, and is then hurled out. The velocity of the water underneath him at this point is intense enough to fling him so far that he lands outside of the vortex entirely. For a while, he is no longer even moving slowly at the outer edges (which is where he came in); rather, he has fallen on the other side of the periphery, where he lies in a state of floating suspension, disengaged from the reality which has broken him. His battered body floats in another part of the water which is stagnant, rather than calm.

In a way, Mrs. Compson lies perpetually outside reality. Most of the liers, however, are exhausted runners who have been ejected from the vacuum; all the runners I have mentioned, in fact, go through this stage. Quentin, of course, will illustrate this literally, but the characters who go on living pass through a similar period

4. William Faulkner, *The Hamlet* (New York: Random House, 1940), p. 228. All future page references, cited in parentheses, are to this edition.

of unconsciousness which in some cases is very much like a death
before rebirth. Mink, for example, after he has been caught,
makes one attempt to escape by jumping from the sheriff's wagon, and as he hangs over the side, we get a vivid description of a
man at the vacuum; but once pulled back into the wagon, he is
clearly outside of the whirlpool:

and he felt the surge of the surrey and he even seemed to see the sheriff
leaning over the seat-back and grappling with the raging deputy; choking, gasping, trying to close his mouth and he could not, trying to roll his
head from beneath the cold hard blow of the water and there was a
bough over his head against the sunny sky, with a faint wind in the
leaves, and the three faces. . . .
They approached the jail from the rear and drove into the enclosed
yard. "Jump," the sheriff said. "Lift him out."
"I'm all right," he said. But he had to speak twice before he made any
sound, and even then it was not his voice. "I can walk."
After the doctor had gone, he lay on his cot. . . . (P. 262)

The passage depicts a drowning man suddenly flung back onto
dry land, utterly spent.

Jason Compson's hunt for his niece finally leads him into a
circus trailer, where he is nearly killed by an old performer:

His breath made a hah hah hah sound and he stood there trying to
repress it, darting his gaze this way and that. . . .
He grasped at the hatchet, feeling no shock but knowing that he was
falling, thinking So, this is how it'll end, and he believed that he was
about to die, and when something crashed against the back of his head
he thought How did he hit me there? . . . and he thought Hurry. Hurry.
Get it over with, and then a furious desire not to die seized him and he
struggled, hearing the old man wailing and cursing in his cracked voice.
He still struggled when they hauled him to his feet, but they held him
and he ceased. (P. 387–388)

Jason is so exhausted by his experience that he is not even able to
drive home. And as with Mink, Jason's last struggle ejects him
from the vacuum to a point outside of even normal activity (that
part of the whirlpool which would be its rim). Instead, he gets
back into the automobile and just sits there, waiting for someone
or something to move him back into the circle of action:

He sat there for sometime. He heard a clock strike the half hour, then
people began to pass, in Sunday and Easter clothes. Some looked at him
as they passed, at the man sitting quietly behind the wheel of a small car,
with his invisible life ravelled out about him like a worn-out sock.
(P. 391)

That last image reveals a very different Jason—a defeated man. Finally, *he* is victimized when he has to pay the asker's price to get someone to drive him home. The self-destruction is complete.

On June 2, 1910, Quentin Compson circulates through Cambridge and its environs: the city is a whirlpool of trolley cars, clocks, fast-moving people, and associations that repeatedly pull his mind back into the past. Amid all the swirling life lies the river—clear, still, and deep—and as Quentin stands on the bridge overlooking it, he knows he will be able that day to propel himself into the unconscious peace of death. Because his mind rejects the very notion of "temporary," which his father uses to characterize his despair, Quentin's stasis must be permanent—a fact which he can insure only by his suicide.

Joe Christmas, Faulkner's long-distance runner, repeats the process I have been describing several times throughout *Light in August*. After his desperate running from the dance hall where he has killed his stepfather to his house where he takes his stepmother's savings, then back to town and Bobbi's room, Christmas finally approaches the vortex when he fights Max and the stranger. The vortex, we have seen, is very often delineated through a physical force which sends its victim spinning so rapidly that he soon loses his stance, flails in the water, is sucked into it, and is just on the verge of utter destruction when he is ejected from it by the tremendous thrust of pressure in the vacuum. This happens to Joe when he is beaten by the two men and lies motionless on the floor while the others pack up their belongings and prepare to leave. After they have gone,

he lay quietly, on his back, with open eyes, while above the suspended globe burned with aching and unwavering glare. . . . He did not know how long he lay there. He was not thinking at all, not suffering. Perhaps he was conscious of somewhere within him the two severed wire-ends of volition and sentience lying, not touching now, waiting to touch, to knit anew so that he could move. (P. 192)

Finally, Joe does get up and re-enters life by walking out the door and into the street he is to follow for the next fifteen years. The road leads him through devious turns, but somehow it always carries him back to the vortex. His relationship with Joanna, for example, slowly leads him into a heart of darkness and by this time, the current is strong enough to sweep him along without his will's being involved, almost without his own consent. That is why he thinks something is going to happen to *him* when he goes to murder her—he feels himself being pushed to disaster, and his body used as an agent for more powerful, though undefinable forces. The moment he kills her, he enters the vortex again and is soon running over the palpitating earth. Like the river in *Old Man* which contains debris of all sorts and matter, swirling around in rapid succession, Faulkner's earth literally contains the past (in the dead bodies buried under its surface) as well as voices, smells, and gravitational tugs. The earth becomes the same maelstrom for Christmas that the river had been for the convict. As Joe flees,

it seemed to him that he could see himself being hunted by white men at last into the black abyss which had been waiting, trying for thirty years to drown him and into which now and at last he had actually entered, bearing now upon his ankles the definite and ineradicable gauge of its upward moving. (P. 289)

That "black abyss" is the vacuum into which he has been thrown, and we have already seen that the character never stays in it long: once he hits dead center, he is cast out by its thrust, which leaves him stunned, breathless, and beaten. It is not surprising, then, that as soon as Joe sees himself entering the abyss, his mind blacks out as his body drops to the ground and he lies in a comatose state. When he awakens,

it is just dawn, daylight: that gray and lonely suspension filled with the peaceful and tentative waking of birds. The air, inbreathed, is like spring water. He breathes deep and slow, feeling with each breath himself diffuse in the neutral grayness, becoming one with the loneliness and quiet that has never known fury or despair. "That was all I wanted," he thinks in a quiet and slow amazement. "That was all, for thirty years." (P. 289)

It is fury and despair which motivates and drives the runner, so that he can attain peace of mind only when these have been purged from his system. But they are finally purged only at the expense of all sentience: the world he wakes up to is lonely, quiet, gray, and suspended.

Hightower, in the same novel, is a strange case of the sitter turned runner. He is sedentary through most of the novel, but he differs from such sitters as Ratliff because he is not functioning fully as a human being: he sits uneasily because, like his grandfather who stormed the South during the Civil War, Hightower is essentially a man of action, and action in Faulkner sooner or later means running. Actually, we could say that Hightower had already been a runner, and as soon as he began preaching, started to eddy toward the center of the whirlpool. It is obvious from the compulsive intensity of his sermons that the man is "possessed," being swept along by the force of the past as it works through his imagination and dominates his being. Like Quentin's, Hightower's running is mental but still shares all the qualities of the physical runner. His ejection from the vacuum is, no doubt, when the townspeople have him locked out of the church (for him, the maelstrom of desperation). He, like the other runners, lands outside the spiral, but what was a rest for Joe Christmas becomes a life for Hightower. What is important is not that he is always sitting, but that his total withdrawal from the affairs of the town, his isolation, his refusal to feel or become involved again (which means living or entering the peripheral currents of the whirlpool once more) make him a lier. Finally, though, he is pushed back into active life by Byron, and we see the vortex syndrome almost immediately:

He leaned forward against the counter, above his laden basket. He could feel the counter edge against his stomach. It felt solid, stable enough; it was more like the earth itself were rocking faintly, preparing to move. Then it seemed to move, like something released slowly and without haste, in an augmenting swoop, and cleverly, since the eye was tricked into believing that the dingy shelves ranked with flyspecked tins, and the merchant himself behind the counter, had not moved; outraging, tricking sense. And he thinking, "I won't! I won't! I have bought immunity. I have paid. I have paid." (P. 270)

But no one can buy immunity from life: a human being is never finished suffering, and Hightower unwillingly gets swallowed up by the current again, getting closer and closer to the center of action until he is once more swept out of it by Percy Grimm as he comes rushing through the house after Joe Christmas. They "raised Hightower, his face bleeding, from the floor where Christmas, running up the hall, his raised and armed and manacled hands full of glare and glitter like lightning bolts, so that he resembled a vengeful and furious god pronouncing a doom, had struck him down " (p. 406). After this, Hightower, bandaged, sits in his chair while his past life parades through his mind.

It does seem that once a man who has already suffered reenters the whirlpool, his ride to the center is so fast as to be almost instantaneous. Such men are accident-prone types, extraordinarily vulnerable; they seem to have unlimited potential for pain. We hardly blame Hightower for becoming a sitter again after his disastrous re-entry into active life. The sensitive man gets hurt too much, too quickly, too often—and we are, I think, glad to grant him whatever refuge from pain he can find.

Byron Bunch is another quiet man who turns runner. Like Hightower's, the serenity of his life is an indication of its emptiness; he lives on the sidelines, uncommitted if not unconcerned. But he falls into the maelstrom of feeling as he follows Lena, and then moves faster and faster as he becomes more deeply involved with her. It is after she gives birth that Byron's action starts speeding up, along with his mind ("and thought was going too fast to give him time to think. That was it. Thought too swift for thinking," p. 349). Almost all the runners experience this new acceleration of the mental process, and I think this can be equated to the convict's waiting for an opportunity to scream in *Old Man*—the mind, in short, starts running along with the body, and goes through parallel stages at each point of the process. It finally breaks down, for example, just as the body collapses, and then enters a comatose state in which there is neither action nor movement. In all the passages cited pertaining to this stage, we have seen that the mind of the lier has emptied itself of all thought just as Darl, in *As I Lay Dying*, must empty himself of his identity before he can fall asleep.

Finally, Byron hits the vacuum of the vortex when he decides to fight Brown, knowing in advance that he has not the slightest chance of beating him. He rushes in and quickly gets knocked back outside the whirlpool's rim:

It lasted less than two minutes. Then Byron was lying quietly among the broken and trampled undergrowth, bleeding quietly about the face, hearing the underbrush crashing on, ceasing, fading into silence. Then he is alone. He feels no particular pain now, but better than that, he feels no haste, no urgency, to do anything or go anywhere. He just lies bleeding and quiet, knowing that after a while will be time enough to re-enter the world and time. (P. 385)

It would seem that one must endanger himself if he is to become involved—if one is to experience life, he must be willing to be bruised by it. For both Byron and Hightower, the state of quiet isolation after they have been thrown back from the turbulence of life is quite different from their earlier states of torpor and inactivity: they are, after all, bleeding now.

Lying, therefore, permits the runner a rest outside of time and space; consciousness recedes and there is a gradual clearing of the senses after the jumbled confusion of the whirlpool's vacuum. The lier is always completely alone at this time. Eventually, a new sense of direction emerges, and the character slowly and serenely walks back into life and commitment. The whole world seems to become calm again now that chaos has been purged from the system, and sensations no longer rush headlong into one another, but now become distinct. Even such a young runner as Vardaman in *As I Lay Dying* feels newly soothed and comforted when, after his mad flight from the house to the barn—during which his tears have mingled with the dust and the stick with which he strikes wildly at Peabody's team—his mind calms down to the point where his mother and the fish become separate entities again. Now, at last, the barn is quiet.

It is dark in the barn, warm, smelling, silent. I can cry quietly, watching the top of the hill.
... I am not crying now. I am not anything. Dewey Dell comes to the hill and calls me. Vardaman. I am not anything. I am quiet. You, Vardaman. I can cry quiet now, feeling and hearing my tears. ...
It is dark. I can hear wood, silence: I know them. ... I am not afraid.[5]

Finally, the whirlpool slows down and stops, and the world becomes once more a place of recognizable shapes, ordered and still.

This, then, is the pattern: a character floats with the current until somehow he loses the rhythm of its movement, and as he splashes and flails, gasping for breath, the force of the current builds around him and sends him spinning forward, usually into the direct path of another life which he knocks over (so Quentin, whose memory-fantasies are pushing him into an attack on Dalton Ames, finds his body leaping at Gerald). He is then drawn into the vacuum where he begins spinning with such velocity that the world around him loses order and solidity as all sensations run together, leaving the agitated mind hopelessly confused. Then just at the moment he is being sucked under and drowning seems imminent, the vacuum springs up beneath him and ejects him with such force, that his body lands outside of the whirlpool, where it floats in suspension, the mind dazed, con-

5. William Faulkner, *As I Lay Dying* (New York: Random House, 1957), p. 55. All future page references, cited in parentheses, are to this edition.

scious but blank, the body lifeless. Gradually, as his breath returns, his mind begins sorting again with a new serenity—the
formal feeling, perhaps, that follows great pain—and he opens his
eyes on a world where all objects have quietly settled back into
their proper places:

The broken flower drooped over Ben's fist and his eyes were empty and
blue and serene again as cornice and facade flowed smoothly once more
from left to right; post and tree, window and doorway, and signboard,
each in its ordered place. (P. 401)

The Sound and the Fury ends with these lines, and everything
is told in them. Order has been recovered and the world moves
slowly once more, but only at the expense of such pain that it
leaves a man's soul dark and empty.

Since Faulkner's fast-moving characters verge frequently on
hysteria, they are doomed to be thrown about in a universe
which constantly dislodges them from any fixed position. It is not
surprising, therefore, to note how frequently Faulkner uses water
images and metaphors to delineate man's peculiar helplessness.
As a natural element which makes no accommodations to man's
need for stability, the river suggests a philosophical equivalent of
an alien environment. Once in the water, a character loses all
control over his movements, and this increases not only his own
vulnerability, but that of others around him, as one body bumps
into another and pushes it under. Thus, disruption becomes so
rampant that even those who have been treading water successfully are endangered by those trying to swim against the current.
All men, finally, are victims destined to be destroyed by a chain
reaction of catastrophe. Such, indeed, is the destiny of the Sutpen
family

which for twenty years now had been like a lake welling from quiet
springs into a quiet valley and spreading, rising, almost imperceptibly
and in which the four members of it floated in sunny suspension, felt the
first subterranean movement toward the outlet, the gorge which would
be the land's catastrophe too, and the four peaceful swimmers turning
suddenly to face one another, not yet with alarm or distrust but just
alert, feeling the dark set, none of them yet at that point where man
looks about at his companions in disaster and thinks When will I stop
trying to save them and save only myself? and not even aware that that
point was approaching.[6]

6. William Faulkner, Absalom, Absalom! (New York: Random House, 1951),
p. 74.

We have only to imagine the waters turning rougher and knock-ing their bodies together to get an accurate visual metaphor for what happens in *Absalom, Absalom!* The Sutpens' actions seem inevitable, and the feeling of Fate is strong, as in a Greek tragedy. Perhaps that is why we feel fear and pity, rather than hatred for most of Faulkner's harmful people. This would apply to Joe Christmas, for example, who arouses our indignation until we find it difficult to connect him with his own actions, and there-fore to hold him responsible for them. As Joe is on his way to kill Joanna, Faulkner describes his actions in terms quite similar to the above passage from *Absalom, Absalom!* The swimmer loses control as the water sends his body in its own direction:

Yet when he moved, it was toward the house. It was as though, as soon as he found that his feet intended to go there, that he let go, seemed to float, surrendered, thinking *All right, All right* floating, riding, across the dusk, up to the house and onto the back porch and to the door by which he would enter, that was never locked. (P. 207)

In the world Faulkner has created for us, it does not seem strange to observe a character watching his own actions in a total-ly detached way. After all, he is not only helpless to resist the current carrying him off, but can expect no rescue either from even the best-intentioned bystanders, who are equally powerless to prevent the catastrophe they watch in horror. Such is Tull's feeble position in *As I Lay Dying,* as he fixes on the commotion in the river:

We could watch the rope cutting down into the water, and we could feel the weight of the wagon kind of blump and lunge lazy like, like it just as soon as not, and that rope cutting down into the water hard as a iron bar. We could hear the water hissing on it like it was red hot. Like it was a straight iron bar stuck into the bottom and us holding the end of it, and the wagon lazing up and down, kind of pushing and prodding at us like it had come around and got behind us, lazy like, like it just as soon as not when it made up its mind. There was a shoat come by, blowed up like a balloon: one of them spotted shoats of Lon Quick's. It bumped against the rope like it was a iron bar and bumped off and went on, and us watching that rope slanting down into the water. We watched it. (P. 148)

Man here is totally at the mercy of indifferent objects, and Tull seems cognizant of his absurd position: he may have the volition and mind that the wagon lacks, but that does him little good in a situation where the only string he holds is a rope whose end he cannot even see. Underneath the surface of the water, beneath the conglomeration of human, animal, and inanimate forms, the river works its independent will. The man who jumps in immediately becomes subservient to it, while the one who remains standing on the bank can do nothing more constructive than watch.

As one of the central images in Faulkner's novels, then, the river becomes a perfect symbol of the chaos pervading men's lives. Its natural fluidity keeps form indistinct and transient; its wild, indifferent will poses a constant threat to men who cannot hope to thwart it; its gushing, sucking, swirling dynamics are all characteristics of a mysterious, hostile force so versatile in its ability to disrupt and destroy, that it inevitably overwhelms anything moving in a counter-direction.

I have said that Faulkner's vision of life resembles a powerful maelstrom which sweeps its people along and overwhelms them as soon as desperation drives them to swim against the current. Since the world is in constant and furious motion, past, present, and future converge, and nature itself swarms around a man, throbbing with its own vitality. The importance of this vision as it recurs in so many of Faulkner's novels is that it conditions theme, characterization, and human values, as well as style and technique. Thematically, chaos is used as a catalyst to detonate the reader's awareness of and concern for the basic problem of men's lives: the difficulty (which we gradually infer to be the impossibility) of trying to create meaning in the face of forces we can neither understand nor cope with satisfactorily. It is in his direct confrontation with chaos that man's inability to know truth, to arrange his life in a purposeful way, and to control his destructive tendencies is reflected. The futility of attempting to combat a chaotic world becomes the main theme of many of Faulkner's novels.

But if life offers no meaning, it does still offer human relationships, and it is here that some conclusions can be drawn and a code of behavior established. Again, though, Faulkner's vision of chaos determines his treatment of this aspect of our lives, for we must understand what *can* be done in such a world before we can decide what *should* be done. Since Faulkner characterizes his people by defining them against chaotic conditions, their movements take on great significance as typifying different patterns of response.

Since the amount of chaos in a person's life grows in proportion to his ability to perceive it, superior perception almost always guarantees a more chaotic life; the existence of chaos cannot be divorced from its mental and psychological origins. Therefore, we should make a distinction here between those characters with awareness and those without it: we must put the latter group outside of the whirlpool altogether, for they are not engaged in living. These people are usually depicted as bovine creatures— they never move, which means they never struggle, which means they never become defined morally (though naturally, their struggle may be a quiet one and still qualify: Dilsey, for example, is the great endurer, but even she struggles against Jason on behalf of Quentin).

It would seem that the most a person could be expected to do is endure without dragging others down—and further, to support them, if possible. Dilsey, again, is a perfect representative of the person in total harmony with the rhythm of nature: we never have the sense of her being carried by the current against her will. She moves slowly, but with a purpose controlled by her own volition. Dilsey can say, "I seed de first en de last" because past and present are not confused in her mind; she always knows the time, and her life is a quiet pattern of regular routine. From the time she enters the house in the morning, starts the fire and makes breakfast, until she leaves in the evening, Dilsey's habitual activities structure her life in an orderly way. Like the Sutpens, the Compson family does such a thorough and effective job of destroying one another that it is little wonder Dilsey's endurance emerges as the most admirable human quality in *The Sound and the Fury.*

Ratliff's life also consists of a quiet and regular pattern, and his movement too is controlled by his will. Even if we hesitate to call him the hero of *The Hamlet,* he does finally emerge as its chief character because he seems most unselfishly involved in the lives of others. Also, his good will and sympathy impress us as the most admirable qualities one can possess in an exploitive society. Surely, *The Hamlet* offers no preferable alternative.

Lena, in *Light in August,* has little awareness, but her ability to endure gives her a kind of stature and dignity. She, too, moves slowly and willfully: she does make her own decisions and will not be dissuaded by others. Her good nature wins us over to her, and we admire her steadfast resolve, her sense of purpose and direction, and her refusal to hurt others.

Dilsey, Ratliff, and Lena are three slow movers of exemplary type. We cannot call any of them heroes or heroines, and yet when we look for values in Faulkner, these people seem the most virtuous, the most worthy of our respect. In such a world, after all, what can one do but live quietly, go about his business, and endure his burden of life without making others suffer for it? It *is* important, though, that they do move around, no matter how slowly, for it is this which distinguishes them from the sitters—Hightower, Old Varner, and Jason Compson Sr., for example—who are so withdrawn from the mainstream of life that, while they do not hurt others directly, they exhibit too little positive action to evoke our admiration. The liers would fall into this class, too, although their state is usually only temporary.

The runners, we have seen, are the men of action who define themselves morally by impressing their identity upon others. What is important about them is that their bodies are not regulated to their wills, that they are peculiarly possessed, and that they suffer. Indeed, their despair itself makes them sympathetic, even when their action has been destructive. The fact is that the runners tend to be the most interesting and memorable characters because, although their energies have been misguided and perverted, they do have great vitality and potential which we feel have been thwarted. They are as close as we can ever come to traditional heroism in Faulkner, for they are the ones who define themselves most clearly against the murky world they inhabit. By fighting the tide, they offer some resistance to an intolerable universe in which man is always hopelessly lost, even if they seem simultaneously to be insuring their own destruction.

The values in Faulkner's world tend, therefore, to be passive ones, because a man's attempts to assert his importance as a creature of will are almost always futile. Courage, of course, is important, but its meaning is restricted primarily to patience, acceptance, endurance, and humility. The reason for this is clear when we consider that as soon as a character tries to contest the malignant forces of his universe, he becomes possessed—doomed by his own nature, which carries him to disaster as he looks on helplessly. Yet since he cannot hope to change his nature, we find it difficult to hold a man entirely responsible for acts which seem inevitable. Perhaps that is why Faulkner has *not* prescribed a code of behavior for the sensitive man. If he fights, he loses, and if he refuses to fight, he ends up not having lived.

Faulkner, then, places his people in a world so full-bodied, fast-moving, and threatening that both his characters and values seem frequently to become revealed through and defined by their manner of adjustment. This technique tends to minimize character and value formation by presenting the positive elements always silhouetted against a rushing background; as a result, it is the form, rather than the particular individual, which becomes outlined. (Even when depicting the intimate act of love-making, Faulkner rarely gives us a strong sense of two individuals; instead, they seem to be rolling about also with their mothers and fathers and sisters and ancestors and the earth and the smell of jasmine and honeysuckle.) Because we are unable to consider the characters apart from the aggregate influences accounting for their actions, we tend to see them instead as embodiments of all mankind: mythic symbols of the human spirit. Thus, it is not surprising that Faulkner's convict in *Old Man* remains nameless, because he never becomes sufficiently individualized but rather seems to represent Man fighting for his life in the elements. The convict is too deeply immersed in the movement of the river to be clearly outlined against it; only his insignificance is emphasized as he's swept along, and since the most he can do is keep his head above water, it is not his character which is defined by the struggle so much as his human impulses. The river carries everything before it, and if a man manages to survive, it is because his instincts have been successful in confronting the threat of the immediate situation. We feel that he has acted from these instincts rather than will, and so his behavior seems less admirable than inevitable. Survival, therefore, is the only thing to be gained from a tough struggle—no higher moral value is possible when man's will is based on intuition rather than free choice of good action over bad. This does not mean that we cannot admire his courage, ingenuity, and endurance—it is important, indeed, that we do so—but we tend to admire them as general tendencies in man rather than as virtues of this one character. In short, because Faulkner characterizes his people *in* motion and *through* their motions, his technique rarely highlights the individual man, but tends instead to weave that man's responses into a complex, patterned design in which he is seen from a greater distance—so great, indeed, that he finally becomes inseparable from all men who have ever lived and suffered.

We have seen how characters suffer in chaos, but how much does the novel suffer from Faulkner's vision? Obviously, not at all. Since Faulkner's world is kinetic, circular, dynamic, and multidimensional, his style, structure, narrative technique, and method of characterization reflect the same qualities—but reflect them brilliantly, powerfully, and with full aesthetic control. It is not necessary to dwell upon Faulkner's artistic methods as appropriate means of expressing his vision—most of them are obvious and have been dealt with often before—but we may simply note their suitability to the sweeping, whirlpool movement I have used to describe that vision.

Faulkner's style is typified by circling sentences that push us precipitantly through the narrative. Once we enter a character's consciousness, we are swept along as if enclosed within a tornado; we feel the tremendous thrust, power, and impetus of a dynamic force that spirals inward, and we are kept in continuous motion by long, involved, convoluted sentences that hurl us along at an almost frightening pace. The very confusion we so often feel is, in fact, a pertinent part of that effect, of the sheer volume of energy embodied in Faulkner's chaotic vision.

Also, the natural fluidity of the stream-of-consciousness technique becomes a perfect instrument for Faulkner to push us along in his spinning world, and the whirlpool effect is reinforced by the repetition of certain words and fragments of past events: they eddy around us, and we remember having passed them before. This is especially true in such works as *The Sound and the Fury*, and particularly in the first two sections, where fragments of the past keep whirling by until they can hardly be distinguished from the action in the present. Each incident comes into focus only after we have passed it by a number of times. Our first impressions of it are vague because it is lost in or dimmed by the motion of the present, and our minds are not given enough time to register this impression fully enough to grasp its meaning. It is only after we have become familiar with recurring glimpses of them, that the forms around us slowly become defined, and we begin to see how they fit in. We grab at recurring words, images, and events as if they were pieces of driftwood on which we might steady ourselves long enough to recover our bearings. If, as in most of the novels, we feel that we never have recovered ourselves sufficiently to apprehend fully what has happened and why it has happened, then that also only attests to the integrity of

Faulkner's structure, which allows us to know only what *can* be known in the course of human events, and in the only way we come to know it in reality. Spirals, after all, end only in infinity.

Faulkner's narrative technique is also suitable to the circular action and structure of his stories. Almost all of his novels present an accumulation of points of view; we see the situation and come to know it from both relevant and seemingly irrelevant perspectives. In *Light in August, The Sound and the Fury, As I Lay Dying,* and *Absalom, Absalom!,* the past becomes only gradually explicit as we put together the parts from all the limited perspectives of the various narrators. Yet Faulkner's point of view is strikingly unusual because the multiple perspectives are not necessarily pertinent as means of revealing the character of the narrator. The last section of *Light in August,* for example, is related to us by a man never identified who is speaking to his unidentified wife; neither of them is relevant to the action—they are important only in getting the story *told.* But why, then, has Faulkner not used an omniscient point of view? Why introduce characters for no other reason than to get the story told? The answer would seem to be that our final knowledge of any situation or event is the totality of various responses to it; we can know it, therefore, only as an aggregate of perspectives. Again, the use of myriad narrators gives us a dynamic, rather than stationary view of the action: as we move constantly from one point of view to another the result is a multidimensional, cubistic kind of observation which forces us continually to shift, adjust, and reorient ourselves to new lines of vision opening up new possibilities of interpretation. In this way, however, our experience as reader parallels and reflects the chaos in Faulkner's novels and characters. Through his method of relating his stories, Faulkner communicates his idea of mental chaos partly by reproducing in us the difficulties faced by his characters in trying to perceive a situation clearly, apprehend truth, and distinguish psychological reality from its external equivalent.

Like Melville in *The Confidence-Man,* Faulkner is obviously unwilling to trust anyone—even himself—as the proper interpreter of a complex situation. Truth, in the end, always eludes the most perceptive mind and so must be forever unknowable. Unlike Sterne, who always holds the final card (although he may present it at his own discretion), Faulkner almost never gives us a "last word" on the action he is presenting; his role as narrator is restricted to an articulate voice expressing thoughts and feelings which are beyond his characters' capabilities to communicate, even to themselves. This is not to say that Faulkner fails to control his reader's responses very carefully and deliberately, but he does this primarily through tone and emphasis. Still, as articulator, he is under no obligation to interpret, and the reader is left on his own to draw meaning from the events he observes. Even so, Faulkner seems to me a very different kind of artist from the Melville of *The Confidence-Man,* who consciously forces his reader into a stalemate of ambiguity where nothing can be reconciled or resolved. Faulkner's purpose does seem to be to clarify rather than confuse—but only so much as is humanly possible.

And how much *is* humanly possible? How much can ever be known about human beings—their complicated, subtle feelings; their vague and ambiguous motives, their seemingly self-destructive desires? By getting into the minds of his characters, Faulkner takes us far indeed, yet the result is more often than not only a deeper awareness of chaos. In *As I Lay Dying,* the reader has all the information he needs to understand the motives and mentalities of the Bundren family, but the information leaves him hopelessly perplexed as he tries to sort out the reasonable from the unreasonable, the tragic from the comic, the reality from the appearance. The knowledge supplied by Faulkner clarifies the ambiguity but never resolves it. Facts may be known, but truth remains unknowable, since it is relative to perspective and levels of awareness: the situation or idea that seemed idiotic and ludicrous from one point of view seems sensible and even heroic from another. Finally, Darl, the narrator we most respect and identify with, turns out to be the one who is taken to Jackson— and while we may enjoy the irony for a while, we feel less secure and comfortable in it when Cash remarks that we can not after all just let a person go around burning people's barns. We may like and respect Darl, but can we afford to empathize with him? If his insanity seems more attractive than the stupidity of the sane, are we to justify him? No matter which direction we take, our values start floundering until we are forced to surrender them altogether.

In most of his important works, then, Faulkner seems intent on producing a world of sound and fury, which finally signifies only what the reader can presume to conclude from a series of complex impressions. As readers, we are ourselves thrown into a whirlpool-like experience, where we find sensations rushing to-gether, judgments falling apart, and our sense of life intensifying as chaos closes in. Tapping this source of energy at the hub of our lives, Faulkner, like only the very greatest writers, is able to bring it closer to us for inspection by capturing it aesthetically with all its dynamism intact. Spinning in the eye of the maelstrom, how-ever, the reader must then adjust to a disturbing idea: that the novel can be used to lead us *into* chaos just as effectively as it was once used to lead us out of it.

5

The Tension of Stalemate

Art and Chaos in Virginia Woolf's To the Lighthouse

M*any contemporary novelists* have surrendered a good deal or all of their artistic control to the belief that a chaotic vision of life can be truly represented only by a chaotic form. To the extent that artifice is falsification, its presence would seem to undermine the confusion that the author is trying to project. But must all aesthetic order dissolve before a philosophical sense of disorder can be communicated? If so, then the novel may be as dead as it has been rumored to be. But if the novel is flexible enough, it may be saved by the very artifice which has threatened to stifle it. In short, the novel can provide illusions of devastating experience without subjecting itself to the inevitable destruction that the experience itself might lead to. The trick is to know how to handle artistic freedom—and that in itself implies a discipline that many contemporaries are evading or willfully abdicating. Just as Marlow in *Heart of Darkness* can peer into Kurtz's abyss without *falling* into it, so the reader can be mentally jarred by the appearance of chaos without being thrust into its real-life equivalent. The author may very well want to give us the sensation of slipping occasionally, but once he pulls us over the precipice, art becomes indistinguishable from life and is therefore rendered superfluous. If art is to heighten and sharpen our awareness of reality, it must provide sufficient stability and de-tachment to enable the reader to use all his resources in coming to terms with the author's vision—no matter how chaotic that vision is. Otherwise, the reader becomes so helplessly lost in the chaos itself that he is no longer free to feel the kind of impact that art makes possible. The view from Kurtz's psyche may have the advantage of greater immediacy, but that same experience for-malized through Marlow's intellect and disciplined by Conrad's artistic devices, gains universality and provides a basis for evalu-ating that experience. Art, then, need not falsify chaos in order to rescue something from it.

Like Joseph Conrad, Virginia Woolf values anything that art can salvage from a world that is "too dark altogether," yet like him too, she is careful not to make too large a claim: the darkness she depicts can never be dispelled. She is under no illusions that the resistance art can offer is tantamount to triumph, but even a stalemate is sufficient assurance for her of art's value in our lives. Here, I think, is where her chief importance lies for us today, both as an artist and as an aesthetician for modern practitioners of the chaotic novel. In her, we may find hope for the future of a form currently in danger of being swallowed up by a vision that sees the futility of artistic control as the end rather than the be-ginning of a perpetual struggle.

In *To the Lighthouse,* Virginia Woolf handles chaos with such delicacy that the work seems almost too well-made to reflect her disturbing vision. Nevertheless, the balance between construc-tive and destructive forces is kept at such a teetering tension throughout, that the novel becomes an exciting, if subdued, con-test between art and reality. If art's ultimate victory is tentative and precarious, it is still legitimate, for Virginia Woolf has not underestimated the power of her opponent. While her character-ization of chaos lacks the terrifying aggressiveness accorded it by many contemporary writers, it is every bit as eerie, menacing, and devastating. Quietly seeping through the roots of our lives, it extirpates us quite as efficiently as much wilder forces, for it works from within *and* without. Like dusk descending slowly and silently, it settles over a scene until all forms become obliterated, and man himself is left a "wedge of darkness."

Because the darkness surrounding our lives originates in the pores of the human personality, we cannot say that it prevents us from knowing ourselves, but rather that this darkness is the deepest thing we *can* know about ourselves. Like Darl in *As I Lay Dying*, who must empty himself out for sleep, Mrs. Ramsay also feels the falseness of her identity in active life when, alone, she divests herself of her various roles, which slip away into the night. Only now

she could be herself, by herself. . . . To be silent; to be alone. All the being and the doing, expansive, glittering, vocal, evaporated; and one shrunk, with a sense of solemnity, to being oneself, a wedge-shaped core of darkness, something invisible to others. . . . our apparitions, the things you know us by, are simply childish. Beneath it is all dark, it is all spreading; it is unfathomably deep; but now and again we rise to the surface and that is what you see us by.[1]

It would seem, then, that all appearances are essentially false suggestions of a unified personality. By implying that we can be known and reached, these outward projections of our internal realities are deceptive and ultimately illusory. For the artist who hopes to penetrate facades, therefore, acknowledgment of chaos is mandatory. Lily Briscoe, never deceived by public forms of personality, tries desperately to grasp the private world of Mrs. Ramsay, but recognizes the futility of her efforts when she finds intimacy itself an impossibility. Leaning her head on Mrs. Ramsay's knee, she is shocked to discover that

Nothing happened. Nothing! Nothing! . . . And yet, she knew knowledge and wisdom were stored up in Mrs. Ramsay's heart. How then, she had asked herself, did one know one thing or another thing about people, sealed as they were? (P. 79)

It is this question that haunts Lily throughout the novel, and her determination to deal honestly with it that dictates Virginia Woolf's themes and techniques, as both author and her fictional counterpart contemplate the chaos separating all human beings from themselves and from one another.

By slipping in and out of her characters' minds, Virginia Woolf reveals all the subtle shifts in mood, idea, and response attesting to the fluidity of human consciousness; and her omniscient point of view enables her to define the remoteness of one mind from another with depressing clarity. We see one person flowing through a rainbow of moods, changing thoughts with the ease of a

1. Virginia Woolf, *To the Lighthouse* (New York: Harcourt, Brace and World, 1955), pp. 95–96. All future page references, cited in parentheses, are to this edition.

chameleon changing color, and continually sliding out of one self into another with such protean elusiveness that even the most astute observer must remain forever locked out of another's identity. Furthermore, the observer himself is affected and his own identity frequently modified or significantly altered by what he has perceived in the other person—and that perception itself is hardly constant, but influenced by the perceiver's particular mood, thoughts, and feelings at the moment. Because all this takes place in seconds, we see that even the form of chaos changes from one moment to the next. If truth is to be found at all, then, it is the truth of an instant—those spots of time when we suddenly rise to the surface to become one with our appearance.

Since Virginia Woolf defines the self as a wedge of darkness invisible to others, we may wonder if it is inaccessible as well. Certainly, it would seem that if her people, like Conrad's, are inevitably sealed off from one another and if, like Faulkner's, their own identities block accurate perception, then interaction is apt to be a haphazard collision at best. Like planets revolving in different spheres, all her characters seem separate worlds divided by vast chasms of darkness which absorb most of the signals sent from one body to another. To what extent does such a universe render meaningful communication possible?

one could say nothing to nobody. The urgency of the moment always missed its mark. Words fluttered sideways and struck the object inches too low. . . . For how could one express in words these emotions of the body? express that emptiness there? (P. 265)

Even if, by chance, the words were to hit their target, their meanings would still be lost by the time they worked their way down into the emotional fabric of the receiver. The words emerging from one sensibility are necessarily distorted in the process of filtering through an entirely different sensibility; even when Mrs. Ramsay puts a relatively simple question to her daughter, "the words seemed to be dropped into a well, where, if the waters were clear, they were also so extraordinarily distorting that, even as they descended, one saw them twisting about to make Heaven knows what pattern on the floor of the child's mind" (p. 84). One must obviously objectify his feelings if they are to traverse the void successfully and reach another's mind intact, but since any kind of objectivity is impossible in such a world, words do indeed seem to be useless vehicles for the transmission of deep currents of feeling. This is why Lily sees the Ramsays without Mrs. Ramsay as "a house full of unrelated passions" (p. 221). Members of the family talk to one another, but no one seems to reach anyone else.

Words are not, however, the only means of trying to reach other people, and Virginia Woolf implies that feelings often *can* be communicated, even when language fails. The first section of the novel ends with Mrs. Ramsay's triumph in communicating her love to her husband without having to articulate it; and moments after Lily has seen the Ramsay household as one of unrelated passions, she watches the procession of the family across the lawn "drawn on by some stress of common feeling which made it, faltering and flagging as it was, a little company bound together and strangely impressive to her" (p. 231). Just as Marlow in *Lord Jim* can understand more than he can express and intuit more than he can comprehend about Jim simply because Jim is "one of us," so, too, does Virginia Woolf suggest that shared instinctive feelings can often overtake chaos to a greater extent than would at first seem possible considering the ultimate isolation of each person. Though words are always inadequate conveyors of one's feelings, communication based on shared sympathies is always possible. When relationships are working well, silence will always transcend speech in eloquence of expression and exactness of thought.

The chaos emanating from within the human personality may, then, restrict self-knowledge and hamper relationships, but shared instinctive feelings can mitigate, if not overcome, the difficulty of having to live and love in such a world. Still, our lives are far more complicated than inner chaos alone would make them; to consider the other half of Virginia Woolf's vision, we must recognize the existence of outer chaos as well, which constantly undermines any order we may try to impose on the universe. This outer chaos is as quiet and invisible as the wedge of darkness at the core of our selves, but its presence is the most distressing fact of our existence because it denies everything we want to affirm, negates the value of our lives, and crushes out meaning with shocking swiftness.

When Lily and William Bankes, while watching a sailboat moving on the waves, feel a "common hilarity," their silent communication promises to dispel the threat of inner chaos; yet both are cut short in their enjoyment by a sudden movement that turns them toward the dunes far away. They immediately become melancholy "partly because distant views seem to outlast by a million years (Lily thought) the gazer and to be communing already with a sky which beholds an earth entirely at rest" (p. 34). In the middle of a beautiful moment, then, Lily and William are shaken by sudden awareness of their insignificance in time. Their sense of spatial vastness suggests a temporal infinity as well; and they are so dwarfed by both dimensions that even the union of two wedges of darkness cannot combat the realization that they have no share in the world's permanence but must remain strangers all their lives to a universe that will tolerate them only for an instant before swallowing them up. Time is one important component of chaos because it gnaws away at our sense of stability, suggesting how little we can hope to know about life when the most that can be known in one lifetime is worth virtually nothing over the ages which will cover and forget us, bury our bodies and our knowledge as effectively as if we had never existed at all. Our place in life is as significant as the position of an ant on a desert, and our minds can never be at home in such a world.

Another aspect of the outer chaos threatening us is the fluidity of the universe, which constantly undermines our sense of structure and security. For a human being to feel unanchored in the general drift of life is intolerable. Just as our feet were not made to walk in quicksand, so our minds cannot contemplate eternal fluidity without going under; we must presume stability before we can determine order, and we must be assured of order before we can hope to find meaning. The natural fluidity of all things is in direct opposition to the spiritual cravings of our souls, to the philosophical tendencies of our minds, and to the unifying obsessions of our imaginations. Unmoored in a shifting reality, man can acquire neither wisdom nor tranquility but can hope only to keep his balance; and it is the stability of his common cause with fellow human beings that alone can help him resist the hostile element in which he finds himself. Like Faulkner's runners, the sensitive characters in *To the Lighthouse* often feel as if they had been thrust into a mental and emotional whirlpool where they can never hope to establish order or feel safe. Fortunately, though, they are usually spared immersion by their feelings of fellowship. Even a scene as simple and familiar as the one at the dinner table can, in Virginia Woolf, evoke these feelings:

Now all the candles were lit up, and the faces on both sides of the table were brought nearer by the candle light, and composed, as they had not been in the twilight, into a party round a table, for the night was now shut off by panes of glass, which, far from giving any accurate view of the outside world, rippled it so strangely that here inside the room, seemed to be order and dry land; there, outside, a reflection in which things wavered and vanished, waterily.

Some change at once went through them all, as if this had really happened, and they were all conscious of making a party together in a hollow, on an island; had their common cause against that fluidity out there. (Pp. 146–47)

Inner chaos seems insignificant when people who can never know one another much better than they can know the universe itself band together and feel a common unity in their mutual fear of an antagonistic world.

A third aspect of chaos is emphasized in the second section of the novel when time and fluidity become synonymous with decay, disintegration and entropy; chaos here infests man's systematic life to the point where it erodes his most basic assumption of self-importance. As darkness infiltrates the Ramsay's summer home, swallowing up the forms of man's existence,

not only was furniture confounded; there was scarcely anything left of body or mind by which one could say, "This is he" or "This is she." Sometimes a hand was raised as if to clutch something or ward off something, or somebody groaned, or somebody laughed aloud as if sharing a joke with nothingness. (P. 190)

The tenuousness of man's significance is felt keenly as Mrs. Ramsay, her daughter, and her son die in parentheses—victims of time, chance, and the general entropic drive of the universe. As the darkness eats away at the products of a man's life in bigger and bigger gulps, both people and things sink into the chaos with remarkable impartiality. Man's values, dreams and creations are swept off into the chaotic flood which renders them inconsequential and meaningless, while his philosophical, moral, social, and spiritual systems are wiped out as so much presumption. Using Nature and Time as its primary instruments, the dark forces of chaos dominate, then demolish all the order man has brought to his uncertain life:

Listening (had there been anyone to listen) from the upper rooms of the empty house only gigantic chaos streaked with lightning could have been heard tumbling and tossing, as the winds and waves disported themselves like the amorphous bulks of leviathans whose brows are pierced by no light of reason, and mounted one on top of another, and lunged and plunged in the darkness or the daylight (for night and day, month and year ran shapelessly together) in idiot games, until it seemed as if the universe were battling and tumbling, in brute confusion and wanton lust aimlessly by itself.

In spring . . . the stillness and brightness of the day were as strange as the chaos and tumult of night, with the trees standing there, looking before them, looking up, yet beholding nothing, eyeless, and so terrible. . . . (the garden was a pitiful sight now, all run to riot, and rabbits scuttling at you out of the beds). (Pp. 202–3, 204)

It would seem that man's chief responsibility in a hostile universe is to subdue chaos with all the energy he can muster, for the second he stops resisting it, it takes over and annihilates him, crushing out all the signs and symbols of his existence.

For now had come that moment, that hesitation when dawn trembles and night pauses, when if a feather alight in the scale it will be weighed down. One feather, and the house, sinking, falling, would have turned and pitched downwards to the depths of darkness. In the ruined room, picnickers would have lit their kettles; lovers sought shelter there, lying on the bare boards; and the shepherd stored his dinner on the bricks, and the tramp slept with his coat round him to ward off the cold. Then the roof would have fallen; briars and hemlocks would have blotted out path, step, and window; would have grown, unequally but lustily over the mound, until some trespasser, losing his way, could have told only by a red-hot poker among his nettles, or a scrap of china in the hemlock that here once some one had lived; there had been a house.

If the feather had fallen, if it had tipped the scale downwards, the whole house would have plunged to the depths to lie upon the sands of oblivion. (Pp. 208–9)

But it is just at this moment, of course, that "slowly and painfully, with broom and pail, mopping, scouring, Mrs. McNab, Mrs. Bast, stayed the corruption and the rot" (p. 209). And so man regains his precarious supremacy over chaos through hard work and conscious will power.

We may leave the hard work to the cleaning ladies for a while, and concentrate on the more complicated mental process involved in combatting and finally controlling chaos. It is obvious that for Virginia Woolf, art represents the ultimate resistance of the mind to the disordered life around us—it keeps airborne that treacherous feather which, once fallen, will upset the scales against us. Although the second section of the book stresses natural chaos, it also embodies the social chaos of a world war and the philosophical and spiritual chaos of a cosmos which refuses to honor man's most prized values, concepts, and beliefs—all of which are founded on an assumption of some order. By facing squarely the aspects of chaos which threaten our security, art attempts to rescue for our benefit what the darkness is continually trying to remove. Thus, we see how the natural pull toward oblivion is met by the artist's struggle to pin down time and make it memorable; the tug toward fluidity is stayed by the permanence of the written word or painted line; the progress of decay is resisted by the vision which unifies and endures. The suction of natural things into a whirlpool of disarray is arrested by the imposition of aesthetic order which freezes reality; and the impulse of nature toward disintegration into unidentifiable atoms is thwarted by the unifying process of creativity.

The struggle of art against chaos is, then, a constant, agonizing, and intense one—infinitely exhausting, yet never futile. To shine a beam of light into the darkness and locate a truth which may be solidified into vision demands all of man's willpower and energy, but the war must be fought before man can ever satisfy his need for meaning. Because "the vision must be perpetually remade" (p. 270), the battle must be perpetually waged; and while any kind of lasting victory must remain impossible, those moments of mastery are enough to provide life with some semblance of order and to offer man the solace of meaning.

I have already mentioned the futility of words as instruments of communication between wedges of darkness, yet the novel does offer simultaneously a vindication for language founded on its permanence, if not its precision. While Lily stands looking at her picture and reflecting on what Mr. Ramsay would have said about her failure to capture her vision on canvas,

a curious notion came to her that he did after all hear the things she could not say. . . . She looked at her picture. That would have been his answer, presumably—how "you" and "I" and "she" pass and vanish; nothing stays; all changes; but not words, not paint. Yet it would be hung in the attics, she thought; it would be rolled up and flung under a sofa; yet even so, even of a picture like that, it was true. One might say, even of this scrawl, not of that actual picture perhaps, but of what it attempted, that it "remained forever." (P. 267)

Lily is humble enough to realize that no fantastic claims can be made for the art she is trying to create: its value is uncertain, perhaps even negligible, in a world that can never be grasped or defined. At the most, art's domination of a moment is still such a difficult process that the moment is a thing of the distant past long before art has mastered it. Still, it is the creative process itself which raises man's position from victim to challenger, and so *his* significance is ascertained independently of the success of his accomplishment.

By inserting the artist into her novel—at first in the background, then later into the foreground—Virginia Woolf is able to duplicate metaphorically her own frustration in the formidable process of wresting shape from chaos. Lily Briscoe may be a good, fair, or poor artist, but her integrity cannot be questioned as she strives to objectify her vision into universal symbols which alone can organize and express what she feels.

But conception and execution are separated by hours of anguish which attest to the difficulty of objectification. How does one translate vague, chaotic feelings into structured, coherent forms? How shed light on darkness without falsifying that darkness? In a passage filled with artistic *angst*, and strongly reminiscent of Sterne's descriptions of John de la Casse's exasperation while working on his *Galateo*, Virginia Woolf depicts Lily's effort as an incredible struggle of the will to project an ordered vision onto nothingness:

She could see it all so clearly, so commandingly, when she looked: it was when she took her brush in hand that the whole thing changed. It was in that moment's flight between the picture and her canvas that the demons set on her who often brought her to the verge of tears and made this passage from conception to work as dreadful as any down a dark passage for a child. Such she often felt herself—struggling against terrific odds to maintain her courage; to say: "But this is what I see," and so to clasp some miserable remnant of her vision to her breast, which a thousand forces did their best to pluck from her. (P. 32)

The artistic temperament suffers as the tension increases between its efforts to objectify feelings and the efforts of chaotic forces to elude formalization. Lily's struggle becomes more desperate as the novel progresses, but even after ten years have gone by, she remains dedicated to her task. Even though "it was a miserable machine, an inefficient machine, she thought, the human apparatus for painting or for feeling; it always broke down at the critical moment; heroically, one must force it on" (p. 287). In her refusal to ever consider the possibility of surrender, Lily as artist becomes the genuine hero of the novel.

Heroism never comes easily, however, and Lily hovers on defeat throughout the novel: as her emotions build in intensity, so does her frustration, until the canvas itself "seemed to rebuke her with its cold stare for all this hurry and agitation; this folly and waste of emotion. . . . She looked blankly at the canvas, with its uncompromising white stare" (p. 234). That white void is similar to the whiteness of Melville's whale in its suggestion of meaninglessness—the chaotic vision that mocks man's attempts to interpret the truth beyond appearances by implying that there is nothing really to interpret. "For what could be more formidable than that space?" Lily thinks as she decides to run the risk of filling it (p. 236)—and even the few nervous lines she finally puts there have a soothing effect on her as she watches them enclose and eventually define space. And arbitrary as this might seem, it is not artifice for its own sake, for as soon as the canvas begins to represent appearances, Lily feels a truth, a reality behind them that becomes the new focus of her concentration. It is not *the* truth which she senses, but *a* truth of this particular scene at this particular moment; still, it is a genuine reality she has discovered in her invasion of space—that space which represents chaos, yet which can be made to reflect meaning so long as man is willing to impose his imagination upon it.

The fact that chaos can be shaped to yield meaning does not imply, however, that the chaos itself is only an illusion; *its* inexplicability cannot be contested without gross falsification, and as a result, we must make sure that the process of formalizing never becomes too representational. That would constitute artifice rather than art, because as soon as chaos becomes defined, it disappears; and as soon as it disappears, we have a false sense of knowledge which leads us away from truth, rather than toward it. Chaos remains the reality behind appearances, *not* simply another appearance. Objectification is crucial, therefore, for *rendering* chaos only: it should not work to dispel it. This is probably the reasoning behind Lily's abstract method of painting, for a valid aesthetic principle must be an outgrowth of vision, and Lily's vision is one that acknowledges the reality of chaos, even while seeking to defeat it. When William Bankes asks her why she has depicted Mrs. Ramsay and James as a purple shadow rather than as identifiable human shapes, Lily replies that she has made no attempt at likenesses because her picture was not so much of them as of her *sense* of them. Her abstract techniques are, then, objectifications of her thoughts and feelings, not of the subjects which have evoked them. Art attempts to demonstrate perception rather than to delineate appearances, and so it must be able to mirror the chaos it perceives as an integral part of its vision.

Art, though, does more than reflect chaos; it also conquers chaos in the very act of rendering it. By capturing the symbolic moment that embodies enduring truth, the artist may apprehend a coherence in things that normally remains hidden behind the disarray of appearances. And again, it is not a matter of dispelling chaos, but simply of selecting from it that which is palatable to the human imagination and workable for the human mind. In the fluidity of time, truth—when it is found—exists only for the moment, but even so, these moments are to be treasured for the meaning they contain. Lily recognizes such a moment early in the book when she sees the Ramsays watching their children play ball:

And suddenly the meaning which, for no reason at all, as perhaps they are stepping out of the Tube or ringing a doorbell, descends on people, making them symbolical, making them representative, came upon them, and made them in the dusk standing, looking, the symbols of marriage, husband and wife. (Pp. 110–11)

And later in the day, while sitting at dinner, she experiences a similar sensation as the kernel of another moment explodes to reveal a harmony symbolizing a universal pattern of coherence:

Nothing need be said; nothing could be said. There it was, all around them. It partook, she felt . . . of eternity; as she had already felt about something different once before that afternoon; there is a coherence in things, a stability; something, she meant, is immune from change, and shines out (she glanced at the window with its ripple of reflected lights) in the face of the flowing, the fleeting, the spectral, like a ruby; so that again tonight she had the feeling she had had once today, already, of peace, of rest. Of such moments, she thought, the thing is made that endures. (P. 158)

These, then, are the moments that art must capture in order to transform life into tiny chunks of meaning which help to stay the chaos of the next moment.

While these moments may be sensed instinctively, they can be expressed only through the indirect means of re-creation; and since the meaning emanated not from the moment itself, but from the sensibility of a sensitive perceiver, the truth cannot be caught through a simple depiction of the moment, but must be

molded into a vision embodying it as the moment's inner structure. Art may be constructed from chaos, but only through the
painstaking process of selecting, organizing, and filtering impressions of reality through vision. As Lily realizes, the total subjectivity of perception, once disciplined and formalized, can refine life
by unifying what exists in its raw state as so much disorganized
matter: "There might be lovers," she thinks, "whose gift it was to
choose out the elements of things and place them together and
so, giving them a wholeness not theirs in life, make of some
scene, or meeting of people (all now gone and separate), one of
those globed compacted things over which thought lingers, and
love plays" (p. 286).

It is in the act of transmitting a moment into vision that art
assumes a philosophical value, for the moment must be arrested
before it can be contemplated; and only art can halt time long
enough for us to discern shape, form, and the kernels of meaning
that the fluidity of our lives keeps submerged. Lily sees her function as artist at the same time she realizes why Mrs. Ramsay is the
great woman she has always thought her to be; for Mrs. Ramsay is
herself like a work of art in her ability to hold back life long
enough for it to yield answers to our one most desperate question:

What is the meaning of life? That was all—a simple question, one that
tended to close in on one with years. The great revelation had never
come. The great revelation perhaps never did come. Instead there were
little daily miracles, illuminations, matches struck unexpectedly in the
dark; here was one. This, that, and the other; herself and Charles Tansley
and the breaking wave; Mrs. Ramsay bringing them together; Mrs. Ramsay saying, "Life stand still here:" Mrs. Ramsay making of the moment
something permanent (as in another sphere Lily herself tried to make of
the moment something permanent)—this was of the nature of a revelation. In the midst of chaos there was shape; this eternal passing and
flowing (she looked at the clouds going and the leaves shaking) was
struck into stability. (Pp. 240–41)

Suddenly perceiving Mrs. Ramsay as a synthesizing agent, Lily
has an almost mystical revelation, which dismisses the relevance
of ever again asking the meaning of life. The "little daily miracles" are the closest we can ever come to finding answers, for the
conception of life as a whole is only another of man's illusions;
reality contains only a series of seconds which may be known and
even universalized as typical, but which can never be consolidat-

ed as if they then formed a unity which they never contained separately. One cannot get at *life* because that is an abstraction of the intellect; but *moments,* since they partake of the fluidity of time, are real.

Through her revelation, Lily gains an increased understanding of art's potential in a world of flux. The truth of life is in the moment and capturing the reality of the moment is therefore a miracle. But like Joseph Conrad, Lily sees the immense difficulty of rescuing the moment from its fluid setting:

One must keep on looking without for a second relaxing the intensity of emotion, the determination not to be put off, not to be bamboozled. One must hold the scene—so—in a vise, and let nothing come in and spoil it. One wanted, she thought, dipping her brush deliberately, to be on a level with ordinary experience, to feel simply that's a chair, that's a table, and yet at the same time, it's a miracle, it's an ecstasy. The problem might be solved after all. (Pp. 299–300)

Art must put life into a vise and hold it there until its reality becomes discernible, making sure, however, not to tamper with that reality by detaching it from the flux in which it lives. Virginia Woolf suggests her own technique for controlling chaos by describing Lily's conception of the painting which acknowledges chaos on one level while defeating it on another:

Beautiful and bright it should be on the surface, feathery and evanescent, one colour melting into another like the colours on a butterfly's wing; but beneath the fabric must be clamped together with bolts of iron. It was to be a thing you could ruffle with your breath; and a thing you could not dislodge with a team of horses. (P. 155)

To have harnessed the strength necessary to bring chaos within the structured and eternal domain of art is already enough to signify that the artist has won the battle of the moment through sheer persistence. We do not, of course, tame chaos simply by capturing it, but we do at least hold it back for a while, and in this sense, the artist of chaos has done all that can possibly be done.

Virginia Woolf's concept of reality is introduced in the very title of the book, which emphasizes not the Lighthouse itself, but the movement toward it, producing an accumulation of multiple relative meanings as we watch it refracted through a succession of different perspectives and points of view. This mode of presentation characterizes every person, scene, and object that we encounter in the novel, and becomes ultimately the only way we can approach its reality.

The bay separating the Ramsay family from the Lighthouse is, for example, a perfect symbol of pure chaos: in its perpetual fluidity, its potential destructiveness as an erosive force, its overwhelming immensity, which devours a man's sense of significance, its flowing rhythms of eternality, which swallow him up in time as well, the sea—now peaceful, now turbulent, soothing or shattering one's nerves—serves as a continual reminder of the undertow beneath all our lives. Yet our sense of this reality is not static, but flickers in and out as our concentration is affected by constant shifts in the other layers of our realities. Early in the book, Mrs. Ramsay suddenly becomes conscious of an inner correspondence to the sound of the waves crashing outside:

> The gruff murmur . . . this sound, which had lasted now half an hour and had taken its place soothingly in the scale of sounds pressing on top of her, such as the tap of balls upon bats, the sharp, sudden bark now and then, "How's that? How's that?" of the children playing cricket, had ceased; so that the monotonous fall of the waves on the beach, which for the most part beat a measured and soothing tattoo to her thoughts and seemed consolingly to repeat over and over again as she sat with the children the words of some old cradle song, murmured by nature, "I am guarding you—I am your support," but at other times suddenly and unexpectedly, especially when her mind raised itself slightly from the task actually in hand, had no such kindly meaning, but like a ghostly roll of drums remorselessly beat the measure of life, made one think of the destruction of the island and its engulfment in the sea, and warned her whose day had slipped past in one quick doing after another that it was all ephemeral as a rainbow—this sound which had been obscured and concealed under the other sounds suddenly thundered hollow in her ears and made her look up with an impulse of terror.
>
> They had ceased to talk; that was the explanation. (Pp. 27–28)

Although the sound of the waves has not changed, Mrs. Ramsay's perception of it has; the sudden cessation of distracting noises in the foreground brings the background up to a higher level of her consciousness, and her refocused attention and concentration lead her to intuit a new meaning from a familiar sound: this fresh awareness of the emptiness at the core of her life. This reminder of her insignificance, her mortality, her vulnerability both pains and terrifies her, so that while she has not moved from her chair, her entire system has been shocked, her sensibility unstrung, her life changed.

Action is unimportant in the writing of Virginia Woolf because the movement of our bodies cannot change our realities; these are created, changed, and carried exclusively in the mind. In a world of flux, every perception is relative to all the conditions converging at that instant to produce a particular impression in the imagination which alone constitutes its apprehension of reality at that moment. It is in our mental processes that we live out our lives. And there is no ultimate truth to be discovered, only a progression of perspectives to be held simultaneously in the mind. As James finally gets close enough to the Lighthouse to be able to observe all its details, he responds at first with disappointment, until he realizes that his present perception does not negate, but can only modify his previous ones:

So that was the Lighthouse, was it?
　No, the other was also the Lighthouse. For nothing was simply one thing. The other Lighthouse was true too. (P. 277)

And Lily, watching from the shore, finds that the constancy of her angle of vision offers no real advantage in her attempt to keep reality frozen long enough to capture it on canvas:

But the wind had freshened, and, as the sky changed slightly and the sea changed slightly and the boats altered their positions, the view, which a moment before had seemed miraculously fixed, was now unsatisfactory. The wind had blown the trail of smoke about; there was something displeasing about the placing of the ships. (P. 286)

Thus does Virginia Woolf keep time flowing through her novel, and insure the constantly shifting perspectives characteristic of cubism as artistic process. The reality of the Lighthouse is never shown in stasis, but in constant revolution as the focal point for each mind trying to find its way out of chaos, but having to refocus, recenter, restructure, and rebuild its reality moment by moment. Even those rare moments of coalescence which solidify experience, unify relationships, and reveal a truth through structure are never presented as ultimate, permanent, or static, but are shown to shatter the second the mind has seized them. Like people posing for a group portrait who disband the instant they hear the camera click, all the atoms flowing together to create the molecule of the moment scatter instantaneously in a release toward entropy. Thus, as Lily's observation of Mr. and Mrs. Ramsay watching their daughter throwing a ball turns into a revelatory moment in which they suddenly become symbolic of the ultimate meaning of marriage—the inner union between husband and wife—she finds that "after an instant, the symbolical outline which transcended the real figures sank down again, and they became . . . Mrs. and Mrs. Ramsey watching the children throw catches" (p. 111). Like a bubble breaking on contact with a hard surface, the moment bursts just when the mind seems to have caught it. It can be perceived in flight, but any attempt to arrest its motion will end by losing it altogether. Our perceptions, our very realities cannot be detached from time.

I have discussed Virginia Woolf's vision of chaos as a quiet but powerful, persistent entropic force which moves so slowly and subtly that one can never truly distinguish it from the general currents of a fluid universe. Such a vision seems entirely consistent with the "feathery," "melting," "evanescent" quality of the book which distinguishes its style, tone, and movement, and which Virginia Woolf has cited as the natural embodiments of her vision. But where in the novel are the clamps and iron bolts which hold this seemingly flimsy fabric together and fasten it onto the matrix of artistic expression? If art's great value is, as Lily comes to believe, its synthesizing function, how has the author managed to "unify" the chaos she sees at the deepest levels of our lives?

Since chaos is a *mental* reality, it is the mind, too, which must struggle to provide relief through proper discipline of its own impulses toward order. Reality can be fixed only when the mind can concentrate on a focal point which gathers to it all the lines of diverse energies usually running rampant. Ordinary moments are characterized by parallel lines of thought which never converge, but move independently in separate spheres. Thus, Mrs. Ramsay, walking with her husband, dissipates her mental energies by pursuing two lines simultaneously:

then, she thought, intimating by a little pressure on his arm that he walked up hill too fast for her, and she must stop for a moment to see whether those were fresh molehills on the bank, then, she thought, stooping down to look, a great mind like this must be different in every way from ours. All the great men she had ever known, she thought, deciding that a rabbit must have got in, were like that, and it was good for young men . . . simply to hear him, simply to look at him. But without shooting rabbits, how was one to keep them down? she wondered. It might be a rabbit; it might be a mole. Some creature anyhow was ruining her Evening Primroses. (P. 108)

Obviously, the mind must steady itself before it can organize its impressions long enough to apprehend a controlling idea; but although Mrs. Ramsay is remarkably effective on the level of action, her mind is never terribly successful in combatting the chaos that unsettles her so at the core of her being. It is here, I think, that we can finally come to understand Mrs. Ramsay's enormous respect for her husband, whom she genuinely and consistently considers a "great man," even though the reader tends to regard him far less favorably. Even Lily Briscoe, for all her superior powers of perception, cannot comprehend until quite late in the book, the "greatness" ascribed to Mr. Ramsay or the basis for his wife's love and devotion for a man so obviously her inferior. But Mrs. Ramsay's respect for her husband has little to do, really, with what he *is*. Rather, his real value for those who admire him is as an ordering principle, a resistance to the chaos:

It was his fate, his peculiarity, whether he wished it or not, to come out thus on a spit of land which the sea is slowly eating away, and there to stand, like a desolate sea-bird, alone. It was his power, his gift, suddenly to shed all superfluities, to shrink and diminish so that he looked barer and felt sparer, even physically, yet lost none of his intensity of mind, and so to stand on his little ledge facing the dark of human ignorance, how we know nothing and the sea eats away the ground we stand on— that was his fate, his gift. . . . he kept even in that desolation a vigilance which spared no phantom and luxuriated in no vision, and it was in this guise that he inspired in William Bankes (intermittently) and in Charles Tansley (obsequiously) and in his wife now, when she looked up and saw him standing at the edge of the lawn, profoundly, reverence, and pity, and gratitude too, as a stake driven into the bed of a channel upon which the gulls perch and the waves beat inspires in merry boat-loads a feeling of gratitude for the duty it is taking upon itself of marking the channel out there in the floods alone. (Pp. 68–69)

In his capacity to confront chaos head-on without being effaced by it, Mr. Ramsay becomes worthy of his wife's awe. Of course, just as courage can often be ascribed to a person's inability to recognize the real danger of his situation, we sense the very limitations of his perception to account for Mr. Ramsay's distinction as a still point in a turning world. While his philosophical investigations do demonstrate one kind of inroad against chaos, his confidence in his discipline impresses us more as presumption than wisdom. Nevertheless, his very presumption makes him a stalwart guardian of order and control which, embodied visually, makes a lasting impact on those who know him. Even Lily is finally able to admit that the man has something about him which causes chaos to recede in his presence. Foolhardy or not, his resoluteness represents something valuable.

Mrs. Ramsay is, of course, too aware to presume that she can contest the chaos she feels in the deepest levels of her mind, but as a mother and hostess, she does achieve in her own life that extraordinary sense of authority which characterizes her, too, as a stake driven into the flood, a marking point for others. Watching her leave a room, Lily notices that "directly she went a sort of disintegration set in; they wavered about, went different ways" (p. 168). Like her husband, then, Mrs. Ramsay provides a point of concentration for others around which otherwise dissipated energies gravitate and lock together to form a meaningful, symbolical, ordered image which makes an imprint on the observer's mind that endures long enough to outlast the chaos. Lily's gratitude and respect for Mrs. Ramsay parallels that lady's feelings for her husband: as marking points in the flood, both blend into the central image of the Lighthouse as an ordering principle, a beacon, a refuge, a resistance to the dark, fluid formlessness which underlies our lives. But if Mrs. Ramsay is the chief synthesizer in the novel, how can we explain the continuous presence of Lily Briscoe, who ultimately seems as least as significant as the woman she so admires?

Obviously, the novel is working toward two objectives at once: (1) the delineation of a reality represented by human characters, and (2) the working out of an artistic theory as symbolized by Lily's effort to project her vision of reality onto a blank canvas. I have already noted Lily's revelation that Mrs. Ramsay's greatness was in her ability to provide a unifying point around which the chaos made up of other people fell into a harmonious pattern; but why, then, is her painting not finished at this point? The answer would seem to be that reality cannot be reflected by direct depiction; it can be grasped only when represented indirectly, as it filters through a selective consciousness. It is Lily who has the vision, yet so long as Mrs. Ramsay is alive, she cannot finish her picture because the immediate reality prevents her from achieving the distance requisite to capturing it aesthetically—that is, "ensnaring" it through the indirectness of metaphor. It is only in the third part of the book, when Mrs. Ramsay's charismatic presence is felt solely as a memory, that Lily feels she can finish her painting.

It is no coincidence that her vision crystallizes immediately after she has been contemplating the Lighthouse, for it is only then that she deliberates on how to make the parts of her painting coalesce. As unifying concepts merge unconsciously in her mind, the Lighthouse suddenly becomes a synthesizing symbol for the fluidity surrounding it in exactly the same way that both Mr. and Mrs. Ramsay have functioned in the first part of the book. Like the jar that Wallace Stevens places in Tennessee, the Lighthouse becomes an organizing principle in a sea of chaos. Lily herself has not yet seen it this way, but she does make the decision to move the tree into the middle of her picture, thereby showing an as yet unconscious awareness of the principle: the particular object being placed in the center is an arbitrary choice, but once that object becomes the central focus, everything immediately gathers around it and becomes ordered.

In the last section of the book, the Lighthouse is seen from all perspectives: from Lily's distant view and from the increasingly closer views of James, Cam, Mr. Ramsay, and the Macalisters as they approach this stark tower in the middle of the water. Seen from multiple perspectives (both psychologically and spatially), the import of the Lighthouse shifts, however slightly, each second that the boat draws nearer (we recall that the vision must be perpetually remade) as one observer surrounds it with his own psychological associations, another sees it as an unapproachable ideal, another as an artistic symbol, and so on. When, in the last chapter, it is seen closeup for the first time, it seems surprisingly insignificant; James is amazed to discover that his enchanted vision from the distance of the shore is nothing but "a stark tower on a bare rock" now that he is face to face with it. Divested of subjective interpretations, the Lighthouse, regardless of proximity, is as meaningless as any building on shore, but that is unimportant: what does count is the meaning people find in it, which renders it as significant as Mrs. Ramsay herself, with whom Lily finally equates it. As the Ramsay family reaches the Lighthouse, Lily suddenly represents it in her picture by drawing a line in the center—and that line is at once the metaphorical expression of both Mr. Ramsay and the Lighthouse. As such, it instantly controls and contains the inner chaos of the human lives on shore, and the outer chaos of the bay's fluidity. Lily is able to say, "I have had my vision" only when she had found a metaphor for it—a symbol to concentrate, centralize, and clarify meaning.

And Virginia Woolf works in exactly the same way: because she has rendered chaos so effectively as a major, ubiquitous element of reality, she must allow her reader, as she has her characters, an axis to keep the centrifugal forces from spinning out of control. This the reader finally finds in Lily herself, for her perception becomes the fundamental organizing principle to which the rest of the novel coheres. It is Lily's imagination which steadies the novel for us, and completes its experience as a meaningful investigation of reality.

Fluid and formless, chaos quite naturally resists our attempts at order, but every time we freeze or structure reality for an instant, we are gaining ground in the struggle to keep our minds on top of the confusion. And this is just what Virginia Woolf does for us as she rescues one image after another from the flood and turns them into powerful symbols which help mark the chaotic channels of our own minds: Lily represents the artist of chaos; the Ramsay home without man symbolizes the infiltration of chaos in our lives, and the Lighthouse functions as the ultimate, conglomerate metaphor for the centralizing factor which resolves the chaos of the author's vision. Such strikingly appropriate, brilliant metaphors are what finally constitute the bolts of iron which clamp the book together. As James Ramsay rides out to the Lighthouse he has been wanting to visit since the first page of the novel, he feels a terror and hatred which he cannot define, but which rests securely at the bottom of the dark abyss within him. Instinctively, he works toward a control of his inner chaos, as

turning back among the many leaves which the past had folded in him, peering into the heart of that forest where light and shade so chequer each other that all shape is distorted, and one blunders, now with the sun in one's eyes, now with a dark shadow, he sought an image to cool and detach and round off his feeling in a concrete shape. (P. 275)

Nowhere can we find a better statement of the necessity for metaphor to control chaos, and nowhere can we find a more accurate explanation for the powerful projection of chaos in this book where art earns every bit of meaning extracted from its exhaustive struggle. Even so, the artistic triumph is never anything more than temporary relief from the struggle which defines the sensitive life. There is no more touching testimonial to this depressing truth than Virginia Woolf's own death: walking into the sea, she finally found the only possible permanent relief by submerging herself in the chaos which closed over her at last, drowning out anguish, fatigue, and life itself.

6

Waking into Nightmare

Dream as Reality in Kafka's The Trial

*T*he world of Franz Kafka is immediately familiar to anyone who has ever had a nightmare. Here are our everyday lives transformed into strange yet recognizable aspects whose reality is so overpowering that we never think to question the outrageous situations in which we suddenly find ourselves. A man turns into a bug and wonders not how such a thing could have happened, but only how he can best maneuver his new body. In a world where probabilities are replaced by possibilities, we are kept too busy adapting to new contexts and assumptions to waste time on useless speculation. If, in our dreams, we find ourselves in a river infested with alligators, we immediately become too preoccupied with getting out alive to consider how we got there in the first place, or just how unreasonable our predicament is. Reasonable or not, our lives are in terrible jeopardy, and we had better concentrate on getting back safely to land.

Or a man is arrested and, from that moment on, finds his life a series of unprecedented crises which he can neither cope with nor understand. As a result, he loses ground steadily until he is finally hauled away to be killed—at which point he does not wake up, but simply dies. The consequences, then, are real, so the situation must be real, too. We need justify it no further: it simply exists, and we must confront it on its own terms.

What seems to me most significant about Kafka is the utter integrity of his vision—his refusal to apologize for it or somehow make it more palatable for the conventional reader. He simply propels us into his world without explanation and shows us what goes on there without comment or interpretation. Whether it resembles our literal reality or not, it contains a psychological reality which enables us to accept it without question. In this completely chaotic atmosphere, our concern must be with survival, not edification. Kafka's novels do have a philosophical dimension, but their power lies elsewhere. It is the intensity of his vision which holds us, the unremitting emotional force with which he keeps us trapped in his reality.

The Trial is surely one of the most unrelenting works of chaos created in the first half of this century, and critics have done it the honor of interpreting it on many levels of significance, including the view that implies it is a rather tame novel dramatizing specific institutions and their effect on the individual. But while the book certainly invites interpretations of a social, political, and religious nature, Kafka seems to have wanted it to evade any facile explanation. It is important that we make no attempt to reduce the unknown in his world to manageable analogies of the known in *our* world. Almost all of those passages unfinished or deleted by the author have in common an explicitness very much at odds with the general tenor of what Kafka had finally considered genuine parts of the book he was writing. It seems to have been his intention to create a world in which things happen arbitrarily to people whose only fault is in being there at the time. Joseph K. may or may not deserve his fate more than another man, but once we decide that he has been chosen by hostile forces for particular reasons, we have forced a meaning onto his experience that Kafka has taken great care to prevent. As soon as we find causes to justify effects, things start making sense in a reassuring way that dispels the chaotic potential in our lives and stills terror until it is made to submit to our intelligences. Like all our dreams, *The Trial* embodies enough elements from our everyday realities to tempt us to search for meanings as we would during a normal day when the intellect seems adequate to interpreting events. But it is obvious that Kafka has no intention of providing this kind of security for the reader: those passages which seem to explain why K. should be an appropriate victim have been purposefully deleted to discourage us from viewing his plight as an expressionistic examination of his own repressed guilt. Certainly, the trial itself is a metaphor, but to what extent can we explicate it without falsifying Kafka's vision? To answer that, we must first consider the assumptions operating in the novel's "world."

In one of the passages deleted by the author, K. explains to the Inspector on the day of his arrest why this event fails to surprise him:

As someone said to me—I can't remember now who it was—it is really remarkable that when you wake up in the morning you nearly always find everything in exactly the same place as the evening before. For when asleep and dreaming you are, apparently at least, in an essentially different state from that of wakefulness; and therefore, as that man truly said, it requires enormous presence of mind or rather quickness of wit, when opening your eyes to seize hold as it were of everything in the room at exactly the same place where you had let it go on the previous evening. That was why, he said, the moment of waking up was the riskiest moment of the day. Once that was well over without deflecting you from your orbit, you could take heart of grace for the rest of the day.[1]

The lack of subtlety in the passage may well justify Kafka's decision to leave it out, but these words would also be terribly inappropriate coming from K., whose chief failure is his inability to adapt himself gracefully to a whole new state of affairs. Essentially, *The Trial* is really about one man who did not "make it"upon waking up one morning; in this riskiest moment of the day, he finds his life completely altered by the fact of his arrest. Physically, of course, his situation is little different from that of the day before, and it is this which misleads K. into thinking that he is still living in the same world, predicated on the same laws, values, and assumptions. Therefore, he continues to lead his previously normal life and to regard his strange arrest in the light of everyday reality. As such, it is probably a mistake, possibly a ruse; certainly a problem and inconvenience—but something, in any case, that can be dealt with in a sensible, rational way. From this point on, he continues to fight his case by appealing to authorities, arguing as his own counsel, finding connections in the court, gath-

---

1. Franz Kafka, *The Trial*, trans. Willa and Edwin Muir (New York: Schocken Books, 1968), pp. 257–58. All future page references, cited in parentheses, are to this edition.

ering information, hiring and then firing a lawyer, etc.—all reasonable actions to take in such a dilemma. But why, then, are
they all ineffective? Why does K. get nowhere in his struggle to
defend his innocence?

Here is where we can talk about his own repressed feelings
and see the trial as an expressionistic metaphor for K.'s guilty
conscience, and his death at the end as the fulfillment of a suicidal impulse based on his self-judgment. Or we can talk about the
forces pushing K. around and identify them as certain definable
institutions which call a man to judgment and demand that he
pay the price for his sins. Certainly, the novel presents all these
possibilities, and we cannot ignore them, but we must be on
guard, too, against translating the chaos in Kafka's work into our
own orderly frames of reference, for the theme of the book seems
to be inextricably bound up with a vision of total chaos.

From the moment K. is placed under arrest, his previously
secure world is replaced by one filled with unknowns. Even
though his arrest leaves him free to continue his normal life, K.'s
life is never the same again because he can never accept his new
mysterious condition. Although he insists on his innocence
throughout, he never even learns of the charges against him, and
so he can never know what is helping him or hurting him in his
mad effort to defend himself. In this new context, he never
knows who his judges are, what their criteria may be, and what
new rules he must follow to impress them favorably. Yet the silence of his opposition drives him into a frenzied activity that is
totally gratuitous. Again and again he vows to remain detached
from this intolerable situation, but finds this psychologically impossible; as a result, he continues to take the initiative until he is
sucked into a state of total obsession with his case. In a way, he is
condemned finally by his own inability to accept an unknown
factor as a permanent part of his life. He eventually becomes so
aggressive in his struggle to reach and identify the higher officials
that he seems to be pulling destruction down upon himself; more
and more his fight resembles shadowboxing, as his prosecutors
retain their silence and anonymity. Their invisibility works increasingly on his imagination, forcing him to become more and
more deeply involved as each day fails to bring any new progress.
At first annoyed by the mystery of his trial, he is later haunted by
it and finally plagued by it, until it becomes the sole concern of

his life. He is trapped in a void by his own imagination, tormented by his own intelligence, and defeated by his human nature.

There seems to be no hint in the novel that, beyond the first
mere statement of arrest, the court intends to take an active role
in bringing K. to trial. Had he accepted the fact of his arrest
without question, he might have continued his routine life until
his natural death, for there is never any suggestion that the court
imposes punishment after its judgments. One remains under the
court's power for his whole life, but that need not restrict his
movements, alter his life style, or cause him undue concern. But
psychologically, of course, such a situation is intolerable, and it is
also intellectually untenable. Our minds cannot rest in the face of
mystery: they insist on finding the proper causes for effects, resolving contradictions into some form of useful knowledge, and
providing faces and features for the unknown. The concept of
nothingness is insupportable for an intelligence that needs to presume the validity of logic before it can go to work.

When K. goes to the lawyer for advice, the information he
receives is entirely worthless because his mind simply cannot
work with it. There are qualifications—endless ones—to every
point, and so many ramifications that it becomes impossible to
predict which line of action will be most beneficial in the long
run. This new context is devoid not only of certainties or even
probabilities but of any *a priori* principles which might lead
eventually to some minimal form of empirical knowledge. The
lawyer's every statement sags with contradictions which frustrate
all efforts at interpretation, and since any action based on them
could well antagonize the officials and set back his case even
further, K. can do nothing but wait—which is the condition he
has already found unbearable.

Again, when he rushes in desperation to Titorelli, the painter
puts him through the same maze—though it is his emotions rather than his intellect which are overwhelmed here. While trying
to offer him hope and encouragement for acquittal, Titorelli's
every assertion contradicts his previous ones, until K. must leave
as dejected as when he came in. And even as he is leaving, K.'s
bewilderment is compounded, as Titorelli tries to sell him copy
after copy of the exact same picture; as artist, Titorelli repeats his
role as legal advisor by implying distinctions which K. can't see at
all. At this point, K.'s emotional and intellectual exhaustion is

complete, and he resolves to brush away the so-called authorities and handle the case himself.

And as his independence becomes more fierce, his isolation becomes more complete; he is so frustrated by and obsessed with the technicalities of his case, that he slowly and unconsciously withdraws from even the minimal protection of other human beings. Hitherto, his work had provided some diversion and solace from his court battle, but now it all seems as irrelevant as anything else that predated his arrest—which includes all of his relationships with business associates, fellow tenants, relatives, and women. To be sure, K. never seems to have had close, rich relationships in his past, but even so, he seems much more alone as the novel progresses. In the earlier chapters, he almost clings to people for the information they may be able to give him, but as each source fails to help him, he moves farther away from their contact until he stands alone in the dark cathedral where he receives the last word on his predicament in the form of a parable from the prison chaplain.

The parable of the doorkeeper seems to reemphasize the ultimate isolation of the man who knocks at the door of the Law, since each door is intended for only one man. But the parable also sums up K.'s situation from the beginning of the novel, as the doorkeeper becomes the spiritual equivalent of the inspector, the lawyer, the painter, and various women such as Leni (who guarded the entrance to the lawyer's rooms). The parallels become more and more striking as the parable progresses, until the court seems to embrace all the institutions that evaluate man; whether personal, political, social, artistic, or theological, all become analogous with and implicit to the court where K. seeks admittance. Yet this story is subject to so many alternative interpretations that K. finally finds it as impossible to cope with as the lawyer's technical advice. It is not surprising when, upon turning to leave the cathedral, he reaches a nadir of confusion, helplessness, and despair as he pathetically discovers that he cannot find his way alone in this darkness. As in the last chapter of Melville's *Confidence-Man*, the darkness becomes an immediate metaphor for man's basic condition in this world.

The priest does, however, advise K. more soundly and clearly that anyone else has when he says, "it is not necessary to accept everything as true, one must only accept it as necessary" (p. 220) and later that "the Court wants nothing from you. It receives you when you come and it dismisses you when you go" (p. 222). The first statement K. rejects as too "depressing," but it pretty well sums up his chief mistake, which has been to accept only what he can make sense of rather than what is crucial to accept simply because it is given, it is real, and it is powerful enough to destroy anyone who tries to resist it. One cannot afford to choose which elements of reality he will comply with without endangering his life; one must be willing to accept far more than he can ever hope to understand if he is to survive. The second statement, by asserting the Court's indifference, seems also to imply its nonexistence as an entity distinct from the human personality which creates it and willingly submits to it. K. is free from the Law so long as he feels no compulsion to seek it out and provide it with the authority to judge him and the power to destroy him.

If we accept the validity of the chaplain's last words, then the final chapter of the book is indeed puzzling unless we interpret K. himself to be his own judge and executioner. Certainly there is some evidence for this: after his initial struggle with the men who have come to take him to his death, K. suddenly gives in and for the first time realizes the futility of resistance.

"The only thing I can do now," he told himself, and the regular correspondence between his steps and the steps of the other two confirmed his thought, "the only thing for me to go on doing is to keep my intelligence calm and analytical to the end. I always wanted to snatch at the world with twenty hands, and not for a very laudable motive either. That was wrong, and am I to show now that not even a year's trial has taught me anything? Am I to leave this world as a man who has no common sense? Are people to say of me after I am gone that at the beginning of my case I wanted to finish it, and at the end of it I wanted to begin it again? I don't want that to be said. I am grateful for the fact that these half-dumb, senseless creatures have been sent to accompany me on this journey, and that I have been left to say to my self all that is needed." (Pp. 225–26)

As soon as he resolves to be cool and logical to the end, K. for the first time becomes his own judge, and from then on, *he* begins to lead his captors, who immediately fall into perfect rhythm with his own footsteps as the three move harmoniously as one "solid front." Yet how are we to interpret this new resignation on K.'s part? Does it make him more or less admirable than he had seemed before? In one sense, we respect his new position of leadership—at last he is no longer a victim, but the instigator of his own judgment. Or is he really more a victim now than he ever was? By accepting and justifying his guilt, he has merged into the very force he had been fighting and finally becomes indistinguishable from the Court itself. Furthermore, his intention to keep his intelligence calm and analytical to the end would suggest that he has still not recognized its uselessness in trying to clarify a situation it cannot comprehend. Chaos cannot be analyzed intelligently *or* calmly; it must simply be accepted, as the priest said, so that one can adapt to it, condition himself to it, and live with it as an integral part of life. From the moment of his arrest, K. has searched desperately for a reasonable explanation to account for it and found nothing at all that would satisfy his sense of logic. Yet now, when he is being carried away to his punishment, he suddenly finds a justification for it, declares himself guilty, and reasserts the value of his common sense. But in what way has his world proved worthy of common sense? Everything has degraded and defeated it, rendered it irrelevant and worthless. Apparently, the world operates on very different terms—terms which confound human reasoning at every step and seem to mock the person attempting to impose a meaningful system upon it. We may assume, if we wish, that the universe moves according to certain laws, but only if we acknowledge these laws to be unknown and utterly foreign to our minds, which run on limited logical tracks. K.'s inability to resist the temptation of discovering and defining these laws rather than accommodating himself to them is what has drawn him into his trial, and now his reassertion of those same values is leading him to his death. Yet it is not even ironic, really, that he should feel strangely soothed by the thought of that punishment he has fought so hard against, for he *has* managed finally to impregnate it with meaning: in this world, a man must be judged by his superiors, and the guilty must be condemned to death. Only the innocent deserve to live, and he simply has not been innocent enough, apparently.

K. lives with this common-sense meaning and is comforted by it only for a few minutes because, as he later lies on the ground watching his executioners prepare for his slaying (and feeling too fatigued to take the knife from them—as he realizes he is supposed to do—to plunge it into his own breast), he suddenly notices a human figure standing at the casement window with both arms stretched forward.

Who was it? A friend? A good man? Someone who sympathized? Someone who wanted to help? Was it one person only? Or was it mankind? Was help at hand? Were there arguments in his favor that had been overlooked? Of course there must be. Logic is doubtless unshakable, but it cannot withstand a man who wants to go on living. Where was the Judge whom he had never seen? Where was the High Court, to which he had never penetrated? He raised his hands and spread out all his fingers.

But the hands of one of the partners were already at K.'s throat, while the other thrust the knife deep into his heart and turned it there twice. With failing eyes K. could still see the two of them immediately before him, cheek leaning against cheek, watching the final act. "Like a dog!" he said; it was as if the shame of it must outlive him. (Pp. 228–29)

This ending seems hopelessly ambiguous, but K.'s sudden change of heart is quite clear. Suddenly all his old doubt returns to torment him—although this time he challenges the supremacy of logic, which cannot withstand a man who wants to go on living but must submit to a higher authority of human instinct and will that ultimately holds life above reason. Unreasonable living is preferable to reasonable dying—and what is reason anyway but an arbitrary way of looking at things which are, from all accounts, invisible to begin with? What proof had he, after all, of the Court, of the Judge, of all those presences and forces which preyed upon his mind, yet had, perhaps, no real existence outside of that mind? Since the priest has denied the Court's interest in K. ("The Court wants nothing from you. It receives you when you come and it dismisses you when you go"), he might really have doomed himself to this wretched death by failing to acknowledge the total absence of all authority higher than himself. Instead he had created laws to fill the vacuum and had become so entangled in them that they ended by controlling his life and death.

But is the priest really any more reliable than all the others who had advised K.? It would seem not, for acknowledgment of his freedom in an existential void has obviously not rescued K. from his killers. Since K. is certainly not killed by a figment of his imagination, this can mean only that the Court and its messengers do have an independent existence after all. The promise held out by existentialism must be seen as just another delusion.

Shortly before, K. had resigned himself to the futility of all resistance, and had determined to keep his intelligence "calm and analytical to the end" (a promise he had made and broken many times before). Yet he has almost immediately slipped back into the struggle by trying to interpret another inexplicable phe-

nomenon: the man with outstretched arms standing at the casement window. Certainly the figure is evocative—but so too are all
the phenomena of our lives: the danger lies in attempting to *interpret* them as symbolic messages from some higher authority.
In *The Odyssey*, a pair of flying eagles signals a whole flurry of
interpretations as one seer reads in them a good omen, another
prophesies doom, etc. Thus can man read all phenomena like a
series of Rorschach tests or content himself instead, as the priest
advises K. to do, with accepting everything as necessary rather
than true. But as soon as K. sees the figure in the window, he
launches into an interpretation, and the possibilities build so
quickly that he has in an instant transformed it into a symbol of
all mankind with help at hand. Immediately forgetting his earlier
resolution, he begins both mentally and physically to respond to
this new "truth" just in time to be cut down by the "necessary"
knife plunging into his heart. There may be no truth involved in
this latter action, but it kills him just the same. Life and death, we
conclude, are not determined by truth but by necessity. Cancer
(or in Kafka's own case, tuberculosis), an accidental gunshot, or a
truck careening out of control would have been no more truthful,
but would have done the job just as well.

If we learn nothing else from K.'s struggle, we are at least
forced to recognize the futility of trying to work with a world that
simply will not relate to our rational faculties. Things *happen*
regardless of whether we can account for them, and we cannot
expect to bargain our way to a more comfortable position, a more
tolerable destiny. Our freedom, if real, *is* limited. Life finally *is* a
nightmare, because there are inscrutable forces beyond our control that no amount of psychological health can protect us from.
Annihilation is not a choice but a fact; the only choice left to us is
whether to accept it or continue to struggle against it. We die
either way, but the implication is that K. might have died with a
little more dignity than a dog.

K.'s death ultimately is as inexplicable as his arrest, for the
reader, like K., must finally accept what he cannot understand. It
seems fitting, though, that the book ends as inconclusively as K.'s
life, because our resultant discomfort is really the most suitable
response to Kafka's vision of reality.

Because *The Trial* must be called an unfinished work at last, it
is not surprising that we will find it impossible to resolve many of

the questions raised in this discussion. It does seem clear to me, though, that a consideration of those passages and chapter fragments that Kafka either deleted or left unfinished reinforces the idea that the author wished to emphasize his chaotic vision as much as possible, and intended to *de*emphasize whatever material might lead to facile explanations of what must otherwise remain mysterious. Just as Michelangelo decided he preferred the four unfinished Slaves of the Boboli Gardens in their incomplete forms, Kafka seems to have left unfinished those chapters which would polish off his tale too smoothly by suggesting a metaphorical or allegorical method (such as the chapter in which Titorelli is seen too clearly as a symbol of the artist leading man to an intuitive and aesthetically spellbinding kind of enlightenment) or by providing psychological justifications for his character's behavior. Thus, he leaves out a seemingly complicated history of K.'s relationship to his parents which might have restricted K.'s guilt by defining it too explicitly. Of course, the lack of such expository material makes K. a thinner, more remote, and possibly less interesting character than he would otherwise have been, but Kafka might well have considered K.'s background irrelevant anyway, since the context of K.'s world after his arrest breaks him off from his past completely. If today is essentially different from yesterday, then we cannot learn from yesterday's experiences; they cannot be carried forward into a new context, but must be dismissed as irrelevant to the experience of today.

No matter how we interpret *The Trial*, we must be careful to consider Kafka's themes within the terms of his chaotic vision. Even though the novel is aesthetically well ordered, tightly structured, and highly unified by images (such as doors), metaphors, and symbolical parallels which permit us to find legitimate analogies and allegories, we cannot restrict ourselves to the development of one or two to the exclusion of the others or force onto the book a more explicit meaning than can possibly be justified. While the Court can well represent a theological, legal, political, social, and psychological system, it must represent them all at once and yet none of them completely. For the chaos in Kafka's world is chaotic chiefly because it evades human classification and identification as any known, familiar or clearly describable thing in our reality. In a world of unlimited and terrifying possibilities, probabilities and empirical laws must be dismissed as artificial, irrelevant creations of the human mind's need to dispel shadows wherever it finds them and fill spaces with faces and facts.

In our most alarming dreams, we are haunted, paralyzed, and often caught in the clutches of strange people and animals that we rarely, if ever, encounter in our routine lives. At such times, we do not dominate our fear by attempting to alter their prospects into something familiar and harmless—we simply run from them with every bit of energy we have. And in the world of Franz Kafka, too, we shall get nowhere by trying to define and domesticate the unknown forces which thwart our logic by impelling us into strange, unfamiliar, and unreasonable situations which men cannot hope to cope with. Instead, we must enlarge our conception of reality to include such unknowns, and then continue living as if they were not there—though if one feels the full power of Kafka's vision, that will no longer be possible.

Part II
The Novel in Chaos

7

The Thing Itself

The Reductive Art of Samuel Beckett

> Thou wert better in a grave than to answer
> with thy uncover'd body this extremity of the
> skies. Is man no more than this: Consider him
> well. Thou ow'st the worm no silk, the beast no
> hide, the sheep no wool, the cat no perfume.
> . . . Thou are the thing itself; unaccommodat-
> ed man is no more but such a poor, bare, forked
> animal as thou art. Off, off, you lendings! come,
> unbutton here.
>
> —*King Lear*

By stripping man to his essence and working exclusively on this level where "the thing itself" is divested of its familiar appearances, Samuel Beckett presents us with the lowest common denominator of everything: man himself is no more than a clumsy organism whose parts fail, resume working order, then fail again; the universe is represented by a patch of land or a vacuum; the movement of time by the presence or lack of a leaf on a tree. The progress of Beckett's work as a whole can be depicted as a constant chiseling away of all the nonessentials that constitute the mass and movement of our lives in order to reach the quintessence of the problem, the fundamental level of reality. It is also at this level, however, that "everything oozes," and since life is in constant flux, man's desperate attempts to impose arbitrary structures of time, place, and identity onto his world are seen as useless, pathetic, and funny; because man, for all his efforts to order existence, finally flows into the muck along with everything else. And as not only humanity, but the novel form itself is swept off into a dark region of dissolving structures where the reader loses all sense of time, setting, character, plot, and theme, Beckett's novels become progressively a blur in which a few movements may be discernible but never meaningful. It is the art, perhaps, of stagnation: nothing moves, nothing speaks, nothing fits, nothing matters. In a void, even art can go nowhere.

Of Beckett's novels, *Murphy* comes closest to representing a world we can recognize: the characters, after all, have human traits, and they live in an atmosphere which resembles our own. Society is present; the sense of location is strong; people talk, act, and fumble with different kinds of relationships. Yet at the center of the novel is a character so enigmatic that he seems entirely unrelated to the life circulating around him. Even the woman who loves him cannot understand him: whereas Celia expects language to express thought, for example, Murphy's speech is equivalent, really, only to silence, "since what he called his mind functioned not as an instrument but as a place."[1] That place is a quiet sanctuary from reality: sitting in his rocking chair, Murphy gradually and consciously retreats from the irritating world of forms.

Like Lily Briscoe, Murphy is the center of a novel reflecting confused relationships, but unlike her, he has found peace in surrendering to chaos. Slipping deep into the recesses of his mind, he relaxes in the vacuum and makes no effort to dispel its darkness. The light zones signify no victory, but only a different atmosphere, a void of a different color. Neither is his silence a sign of defeat, but rather an affirmation of a life which has nothing to tell us.

As Murphy "lapsed in body he felt himself coming alive in mind, set free to move among its treasures" (p. 111), but once inside Murphy's mind, the reader will find few treasures he can identify as such. Nothing, in fact, seems to be going on here:

There were the three zones, light, half light, dark, each with its speciality.

In the first were the forms with parallel, a radiant abstract of the dog's life, the elements of physical experience available for a new arrangement. Here the pleasure was reprisal, the pleasure of reversing the physical experience. Here the kick that the physical Murphy received, the

1. Samuel Beckett, *Murphy* (New York: Grove Press, 1957), p. 178. All future page references, cited in parentheses, are to this edition.

mental Murphy gave. . . . Here the whole physical fiasco became a howling success. (P. 111)

How well this zone describes the province of the compensatory
novel (see Introduction) in which the artist rearranges experience
in order to rebuild it into meaningful structures which ultimately
defy a chaotic universe. As it transforms reality into art, the imagination transcends its material, turning chaos into control, fiasco
into success. But Murphy's mind does not stop here.

In the second were the forms without parallel. Here the pleasure was
contemplation. This system had no other mode in which to be out of
joint and therefore did not need to be put right in this. Here was the
Belacqua bliss and others scarcely less precise. (P. 111)

It is at this level that the nonanalogical author is able to accept
those tones of half light and half dark, without trying to make one
dominate or hold back the other. The result of this would be a
nonrepresentational work in which the mind exalts in a world of
its own creation, totally independent of literal reality. Opposites
are accepted, rather than reconciled or synthesized, and the
mind no longer functions as an instrument of reconstruction, but
simply as a place with its own pleasures where it need be faithful
to nothing but itself. It can create forms "without parallel" which
satisfy in themselves and seek no higher end.

The third, the dark, was a flux of forms, a perpetual coming together and
falling asunder of forms. The light contained the docile elements of a
new manifold, the world of the body broken up into the pieces of a toy;
the half light, states of peace. But the dark neither elements nor states,
nothing but forms becoming and crumbling into the fragments of a new
becoming, without love or hate or any intelligible principle or change.
Here there was nothing but commotion and the pure forms of commotion. Here he was not free, but a mote, he was a point in the ceaseless
unconditioned generation and passing away of line. (P. 112)

Murphy considers the pleasures of each level in his mind, and
finds those of the third by far the most satisfying:

It was pleasant to kick the Ticklepennies and Miss Carridges simultaneously together into ghastly acts of love. It was pleasant to lie dreaming
on the shelf beside Belacqua, watching the dawn break crooked. But
how much more pleasant was the sensation of being a missile without
provenance or target, caught up in a tumult of non-Newtonian motion.
So pleasant that pleasant was not the word.

   Thus as his body set him free more and more in his mind, he took to
spending less and less time in the light, spitting at the breakers of the

world; and less in the half light, where the choice of bliss introduced an element of effort; and more and more in the dark, in the will-lessness, a mote in its absolute freedom. (Pp. 112–13)

Murphy, then, finally opts for the joys of passivity, stagnation, and tranquility. Tired of urging his intellect to struggle against the life he cannot bear, and even the effort of nudging his imagination toward the creation of independent forms to replace the world he cannot live in, he finds his greatest solace in surrending himself to the vacuum where he can float freely and comfortably, released from responsibility. If his very identity falls apart in the process, this too is a relief not to be underestimated.

In summary, we can equate the first level—which consists of building parallels into blocks of meaning—with chaos *in* the novel, which becomes controlled through aesthetic form; the second level, with the nonrepresentational novel, which seeks to build an independent reality from and within the imagination; and the third level, with the novel in chaos, in which the author watches peacefully while forms dissolve and expresses his equivalent of silence through relinquishment of control. The novel itself becomes a place, rather than an instrument—and a place, furthermore, wherein reflection is passive, unmotivated, and undirected. It is a solipsistic paradise.

Murphy's mind pictured itself as a larger hollow sphere, hermetically closed to the universe without. This was not an impoverishment, for it excluded nothing that it did not itself contain. Nothing ever had been, was or would be in the universe outside it, but was already present as virtual, or actual, or virtual rising into actual, or actual falling into virtual, in the universe inside it. (P. 107)

Beckett goes on to describe Murphy's discriminations between the actual—which represents his physical existence—and the virtual, which represents the unlimited workings of the mind. This dichotomy of human life has, of course, been at the heart of most philosophical and artistic systems, which then go on to work with the conflict by establishing some relationship between the mind's yearning and the body's impulses, between will and action, imagination and reality, the internal and external world. It is here that Beckett parts company with the other writers we have discussed, for he refuses not only to resolve the conflict, but even to work with it. The two systems, he insists, have nothing to do with each other and should not interact. The mind, in short, cannot impose meaning on the outside world.

The mental experience was cut off from the physical experience, its criteria were not those of the physical experience, the agreement of part of its content with physical fact did not confer worth on that part. It did not function and could not be disposed according to a principle of worth. It was made up of light fading into dark, of above and beneath, but not of good and bad. It contained forms with parallel in another mode and forms without, but not right forms and wrong forms. It felt no issue between its light and dark, no need for its light to devour the dark. The need was now to be in the light, now in the half light, now in the dark. That was all. (P. 108)

The philosophical and theological consequences of this passage are quite clear: no ethical or spiritual system can be formulated from a mind content to observe rather than synthesize the irreconcilables of existence. The aesthetic consequences of such a view, however, are even more disturbing, and may help us understand why Beckett's novels operate so differently from those of his predecessors in the "chaotic" tradition.

Murphy itself does not seem to me a chaotic novel, because it does depict some minimal form of conflict. Murphy may be spending more and more time in the darkest levels of his mind, but he is still a visitor there; he can never stay long enough to become as remote from the outer world as he would have to in order to qualify as a permanent resident. It *is* true, of course, that the more he sees of outer reality, the less he cares to deal with it, and the more lucrative and sensible seems the idea of descending permanently into the darkest areas of his mind:

He would not have admitted that he needed a brotherhood. He did. In the presence of this issue (psychiatric–psychotic) between the life from which he had turned away and the life of which he had no experience, except as he hoped inchoately in himself, he could not fail to side with the latter. . . .

Thus it was necessary that every hour in the wards should increase together with his esteem for the patients, his loathing of the text-book attitude towards them, the complacent scientific conceptualism that made contact with outer reality the index of mental well-being. Every hour did. (p. 176–77)

In short, the psychoses of the patients seem to him far healthier and more reasonable than what is regarded as the saner way of looking at things. Sanity, Murphy discovers, is simply a matter of staying in contact with outer reality.

On this basis the patients were described as "cut off" from reality, from the rudimentary blessings of the layman's reality, if not altogether, as in the severer cases, then in certain fundamental respects. The function of treatment was to bridge the gulf, translate the sufferer from his own pernicious little private dungheap to the glorious world of discrete particles, where it would be his inestimable prerogative once again to wonder, love, hate, desire, rejoice, and howl in a reasonable balanced manner, and comfort himself with the society of others in the same predicament.

All this was duly revolting to Murphy, whose experience as a physical and rational being obliged him to call sanctuary what the psychiatrists called exile and to think of the patients not as banished from a system of benefits but as escaped from a colossal fiasco.

The issue therefore, as lovingly simplified and perverted by Murphy, lay between nothing less fundamental than the big world and the little world, decided by the patients in favour of the latter, revived by the psychiatrists on behalf of the former, in his own case unresolved. (Pp. 177–78)

Murphy, then, remains suspended between the big public world and the small private one, unable to commit himself to either, though he does favor the latter. Yet Murphy is disturbed to find "frequent expressions apparently of pain, rage, despair" on the faces of the patients, which suggest that even while each man is locked in his own private universe, his psychosis can cause him just as much grief as the layman suffering "out there" in the real world. The mental systems may differ, but they have essentially the same effect: suffering becomes commonplace, decomposing the spirit and destroying the will to live.

Finally, though, Murphy does lose contact completely with the outer world. While playing chess with Mr. Endon, "Murphy began to see nothing, that colourlessness which is such a rare postnatal treat, being the absence . . . not of *percipere* but of *percipi*. His other senses also found themselves at peace . . . not the numb peace of their own suspension, but the positive peace that comes when the somethings give way, or perhaps simply add up, to the Nothing, than which in the guffaw of the Abderite naught is more real" (p. 246). The revelation is so shattering that Murphy never recovers from it. Afterwards, he tries vainly to call up images from the outer world, but his mind throws back only the nothingness. He has now truly entered the void for good:

unable to find parallels in his mind to the reality outside of it and unable, too, to replace the void with creations of his own imagination (which would be the state of the psychotic), he finally sinks down to the darkness at the bottom of his mind, finding permanent peace and death at the same time.

Earlier in the book, Beckett has equated gas with chaos, so that when Murphy meets his death as a result of the gas seeping into his system, the philosophical implications are clear: Murphy's system has been racked and now wrecked by the forces of chaos. By surrendering to these forces so early, he is no longer able to define himself against them, and so becomes a part of the void that has tempted him all along.

He tried with the men, women, children, and animals that belong to even worse stories than this. In vain in all cases. He could not get a picture in his mind of any creature he had met, animal or human. Scraps of bodies, of landscapes, hands, eyes, lines and colours evoking nothing, rose and climbed out of sight before him, as though reeled upward off a spool level with his throat. (P. 252)

Murphy has finally blurred into the blankness, darkness and silence which had become his only reality.

After Murphy's death, we are apt to be shocked at Beckett's irreverent treatment of his remains:

Some hours later Cooper took the packet of ash from his pocket, where earlier in the evening he had put it for greater security, and threw it angrily at a man who had given him great offence. It bounced, burst, off the wall on to the floor, where at once it became the object of much dribbling, passing, punching, trapping, shooting, heading, and even some recognition from the gentleman's code. By closing time the body, mind and soul of Murphy were freely distributed over the floor of the saloon; and before another dayspring greyened the earth had been swept away with the sand, the beer, the butts, the glass, the matches, the spits, the vomit. (P. 275)

Truly it is an ignoble end for Murphy, who has now become part of the chaos he had not tried to resist.

Because the whole progression of the novel has been leading steadily to Murphy's immersion in chaos, the book itself is not chaotic but rather follows a conventional line of development, controlled by the author's vision, tone, and structural devices. Yet *Murphy* remains strikingly different from any of the works previously discussed. For the first time, the hero exits without a shred of dignity; for the first time, we can detect no signs of a battle against those forces which unknit a man's identity and loosen the framework of his existence. The role of the traditional hero in the chaotic novel has been that of contestant, creator, even victim, but never accomplice. Thus, while he may not be a genuine hero, he has at least *struggled* heroically to extricate himself from the chaos swarming in upon him. He has opposed a formless universe by formalizing—through art, philosophy, or sheer will—products in his mind to counterbalance the vision he cannot accept. Murphy, however, accepts as inevitable the natural confusion of all things and allows his own mind to become part of the general void. He abdicates any responsibility to impress his identity upon the cosmos; instead, the chaos of the outer world is assimilated into his own identity, and he becomes indistinguishable from cigarette butts and vomit. Man can acquire no stature whatever when he is inseparable from the muck surrounding him.

If Murphy is our first victim of chaos (one who loses the battle on every level), then Watt may be seen as our first clown, for he never even enters the battle against meaninglessness, but accepts his absurd situation as the given relationship of man to the universe. As a result, he finds that each incident in his life begins eventually to resemble all the others "in the vigour with which it developed a purely plastic content, and gradually lost, in the nice processes of its light, its sound, its impacts and its rhythm, all meaning, even the most literal."[2] Unlike Murphy, Watt has no desire to rock himself out of the external world and into the comforting silence of his mind, because there is never anything of interest going on in that mind, and Watt can find as much solitude in society as Murphy ever found in his rocking chair. His life remains uncomplicated by relationships, because nothing impresses him enough to distract him. He is unable to find any meaning behind events, and so all his experience is reduced to shadowy sense impressions.

This fragility of the outer meaning had a bad effect on Watt, for it caused him to seek for another, for some meaning of what had passed, in the image of how it had passed.

The most meagre, the least plausible, would have satisfied Watt, who had not seen a symbol, nor executed an interpretation, since the age of fourteen, or fifteen, and who had lived, miserably it is true, among face

2. Samuel Beckett, *Watt* (New York: Grove Press, 1959), pp. 72–73. All future page references, cited in parentheses, are to this edition.

values all his adult life, face values at least for him. Some see the flesh before the bones, and some see the bones before the flesh, and some never see the bones at all, and some never see the flesh at all, never, never see the flesh at all. But whatever it was Watt saw, with the first look that was enough for Watt, that had always been enough for Watt, more than enough for Watt. And he had experienced literally nothing, since the age of fourteen, or fifteen, of which in retrospect he was not content to say, That is what happened then. (P. 73)

Watt has no interest in symbols, because whatever they might disclose to him is arbitrary. Meanings melt away, leaving behind only a memory of flat details. His whole life seems composed of incidents "of great formal brilliance and indeterminable purport" (p. 74).

Appearances, then, may be suggestive, but because they never signify anything definite, Watt is content to leave them alone and make his way among them as best he can. After all, why seek explanations if you can never stop at one, but can always find sufficient mutually exclusive alternatives to defeat any single interpretation? Rather than work with countless possibilities, one might just as well work without any, since the result is the same: inability to know anything. Once this position is accepted, the mind finds peace in surrender, as outward forms relax into dim sensations (which is not to suggest that the emotions can enjoy what the mind has rejected; Watt hates the sun and the moon, the earth and the sky with admirable impartiality). What remains, therefore, is a world stripped not only of meanings, but also of most pleasure and pain. The resultant void—which Murphy had to use effort and concentration to reach—is then reflected in Watt's mind as indifference, which should in turn render him immune from suffering.

It is clear, however, that Watt *does* suffer, because he is never able to achieve the restful state characterizing surrender; the void remains as unattainable as meaning. While Watt is content to accept a phenomenological view of the universe, he finds that the mystery of each phenomenon haunts him until it has been explained away—"exorcized," as he terms it. His mind cannot eliminate an event until it has been flattened into nothingness through deflation of mystery, yet the mind continually finds it impossible to reduce to nothing that which has the form of *some*thing. The mind tries desperately to empty itself, but phenomena keep pouring in, meaning nothing but always suggesting, representing, appearing as something.

> What distressed Watt . . . was not so much that he did not know what had happened, for he did not care what had happened, as that nothing had happened, that a thing that was nothing had happened, with the utmost formal distinctness, and that it continued to happen, in his mind, he supposed, though he did not know exactly what that meant, and though it seemed to be outside him, before him, about him, and so on. . . . Yes, Watt could not accept . . . that nothing had happened, with all the clarity and solidity of something. . . . If he had been able to accept it, then perhaps it would not have revisited him, and this would have been a great saving of vexation, to put it mildly. But he could not accept it, could not bear it. One wonders sometimes where Watt thought he was. In a culture-park? (P. 77)

Watt's mind can neither work with emptiness, nor shut itself off; not only does it reflect forms, but it *remembers* them long after their departure. Constantly pulling forms back into the mind, the memory fills as much void as it finds, so that Watt can never clear away the useless litter left by experience.

That is why Watt continues to search for meanings, even when he refuses to believe in them. "But what was this pursuit of meaning, in this indifference to meaning? And to what did it tend? These are delicate questions" (p. 75). They are delicate indeed, for Watt seems paradoxically to need those forms suggesting meaning just in order to negate them. Once drained of meaning, phenomena begin to recede until they can no longer be recalled, and while Watt is beyond caring to know the meaning of an event, he still does want to be assured that "that is what happened then," so that the event can then be dismissed from his mind. Something must exist before it can be negated, however, and affirmation of negativity is crucial to dispensation of meaning. Let us try that again: Watt needs to know what has happened because "if then he could say that, then he thought that then the scene would end, and trouble him no more" (p. 77). Now since phenomena cannot be retained in the mind unless inflated with suggestions of some meaning, Watt must strive for meaning in order to conceptualize what he wishes to deny, "for the only way one can speak of nothing is to speak of it as though it were something" (p. 77). Nonexistence by definition cannot be negated, so Watt must work to create what he then intends to destroy.

It is at this point—when he must create objects and symbols to signify the nothingness and meaninglessness of his universe—that Watt runs into trouble, and here it becomes apparent that in Watt we can find a metaphor for the artist creating a novel of chaos, devising phenomena in order to divest them of their significance, constantly seeking symbols in order to puncture their import and deflate them to nothingness, their only real existence. For one needs to be able to conceptualize his nothingness in order to speak of it, and this can be done only through the process of formalizing the void at the core of the vision. Thus, the novel of chaos is itself a paradox, for it signifies this formalization of a vision denying form—a creation to articulate destruction, a structure to disintegrate into the nothingness it holds.

The act of creating art out of, within, and for purposes of expressing a vacuum is a difficult one for Watt. After all, who more than Beckett would realize that "to elicit something from nothing requires a certain skill" (p. 77)? The results in Watt's case are mixed: "in foisting a meaning there where no meaning appeared," (p. 77) Watt sometimes succeeds, sometimes fails; but since all his successes are subject to change, and since all his failures are also subject to change, and since even his successes only succeed in negating meaning, and his failures fail by affirming meaning, it is impossible, really, to assess his progress. When he does find meaning, it is totally arbitrary because it slips in and out of focus, becomes changed, transformed, negated, and reaffirmed:

But generally speaking it seems probable that the meaning attributed to this particular type of incident, by Watt, in his relations, was now the initial meaning that had been lost and then recovered, and now a meaning quite distinct from the initial meaning, and now a meaning evolved, after a delay of varying length, and with greater or less pains, from the initial absence of meaning. (P. 79)

Beckett makes it clear, then, that any meaning Watt finds evolves from his own ingenuity at eliciting something from nothing, and is therefore false. Still, the struggle goes on as

Watt now found himself in the midst of things which, if they consented to be named, did so as it were with reluctance. And the state in which Watt found himself resisted formulation in a way no state had ever done, in which Watt had ever found himself. . . . (P. 81)

Of course the only language suitable to express a void is silence, but since silence, which signifies the nonexistence of words, cannot be used to negate words, and since the words must be negated before the mind can whisk them out and rest in silence, Watt is faced with quite a problem, indeed: how to *render* nothingness when it can be done only through forms which seem to falsify the nothingness they are intended to express because they *will* not stop suggesting something. The forms become phantoms plaguing their creator because they will neither disappear nor yield to a formulation which would make it possible for one to live with them.

Finally, though, Watt does begin to learn: as words begin to fail him, allowing the objects they represent to slip away into the soundless void, the structure of his language becomes increasingly private and incomprehensible. Certainly, this does seem to represent some progress in Watt's ability to resist formulation.

Watt learned towards the end of this stay in Mr. Knott's house to accept that nothing had happened, that a nothing had happened, to bear it and even, in a shy way, to like it. But then it was too late. (P. 80)

It seems fair to exploit Beckett's puns in this book, and thus it becomes clear that Watt represents the question to which Mr. Knott provides the ultimate negative answer. In this way, Watt's stay at the house of denial is profitable for him, since he learns to accept his position of total ignorance. Since logic will not work for him here, he is finally able to dismiss it as worthless. Although his experiences continually frustrate reasonable explanations and all sense of probabilities, he eventually comes to prize the freedom implicit in such a world. Since all symbolical, structural, and logistic systems are arbitrary and unhelpful, Watt is content to remain independent of them. His mind detaches itself from the world of forms and finds the peace of abdication and utter alienation. Released at last from the trauma of conceptualizing and communicating, he divests his mind of all forms and sinks with relief into the silent void. He is now one with nothingness because all interferences have been swept away with the disappearance of mental forms. Unable to conceive them, he is also unable to remember them, and so is free of them forever.

To think, when one is no longer young, when one is not yet old, that one is no longer young, that one is not yet old, that is perhaps something. To pause, towards the close of one's three hour day, and consider: the darkening ease, the brightening trouble; the pleasure pleasure because it was, the proud, the proud acts growing stubborn; the panting the trembling towards a being gone, a being to come; and the true true no longer, and the false true not yet. And to decide not to smile after all, sitting in the shade, hearing the cicadas, wishing it were night, wishing it were morning, saying, No, it is not the heart, no, it is not the liver, no it is not the prostate, no, it is not the ovaries, no, it is muscular, it is nervous. Then the gnashing ends, or it goes on, and one is in the pit, in the hollow, the longing for longing gone, the horror of horror, and one is in the hollow, at the foot of all the hills at last, the ways down, the ways up, and free, free at last, for an instant free at last, nothing at last. (Pp. 201–2)

Nothing at last, Watt is victorious at last—but victory, alas, is not permanent: the mind can know and the emotions feel nothingness for exhilarating instants only before the vacuum again becomes invaded by forms. This is not necessarily a regression for Watt, however, because forms deny nothingness only when one can no longer resist the temptation to interpret them. If one accepts them as appearance only, they simply add shadow or light to the void—become, in short, simple stage props providing atmosphere, but never meaning.

While walking to the train station after having left the employment of Mr. Knott, Watt, watching with mild curiosity as a figure approaches, desires simply to discern the nature of this form. The figure, he feels, need not draw near enough to be identified very accurately, but just moderately close enough for Watt to be able to see what *kind* of figure it is:

For Watt's concern, deep as it appeared, was not after all with what the figure was, in reality, but with what the figure appeared to be, in reality. For since when were Watt's concerns with what things were, in reality? (P. 227)

Watt, then, does seem to have succeeded in incorporating his phenomenological views into his life style, realizing that he must limit his concerns to appearances since reality itself is unknowable and therefore irrelevant to his mind. There are backslidings, of course, for "he was for ever falling into this old error, this error of the old days when, lacerated with curiosity, in the midst of substance shadowy he stumbled" (p. 227). Victory is temporary, incomplete—yet possible from one instant to the other as long as the mind is willing to yield its feeble, useless powers and be content with the role of observer of appearances rather than interpreter of appearances for the end of discovering reality. Reality is nothingness, colored (in subtle shadings of black, gray, and white) by appearances perhaps, but never rendered meaningful through them.

It is obvious that Beckett's view of the mind's role in a mysterious universe forms a stark contrast to that of Virginia Woolf. Whereas her response to the mind's fatigue in finding meanings is that "one must push it on," Beckett sees this as futile activity; he finds value only in the mind's surrender to what it cannot hope to work with. Lily Briscoe's few successes would be in Beckett's world her moments of greatest defeat. For him resignation is the only heroic stance, and perseverance the surest sign of failure.

We have only to consider the flimsy plot of *Watt* to realize that the book is not really about its main character and his eventual outcome in a meaningless universe. For one thing, while Watt's end must be seen as sorrowful, the novel seems essentially comic; the tone here does seem at odds with the bleak implications of Watt's increasing alienation and his failure to find meaning or fulfillment in a spiritual vacuum. The truth is that the main character here is *not* a human one, but a mental one—not Watt but the author's imagination, which pounces on the occasion to romp freely in the void Beckett has provided for its amusement. In direct contrast to the workings of Ishmael's imagination, which provide the impetus toward meaning in *Moby-Dick*, Beckett uses *his* novel to unravel logic by exploring *ad absurdum* endless possibilities, sequences of reasoning, combinations and complications of thought processes to celebrate and demonstrate the ingenuity of imagination leaping about in a vacuum. Beckett's point seems to be that the more one considers, the less he has to say, so it is appropriate that the extent to which the mind can consider alternatives becomes, really, the subject proper of the book. As negative capability frees the artist from limiting his vision in advance, thought sweeps on to its inconclusive ends, which always turn out to be middles, from which one can spring off to new beginnings.

Given Beckett's view that it is futile to investigate the meaning behind forms, even while we *may* be engaged for a while with the peculiarities of a particular form, we can see how irrelevant the major components of the traditional novel will be to him. Characterization, for example, will necessarily be absent, for it is impossible to explain the man who may perhaps be hiding

behind his form as man. Since all explanations are proved farcical
in this book, the author who attempts to provide sensible motivations for characters' actions is as much a fool as the philosopher.
Can we ever know *why* Watt feels as he does? Well, perhaps it is
one thing and perhaps another, but why speculate when we
know that any real knowledge is impossible to come by? Let us,
instead, simply accept Watt and his situation as curious forms—
interesting, perhaps, but hardly significant. Forget reality, because there is no such thing; appearances hide nothing. Do not
expect a fat person to represent anything but a person who appears fat; do not expect to know him as anything but a fat form.
True, if he sits in the moonlight, his form may become slightly
different as parts of it slip into the shadows while other parts are
illuminated. The moon itself may shed a little light, a tree nearby
may shed or sprout a leaf—but nothing has been changed but the
form. Life, then, is nothing more than a kaleidoscope of constantly shifting, meaningless patterns.

Thus, Beckett has drained his novel of psychological import,
philosophical investigation, spiritual significance, moral purpose,
and symbolical implication. Because the void provides context for
everything—rendering all objects dim, hollow, and colorless—life
reduced to its formal common denominators is flat and silent.
And so the novel itself purports to tell us nothing at all beyond
the fact that it has nothing to say. Beckett expresses his sense of
nothingness by finding forms to represent it, but while the forms
(of logic, structure, setting, etc.) do exist qua forms, they add up
to nothing, boil down to nothing, lead to nothing. The novel,
therefore, is aesthetically meaningful as it conjures up appearances, then deflates them to the common denominator of zero.
Chaos has infiltrated the novel so completely that its form has by
now become barely distinguishable from its vision.

With each successive novel, Beckett cuts away more and more
of the external world until the reader can hardly distinguish the
narrator's mental processes from the mass outside. Whereas Conrad takes the story of *Lord Jim* away from Jim's consciousness
(because of Jim's limited potential for understanding himself) and
presents it through the more detached perspective of Marlow,
Beckett has done just the opposite in moving from *Watt* to *Molloy*. The detachment of the third-person point of view in *Watt*
enabled us to see Watt's alienation from his world, but at the

same time the reader was kept at sufficient distance to see both Watt and his world as two separate entities. Since Beckett views the world as "oozing," however, it is inevitable that he would eventually try to get closer to the confusion and farther from the conventional world of appearances by adopting the first-person point of view, which by supplying less verifiable information than the more detached one, dims any distinctions between the world itself and the mind through which it filters.

"It is in the tranquillity of decomposition that I remember the long confused emotion which was my life,"[3] says Molloy; and if we are tempted to think that such tranquillity might lead to a sense of stability from which earlier impressions could assume a new order, Molloy later asserts: "The fact is, it seems, that the most you can hope is to be a little less, in the end, the creature you were in the beginning, and the middle" (p. 32). Creativity, then, is now working in reverse; its new goal is to deflate, diminish, and ultimately undo entirely the impact and significance of a man's life. We can see, however, that if composition itself succeeds only in falsifying (through deceptive appearances implying meaning), the art of *de*composition—one which attempts to strip away all the false layers clarifying cloudy issues—is no less valid an aesthetic form. Like Lily Briscoe, Beckett seems to feel that one must force on the creative apparatus (or rather, that since it forces itself *on* one, he might as well exploit it in order to stop it), but in *his* world value is judged by how much meaning has been drained rather than sustained through the artistic process. The ends may be different, but there is a purposeful process involved in both the art of composition and the art of decomposition. Of course, Lily is far more successful than Molloy's counterpart, Moran—for try as he may to resist the imagination's impulse to mold, transform, and re-create reality in the form of art, Moran does finally succumb: "Then I went back into the house and wrote. It is midnight. The rain is beating on the windows. It was not midnight. It was not raining" (p. 176). Like a volcano verging on eruption, the imagination's potential to explode through reality is always imminent, and Moran's attempt to push it back is as futile as the finger stuck in the dike. The imagination cries for room, expansion, materials with which to work its will into a dif-

3. Samuel Beckett, *Molloy*, trans. Patrick Bowles, in *Three Novels by Samuel Beckett* (New York: Grove Press, 1965), p. 25. All future page references, cited in parentheses, are to this edition.

ferent world, but Moran wants truth, not fantasy, so he tries to starve his imagination of the nourishment it needs to create. Since truth is the void itself, only the eventual disappearance of structure, appearances, and meaning, which characterizes the process of decomposition, can lead us to that truth. In this way, Molloy's seemingly arbitrary presentation of his life disguises a method of progression—a use of aesthetic formulae to structure, represent, and project a vision of nothingness.

First, *Molloy* is full of allusions to the atmosphere in which Molloy's body struggles, but the difference between the various settings is the difference between muck, scum, and shit. Time and place too are flattened out as falsifying structures implying diversity, progression, order. Instead, "however far I went, and in no matter what direction, it was always the same sky, always the same earth, precisely, day after day and night after night" (p. 65). Whether in Tibet or Nebraska, man is stranded in the same universe, and whether the day is Tuesday or Thursday, he suffers in the same way he did on Monday.

Since composition is a formalizing process, decomposition must melt down structures to their essential ingredients before the false sense of man's control can be dispelled. Thus, what men call forests, mountains, jungles, or prairies can all be reduced to "land"; while his oceans, rivers, bays, streams, and lakes can be simply equalized as "water." Then, we can go even further by mixing the two atmospheres together and getting mud, muck, scum, shit, or whatever. This explains the great amount of local colorlessness in Beckett's world: in both color and substance, the environment is defined by its lack of meaningful detail and individualizing qualities. All we have to do is think of the novels of Faulkner, Woolf, Melville, Conrad, Kafka, and Sterne to realize that Beckett, by squashing atmosphere into unrecognizable, formless matter, has sidestepped the world of appearances completely, thereby removing the setting that constituted an important part of the traditional novels of chaos—the impression and effect of the particular moment in a particular place. Beckett has already gone far beyond the other novelists discussed in erasing the world of appearances in which most of us think we live.

In most of Beckett's work, revelations lead to resolutions which make absolutely no difference in a person's life. Think of Lord Jim's or Lily Briscoe's revelations, both of which lead to resolutions shaping values and changing life styles, and we can see the traditional importance of self-knowledge both as literary climax and basis for action in the novel. But again, Beckett's art moves in a different direction.

For to know nothing is nothing, not to want to know anything likewise, but to be beyond knowing anything, to know you are beyond knowing anything, that is when peace enters in, to the soul of the incurious seeker. (P. 64)

Molloy's quest, then, is not for any kind of self-knowledge, but for the state of mind that has no concern for knowledge. He does not have to discover that all knowledge is useless—he *knows* it—but his mind will not stop working, even though it always leads him to the same dead end. A dead end, however, is not a real end unless the mind accepts it as such, and since Molloy's mind can neither conceive of nor accept any sense of an ending, the traditional concept of structure must be rejected. The novel of action gives way to the novel of *in*action, which finds all stops and climaxes arbitrary, with the exception of death. To outlive a crisis is to break out of the frame that made it seem critical.

You think you have your bellyful but you seldom have it really. It was because I knew I was there that I had my bellyful, a mile more to go and I would only have had my bellyful an hour later. Human nature. (P. 35)

In conventional tragedy, action seems meaningful and important because it leads to the hero's death. But most of us fail to die at the moment when death would be a legitimate climax to the primary concerns of our lives. Instead, as in *Waiting for Godot*, the characters are left still standing there the moment after they have uttered their final words of despair. When the curtain does come down finally, the ending is arbitrary and meaningless, anticlimactic and hollow. What seemed the natural ending has turned out to be only another middle-muddle, for life keeps going on, "oozing" out of formal frames into its natural state of chaos. There are no real climaxes, therefore: nothing to be learned, no definitive statements ever to be made until the final one—and that is immediately turned into silence by death.

The artist's main concern should be with life, but Molloy sees that the traditional artist has ignored life as we know it and live it, and has focused instead on the falsities created by his own form. Because man longs to interpret the events in his life, and because these events cannot be meaningfully interpreted until that life is over, all evidence is in, and conclusions can be drawn that take everything into account, man turns to art as a means of discovering, through the form that art makes possible, those explanations he can never hope to find in his own oozing existence. By providing its climaxes in logical places, art crystallizes and intensifies existence, thereby rendering it palatable to the mind. Molloy, however, by placing these climaxes in their natural context of life's continuous movement, renders them inconsequential: "But these were mere crises, and what are crises compared to all that never stops, knows neither ebb nor flow, its surface leaden above infernal depths" (p. 79). The drama of crisis is no longer valid as a statement on life; only the oozing deserves to be depicted, for that is where most of our lives are spent; and only the ultimate statement is worth making, because it alone takes the oozing into account. The chorus in *Oedipus Rex* warns us not to make a judgment on any man while he remains alive, for the next second might produce changes which must alter drastically any previous impressions, and Molloy is really saying the same thing when he asserts that he cannot make sense of his life, can provide no meaningful comment on it as long as he remains in the middle of it:

So I wait, jogging along, for the bell to say, Molloy, one last effort, it's the end. That's how I reason, with the help of images little suited to my situation. And I can't shake off the feeling, I don't know why, that the day will come for me to say what is left of all I had. But I must first wait, to be sure there is nothing more I can acquire, or lose, or throw away, or give away. Then I can say, without fear of error, what is left, in the end, of my possessions. For it will be the end. And between now and then I may get poorer or richer, oh not to the extent of being any better off or any worse off, but sufficiently to preclude me from announcing, here and now, what is left of all I had, for I have not yet had all. (P. 82)

If one were to comment on Oedipus the moment before he became aware of his father's slayer, if Joseph K. were to assess his life the evening before he awoke to learn of his arrest, or if Molloy were to present a summation of his life the moment before . . . what?—then all our hard-earned conclusions would have been worthless. One must wait until death to know what he has to say, and of course, once death has come, he will have nothing to say. Nothing is, then, the ultimate statement on all our lives, and Molloy wants to be able to make this statement by remaining silent. Yet he continues to talk and so can never say the one thing that needs to be said, the one thing genuinely worthy of being said—

which is nothing. Silence is success; speech is failure—so we seem to have our choice between truth and a novel which, by the very act of language which brings it into creation, can never attain truth. The novel cannot hope to help us toward the truth, since it expires at the very second truth is reached.

The novel's existence, therefore, is sufficient proof that truth has not been won, and that is why all of Molloy's efforts are concentrated toward stopping his creation, even while it is working to stop *him* in his pursuit of truth. It is this conflict between the artist and his own self-defeating material which provides both tension and theme in *Molloy* and which dictates Beckett's structural formulae for the novel. Since all roads lead to the same end, and since that end shifts to become a middle and then a new beginning, Beckett has based his structural principle on the one geometric shape that can project his vision without falsifying it. In his journey, Molloy feels at times that he is making some progress,

but from time to time I came on a kind of crossroads, you know, a star, or circus, of the kind to be found in even the most unexplored of forests. And turning then methodically to face the radiating paths in turn, hoping for I know not what, I described a complete circle, or less than a circle, or more than a circle, so great was the resemblance between them. (P. 83)

This circular structure created by Beckett enables Molloy to think he is changing direction in the very process of writing (concerning the impressive list of his weaknesses he intends to draw up, he says: "No, I shall never draw it up, yes, perhaps I shall," p. 80), but since he ultimately always returns to the same point and always leaves it only to travel the circle once more, it is clear that Beckett has also structured his novel to depict the futility of having written it.

Molloy's whole journey thus becomes a metaphor for the mind's quest for an oasis, a final resting place where it can drift in silence, suspended in stillness. But of course there are no final resting places—just as there are no true climaxes—so long as time keeps moving; even if *we* continue to stand still, our context changes and our identity shifts with each second. The quest for finality of some sort is doomed because, just as every synthesis immediately becomes a new thesis, so each of those moments we judge to be endings ooze into other moments, providing the new perspective which makes them middles. Molloy cannot even find a way of talking about a life which continues to float in time:

My life, my life, now I speak of it as something over, now as of a joke which still goes on, and it is neither, for at the same time it is over and it goes on, and is there any tense for that? (P. 36)

If there is no tense to capture the movement of time within the arrest of motion, Beckett has at least found a structural principle that duplicates the cross purposes of a man pursuing a goal in an elusive reality. Molloy's circle is a purposeful one, for having learned "that when a man in a forest thinks he is going forward in a straight line, in reality he is going in a circle, I did my best to go in a circle, hoping in this way to go in a straight line" (p. 85). Trying to outwit the universe in this way, Molloy has come up with a clever device which makes little sense, especially when we consider that he rarely remembers where he is going. Still, his method is intentional and represents a logical way of dealing with an unreasonable world, just as Beckett's structure seems the only way for *him* to delineate the shape of chaos while trying to make his way through it. If neither he nor Molloy ever *does* succeed in getting anywhere, then that failure must be acknowledged as the main point of a novel patterned faithfully on chaotic vision.

By shaping chaotic forces, Lily Briscoe in *To the Lighthouse* is able to keep them under artistic control, and this management stablilizes reality for her. Beckett also gives chaos a certain form, but his form has no philosophical value: all we can say is that it leads us nowhere in an interesting way. The structure offers us no security because it provides no clue to meaning and implies no control over the confusion of events. If we consider the two parts of *Molloy,* for example, we find strong parallels which suggest meaningful patterns, without elucidating the mystery they formalize. Thus, Moran's section begins at the end, and ends back at the beginning, but the structure itself gives us no insight beyond the relationships it sets up. It is obvious that Moran's journey parallels Molloy's, and it is quite possible that it precedes Molloy's or even becomes Molloy's, but that does not help us decipher the meaning of either narrative.

This is not to say that Beckett has failed to provide us with a wealth of possibilities. We have, for example, much evidence to support an interpretation of Moran as the artist pursuing and struggling with his subject matter. Moran is at first depicted as

the opposite of Molloy, for his whole life has been built on a rigid
concept of order and routine which is never seriously disrupted
by the relationships which so often complicate our lives. "Vague-
ness I abhor," he says (p. 99) when his son, questioned as to where
he has been, replies only, "out." Moran cannot tolerate inadequate explanations; he wants to be in complete control of all the
facts before he makes a decision. Contemplating his journey, he
says:

I had a methodical mind and never set out on a mission without prolonged reflection as to the best way of setting out. It was the first problem to solve, at the outset of each inquiry, and I never moved until I had
solved it, to my satisfaction. (P. 98)

He sees right away, however, that this mission threatens to be
different, "for how can you decide on the way of setting out if
you do not first know where you are going, or at least with what
purpose you are going there?" (p. 98). In spite of this, Moran tries
to approach this mission as he had the others: he makes arrangements, gives instructions to his son, packs, locks his door, and
leaves as scheduled. Quickly and surely, he makes his way into
the dark forest where he immediately loses the confidence, control, and detachment which had made him such an effective
agent. Is this the artist struggling with his material, pursuing the
character he has created ("For who could have spoken to me of
Molloy if not myself and to whom if not to myself could I have
spoken of him?" p. 112) in order to save him, through art, from
the chaotic conditions of the author's imagination?

Far from the world, its clamours, frenzies, bitterness and dingy light, I
pass judgement on it and on those, like me, who are plunged in it beyond recall, and on him who has need of me to be delivered, who cannot
deliver myself. . . . The blood drains from my head, the noise of things
bursting, merging, avoiding one another, assails me on all sides, my eyes
search in vain for two things alike, each pinpoint of skin screams a different message, I drown in the spray of phenomena. (P. 111)

The author can do no more for his character than he can manage
to do for himself. Faced at first with the universal disorder on
which he tries to impose unity, he does finally meet with astounding success in finding likenesses, but the likenesses are strong
enough to cause him to merge with his own creation and then
with the dark mass outside which obliterates all distinctions of
identity. He eventually becomes consumed by the same darkness

from which he had meant to rescue his character. Or *was* the character created to be rescued? Moran wonders what he is supposed to do with Molloy once he comes upon him.

If life is darkness, then the value of the imagination may lie in accepting the challenge to dispel it. Moran at one point gives thanks "for evening that brings out the lights, the stars in the sky and on earth the brave little lights of men" (p. 159). Later, however, when he wearies of his pursuit, he begins to hope that since he will never reach Molloy, perhaps Molloy will come to him like a friend or a father and help him do whatever he has to do in order to avoid being punished by Youdi. As he begins to identify more and more with Molloy's situation, Moran's values undergo a radical change: now, when turning to the lights of the city below in which he had previously found comfort, he sees the "foul little flickering lights of terrified men" (p. 162). And by the time he gets back to his own house, he finds that "the company had cut off the light. They have offered to let me have it back. But I told them they could keep it. That is the kind of man I have become" (p. 175).

Earlier, Moran had said:

The more things resist me the more rabid I get. With time, and nothing but my teeth and nails, I would rage up from the bowels of the earth to its crust, knowing full well I had nothing to gain. And when I had no more teeth, no more nails, I would dig through the rock with my bones. (P. 156)

As soon as he sets out for home, however, he finds his resistance crumbling, and feels lured, instead, by those forces after his destruction. And so what kind of man has Moran become by the end of his journey? No man at all, it seems: "I have been a man long enough. I shall not put up with it any more, I shall not try any more. I shall never light this lamp again. I am going to blow it out and go into the garden" (p. 175). Moran, we find, has followed the pattern of Molloy's decomposition, and in so doing, has learned the value of surrender, the only one he can assert with conviction in his weakened state. He has not caught Molloy, but he has embodied him.

After receiving a letter from Youdi "in the third person, asking for a report" (p. 175), Moran discovers that he will be able to write it in the language he has come to understand from that inner voice which seems to be his projection of Molloy's inner voice (which Molloy found welling up in him at the end of his section):

I have spoken of a voice telling me things. I was getting to know it better now, to understand what it wanted. It did not use the words that Moran had been taught when he was little and that he in his turn had taught to his little one. So that at first I did not know what it wanted. But in the end I understood this language. I understood it, I understood it, all wrong perhaps. That is not what matters. It told me to write the report. Does this mean that I am freer than I was? I do not know. I shall learn. Then I went back into the house and wrote. It is midnight. The rain is beating on the windows. It was not midnight. It was not raining. (P. 176)

It is odd that Youdi's request for a report was written in the third person, yet Moran responds in kind: as soon as he feels he understands his inner voice, it seems to take control of him so that he too speaks of himself in the third person. Does this mean that Moran has been the persona for Beckett all along? Is this closing passage the author's apology for the artifice of his craft, or is it an explanation of why he handled the story as he did? Were the inner voices of Molloy really the thoughts of his creator, and has Moran, in turn, been able to produce his report only after he has captured Molloy in his imagination?

And is it fair to equate Moran, the persona, with Beckett, the author? Ordinarily, this would seem risky business, and yet Moran himself has said earlier:

Oh the stories I could tell you, if I were easy. What a rabble in my head, what a gallery of moribunds. Murphy, Watt, Yerk, Mercier and all the others. I would never have believed that—yes, I believe it willingly. Stories, stories. I have not been able to tell them. I shall not be able to tell this one. (P. 137)

This echoes Molloy's lines earlier in the first section: "I've disbelieved only too much in my long life, now I swallow everything, greedily. What I need now is stories, it took me a long time to know that, and I'm not sure of it" (p. 13). Is Beckett, then, addressing the reader directly? Is he describing the therapeutic value of his art, or simply presenting the rough material of a story he refuses to shape into coherent order? Is he concerned with the chaos in his imagination, his psyche, or his universe? Is he creating art or mocking it?

We have seen in *Watt* that a wealth of possibilities cannot be successfully reduced to one probability (note in the above quotation how even certainty immediately spawns a qualification which makes it melt away). As in Kafka, the world of Beckett throws us off balance, stimulating us to search for answers, yet frustrating us at every turn. Beckett's relation to his characters and to his readers is as confusing as the characters' relations to one another. We are endlessly fascinated and endlessly puzzled. Whereas in *The Trial*, Kafka keeps himself out of the picture entirely, Beckett throws his narrative into the same uncertainty that characterizes his characters' situations. If nothing can be known (and this is a positive as well as a negative statement), then the distinction between author and subject, narrator and persona, the artist and his material may also be legitimate cause for conjecture. Where is all the chaos coming from? Is it matter itself which is chaotic, or man's mind, or the combination of the two which throws everything out of joint? As soon as Moran becomes sufficiently detached from his own secure surroundings (which includes his earlier self-conception), he is able to accept nihilism and create a report founded on, even embracing uncertainty. Knowing nothing of his motivations, his victim, or his purpose, he is willing to create in order to follow the form of his ignorance. If his journey had no meaning, it did have a form which he can still regard with interest. Previously a man who refused to act without complete knowledge of all the facts of his situation, he now consciously throws away his light, and resolves to affirm the uncertainty behind everything. He shall use his form (the report) not to clarify experience, but to formalize its obscurity.

If Beckett is doing much the same thing, should we consider Moran to be Beckett? It would be difficult, because in spite of the many similarities, there remain many qualities peculiar to Moran, and many incidents in his story that would have no relevance at all to this interpretation, along with too many hints linking him more closely to Molloy than to the author that would have to go unheeded. Let us do Beckett the justice of remaining mystified.

In discussing *To the Lighthouse*, I have said that outer chaos is only half the problem in man's difficult adjustment to the universe, since much of the darkness stems from the incredible complexity or his inner life. Still, the characters in that novel emerge as distinct individuals, and the reader himself, because he can explain motivations for action, is not subject to the gap in communication that alienates the characters from one another. In *Molloy*, however, the reader cannot benefit from his detached perspective: he remains a stranger to everyone encountered in the novel, including the narrator, who is as honest with us as we could demand. Beckett's refusal to make his characters comprehensible may present the greatest stumbling block to the reader who, in trying to gain some control over the confusion, seeks the stability of human identity.

Not that identity has ever been so stable. We are willing to concede the difficulty of ever knowing enough about anyone, or even ourselves for that matter. Still, Beckett's unwillingness to help us here is remarkable, for we cannot make even the most basic statement about a character—that is, whether he is male or female, alive or dead, real or imaginary. In trying to conceptualize Molloy, for example, Moran sees that more than one person is involved:

The fact was there were three, no, four Molloys. He that inhabited me, my caricature of same, Gaber's and the man of flesh and blood somewhere awaiting me. To these I would add Youdi's . . . for could it seriously be supposed that Youdi had confided to Gaber all he knew, or thought he knew . . . about his protégé? Assuredly not. He had only revealed what he deemed of relevance for the prompt and proper execution of his orders. I will therefore add a fifth Molloy, that of Youdi. (P. 115)

This of course presents problems, but not necessarily insurmountable ones, because the reader has, after all, already been given a first-person account of Molloy, and should therefore have his own conception of him, even if his first impression might be modified by other points of view (a method similar to Virginia Woolf's cubistic presentation of character). But our confusion goes far beyond that, for Molloy himself is unable to account for his actions. His motivations remain as great a mystery to him as they would to the most disinterested bystander. Consider the following:

Yes, my resolutions were remarkable in this, that they were no sooner formed than something always happened to prevent their execution. . . . But to tell the truth (to tell the truth!) I have never been particularly resolute, I mean given to resolutions, but rather inclined to plunge headlong into the shit. . . . (P. 32)

And when I talk of preferring, for example, or regretting, it must not be supposed that I opted for the least evil, and adopted it, for that would be wrong. But not knowing exactly what I was doing or avoiding, I did it and avoided it. . . . (P. 55)

Now as to telling you why I stayed a good while with Lousse, no, I cannot. That is to say I could I suppose, if I took the trouble. But why should I? In order to establish beyond all question that I could not do otherwise? For that is the conclusion I would come to fatally. (Pp. 50–51)

It came back to my mind, from nowhere, as a moment before my name, that I had set out to see my mother, at the beginning of this ending day. My reasons? I had forgotten them. (P. 27)

And of myself, all my life, I think I had been going to my mother, with the purpose of establishing our relations on a less precarious footing. And when I was with her, and I often succeeded, I left her without having done anything. And when I was no longer with her I was again on my way to her, hoping to do better the next time. (P. 87)

Analysis of motivation is useless because it does not get us any-where. We cannot explain what we do not understand, and we do not understand what we cannot justify as logical behavior. Since Molloy rarely remembers where he is heading, and when he does, cannot usually recall why he is heading there, and when he does, does not know what he hopes to achieve or why, then we must expect that his actions and motivations will be as enigmatic to him as they are to us.

How can the reader be expected to adjust to this condition of ignorance, helplessness, and frustration? Can Beckett be justified in giving us so little knowledge to work with in coming to terms with his central character? We have seen that Melville's Confi-dence Man left us just as confused, but in that case, the author was writing in the third person, and so did not offer more knowl-edge than such a perspective could have warranted. But Beckett in *Molloy* has had his two (if they are indeed two separate) char-acters tell their own stories with the same baffling results. Fur-thermore, while the Confidence Man is regarded, at least, as an "original," Beckett's characters and consequences seem univer-sal. Even Moran, who at first represents the epitome of self-con-trol, order, and discipline, quickly loses his sense of superiority to Molloy and dashes any hope the reader might have placed in his helping to account for the strange gaps in Molloy's narrative. De-scribing his fight with a stranger, Moran cannot even answer for his own lapses of consciousness:

I do not know what happened then. But a little later, perhaps a long time later, I found him stretched on the ground, his head in a pulp. I am sorry I cannot indicate more clearly how this result was obtained, it would have been something worth reading. But it is not at this late stage of my relation that I intend to give way to literature. (P. 151)

It would seem that no man is ever in a position to make much sense of his life. We constantly operate against our self-interests and can rarely explain why. We follow those inner voices which apparently represent our thinking, and then are amazed at the places they lead us to. We feel the irrelevance of our own wills when our most carefully formed resolutions have no effect whatever on our actions. And finally, we really cannot explain what makes us unique, especially when we seem to have so little influence on the person we watch ourselves becoming.

Molloy realizes that all men die ignorant because partial knowledge is useless to the truth-seeker, and complete knowledge is unattainable. Yet man's inability to accept the apparent chaos of the universe drives him toward some final explanation which, like Vladamir and Estragon, he spends his life waiting for. In this situation, his life resembles the stagnancy of death, but with none of its peace. Molloy questions his motivations, goals, and primary concerns, but the futility of his life negates so much that it does not seem to make much difference, really, what he does with it.

Perhaps there is no whole, before you're dead. An opiate for the life of the dead, that should be easy. What am I waiting for then, to exorcize mine? It's coming, it's coming. I hear from here the howl resolving all, even if it is not mine. Meanwhile there's no use knowing you are gone, you are not, you are writhing yet, the hair is growing, the nails are growing, the entrails emptying, all the morticians are dead. Someone has drawn the blinds, you perhaps. Not the faintest sound. Where are the famous flies? Yes, there is no denying it, any longer, it is not you who are dead, but all the others. So you get up and go to your mother, who thinks she is alive. (P. 27)

Molloy's solipsism may explain his inability to remember those who have had, presumably, a profound effect on him; their reality is so elusive that his memory cannot retain them as clear identities. While recalling the only woman he has ever loved, he says that "she went by the peaceful name of Ruth I think, but I can't say for certain. Perhaps the name was Edith" (p. 56). Then, as he continues to think about her, even her sex becomes uncertain, and finally, the whole experience becomes dim enough for the reader to wonder whether Molloy has not merely invented the few precious memories he clings to. But meanwhile his own identity is so precarious that we cannot say for sure whether *his* existence is any more tangible than those whose reality seems confined to his own mind. Alone in his mother's room, he wonders whether she was dead when he got there, or had died only after he had arrived.

I don't know. Perhaps they haven't buried her yet. In any case I have her room. I sleep in her bed. I piss and shit in her pot. I have taken her place. I must resemble her more and more. All I need now is a son. Perhaps I have one somewhere. But I think not. He would be old now, nearly as old as myself. It was a little chambermaid. It wasn't true love. The true love was in another. We'll come to that. Her name? I've forgotten it again. (P. 7)

There is nothing for the reader to hold onto here. Molloy has become indistinguishable from his mother, just as Moran (his forgotten son?) becomes indistinguishable from Molloy as his situation becomes similar. Age, of course, is simply a matter of time, so it is reasonable that Molloy might have grown into the age of his old mother, that his son has by now grown into the age of his father, and that all old forms of humanity become much the same person. From the fetus to the skeleton, all men progress through the same forms and so may ultimately be considered the same person. And since sex is merely a matter of holes and plugs, that distinction too can be easily lost in the general chaos of all matter. The closer we get to essentials, the less meaningful and significant seem the few peculiarities that make each man unique. Consider their forms, their fears, their needs, their origins, their ends, and the great mass in between which is doubtless composed of experiences of love, suffering, useless thinking, joy, despair—and the differences are insignificant and vague at best. Of course, the one exception is our own lives, which do strike us as strangely significant and special. But Molloy makes no exception for himself; he is willing to throw his own mind and body into the general jumble of human forms and watch his individuality being squeezed out by the pressure of other limbs, heads, and trunks. "I was a solid in the midst of other solids," says Moran (p. 108), and this applies equally to Molloy, who cannot make the most elementary distinctions between the solid he forms and that other solid formed by everything outside of himself:

And even my sense of identity was wrapped in a namelessness often hard to penetrate. . . . And so on for all the other things which made merry with my senses. Yes, even then, when already all was fading, waves and particles, there could be no things but nameless things, no names but thingless names. I say that now, but after all what do I know now about then, now when the icy words hail down upon me, the icy meanings, and the world dies too, foully named. (P. 31)

It is no wonder that Molloy has such trouble remembering even his own name. Because he never sees himself as an individual, the name which so arbitrarily stamps him as such is lost when the conception of identity itself slides out of his mind.

Are we then to make something significant of the fact that Moran finally resembles Molloy, or that Molloy comes more and more to resemble his mother? Only if that fact is itself a significant one. But what importance can it have when it is so common? Would Gaber's story be any different? Or Youdi's? Or Ruth's or whatever her name was? Are pebbles on a beach to be given individual names, and are we to be overcome with a feeling of insight if we find two that match? And if we grind the pebbles down to their essential substance, are we to investigate grains of sand and be surprised to discover their similarity? So in Beckett's reductive world, the individual melts into a conglomeration of individuals, which in turn is finally reduced to a mass of howling protoplasm.

Beckett, then, has scooped out characterization, leaving only hollow forms to reflect what is left of the human personality when it has been flattened down to its basic instincts, drives, and feelings. Whereas the novel's development as a form seems to have paralleled development of methods to penetrate, explore, and analyze the human psyche, Beckett in *Molloy* has cast aside the whole concept of strong characterization as presumptuous nonsense, clarifying falsely through art what always remains inexplicable in life. The idea of free will is absurd when each person lives at the mercy of an inner voice which thinks for him and pushes him into action, unconcerned with what his will has resolved. The idea of providing causes to explain every effect is equally ridiculous; aside from providing evidence of the author's ingenuity, given causes are simply contrivances of will to cover up unknowns and deflate the mystery each person feels about himself, as well as others. Beckett refuses to falsify his chaotic vision by achieving through artifice what can never be found in reality, and so he allows the chaos to seep deeply into his characters until we are as ill-equipped to deal with *them* as they are with the universe which appalls them. By reducing his characters to flesh and thought, Beckett strips them of all misleading appearances, including the notion of identity. What remains is the poor, bare, forked animal that Lear sees in Edgar disguised as Poor Tom. Beckett, like Lear, has lost interest in giving instructions; he now wishes only to consider man well, and since he has concluded that man is indeed no more than this, Beckett intends to show no more than the helpless, trembling, ignorant animal he sees as the deepest truth about us all. If characterization is weak in Beckett, it is simply because he does not regard character as a natural attribute of the human animal.

Since Beckett has deprived the reader of the kind of knowledge the traditional novel always made possible, *Molloy* seems at first to represent an abandonment of those forms and techniques which novelists have utilized to project vision with emotional impact. Art, however, can survive chaos so long as it can control it—not necessarily by defeating it, but by formalizing it into universal expression. If we remember that Beckett's thesis—Nothing is knowable—is a positive, as well as negative statement, we can see that forms are still needed to express his idea. Just as Watt cannot deny what has no mental existence for him, so the reader must be given some sense of form before he can notice its hollow interior. The shell of a deserted house must remain before its emptiness can be felt, and even a vacuum must be conceptualized before it can be defined as such—which is why the dark, empty church in *The Trial* can be felt as such a meaningful symbol of spiritual depletion.

Beckett may have compressed his forms, made them barren and flat, insubstantial and hollow, but the effect is to make them echo the full resonance of the void. One's vision may be that nothing leads anywhere, but one's art must show that everything leads nowhere. This, finally, is what distinguishes chaos in the novel from the novel in chaos: in the one case, form embodies nothingness; in the other, form itself dissolves into nothingness, and art loses its hold on life.

If we characterize Beckett's chaos, it becomes clear that each quality has been rendered through the author's purposeful manipulation of the novel's forms. Life's complexity forces itself upon us much as it did in *Watt:* the narrator tries to work with evidence which contradicts every conclusion until he finally concedes the intellect's inadequacy in coping with a world that defies interpretation. Moran's beehive is a perfect metaphor for this situation: having observed that the bees' various dances seem to represent a system of signals, he takes pains to classify the dances in order to interpret their meanings:

The most striking feature of the dance was its very complicated figure, traced in flight, and I had classified a great number of these, with their probable meanings. But there was also the question of the hum, so various in tone in the vicinity of the hive that this could hardly be an effect of chance. I first concluded that each figure was reinforced by means of a hum peculiar to it. But I was forced to abandon this agreeable hypothesis. For I saw the same figure (at least what I called the same figure) accompanied by very different hums. So that I said, The purpose of the hum is not to emphasize the dance, but on the contrary to vary it. And I had collected and classified a great number of observations on this subject, with gratifying results. But there was to be considered not only the figure and the hum, but also the height at which the figure was executed. And I acquired the conviction that the selfsame figure, accompanied by the selfsame hum, did not mean at all the same thing at twelve feet from the ground as it did at six. For the bees did not dance at any level, haphazard, but there were three or four levels, always the same, at which they danced. And if I were to tell you what these levels were, and what the relations between them, for I had measured them with care, you would not believe me. . . . And in spite of all the pains I had lavished on these problems, I was more than ever stupefied by the complexity of this innumerable dance, involving doubtless other determinants of which I had not the slightest idea. And I said, with rapture, Here is something I can study all my life, and never understand. (P. 168–69)

The bees' dance thus becomes a symbol for the chaos of the natural world which defeats man's attempts at interpretation. And the mind's built-in sense of logic only confuses things further by promoting so many ramifications to each hypothesis that it becomes futile to even *consider* the possibilities. In Beckett's world, complexities can never be resolved because each solution contains so many qualifications that the whole matter must be dismissed as unworkable. But Beckett *has* found an artistic device to express endless speculation spinning along the circumference of nihilism: like Melville's counterfeit detector, the beehive reflects the frustration of man's mind in the face of complexities he cannot deal with.

At a certain point, complexity turns into mystery, and Beckett's conception of chaos includes unknowns lurking behind unknowables. Moran's relation to Youdi is strongly reminiscent of K.'s relation to the High Court in *The Trial*. Who, after all, is

Youdi? Moran can observe his dancing bees, even if he can make little sense of their activity, but Youdi's very existence may be called doubtful at best. If, as his name implies, he represents Death, then he would be similar to The Law in *The Trial:* the supreme authority who can never be appealed to directly, never seen or known, but only heard from through lesser agents. According to Moran, Youdi has the power to punish him, so the relationship must be one of subjugation to a master one can never comprehend, but must please, all the same. But then there is always the possibility that Youdi has no existence outside of Moran's imagination, which would make him merely an expressionistic projection of Moran's own guilt feelings, sense of duty, fear of death, or whatever. It is all so vague, murky, and mystifying that we cannot know for sure just what, if any, threat Youdi poses to Moran, much less what he wants Moran to do with Molloy once he has been hunted down. Youdi's instructions are incomplete and his motives unknown. Also, what is the hold he has over Moran? When did their relationship begin? Or, who is Gaber, for that matter? Is he equivalent to the boy who brings Godot's message to Vladimir and Estragon? Just what are the roles here and what is their significance? Moran's thoughts on the whole affair are infinitely suggestive, but also infinitely puzzling:

Gabor [*sic*] was protected in numerous ways. He used a code incomprehensible to all but himself. Each messenger, before being appointed, had to submit his code to the directorate. Gabor [*sic*] understood nothing about the messages he carried. Reflecting on them he arrived at the most extravagantly false conclusions. Yes, it was not enough for him to understand nothing about them, he had also to believe he understood everything about them. . . . To be indecipherable to all but oneself, dead without knowing it to the meaning of one's instructions and incapable of remembering them for more than a few seconds, these are capacities rarely united in the same individual. No less however was demanded of our messengers. . . . And when I speak of agents and messengers in the plural, it is with no guarantee of truth. For I had never seen any other messenger than Gaber nor any other agent than myself. But I supposed we were not the only ones and Gaber must have supposed the same. For the feeling that we were the only ones of our kind would, I believe, have been more than we could have borne. And it must have appeared natural, to me that each agent had his own particular messenger, and to Gaber that each messenger had his own particular agent. Thus I was able to say to Gaber, Let him give this job to someone else, I don't want it, and Gaber was able to reply, He wants it to be you. And these last words, assuming Gaber had not invented them especially to annoy me, had perhaps been uttered by the chief with the sole purpose of fostering our illusion, if it was one. All this is not very clear. (Pp. 106–7)

Not very clear, indeed! But up to this point, the situation may still be seen as one of overwhelming complexity rather than mystery. Moran's thinking, however, becomes increasingly solipsistic as his speculations get increasingly out of hand:

That we thought of ourselves as members of a vast organization was doubtless also due to the all too human feeling that trouble shared, or is it sorrow, is trouble something, I forget the word. But to me at least, who knew how to listen to the falsetto of reason, it was obvious that we were perhaps alone in doing what we did. Yes, in my moments of lucidity I thought it possible. And, to keep nothing from you, this lucidity was so acute at times that I came even to doubt the existence of Gaber himself. And if I had not hastily sunk back into my darkness I might have gone to the extreme of conjuring away the chief too and regarding myself as solely responsible for my wretched existence. . . . And having made away with Gaber and the chief . . . could I have denied myself the pleasure of—you know. (P. 107)

I suspect that Moran here is contemplating the pleasure of self-extinction. Once he starts doubting the reality of others, the question of his own reality becomes pressing, and if his existence is really all that wretched, then he might as well erase it along with the others.

By putting Moran in this position, Beckett has again found a metaphor to express chaotic vision, although this one is quite different from the dancing bees. After all, Moran, as observer, never doubted his own existence, not to mention the bees'. In his role as agent, however, Moran's mystification results from forces he cannot see, and their invisibility suggests something deeper than complexity: it questions the very nature of reality, the validity of perception, conception, and the most natural of assumptions; and finally, it uproots our identities, and throws them, too, into the area of the unknown. If there is no reality outside of ourselves, then there may be no reality inside, either. Even the most minimal certainties of life are whisked away and the whole world becomes a bad dream, the illusion of a madman. If nothing is knowable, then everything is mysterious, for as in Kafka's world, we can never hope for enough facts to effectively limit the reasonable possibilities. Life then becomes unreasonable, and here is where our minds buckle under and leave us to manage as we can among effects that we ourselves might be causing. It is all too deep for the mind to fathom, so our suffering leads to no realizations, but only fearful feelings about an uncertain, threatening future.

In one of the most pungent, startling, but strikingly appropriate metaphors in the book, Molloy, who is always unable to justify the journey which absorbs his whole life, admits getting back into the saddle with a prick of misgiving in his heart, "like one dying of cancer obliged to consult his dentist." The irony here is bitter and depressing, for surely, the victim of a terminal disease must feel some kind of ultimate absurdity in an aching tooth; after all, why fix a faulty part when the entire system is already rotted beyond repair? And yet the answer would have to be because it *hurts* and we still need to relieve whatever pain we can from our lives. Applied to Molloy, the question becomes: What good are limited objectives when the main journey is no more than a side-trip to nowhere? If one doesn't know where he's going, how is he to know when he's wandering in the right direction? Man's basic existential dilemma immediately and emphatically undermines traditional values, concerns, goals. Molloy must move because the torment of each moment pushes him away from the spot in which he's suffering and drives him to another point on the circle. Molloy's basic condition is incurable, so is it worth the trouble to search out short-term comforts? Renewal of contact with his mother? Marriage? Money? Love? It's really so much easier—since nothing can be done *really* to alleviate his distress—to suck stones. Symbols of sterility, the stones provide no nourishment, but Molloy's use of them becomes a metaphor for the lowest common denominator of all our lifetime goals, which consist simply of trying to get maximum pleasure—otherwise known as happiness—from the thin resources of our world. Molloy's changing of the stones is reminiscent of Sisyphus' rolling of the rock: both actions recognize the absurd but accommodate themselves to it with a purity that we can hardly help admiring. When we stop resisting the mystery of our universe, but begin instead to shape our lives accordingly, we have moved from the tragedy of K. to the absurdity of Molloy—and this sense of absurdity is founded upon a recognition of and reconciliation to chaos as the signification of the fundamental foolishness of our lives.

Another aspect of Beckett's chaos is the disunity of all phenomena. Moran feels assailed by "things," and his eyes "search in vain for two things alike, each pinpoint of skin screams a different message. . . ." Phenomenology asserts that matter, too, is chaotic: things do not fall together in meaningful categories but instead individualize themselves with peculiar and often terrifying possibilities. As in Sartre's *Nausea,* objects lose their everyday identities and can no longer be defined. An apple might be dangerous, a tree might turn killer, a pavement is infinitely mysterious. As phenomena tumble out of the categories established for them by the human mind, chaos reigns in a most vivid and frightening way. Classification is the first step to knowledge, and knowledge is man's first step to safety. Without it, he remains disoriented, unprotected, and vulnerable to anything he does not know—which is everything. All forms are strange, all men are strangers. Moran is able to distinguish "each pinpoint" of his skin as "I drown in the spray of phenomena" (p. 111). This kind of chaos is probably the most devastating, and it is doubtful that one can keep his sanity long in such an atmosphere.

Strangely enough, Beckett's chaos is also characterized by the melting together of all forms into indistinguishable matter. This would seem at first to contradict the dissimilarity of all things which we have just mentioned, but Beckett's universe is much darker than Sartre's so that, while each object may be unique, its *effect* is much the same in the cloudy atmosphere of *Molloy.* While Moran may feel his senses bombarded by phenomena, he considers such sensations illusory, and can therefore enjoy them for the dramatic contrast they offer in an essentially ponderous world, composed of slow-moving masses of matter floating silently around him. By negating the reality of everything outside the self, solipsism causes phenomena to retreat into the pervasive darkness. Thus, while watching A and C moving slowly toward each other, Molloy observes that "they looked alike, but no more than others do" (p. 9), and while speaking of Lousse, he finds himself uncertain of her sex, then confuses her with Ruth, another "old hag," and finally finds his mother's image merging with both of theirs. In Beckett's reductive universe, phenomena and people and places rarely become distinct enough to pose much of a threat; they tend, instead, to recede into shadows where their identities become a mystery, floating out of forms and into the general drift of matter, where everything assumes the same color and sinks into the morass.

A final component of Beckett's chaos involves another paradox: "of finality without end," as Moran calls it (p. 111). Each moment seems the last, each breath terminal, each word final. Yet each breath, moment, and word leads to another, and still another without negating the conviction that nothing will follow after *this* word has been said, *this* moment lived, *this* breath expired. Each instant is a crisis, but combined, their common level denies significant experience. The concept of infinity is enough to throw man's mind into chaos, as is the sensation of living one's last moment; together, they defeat our mental and emotional systems, and hurl us into turmoil—which is exactly where Beckett wants us.

Molloy, then, promotes the impression of chaos through metaphor (communicating complexity, mystery, and absurdity), characterization (communicating solipsism and sameness), and structure (communicating "finality without end"). Beckett seems to have embraced Virginia Woolf's wedges of darkness, Kafka's nightmarish mystery, Melville's nihilism, Conrad's inscrutability, Sterne's non sequiturs, and Faulkner's confusion of time and space. The repercussions of chaotic vision are felt in every aspect of the novel, but aesthetic control is everywhere, too, as Beckett molds his forms into funnels that permit us to watch meaning being filtered out.

We must be careful, though, not to make this sound too neat, for while Beckett's artistry is everywhere evident, so is the suspicion that art cannot much longer contain the chaos before the dam created by form collapses from the corrosive force of its acidic content. It is not so much the strain of creating that Beckett is rebelling against as it is the gratuitousness of formalizing a vision which undermines the significance of forms. Art's value becomes questionable once it ceases to yield meaning, consolation, and control, and becomes useful only as distraction. By articulating silence, organizing the ooze, formalizing the incomprehensible, art falsifies whatever it touches, yet insists on touching even what it cannot transform. When Moran says that he has never been able to tell the stories of Watt, Murphy, Yerk, and Mercier, and that he will not be able to tell this one either, he is implying, I think, that the real stories are silent and the very *telling* of them distorts them. The act of creating does satisfy some need, but it is more a psychological crutch than anything else. Moran's "voice" tells him "that the memory of this work brought scrupulously to a close will help me to endure the long anguish of vagrancy and freedom" (p. 132), but then perhaps a game of cards would do as much. Art exists because silence is intolerable, not because silence is inexplicable. Art does not change the mystery, but simply provides an escape from it. After all, a work that ends back at its own beginning could hardly have been brought scrupulously to a close, and so any comfort Moran gets from it must lie in the means of telling it, not in terms of where it has gotten him.

As in *To the Lighthouse*, though, the creative process is laborious and exhausting. Both Molloy and Moran constantly contemplate giving it up entirely, but as Molloy has said, his resolutions never did have much bearing on his actions. Still, the two narrators (unlike Laurence Sterne) have little sense of obligation to the reader; they want the reader to feel the arbitrariness of their art lest he make the mistake of thinking he might be getting somewhere.

And as to saying what became of me, and where I went, in the months and perhaps the years that followed, no. For I weary of these inventions and others beckon to me. But in order to blacken a few more pages may I say I spent some time at the seaside, without incident. (P. 68)

Molloy's story is directed by his own spasmodic impulses, not by any requirements of aesthetic form. The story itself is gratuitous, for it is in the act of language only that some psychological benefits may be achieved. If the narrator suddenly finds himself in the middle of a plot, that is accidental, and he may turn away from it at will.

The more he turns, however, the more he loses, for anything that keeps the will alive is a move in the wrong direction. In this novel where both truth and balance are unattainable, the one great value is the ability to surrender. Once Moran sees the absurdity of men's lives and of any concept of nobility, he finds himself laughing bitterly and uncontrollably at the weak lights in the town which he had previously found so touching. Man's pathetic attempt to throw a little light onto the darkness is proof of his foolishness, not of his heroism. The only honorable gesture is to throw the light away, and wait to be absorbed into the darkness. It is only his pride that causes man to hug onto his identity and resist the true nature of the world's formlessness; and when Moran feels his resistance ebbing, he discovers a new happiness which mocks the old values of his "wretched existence." Surrender of the will is of course every bit as difficult for Moran as the

exertion of it was for Lily Briscoe, and the relaxation of all efforts
to push back death requires an immense lack of willpower,

but there were moments when it did not seem so far from me, when I
seemed to be drawing towards it as the sands towards the wave, when it
crests and whitens, though I must say this image hardly fitted my situation, which was rather like that of the turd waiting for the flush. And I
note here the little beat my heart once missed, in my home, when a fly,
flying low above my ash-tray, raised a little ash, with the breath of its
wings. And I grew gradually weaker and more and more content. For
several days I had eaten nothing. I could probably have found blackber-
ries and mushrooms, but I had no wish for them. I remained all day
stretched out in the shelter . . . and I crawled out in the evening to have
a good laugh at the lights of Bally. And though suffering a little from
wind and cramps in the stomach I felt elated, enchanted with my performance. And I said, I shall soon lose consciousness altogether, it is
merely a question of time. (Pp. 162–63)

The passage is typical—for Molloy as well as Moran—of the soothing calm resulting from recognition that one cannot alter his basic condition in the universe. All conflict, struggle, and suffering
subside as soon as Moran and Molloy resign themselves to the
absolute futility of trying to do anything to hold back the forces of
death, darkness, annihilation. Dissolution *into* chaos is more reasonable and gratifying than any resistance, art included. Perhaps
this is the most important lesson Moran learns from Molloy, for
whom "all roads were right for me, a wrong road was an event,
for me" (p. 30). It was Moran who had said

the more things resist me the more rabid I get. With time, and nothing
but my teeth and nails, I would rage up from the bowels of the earth to
its crust, knowing full well I had nothing to gain. And when I had no
more teeth, no more nails, I would dig through the rock with my bones.
(P. 156)

Taken together, these last two passages from Moran's narrative
show just how much progress has been made (though we must
remember that this is the process of decomposition). From the
blustery, self-disciplined, willful, calculating man who set out for
Molloy, Moran has reduced his concept of self-significance to that
of a turd and an ash. Scatology becomes a new necessity to destroy outdated conceptions of nobility, and Moran's identification
with turd is a purposeful contrast to the traditional image of
men's clean, well-lighted places in the town below. The ash image is perhaps ambivalent, but Moran seems to be admiring the

ash's ability to move with the slightest wind. The traditional image would of course focus on the fly's influence, frail as it is, and find some solace in the thought that even a fly can disturb the ash, just as man's actions may change the composition of a wasteland. But Moran seems to relate the fly to some higher power (such as Youdi, perhaps) which he can never hope to resist; he reserves the ash for himself because it seems to represent complete surrender of the will.

It is true that Moran ends his narrative with a self-conscious reference to the fact that he is still telling lies, still inventing, still creating. The will has not yet been killed, has not yet abdicated to the inevitable. Once again, art comes out slightly ahead. But this time it does seem to be a Pyrrhic victory: chaos has closed in, and art has been submerged. If it has risen to the surface again, that may mean only that it will bob up twice more, gasping for air, before going down for the last time—typical of the process of drowning. And it *is* a bit frightening to realize that Beckett has two more stories to present before his trilogy is complete.

> "I suppose the wisest thing now is to live it over again, meditate upon it and be edified."
> —*Malone Dies* [4]

Like Molloy, Malone is constantly making resolutions that mean very little, so it is not surprising that the above passage fails to describe the development of *Malone Dies.* First of all, edification remains an impossibility, and meditation a useless endeavor. Also, if there is a concept of wisdom in this book, it would consist in embracing death, not reliving life. Still, one must do something while waiting for death, and Malone decides that this is the proper time to amuse himself. He has already spent too much of his life in futile attempts to find meaning and now regrets his former seriousness: "I shall never do anything any more from now on but play" (p. 180). His games must be restricted, however, for he is still, as he has always been, alone. No matter: he will play by himself. All he needs is his imagination, a few memories, a pencil,

4. Samuel Beckett, *Malone Dies,* in *Three Novels by Samuel Beckett* (New York: Grove Press, 1965), p. 254. All future page references, cited in parentheses, are to this edition.

and some blank sheets of paper that he finds in an old exercise book. He will now enter into the book the exercises of his imagination; his goal is not edification but entertainment.

As the novel progresses, however, Malone's imaginative excursions begin to reflect his own experiences and state of mind, until the world he creates becomes indistinguishable from the one he inhabits. Just as Moran's report on Molloy is more about Moran than Molloy, Malone's fictional characters always become personas for himself. Malone's stories are projections of his own situations, and so his choice of characters is arbitrary: their names change, but they remain the same person. Malone writes: "Nothing is more real than nothing" (p. 192), and the implication is that nothingness can take whatever forms it chooses at random, just so long as the forms do not begin to render meaning, but remain insubstantial, empty. Forms are useful devices for enclosing space, but they must not be used to fill that space.

Malone does have a difficult time of it, though. He no sooner gets into a story than it takes a shape that he did not intend, grows unmistakably eloquent and suggestive, rich with atmosphere and emotion—and he is forced to stop it before it develops into a conventional novel. Artistically balanced phrases, colorful figures of speech, compelling plots—all spring forth effortlessly, until he must with effort cut off the flow of his imagination and return to his own situation. That situation is similar to those of Molloy and Moran, but Malone's is a bit further along in the decomposition process since his body has become completely useless to him and must keep its stagnant position in bed:

and perhaps he has come to that stage of his instant when to live is to wander the last of the living in the depths of an instant without bounds, where the light never changes and the wrecks look all alike. (P. 233)

This is the basic condition which Malone faces and wants to express. The novel is controlled and directed by this vision as Malone uses up his last instant of life trying to capture his impressions through an artistic process that concedes everything to chaos in method, form, and meaning.

It would have to. For the impressions that Malone wants to share are formless, colorless, and silent—indicative of nothing. Thus, no sooner does Malone create a persona than his character begins to duplicate his own condition. Sapo, left alone in a room, tries to focus on the light pouring through the windows, but it entered at every moment, renewed from without, entered and died at every moment, devoured by the dark. And at the least abatement of the inflow the room grew darker and darker until nothing in it was visible any more. For the dark had triumphed. And Sapo, his face turned towards an earth so resplendent that it hurt his eyes, felt at his back and all about him the unconquerable dark, and it licked the light on his face. Sometimes abruptly he turned to face it, letting it envelop and pervade him, with a kind of relief. . . . But silence was in the heart of the dark, the silence of dust and the things that would never stir, if left alone. And the ticking of the invisible alarm-clock was as the voice of that silence which, like the dark, would one day triumph too. And then all would be still and dark and all things at rest for ever at last. (P. 203)

The vacuum that is and has always been Malone's life is characterized by darkness, silence, and stagnation: lack of color, lack of sound, lack of movement. Malone's intention to tell stories is rather whimsical, therefore, because a story *implies* movement, language, and atmosphere. And his little spurts of imagination do begin to create conventional tales with plots, characters, and settings. But Malone immediately tires of his stories when he sees them falsifying reality; sooner or later he either drops them completely or steers them into corners where they parallel his own position. Although he tries at first to depart from himself—to heighten the end of his life by creating new life—he soon finds that all his stories eventually funnel back into their creator.

That must be in the natural order of things, all that pertains to me must be written there, including my inability to grasp what order is meant. For I have never seen any sign of any, inside me or outside me. I have pinned my faith to appearances, believing them to be vain. I shall not go into the details. Choke, go down, come up, choke, suppose, deny, affirm, drown. I depart from myself less gladly. (P. 210)

The drowning metaphor that closed the discussion of *Molloy* seems especially appropriate here, for Malone sees his whole life as having been a series of futile attempts to stay on top of the world of phenomena. Reason, of course, is man's sole means of staying afloat, but Malone's raft is losing air fast, and his mind continues to sink deeper and deeper into the natural disorder of things. He is, in fact, already sufficiently submerged to wonder whether he is still alive, or if he has not already died. He finds it impossible at times to distinguish the state of death from the process of dying (which is simply another term for living).

Since reason has never helped Malone understand his condition, he refuses to let his characters or readers benefit from the use of their minds. That may be why he suddenly changes characters in mid-stream. Without explanation, he abandons Sapo and replaces him with Macmann (although since all names are arbitrary anyway, we cannot assume that the new character is really any different), then immediately shoves him into the same situation that tormented Molloy and Moran. Lying face down in a ditch, Macmann knows only that he is suffering. How he got there, why he chooses to stay there—these are questions Malone will not stoop to answer, for that would imply a knowledge of causes he does not pretend to have. Our knowledge, in fact, is so limited that we cannot even trace the roots of our misery; Macmann *thinks* that his suffering would be greatly alleviated if the rain would stop, but he slowly begins to wonder whether that would make any real difference:

For while deploring he could not spend the rest of his life (which would thereby have been agreeably abridged) under this heavy, cold . . . and perpendicular rain, now supine, now prone, he was quarter-inclined to wonder if he was not mistaken in holding it responsible for his sufferings and if in reality his discomfort was not the effect of quite a different cause or set of causes. (P. 242)

Of course, Malone could (like Lucky in *Waiting for Godot*) try to hypothesize the reasons for Macmann's uncomfortable condition, but he quickly gives that up as a waste of time. After all, what does it matter why man suffers? What can causes tell us as long as the primary cause is always unknown? If we are dying, what difference does it make that we are dying from one thing rather than another? Why trace the origin of our pain? Causes do not matter because they get us nowhere; they cannot account for our situation because that situation existed before we did. The dark, silent, stagnant universe has nothing to tell us, so why must we insist on forming the right kinds of questions? All thinking is finally useless, since we can neither avoid nor transcend our submergence in chaos.

What, then, is the role of art in such a world? Virginia Woolf's conception of art's potential as an ordering principle can be dismissed immediately, for Malone has neither the desire nor the fortitude to take arms against the chaos enveloping him; his mind itself does not contain enough order for use as a controlling agent, and besides, Malone has by now given all that up—he has tried to approach life seriously and wring a bit of meaning from it, but he has met with such failure that he does not care to try again. After the successive defeats, "there comes the hour when nothing more can happen and nobody can come and all is ended but the waiting that knows itself in vain" (p. 241). Waiting, for Malone, carries no hint of expectation—it is a purely passive state deeply in touch with the vanity of striving and the despair of a life used up by something other than living. It is too late now to start living, and yet the tedium of waiting must be relieved, so Malone invents stories simply to pass the time. Previously, he had given no interest to means, but only to ends; now that the end (his death) is certain and close, however, he can disregard *it* and occupy himself instead with the means. But the basic gravity of his nature is not so easily dispelled; Malone eventually comes up with a new purpose: "to live, to invent." Perhaps, through the process of inventing, he can yet squeeze a little life from his existence:

Live and cause to live. There is no use indicting words, they are no shoddier than what they peddle. After the fiasco, the solace, the repose, I began again, to try and live, cause to live, be another in myself, in another. . . . I began again. But little by little with a different aim, no longer in order to succeed, but in order to fail. . . . To show myself now, on the point of vanishing, at the same time as the stranger, and by the same grace, that would be no ordinary last straw. Then live, long enough to feel, behind my closed eyes, other eyes close. What an end. (P. 195)

And so Malone invents the art of failure—that art which concentrates on life at the vanishing point, the instant before one disappears into death. Malone will create for the express purpose of destroying his creation; he will create a resounding affirmation of denial. Later when he says, "my notes have a curious tendency, as I realize at last, to annihilate all they purport to record" (p. 259), Malone seems to have insured his success at a self-negating art. Judged in this way, the novelist's accomplishment seems to lie in the extent to which all his actions and assertions have led to negatives. "I have spoken softly, gone my ways softly, all my days," Malone says, "as behooves one who has nothing to say, nowhere to go, and so nothing to gain by being seen or heard" (p. 253).

It is clear, though, that Malone still seeks something positive in his nihilism; otherwise, there would be no sense in re-creating his condition in a fictional character. If life itself is enough to negate the value of living, why is art necessary if it seeks nothing more? Malone's conception of art, even while aiming at self-destruction, remains conventionally motivated by an urge to control, to gain some power (if not knowledge) over life that is not possible without art.

All I ask is that the last of mine, as long as it lasts, should have living for its theme, that is all, I know what I mean. If it begins to run short of life I shall feel it. All I ask is to know, before I abandon him whose life has so well begun, that my death and mine alone prevents him from living on, from winning, losing, joying, suffering, rotting and dying. . . . (P. 198)

For one who makes no pretense of using his art to gain a foothold on life, Malone here is asking little less of his craft than to make him a god. He wants it to be in his power to create or extinguish life at will, and if he could accomplish this, it would have to grant art a positive potential that had not at first seemed possible. And Malone does end by finding compensation in art for his impotence in life. In the last moment of his life, as death begins to crush him out of existence, Malone experiences a spasm of triumph as the vise tightens:

Macmann, my last, my possessions, I remember, he is there too, perhaps he sleeps. Lemuel

Lemuel is in charge, he raises his hatchet on which the blood will never dry, but not to hit anyone, he will not hit anyone any more, he will not touch anyone any more, either with it or with it or with it or with or

or with it or with his hammer or with his stick or with his fist or in thought in dream I mean never he will never

or with his pencil or with his stick or

or light light I mean

never there he will never

never anything

there

any more (Pp. 287–88)

Lemuel had been inserted into the story about the time Malone had been awakened by a brutal blow on the head from behind. Completely at the mercy of the cruelty of this unknown visitor, Malone fictionalizes him, thereby gaining control over him. Now at the last moment, when Lemuel, like Death, threatens to annihilate Macmann who, like Malone, is in the most vulnerable, defenseless position, out in the sea, in no way able to ward off the blows of Lemuel, Malone realizes his victory as creator: he has saved Macmann from death (which makes it possible for him to remember and list his created character as the last, but surely one of the most treasured, of his possessions) and prevented Lemuel from ever carrying out his schemes of violent destruction. Even while Malone loses the life he never expected to keep, he has managed to wring something from himself in those last moments (days? years?) that consoles him as he finally fades away into the silence. Through his act of language, he has created a life that will outlive him and has found through that life a bit of life in himself. He had asked that his death and his alone prevent someone else from living, and that goal has been achieved when Lemuel is frozen forever with his hatchet raised. Malone dies, but Macmann has been freed. For one whose life has lacked joy, Malone's death seems a strangely happy one. Ultimately, art has not been able to destroy all it created. Something does remain, and—despite Malone's cynicism—it is clear that that something is to be valued.

Moving from Malone to Beckett, we can see that the radical devices used in the novel have been effective techniques calculated to shape vision, communicate chaos, and produce tension. Beckett pushes the reader into a position where he must struggle constantly for the control he finally achieves only at the moment Malone achieves his. Until the significance of Malone's dying thoughts have been impressed upon the reader, he is not permitted to feel the security normally provided even by the chaotic novel—that he is reading a completed work of fiction rather than a rough draft for one that cannot seem to emerge from the chaos it is trying to project. We can say finally that *Malone Dies* is a novel about an artist struggling with his creation in a philosophical void which devalues not only his art but the very struggle to produce it. Malone's failures do not seem meaningful until his final success; and that success would seem too slight to be significant if it were not for the frequent failures that preceded it. Beckett, then, has kept his form submerged in chaos until it seems to have disappeared altogether. When it suddenly bobs up again at the end, we are amazed to find that it has chaos in its clutches; it had seemed all along the other way around.

Nevertheless, we cannot underestimate the damage done by chaos as the novel absorbs it to such a degree that the salvaged form seems shapeless and insubstantial. Whereas the novel has traditionally been an expanding experience, opening up creative possibilities, it now appears to be caving in, as all forms and representations of life are crushed out, reduced to a common denominator which flattens impressions, stifles vitality, and grinds down the particular. Chaos, as a reductive agent, irons out the individual effect until all things reflect only one thing: the vacuum that persists after significance has been washed away.

There is no dialogue in *Malone Dies* because Malone cannot decipher individual sounds in order to know them as voices:

> What I mean is possibly this, that the noises of the world, so various in themselves and which I used to be so clever at distinguishing from one another, had been dinning at me for so long, always the same old noises, as gradually to have merged into a single noise, so that all I heard was the vast continuous buzzing. The volume of sound perceived remained no doubt the same, I had simply lost the faculty of decomposing it. The noises of nature, of mankind, and even my own, were all jumbled together in one and the same unbridled gibberish. (P. 207)

Malone's inability to distinguish the individual voice—including those outside him from those inside of him—means that he cannot represent anything without confusing it with its opposite. He may hear words and write them down, but so long as he is unable to know who said them, the reader is at a loss to evaluate their significance. Traditionally the novel has offered us highly individualized speakers whose particular patterns of expression become an important part of their identity. Here, however, there is only one voice running through the novel, absorbing identities and echoing through every form, no matter how dissimilar. The effect, of course, is just to make these forms resemble one another so closely that they finally converge into an indistinguishable mass, a wall of sound sounding like nothing so much as silence.

Colors, too, melt into one another in Malone's world. Granted, we never had much to work with in Beckett anyway, but there was, in *Murphy* at least, a clear distinction between black and white. Not anymore:

> Yes, no doubt one may speak of grey, personally I have no objection, in which case the issue here would lie between the grey and the black that it overlays more or less, I was going to say according to the time of day, but no, it does not always seem to depend on the time of day. I myself

am very grey, I even sometimes have the feeling that I emit grey, in the same way as my sheets for example. (P. 221)

Again there is no distinction made between human and inanimate forms, or between the source and ultimate manifestations of grayness. It encompasses all, emanates from all, and settles everywhere. That is why, later on, when Malone, in a burst of imaginative fire, starts to describe the setting of the plateau on which Macmann finds himself, he gets no farther than the stream before he cuts it all off with: "but to hell with all this fucking scenery" (p. 277). Since the grayness infiltrates each setting and becomes ultimately the most accurate description of the atmosphere, Malone decides not to bother with the surface details.

Beckett's principle of reduction works on the intellect, as well as the senses. The gray matter in the brain provides no more clarity than the gray matter outside. As Macmann lies in his ditch, "the ideas of guilt and punishment were confused together in his mind, as those of cause and effect so often are in the minds of those who continue to think" (p. 240). Malone, of course, is himself one of those unfortunates, but there is a grace in his acceptance of mental blurs that one can hardly help admiring:

It's vague, life and death, I must have had my little private idea on the subject when I began, otherwise I would not have begun. . . . But it is gone clean out of my head, my little private idea. No matter, I have just had another. Perhaps it is the same one back again, ideas are so alike, when you get to know them. (P. 225)

All concepts, ideas, theories, and distinctions that the mind works so hard to achieve are here disregarded as interchangeable falsifications. In reality, everything is so much alike—even life and death—that the attempt to differentiate is presumptuous and absurd.

In the same way, the whole experience of living can be boiled down to a feeling or two. One suffers, feels frustrated, longs for release, finally gets it—what life amounts to more? Malone mocks his character for implying that reality has more than one dimension: when Macmann cries out, "I have had enough," Malone sees "enough" as the quintessential response to all experience, and so ridicules his creation who spoke without considering what it was he had had enough of, without deliberating on what alternative he had in mind to replace the enough that had become too much, "and without suspecting that the thing so often felt to be excessive, and honored by such a variety of names, was perhaps in reality always one and the same. But there was one reflecting in his place and setting down coldly the sign of equality where it was needed, as if that could make any difference" (p. 278). Macmann is desperate to scale the wall, but Malone sees the absurdity of assuming that his character will find a different reality there. Reality equals itself on either side, so that the very notion of escape becomes ludicrous.

Since reality and experience are repetitive, it is not surprising that people are, too. No matter how many times Malone changes his stories, they all begin to center on the same person. Even when the name is changed, the sufferer remains constant because he too has been reduced to essentials:

It is true the Macmanns are legion in the island and pride themselves, what is more, with few exceptions, on having one and all, in the last analysis, sprung from the same illustrious ball. It is therefore inevitable they should resemble one another, now and then, to the point of being confused even in the minds of those who wish them well and would like nothing better than to tell between them. No matter, any old remains of flesh and spirit do, there is no sense in stalking people. So long as it is what is called a living being you can't go wrong, you have the guilty one. (P. 259)

What Beckett is doing here distinguishes him sharply from the other writers of chaos I have discussed. Whereas Faulkner, Conrad, Melville, and Virginia Woolf have focused on the enigmatic qualities of their characters and the difficulty of ever knowing enough about the human personality to evaluate it properly, Beckett has cut right through the mystery of man and concentrated on the core underlying appearances. He has no interest in specifics, only in the common denominator which characterizes the human condition. The psychological complexities of the individual, the thin line between honorable and dishonorable motivation, the whole problem of ethical behavior—all these matters are dismissed as trivial when compared to the basic drives, fears, and responses uniting us. Underneath our different colors, sizes, shapes, and features flows the same blood, beats the same chunk of meat, lies the same skeleton. We live in different countries but suffer in the same reality; we set up different goals but fail to attain the ones we treasure most; we contain different combinations of good and evil, but feel guilty for the wrong things; we live in different cultures worshiping different gods but feel alienated from the solace and nourishment that social life and religion are supposed to provide. Beckett would never have written *King Lear*, but he might well have written the story of Poor Tom of Bedlam—and even Lear learns the principal lesson of his identity when he realizes that the same shivering fellow exists under all his kingly robes. Nevertheless, it is true that Shakespeare sees man's life as being complicated by his social roles, whereas Beckett no longer seems interested in *any* facet near the surface.

Since man's world is a hostile one and his own condition characterized by struggling and suffering, Malone sees no nobility to be gained from man's contest with the elements. His world is so devoid of values—either moral or existential—that the most he can wish for his character, "since wishing costs nothing," is "sooner or later a general paralysis sparing at a pinch the arms if that is conceivable, in a place impermeable as far as possible to wind, rain, sound, cold, great heat . . . and daylight" (p. 245). There is no sense here of admirable behavior, heroic action, or even the minimal value of endurance. It would simply be nice if Macmann could feel less so that he might suffer less.

It seems, then, that Beckett in this novel has brought his reductive principle to bear on every aspect of the novel: the sensuous, intellectual, ethical, philosophical, and human elements are all put through a vise which flattens form, restricts movement, and compresses value systems until nothing is left but a one-dimensional surface which equalizes meanings. There is no growth, no development, no expansion—only arbitrary shifts in the forms used to represent nothingness. "The forms are many in which the unchanging seeks relief from its formlessness," says Malone (p. 197), and this justifies the creation of new forms as immediate replacements for those which have gone stale. In this way, the novel progresses, but only as it continues to find a variety of images to represent stagnation.

The sole value left, therefore, is the creative impulse itself, although it is difficult to assess its exact importance. Malone, at one point, seems to stress the sheer challenge of the creative act while devaluing the finished product which, made in his image, would be born for failure anyway:

But what matter whether I was born or not, have lived or not, am dead or merely dying, I shall go on doing as I have always done, not knowing what it is I do, nor who I am, nor where I am, nor if I am. Yes, a little creature, I shall try and make a little creature, to hold in my arms, a little creature in my image, no matter what I say. And seeing what a poor thing I have made, or how like myself, I shall eat it. Then be alone a long time, unhappy, not knowing what my prayer should be nor to whom. (P. 226)

It would seem from this that Malone wishes to create for the purpose of companionship. He wants to cut through his isolation, making something resembling himself, but outside himself so that he can hold it, cherish it, and ultimately—out of pity—eat it. After having performed this art-as-cookie-making process, he would still be alone, but he would have had at least the paternal satisfaction of self-sacrifice for something he loved. Yet a bit later, when he feels his character taking shape, he says: "I slip into him, I suppose in the hope of learning something" (p. 226). Does this indicate that Malone is using his art as a means toward greater knowledge, after all? It would be hard to answer this question conclusively, for Malone's attitude is inconsistent throughout. At times, his ambivalence leads to a state of such tension that he cannot seem certain even of his own cynicism:

Yes, I leave my happiness and go back to the race of men. . . . Perhaps I have judged them ill, but I don't think so, I have not judged them at all. All I want now is to make a last effort to understand, to begin to understand, how such creatures are possible. No, it is not a question of understanding. Of what then? I don't know. Here I go none the less, mistakenly. Night, storm, and sorrow, and the catalepsies of the soul, this time I shall see that they are good. The last word is not yet said between me and—yes the last word is said. Perhaps I simply want to hear it said again. Just once again. No, I want nothing. (P.199)

Malone's skepticism here proves only that art's potential has not yet been fully negated, even if he is trying to talk himself into the futility of thinking one more attempt might work where the others failed. Certainly, though, the possibilities of art are played with endlessly in the novel, and Beckett's principle of reduction wavers only on this question of art's value.

I have said that Malone's dying words seem to signify art's triumph as a meaningful force in a meaningless world, but if we look closely at Malone's difficulty in creating, we are forced to recognize the terribly precarious position of an art struggling to formalize chaotic vision. The trouble begins right away: Malone spins out a story in order to get away from himself, yet begins to wonder immediately if he is not still talking about himself. He resolves to be on his guard and continues. It is not long, however, before he stops again: "I have tried to reflect on the beginning of my story. There are things I do not understand. But nothing to signify. I can go on" (p. 189). Already, the author has lost control of his own story. Already it exists as another thing he cannot understand. Aspects of the chaos. But he will not be stopped so easily; he continues. A few more sentences, then another breakdown. He has stated a fact but cannot explain it. Time out for thought, because while a little darkness is nothing, "I know what darkness is, it accumulates, thickens, then suddenly bursts and drowns everything" (p. 190). Malone will not take any chances. He will take a moment to find the explanation so that this little bit of darkness cannot become a threat. Thought. But no result. So Malone will go on without it, after all. But cautiously:

We shall turn our backs on this little cloud, but we shall not let it out of our sight. It will not cover the sky without our knowing, we shall not suddenly raise our eyes, far from help, far from shelter, to a sky as black as ink. That is what I have decided. I see no other solution. It is the best I can do. (P. 190)

Malone is losing control quickly; his authority as author is weakening. And things get worse:

Sapo loved nature, took an interest in

This is awful.

Sapo loved nature, took an interest in animals and plants. . . . (P. 191)

Already his story is full of false starts; he cannot seem to get the momentum going, and meanwhile the darkness is growing from that one unexplained fact in the very beginning. Things are going badly. Still, he pushes on. A few more paragraphs. Good. Some progress now. It's off the ground. Then, a breakdown:

In his country the problem—no, I can't do it.

the peasants. His visits to. I can't. (P. 196)

But he continues. And images begin eventually to take on force; situations turn effortlessly into metaphors both of his own brave attempt to work with chaos and his frequent impatience with the difficult role of artist. Describing Mrs. Lambert's simple act of sorting lentils, Malone grows eloquent as he discovers a metaphor to express his own position:

She set down the lamp on the table and the outer world went out. She sat down, emptied out the lentils on the table and began to sort them. So that soon there were two heaps on the table, one big heap getting smaller and one small heap getting bigger. But suddenly with a furious gesture she swept the two together, annihilating thus in less than a second the work of two or three minutes. . . . To stop in the middle of a tedious and perhaps futile task was something that Sapo could readily understand. For a great number of tasks are of this kind, without a doubt, and the only way to end them is to abandon them. She could have gone on sorting her lentils all night and never achieved her purpose, which was to free them from all admixture. But in the end she would have stopped, saying, I have done all I can do. But she would not have done all she could have done. But the moment comes when one desists, because it is the wisest thing to do, discouraged, but not to the extent of undoing all that has been done. But what if her purpose, in sorting the lentils, were not to rid them of all that was not lentil, but only of the greater part, what then? I don't know. Whereas there are other tasks, other days, of which one may fairly safely say that they are finished, though I do not see which. (Pp. 213–14)

Changing his forms as he goes along, Malone eventually builds up confidence as he comes to accept the arbitrariness of his art and then to relish it:

I simply believe I can say nothing that is not true, I mean that has not happened, it's not the same thing but no matter. . . . Yes, no reflection is needed, before or after, I have only to open my mouth for it to testify to the old story, my old story, and to the long silence that has silenced me, so that all is silent. And if I ever stop talking it will be because there is nothing more to be said, even though all has not been said, even though nothing has been said. . . . Then it will be all over with the Murphys, Merciers, Molloys, Morans, and Malones, unless it goes on beyond the grave. (P. 236)

Malone realizes now that everything he says will be relevant, for it all melts into the general silence that is his theme. Just as all sounds and voices are reduced to a general din, so any sounds he adds to the din will converge easily with the rest of the chaos. Again, one goes on, not because reflection has explained or justified his reasons for continuing, but simply because the voice keeps speaking. Is it quite as arbitrary as all that? Yes. All this nonsense about free will notwithstanding, one does what one does out of inner necessity, not out of conviction or determination. When Sapo leaves home, for example, he follows the dictates of that inner voice which drives him in one direction rather than another. "And when he halted it was not the better to think, or the closer to pore upon his dream, but simply because the voice had ceased that told him to go on" (p. 206). And Malone will create, stop, pick up, or destroy his stories according to the same arbitrary standard: the narrative hangs in suspense moment by moment as the author writes. As long as the words keep coming, he will continue; when they stop, he will stop. As an aesthetic procedure, this is quite shaky, but as a method for capturing (through duplication) the inexplicable qualitites of chaos, Malone's fragments tell just the story he wants to get told: if there is a plot, it is the story of a man living in chaos, writing in chaos, dying in chaos. Malone does learn, finally, how to handle his subject matter.

Another characteristic of Malone's art—and one that follows naturally from the arbitrary narrative method—is its total gratuitousness. Art is a manner of playing; it is not a philosophical tool, not a spiritual staircase, not a handbook for the psyche. It need not attempt to find causes or answer questions:

I shall not answer any more questions. I shall even try not to ask myself any more. While waiting I shall tell myself stories, if I can. They will not be the same kind of stories as hitherto, that is all. They will be neither beautiful nor ugly, they will be calm, there will be no ugliness or beauty or fever in them any more, they will be almost lifeless, like the teller. (P. 180)

This idea recurs frequently throughout the book, as Malone feels the ultimate peace behind wild phenomena—a peace which obviates the necessity for searching, penetrating, analyzing the images which strew themselves on the floor of the mind:

Words and images run riot in my head, pursuing, flying, clashing, merging, endlessly. But beyond this tumult there is a great calm, and a great indifference, never really to be troubled by anything again. (P. 198)

And later: "I must state the facts, without trying to understand, to the end" (p. 249). Art's ultimate uselessness somehow does not deny its value as an intensifier. Malone is obsessed with facts and details, even while he expects to do nothing with them—and this makes him qualify as the Absurd creator defined by Albert Camus in his *Myth of Sisyphus*. Once absurdity has been recognized, Camus says, art's function changes, but it still plays a vital role in man's self-awareness, by helping him experience his own life. According to Camus, the constant tension that keeps man face to face with the world, the ordered delirium that urges him to be receptive to everything leaves him another fever. In this universe the work of art is then the sole chance of keeping his consciousness and of fixing its adventures. Creating is living doubly. . . . All try their hands at miming, at repeating, and at re-creating the reality that is theirs. . . . For the absurd man it is not a matter of explaining and solving, but of experiencing and describing. Everything begins with lucid indifference.

Describing—that is the last ambition of an absurd thought. . . . The heart learns thus that the emotion delighting us when we see the world's aspects comes to us not from its depth but from their diversity. Explanation is useless, but the sensation remains and, with it, the constant attractions of a universe inexhaustible in quantity. The place of the work of art can be understood at this point.

It marks both the death of an experience and its multiplication. It is a sort of monotonous and passionate repetition of the themes already orchestrated by the world. . . .

For an absurd work of art to be possible, thought in its most lucid form must be involved in it. But at the same time thought must not be apparent except as the regulating intelligence. . . . The work of art is born of the intelligence's refusal to reason the concrete. . . . It will not yield to the temptation of adding to what is described a deeper meaning that it knows to be illegitimate. . . . The absurd work requires an artist conscious of these limitations and an art in which the concrete signifies nothing more than itself.

. . . The absurd work illustrates thought's renouncing of its prestige and its resignation to being no more than the intelligence that works up appearances and covers with images what has no reason. If the world were clear, art would not exist.[5]

Malone, then, seems fully aware of his intentions to render life in order to experience its nothingness more intensely, and to be able to fix his experience onto his consciousness. To render life is not, however, to render or imply meaning, or to attempt to transcend the reality we are trying to take into our minds. Malone's art is gratuitous, therefore, because it seeks nothing more than to represent the emptiness it knows to be reality. It does not try to make life any more bearable, but only more visible. It does not try to capture meaning but only to intensify our consciousness of the *lack* of meaning.

5. Albert Camus, *The Myth of Sisyphus and other Essays* (New York: Random House, 1955), pp.69–73.

Still, Malone cannot seem to keep his art from falsifying; he often replaces the word "tell" with "invent," and the word "invent" with "lying." "That is not what I said," he insists at one point, "I could swear to it, that is what I wrote" (p. 209). Yet art's tendency to falsify may be part of its purpose for Malone, who sees it as a pretext foɪ not coming to the point:

But that is all beside the point, like so many things. All is pretext, Sapo and the birds, Moll, the peasants, those who in the towns seek one another out and fly from one another, my doubts which do not interest me, my situation, my possessions, pretext for not coming to the point, the abandoning, the raising of the arms and going down, without further splash, even though it may annoy the bathers. (P. 276)

Once again, as in *Molloy,* art becomes the thin lifeline saving man from his suicidal craving for immersion in chaos (*that,* of course, is the point, while all living is beside and despite the point). As the line wears down, however, drowning becomes imminent. Perhaps Malone is saved by his willingness to struggle for a while yet with his art. At least it is quite clear that once art has lost its battle, all positive values have been lost with it, and the only worthy alternative becomes a ringing affirmation of self-annihilation:

To be buried in lava and not turn a hair, it is then that a man shows what stuff he is made of. To know you can do better next time, unrecognizably better, and that there is no next time, and that it is a blessing there is not, there is a thought to be going on with. (P. 254)

Earlier in the book, Malone has wondered about the right thing to pray for. He finally finds it as he contemplates drowning: "the horror-worn eyes linger abject on all they have beseeched so long, in a last prayer, the true prayer at last, the one that asks for nothing" (p. 277).

Malone's art has provided him with some life to experience before his death, but the compensation of that gain must be severely qualified by what seems an even greater triumph: Malone's final and complete disappearance in the chaos he used his art to pray for.

"Where I am there is no one but me, who am
not."   —*The Unnamable*[6]

As we slip into *The Unnamable,* we seem at the same time to be
slipping out of the novel. Whereas *Molloy* and *Malone Dies* are
elliptical, *The Unnamable* may be unreadable: the novel's immersion in chaos is here so complete that drowning has by now become a fact; it is simply a matter of filling out the death warrant.
The novel of chaos has always been characterized by its skeptical
view of knowledge and its unwillingness to provide the reader
with any sense of complete clarity; there are areas of darkness
that cannot be mastered or even coped with effectively. But consider the area of the reader's ignorance in *The Unnamable:* he
can find no action (much less plot); he cannot identify—even in
the most minimal sense—the narrator, the subject, or the object
of the story; he cannot work with metaphors, interpret forms, or
put the slightest faith in language. Instead, he is confronted with
an experience that seems an exercise in tedium—flat, repetitive,
stagnant, formless, mystifying.

It is clear from the beginning that the book's effects are intentional. The unidentified narrative voice ("I seem to speak, it is not
I, about me, it is not about me," p. 291) explains its procedure as
haphazard:

The best is not to decide anything, in this connexion, in advance. If a
thing turns up, for some reason or another, take it into consideration. . . .
The thing to avoid, I don't know why, is the spirit of system. . . . The best
would be not to begin. But I have to begin. (P. 292)

In his determination to have his work catch the flux of reality, the
narrator is willing to throw the novel itself into the muck and let
it ooze along with everything else. Now this much the reader can
accept with little trouble: Laurence Sterne's narrative in *Tristram Shandy* was also used to reflect the chaotic meanderings of
the mind, and while its progress was purposely elusive, we had
only to adjust some and suspend other expectations for the technique to work effectively. Meanwhile, too, we had the stability of
Tristram's character to balance the caprice of his narrative. But

---

6. Samuel Beckett, *The Unnamable,* in *Three Novels by Samuel Beckett* (New
York: Grove Press, 1965), p. 355. All future page references, cited in parentheses,
are to this edition.

Beckett's narrator is unknown throughout. He might be the author, he might be the persona, he might be a disembodied voice belonging to no one, he might not even exist at all. Even our pronoun is arbitrary, for the speaker is unwilling to take responsibility for what he is saying. He does try to convince us that there is some discipline to his method yet admits immediately that the mind in control may not be his own:

For what I am doing is not being done without a minimum of mind. Not mine perhaps, granted, with pleasure, but I draw on it, at least I try and look as if I did. Rich matter there, to be exploited, fatten you up, suck it to the core, keep you going for years, tasty into the bargain, I quiver at the thought, give you my word, spoken in jest, quiver and hurry on, all life before me, on and forget, what I was saying, just now, something important, it's gone, it'll come back, no regrets, as good as new, unrecognizable, let's hope so, someday . . . I'll forbid myself everything, then go on as if I hadn't. (Pp. 311–12)

It is not simply that the natural chaos of the mind—characterized by stream of association, contradictions, memory lapses, etc.—has been tossed directly into the narrative of the novel but that this particular mind cannot be identified, that makes things so difficult for the reader. Where *are* these thoughts coming from? From the speaker himself, whoever he or she or it is, or from some outside source, whatever that is or they are or he, she, or it is? Obviously, the reader cannot orient himself to the narrative techniques with the ease he was able to in *Tristram Shandy.*

But difficulty is one thing, and futility another. What *can* we do with a voice that says: "To tell the truth, let us be honest at least, it is some considerable time now since I last knew what I was talking about" (p. 323)? Because we cannot conceptualize the speaker, it is hard to see a tongue in anybody's cheek; and if we take it seriously, we are quite lost, for there is no one to take responsibility for this statement. Of course, we can gain some security if we see the voice as a metaphor, but a metaphor for what? Could the following words be the voice of reason itself spinning around in a vacuum?

At no moment do I know what I'm talking about, nor of whom, nor of where, nor how, nor why, but I could employ fifty wretches for this sinister operation and still be short of a fifty-first, to close the circuit, that I know, without knowing what it means. The essential is never to arrive anywhere, never to be anywhere. . . . The essential is to go on squirming forever at the end of the line. . . . (P. 338)

This might represent reason's inability to deal effectively with a world full of unknowns, yet another passage on the same page would seem to make this conclusion a trap:

That the impossible should be asked of me, good, what else could be asked of me? But the absurd! Of me whom they have reduced to reason. It is true poor Worm is not to blame for this. That's soon said. But let me complete my views, before I shit on them. For if I am Mahood, I am Worm too, plop. Or if I am not yet Worm, I shall be when I cease to be Mahood, plop. (P. 338)

Who are "they" who have "reduced" this voice to reason? And can reason be detached from the mind using it? Finally, can reason reasonably deny itself by shitting on its own syllogisms? There are two hypotheses produced in the above passage, yet each is followed by the unmistakable sound of falling turd. The metaphor, then, would have to represent something that shits on reason, not reason itself.

So perhaps the voice is the sound of chaos, overrunning reason and flowing endlessly through and around all forms—pure matter to be contained, shaped, or pounded into something recognizable but always more elusive than the form it takes. Unnamable itself, it resists definition yet might be the raw stuff of life which art works on to control. Has Beckett here refused to embody or formalize chaos but instead permitted it to run rampant so that it can be represented without being captured? At times, the voice does seem to possess substance along with an awareness of its malleability:

Ah if they could only begin, and do what they want with me, and succeed at last, in doing what they want with me, I'm ready to be whatever they want, I'm tired of being matter, pawed and pummelled endlessly in vain. Or give me up and leave me lying in a heap, in such a heap that none would ever be found again so try and fashion it. . . . yet they don't know what they want to do with me, they don't know where I am, or what I'm like. I'm like dust, they want to make a man out of dust. Listen to them, losing heart! That's to lull me, till I imagine I hear myself saying, myself at last, to myself at last, that it can't be they, speaking thus, that it can only be I, speaking thus. Ah if I could only find a voice of my own, in all this babble, it would be the end of their troubles, and of mine. (P. 348)

But before we conclude that chaos has found its own voice at last and need not be falsified by finding itself incorporated into images, we must remember that this voice suffers, that it has a will, and that it yearns for its termination in silence. True chaos would have none of these qualitites: nothingness is static and need not set out on a quest for itself—it is *man* who searches, feels, and reflects. While the voice is ambiguous ("Nothing ever troubles me. And yet I am troubled," p. 293), it has too many qualities which we recognize as human to be a satisfactory representation of chaos unreeling in a void.

Since consciousness is a property of man rather than matter, we are back to a more conventional narrator. Could it be the author himself? Again we have possibilities galore. At the beginning of the book, the voice, while acknowledging his real situation as a solitary in darkness, resolves: "I shall have company. In the beginning. A few puppets. Then I'll scatter them, to the winds, if I can" (p. 292). Enter Malone—or is it Molloy?—while the presence of all those from Murphy on are felt, if not clearly deciphered. Of course we all know not to confuse the author with his persona, but after all, we *know* who created these characters, so why not call the voice Beckett's? He says: "I have been here, ever since I began to be, my appearances elsewhere having been put in by other parties" (p. 293)—and we begin to feel that this surely *is* the author speaking, the ventriloquist finally tired of speaking through others, determined to have *his* own say at last:

All these Murphys, Molloys and Malones do not fool me. They have made me waste my time, suffer for nothing, speak of them when, in order to stop speaking, I should have spoken of me and of me alone. But I just said I have spoken of me, am speaking of me. I don't care a curse what I just said. It is now I shall speak of me, for the first time. I thought I was right in enlisting these sufferers of my pains. I was wrong. They never suffered my pains, their pains are nothing, compared to mine, a mere tittle of mine, the tittle I thought I could put from me, in order to witness it. Let them be gone now, them and all the others, those I have used and those I have not used, give me back the pains I lent them and vanish, from my life, my memory, my terrors and shames. There, now there is no one here but me, no one wheels about me, no one comes towards me, no one has ever met anyone before my eyes, these creatures have never been, only I and this black void have ever been. . . . Nothing then but me, of which I know nothing, except that I have never uttered, and this black, of which I know nothing either, except that it is black, and empty. That then is what, since I have to speak, I shall speak of, until I need speak no more. And Basil and his gang? Inexistent, invented to explain I forget what. Ah yes, all lies, God and man, nature and the light of day, the heart's outpourings and the means of understanding, all invented, basely, by me alone, with the help of no one, since there is no one, to put off the hour when I must speak of me. There will be no more about them. (Pp. 303–4)

If the voice *is* Beckett's, then this passage represents, I think, a crucial point in the development—or disintegration—of the novel. Here metaphor breaks down, and the artist wishes to communicate directly. After all, the characters he had created were all lies, fabrications functioning as metaphors for his own condition, his own problems, his own pain. Finally the mysterious "I" becomes identified as the artist comes crashing through the curtain . . . or does he? It is possible. Certainly, Beckett's relation to the reader is uncomfortably intimate at times, as if all metaphor had indeed perished and the author is now after direct confrontation with his reader. He speaks of the characters he created, which seemed to him the most successful, why they were finally all unsuccessful, etc. Yet the feeling persists (and grows on repeated readings) that this author is but another persona after all, that even while Beckett's voice may be interfused with the jumble of noise pouring forth, the voice is somehow either more or less than the writer's own. After all, can we believe that Beckett himself lived for a while in a jar or experienced many of the other transformations of the "voice"? The most we can say, finally, is that the author may well be one of the voice's transmutations, one of the forms from which the words pour incessantly, but that the voice cannot be restricted to that single identity. Once in the dark (and that is where the author has placed us), we cannot expect to decipher individual voices, any more than Malone was able to. If we think we hear the author at times, our impression is not necessarily wrong, but other voices come galloping at us too, and unless the ventriloquist is throwing his voice into different areas of the darkness (in which case, he *is* again creating metaphors, thus invalidating any assumption that he is addressing us directly), we are forced to acknowledge that the unidentified "I" remains a mystery.

Then what about Mahood and Worm? Two personas *are* picked up along the way, yet they lack the substance and unity of Molloy, Moran, Macmann, and Malone. These seem total abstractions, unencumbered by form. Still, Mahood looks familiar right away. "Before Mahood there were others like him, of the same breed and creed, armed with the same prong" (p. 337), and indeed, he is inseparable from Macmann and all the others who have become so familiar to us by the third book of this trilogy that, like a caricature in which several lines capture the quintessence of a familiar face, just a few suggestions suffice for us to conceptualize him. But Mahood does not become the center of the story; rather he is used as a departure point. As a pupil, he was forced to learn that "Man is a higher mammal," and it is so easy to inject the *n* into Mahood's name that we might as well do it, if only long enough to realize that he becomes Beckett's metaphor for man.

"But Worm is the first of his kind. That's soon said. I must not forget I don't know him" (p. 337.). And neither do we, except as we may presume that if Mahood represents man as a higher mammal, Worm represents the lowest form of life. Yet for this very reason, the voice cannot know him, cannot enter into him. Worm *is* silence, unconscious life, the dark form that does not question the darkness. If there is any conflict in *The Unnamable*, it would be the voice's attempt to enter into and thus become Worm.

Perhaps it's by trying to be Worm that I'll finally succeed in being Mahood. I hadn't thought of that. Then all I'll have to do is be Worm. Which no doubt I shall achieve by trying to be Jones. Then all I'll have to do is be Jones. Stop. (P. 339)

The apprehension of one's identity can be realized only through the indirect method of metaphor, but since each metaphor can be reached only through another metaphor, the voice senses infinity and futility in such an artistic project. Still, some metaphor is needed as a means for the voice to pursue its end, which is the silence signifying lack of consciousness:

There at least is a first affirmation, I mean negation, on which to build. Worm cannot note. Can Mahood note? . . . Yes, it is the characteristic, among others, of Mahood to note, even if he does not always succeed in doing so, certain things, perhaps I should say all things, so as to turn them to account, for his governance. (P. 339)

Although the voice at first announces its intention of using Worm as a means to embody Mahood, it soon becomes clear that Mahood is actually the means to becoming Worm. The voice wants to slide down, rather than scale the hierarchy of conscious life. Gloucester's lines in *King Lear*—"I' th' last night's storm I such a fellow saw, /Which made me think a man a worm" (IV. i. 38–39)—represent a traditional vision of despair at man's insignificance, but the pattern is reversed in Beckett's world: poor Tom o'

Bedlam could be Mahood and Gloucester's horrified response, the voice's highest goal. Gloucester's pain is a result of thought, but the nonthinking worm will never suffer. The voice, then, would represent man's desperate attempt to submerge himself in the silence and stagnation of unconscious forms.

This gives us a plot. The voice does gradually feel itself fading into the figure of Worm,

> for this feeling of being entirely enclosed, and yet nothing touching me, is new. The sawdust no longer presses against my stumps, I don't know where I end. I left it yesterday, Mahood's world, the street, the chop-house, the slaughter, the statue and, through the railings, the sky like a slate-pencil. I shall never hear again the lowing of the cattle, nor the clinking of the forks and glasses, nor the angry voices of the butchers, nor the litany of the dishes and the prices. There will never be another woman wanting me in vain to live, my shadow at evening will not darken the ground. The stories of Mahood are ended. (P. 345)

But conscious victory is false victory. Preconscious Worm cannot note, cannot say his good-byes to a world of remembered images. The voice senses this when it finds that its talking has not stopped; and suspicion grows deeper when it observes that it is still existing as a metaphor, therefore pointing to meanings:

> I should know what is going on now, in order to announce it, as my function requires. It must not be forgotten, sometimes I forget, that all is a question of voices. I say what I am told to say, in the hope that some day they will weary of talking at me. The trouble is I say it wrong, having no ear, no head, no memory. Now I seem to hear them say it is Worm's voice beginning, I pass on the news, for what it is worth. Do they believe I believe it is I who am speaking? That's theirs too. To make me believe I have an ego all my own and can speak of it, as they of theirs. Another trap to snap me up among the living. It's how to fall into it they can't have explained to me sufficiently. They'll never get the better of my stupidity. (Pp. 345–46)

The metaphor rebels? It would seem so. Yet the last few sentences are disconcerting because the voice appears to be victimized by the form (trap), and so cannot be the form itself. Is it, then, a disembodied central intelligence flowing through forms but never retained within the form? But the voice asks: "Is it possible certain things change on their passage through me, in a way they can't prevent?" (p. 346). Now the voice sees itself as object rather than subject and again tends to define itself as metaphor. But a few sentences later, the impression is reversed as the voice becomes the elusive goal (truth?) that metaphor manages to express:

I don't say it's not the right method. I don't say they won't catch me in the end. I wish they would, to be thrown away. It's this hunt that is tiring, this unending being at bay. Images, they imagine that by piling on the images they'll entice me in the end. . . . They, yes, now they're all in the same galley. Worm to play, his lead, I wish him a happy time. To think I thought he was against what they were trying to do with me! To think I saw in him, if not me, a step towards me! To get me to be he, the anti-Mahood, and then to say, But what am I doing but living, in a kind of way, the only possible way, that's the combination. Or by the absurd prove to me that I am, the absurd of not being able. (P. 346)

The voice had previously tried to become Worm; now it says it saw Worm as a step toward itself. What *is* the relationship here, and why does the voice suddenly group Worm with those conscious beings who are trying to trap him?

The voice has no ego but feels one being imposed upon it by "them." By trying to capture it through metaphor, "they" provide the voice with substance and identity, thus falsifying what they assume to have trapped. Perhaps that is why the voice—in its more lucid moments—refuses to take responsibility for its assertions; it knows that any sense of identity it might have comes from without. Now in what sense is Worm a collaborator? The voice had thought him to be a step toward the Unnamable, *not* another metaphor, yet Worm *is* finally a metaphor, so by entering him the voice has been caught in the trap of form; it has assumed an identity—even a name! So the voice squiggles out of the frame, but only to find "the absurd prove to me that I am, the absurd of not being able." If it cannot be Worm, the metaphor for the unconscious, then its very inability proves it to have a conscious existence. It has therefore been defeated anyway.

Now the voice sees that it is not Worm who has been against it all along, but "they" who have been feeding him the thoughts which prevent his becoming Worm:

Worm, to say he does not know what he is, where he is, what is happening, is to underestimate him. What he does not know is that there is anything to know. His senses tell him nothing, nothing about himself, nothing about the rest, and this distinction is beyond him. Feeling nothing, knowing nothing, he exists nevertheless, but not for himself, for others, others conceive him and say, Worm is, since we conceive him, as if there could be no being but being conceived. . . . (P. 346)

The fact that Worm is a metaphor, then, does not prove that he exists, but only that he can be conceived. This means, in turn, that the voice itself may not exist, either, and need only be injected with Worm's identity to be stilled forever:

But it is solely a question of voices, no other image is appropriate. Let it go through me at last, the right one, the last one, his who has none, by his own confession. . . . Is there a single word of mine in all I say? No, I have no voice, in this matter I have none. That's one of the reasons why I confused myself with Worm. But I have no reasons either, no reason, I'm like Worm, without voice or reason. I'm Worm, no, if I were Worm I wouldn't know it, I wouldn't say it, I wouldn't say anything. I don't know anything, these voices are not mine, nor these thoughts, but the voices and thoughts of the devils who beset me. Who make me say that I can't be Worm, the inexpugnable. Who make me say that I am he perhaps, as they are. Who make me say that since I can't be he I must be he. That since I couldn't be Mahood, as I might have been, I must be Worm, as I cannot be. But is it they who say that when I have failed to be Worm I'll be Mahood, automatically, on the rebound? (P. 347)

It would seem that the voice needs form to be negated, just as Watt needed to conceptualize in order to forget his formalizations. But forms cannot be dispelled from the mind, and so continue to exist. Perhaps this does not deny the form's nonexistence, however, but only exposes the failure of the conceiver to do away with the forms he has created.

This leads us to the conclusion that the voice may be a metaphor yet—the metaphor for an empty form that will not disappear. Even though its exact meaning is nothingness, it cannot satisfactorily *be* nothingness as long as it continues to *represent* or *signify* nothingness. "Is not this the place . . . where one finishes vanishing?" (p. 293), the voice asks at the beginning of the narrative, but the novel becomes then the story of its failure to achieve its own destruction. While it does feel an obligation to its creator (the mysterious "they"), it cannot manage to squeeze out its consciousness as a meaningful form of meaninglessness:

Come, come, a little cooperation please, finish dying, it's the least you might do, after all the trouble they've taken to bring you to life. . . . They have put you on the right road, led you by the hand to the very brink of the precipice, now it's up to you, with an unassisted last step, to show them your gratitude. (P. 333)

The metaphor is in trouble because it does not work and yet

cannot stop. Its very image as a voice—disembodied though it is—precludes its submergence into unconsciousness, and so it continues to fight its form while at the same time sensing its inability to abandon it.

Ah if only this voice could stop, this meaningless voice which prevents you from being nothing, just barely prevents you from being nothing and nowhere, just enough to keep alight this little yellow flame feebly darting from side to side, panting, as if straining to tear itself from its wick, it should never have been lit, or it should never have been fed, or it should have been put out, put out, it should have been let go out. (Pp. 370–71)

And so the metaphor, far from annihilating itself, succeeds only in producing other metaphors to express the thin line between man and nothing—that thin line which can be neither erased nor traversed. Just as the flame cannot tear itself from its wick, the voice cannot detach itself completely from its source—the mind of the creator.

The voice, then, may be a metaphor of a sort, but its role in the story (and in this sense we might call it a character) really represents the breakdown of metaphor—metaphor flailing in the chaos, unable to sink or survive:

I haven't stirred, all I've said, said I've done, said I've been, it's they who said it, I've said nothing, I haven't stirred, they don't understand, I cannot stir, they think I don't want to, that their conditions don't suit me, that they'll hit on others, in the end, to my liking, then I'll stir, I'll be in the bag, that's how I see it, I see nothing, they don't understand, I can't go to them, they'll have to come and get me, if they want me, Mahood won't get me out, nor Worm either, they set great store on Worm, to coax me out, he was something new, different from all the others, meant to be, perhaps he was, to me they're all the same, they don't understand, I can't stir. (P. 378)

The inner voice is a pure abstraction which metaphors will no longer be able to drag out. Its existence is too elusive to be caught through forms, rendered conceivable without becoming meaningful. Worm is the metaphor which will not work, but the previous metaphors have not worked either because their very existence invalidates the voice's true quality of formlessness. With this realization, the voice, having eluded all the forms set up to trap it, decides to escape at last and insist on its independent existence as abstraction:

when I think of the time I've wasted with these bran-dips, beginning with Murphy, who wasn't even the first, when I had me, on the premises, within easy reach, tottering under my own skin and bones, real ones, rotting with solitude and neglect, till I doubted my own existence, and even still, to-day, I have no faith in it, none, so that I have to say, when I speak, Who speaks, and seek, and so on and similarly for all the other things that happen to me and for which someone must be found, for things that happen must have someone to happen to, someone must stop them. But Murphy and the others, and last but not least the two old buffers here present, could not stop them, the things that happened to me, nothing could happen to them, of the things that happened to me, and nothing else either, there is nothing else, let us be lucid for once, nothing else but what happens to me, such as speaking, and such as seeking, and which cannot happen to me, which prowl round me, like bodies in torment, the torment of no abode, no repose, no, like hyenas, screeching and laughing, no, no better, no matter, I've shut my doors against them, I'm not at home to anything, my doors are shut against them, perhaps that's how I'll find silence, and peace at last, by opening my doors and letting myself be devoured. . . . What a joy it is, to turn and look astern, between two visits to the depths, scan in vain the horizon for a sail, it's a real pleasure, upon my word it is, to be unable to drown, under such conditions. (Pp. 390–91)

The voice seems here to be fluctuating from a desire for freedom to one of imprisonment: by shutting itself away from the world of forms, it hopes finally to achieve the peace that has been its objective all along; but then it also considers immersion into the chaotic phenomena which promise to devour its identity. By fleeing the forms of events, the voice finally finds refuge in the vacuum, isolated from all the false identities which kept it submerged, away from itself. Now divested of confining forms, it becomes newly bouyant, free-floating, repurified into its existence as an abstraction. Finally formless, it is immune from danger—from all life and death.

But of course the voice continues to drone on until it realizes that its resolution has changed nothing. "I'll speak of me when I speak no more" (p. 392), it says in a saner moment, but it remains determined to evade formalization: "I can't go on in any case. But I must go on. So I'll go on. Air, air, I'll seek air, air in time, the air of time, and in space, in my head, that's how I'll go on" (p. 393). Not many more sentences roll by, however, before the search for air and space becomes a search for *representation* of air, *embodiment* of space. The voice simply cannot speak of itself without being silent, and cannot speak of anything else without projecting forms to conceptualize its subject.

But once again the fable must be of another, I see him so well, coming and going . . . how can I recognize myself who never made my acquaintance . . . I feel the end at hand and the beginning likewise. (P. 398)

And so it decides to make one last attempt to get at silence, and in that instant throws itself right back to where it started. After all, if it does not exist, then it cannot know itself, so must make its acquaintance through another. Off it goes, then, on another quest for the one form in which it will realize itself. The drive toward metaphor can neither succeed nor be stopped, for even while it leads us away from reality, it is still the only possibility for conceptualizing and communicating that inner reality; and because the device is contradictory and self-negating, the voice will be doomed to go on into infinity.

Which leads us back, finally, to the narrative structure of the book. Now that we have identified some possibilities for the narrative voice, we can see the inevitability of its circular movement.

And my course is not heliocoidal . . . but a succession of irregular loops, now sharp and short as in the waltz, now of a parabolic sweep that embraces entire boglands, now between the two, somewhere or other, and invariably unpredictable in direction, that is to say determined by the panic of the moment. (P. 327)

Although this passage is strongly reminiscent of Laurence Sterne's description of his narrative technique in *Tristam Shandy*, there are significant differences in the narrator's relationship to the reader which may account for the reader's difficulty in adjusting to Beckett's novel. First of all, Tristram Shandy's voice is clearly emanating from Tristram himself and carries frequent assurances to us that the writer knows what he is doing and has his story under control at all times. Beckett's voice, on the other hand, is not only unnamable, but indecipherable: our impression of its identity changes from one page to another, and even the voice itself is rarely sure whether its words are truly its own or someone else's merely being echoed through it. Also, while Shandy insists that he is making his own sort of progress (progression through digression), Beckett's voice seems confident only that it is always nowhere and will never arrive at any other place. In contrast to Shandy's delight in the roundabout course of his narrative, the Unnamable emits only hysteria (forced to move along, as it does, by the panic of the moment) and pain in its uncertainty. We cannot, therefore, put much trust in this voice; its lack of confidence begins to affect us too. Finally, though, the most salient distinction between the effect of these two narratives is that, while Sterne does get his story told in just the way he wanted to, the circular direction of Beckett's story is never more than a self-confessed illusion to conceal stagnation. *The Unnamable* has not arrived anywhere; we never really left the landing field. We have stayed in the same spot of ignorance, uncertainty, and tedium during the entire trip. Our suspense has not been enlisted, our interest has not been aroused, our compulsion for completion has not been satisfied. Whereas *Tristram Shandy's* structure delighted us by playing with our expectations, *The Unnamable* disappoints us by taking no cognizance of them. Like a bowling ball wobbling slowly down an endless alley, *The Unnamable* rolls along with tedious regularity. We get nowhere, and there is little scenery along the way to distract us from the monotony of the journey.

All this is not to suggest for an instant that Beckett is not as fully aware of what he is doing as Sterne was; both writers carry out their intentions with full artistic control. We are simply dealing with the problems presented by Beckett's novel, and they are, of course, the same problems as those presented *in* the novel, all arising from the form's attempt to annihilate itself at the moment creation has succeeded. Beckett's novel is built to self-destruct, so the components through which creation engenders vision must be set up to crumble on contact.

We have seen the art of self-negation justified in our discussion of *Watt:* the mind needs to conceive what it intends to destroy, for nothingness must exist in a positive form before its value as nothingness can be affirmed. Just as a double negative becomes a grammatical positive, so a nothingness that does not exist cannot be conceptualized as a negative. The result, in Beckett, is a passionate pursuit for forms that will detonate themselves once the mind has recognized them. That is why the Unnamable (which, because it is unnamed, has not found the form it seeks to negate itself) keeps its ears and eyes alert for any impressions it can receive from the outer world; it needs them "to provide me at least with a vague idea of the elements to be eliminated from the setting in order for all to be empty and silent. That was always the way. Just at the moment when the world is assembled at last, and it begins to dawn on me how I can leave it, all fades and disappears" (p. 334). The voice cannot rest in its vacuum, but must be on a constant series of search-and-destroy missions. "The search for the means to put an end to things, an end to speech, is what enables the discourse to continue. No, I must not try to think, simply utter. Method or no method I shall have to banish them in the end, the beings, things, shapes, sounds and lights with which my haste to speak has encumbered the place" (pp. 299–300). Forms are means to an end, and the end is always the same: to dismiss the forms.

Words too are forms, of course, and this means that the purpose of language in Beckett's novel is also suicidal; it exists only to drop us back into silence. As formalizing agents, words are so absurdly inadequate that they lose their meaning as soon as they are spoken. One has only to say a word to watch it deflate and know how arbitrary is the sound that signifies:

I used them all, all the words, they showed me, there were columns of them, oh the strange glow all of a sudden, they were on lists, with images opposite, I must have forgotten them, I must have mixed them up, these nameless images I have, the imageless names, these windows I should perhaps rather call doors, at least by some other name, and this word man which is perhaps not the right one for the thing I see when I hear it, but an instant, an hour, and so on, how can they be represented, a life, how could that be made clear to me, here, in the dark, I call that the dark, perhaps it's azure, blank words, but I use them, they keep coming back, all those they showed me, all those I remember, I need them all, to be able to go on, it's a lie, a score would be plenty, tried and trusty, unforgettable, nicely varied, that would be palette enough, I'd mix them, I'd vary them, that would be gamut enough. . . . (P. 407–8)

For all that, though, there *is* a value to words as sound that signifies nothing beyond itself. If the word calls a form into the mind, the sound of the word dissipates the form, thus completing the process of creation for negation. Of course the inherent contradiction of this principle applies here, too, for speech, while treasured as a means toward silence, also keeps that silence at bay:

This voice that speaks, knowing that it lies, indifferent to what it says, too old perhaps and too abased ever to succeed in saying the words that would be its last, knowing itself useless and its uselessness in vain, not listening to itself but to the silence that it breaks and whence perhaps one day will come stealing the long clear sigh of advent and farewell, is it one? . . . I have no voice and must speak, that is all I know . . . I know no more questions and they keep on pouring out of my mouth. (P. 307)

Language, then, is useful as it leads us toward silence, but ultimately useless because it manages always to resist silence. Words continue to pour forth long after one realizes he has nothing to say, and the voice is therefore the extension of the mind which prevents the mind from lapsing into unconsciousness. This was the relationship depicted when the voice referred to itself as a little feeble flame unable to extricate itself from its wick. The mind is the voice's origin, and each seeks to be delivered from the other so that peace might be realized at last. But the voice forces the mind to remain conscious of itself, and the mind pushes the voice out into the void, but will not release it long enough for the "flame" to extinguish itself. In short, the voice becomes a metaphor for the mind's frustration at being unable to exhaust itself.

All the components in this novel work in the same way, then: each is set in motion only to realize the utter futility of its motion, and each is unable to stop after the futility has been noted. Metaphors do not work and do not stop. The narrative structure gets nowhere and keeps right on going. Forms negate themselves in the mind, re-create themselves in the memory, and inspire new forms for the mind to negate. The main character of the novel cannot make up its mind whether (1) it has a mind, (2) whether it is the subject, object, or linking passageway to the forms it finds, or (3) whether it seeks extinction or embodiment. After proclaiming that it has silenced itself for once and for all, it continues to make the proclamation over and over until it concedes that silence is as far away as ever, and yet will still be attempted. Language is used to negate its own value, after which it continues to negate its value and asserts that it will never stop talking in order to keep saying that it has nothing to talk about. . . . It is a novel calculated to drive the sanest reader to a point of hysterical anxiety because he cannot step in and just stop the whole process.

Beckett has obviously succeeded in producing the effect he wants, but he has used techniques that seem to me to have important consequences for the novel. Certainly, the need to watch form perish—a basic theme of *The Unnamable*—has been demonstrated within the novel itself, which appears here to be on the threshhold of extinction. Again, these techniques are conscious and purposeful on Beckett's part; but I take note of them to consider both their effect on this particular novel and their implications for the novel of chaos.

I have already discussed Beckett's reductive principle in *Malone Dies,* but *The Unnamable* carries this technique to new depths: the entire outer world with all its forms has been reduced to darkness; the entire cast of characters has been reduced to one unidentified and mysterious voice contemplating a couple of forms; action has been reduced to . . . no, has been totally divorced from the story; and the story has been reduced to a series of circles representing the continuous affirmation and denial by the speaker of its existence. The book's texture is perfectly flat: it is devoid of all atmosphere, all people, all action.

"Here all is clear. No, all is not clear. But the discourse must go on. So one invents obscurities. Rhetoric" (p. 294). The solipsistic voice sees nothing outside of its own imagination and so must invent an external world in its own mind to represent its nebulous sense of its surroundings:

Air, the air, is there anything to be squeezed from that old chestnut? Close to me it is grey, dimly transparent, and beyond that charmed circle deepens and spreads its fine impenetrable veils. Is it I who cast the faint light that enables me to see what goes on under my nose? . . . But may not this screen which my eyes probe in vain, and see as denser air, in reality be the enclosure wall, as compact as lead? To elucidate this point I would need a stick or pole, and the means of plying it . . . I could also do, incidentally with future and conditional participles. Then I would dart it, like a javelin, straight before me and know, by the sound made, whether that which hems me round, and blots out my world, is the old void or a plenum. . . . But the days of sticks are over, here I can count on my body alone, my body incapable of the smallest movement and whose very eyes can no longer close as they once could . . . and no longer look away, or down, or up open to heaven, but must remain forever fixed and staring on the narrow space before them where there is nothing to be seen, 99% of the time. (Pp. 300–1)

Are these environs the obscurities which the voice has invented? Certainly the gray atmosphere is murky enough, but its dimness precludes even suggestions of appearances which may be lurking behind the veils. The voice considers groping in the grayness with a stick, in order to assess the possibilities of life around it; the use of future and conditional participles would help, too, by permitting it to fill the void—if such it found it to be—with forms that once might have been there or may yet appear. But these days (the days of Molloy, Moran, and Malone?) are over: the speaker itself has now been reduced to less than human form. All that remains of the body are two red-rimmed eyes staring straight ahead into space. Because the eyes can neither move nor shut, even the slightest action becomes impossible: the eyes gaze out into the grayness but cannot penetrate it. The means of investigation are so limited, the visibility so restricted (so that there is nothing to be seen 99% of the time), and the fatigue and despair so great that nothing can be allowed to happen in the novel. With all forms evaporated and action immobilized, there is nothing to see, nothing to say, and nothing to do. We might well ask if the novel itself has not at this point been squeezed right out of existence.

"But let us first suppose, in order to get on a little, then we'll suppose something else, in order to get on a little further . . ." (p. 311). With this statement, the voice begins making conscious use of the imagination to work its way back into the world of forms, and the very action involved in spurring the mental process onward makes the novel again possible. Still, progress is sporadic enough to make it a touch-and-go proposition all the way, and the novel wavers on the thin line between existence and extinction throughout the narrative. Even after the imagination has gone to work, its exhaustion is obvious in its willingness to replace re-creating with reciting, expansion with compression, characters with outlines. In the following passage, the voice summarizes before beginning the activity it will go through in order to end where it has not yet begun:

I hope this preamble will soon come to an end and the statement begin that will dispose of me. Unfortunately I am afraid, as always, of going on. For to go on means going from here, means finding me, losing me, vanishing and beginning again, a stranger first, then little by little the same as always, in another place, where I shall say I have always been, of which I shall know nothing, being incapable of seeing, moving, thinking, speaking, but of which little by little, in spite of these handicaps, I shall begin to know something, just enough for it to turn out to be the same place as always, the same which seems made for me and does not want me, which I seem to want and do not want, take your choice, which spews me out or swallows me up, I'll never know, which is perhaps merely the inside of my distant skull where once I wandered, now am fixed, lost for tininess, or straining against the wall, with my head, my hands, my feet, my back, and ever murmuring my old stories, my old story, as if it were for the first time. (Pp. 302–3)

Of course, this is an exact description not only of this novel, but of the two that preceded it. Moran's story turned out to be the same as Molloy's, Macmann's story the same as Malone's—and so the sum of these stories is here reduced to the bare outline of the one story they have all been used to tell. Still, the others have been *told*, not merely hinted at, and Malloy and Malone, while depicted as obtuse remnants of receding consciousnesses, were nevertheless recognizably human—even if as lowest common denominators of the humanity they represented.

Now, however, experience is funneled through Beckett's mind until everything is ground down to the same essence. Put ten different animal carcasses through a meat grinder, and you will extract the basic red meat which is the common, fundamental substance of them all. Beckett does much the same thing when he pours experience through a sieve and humanity through a pulverizer: what comes out is the essence extricated from its appearance, so that we know the product but cannot recognize it.

Closely related to this reductive principle is another technique peculiar to Beckett, which separates him from the traditional novelist of chaos: "ellipse when possible," says the voice, "it saves time" (p. 389). The implications of this statement cannot be underestimated when we apply it to the question of the novel's future. One no doubt saves a great deal of time by not writing novels at all, but once the task has been undertaken, can one afford to court ellipsis as a valid literary procedure? The novel has always worked through re-creation which renders the uniqueness of the individual moment; can it survive the short cuts that eliminate its life blood? The Unnamable can say: "We've gone wrong somewhere, no matter, there is no great difference here between one expression and the next, when you've grasped one you've grasped them all . . ." (p. 388), but the reader may have a hard time working with such a concept. Our own minds are elliptical, to be sure, but that only accounts for the difficulty of accurate communication. One can know exactly how he feels without expressing it, but the moment he wants someone else to understand his state, he must take the trouble to formalize it through metaphor. Otherwise, he ends up with something like: "When I think of the strangeness of life, I feel so . . . you know." At which point, the listener shrugs his shoulders and turns away, none the wiser for what he has been told. Is Beckett's art to be the equivalent of the mental short cut which expresses only confusion to the uninitiated? The Unnamable takes leaps in logic and association that the reader cannot possibly follow. We have vague suggestions of an incident rather than the incident itself, nebulous shadings of a character rather than the character himself embodying his own obscurity.

By presenting pattern without substance, Beckett has robbed the novel of one of its greatest advantages: emotional appeal. Empty frameworks evoke little or no feeling because we can experience emotional involvement only with a work that seems as substantial as our own lives. Confronting concepts like "War is hell" or "Crime does not pay"—no matter how often they are repeated or reaffirmed—cannot be equivalent to the overpowering experience of reading *A Farewell to Arms* or *Crime and Punishment;* the statement that man's life is absurd can never be as touching as the visualization of the two pathetic bums in *Waiting for Godot* who live with it and suffer from it. Strip any novel down to its theme or vision, and you have lost the novel, whose very life is verified by and sustained through the richness of its texture—both atmospheric and human. The intellect can be satisfied with philosophy, but our emotions need to be stirred too, and that is one reason we demand art in our lives. Beckett's radical theory of ellipsis, if carried out, will stifle the novel's potential to bring into play the full range of the reader's sensibilities.

Implicit to the Unnamable's assertion that all stories boil down to the same story and yet one must go on, is the idea that repetition will now replace re-creation in the novel's progression from beginning to end. "I feel nothing, know nothing," says the voice, "and as far as thinking is concerned I do just enough to preserve me from going silent, you can't call that thinking" (p. 307). Knowing that it has nothing to discover, the voice still needs to hear itself speaking; the matter and movement of its discourse are not only idle to consider but also irrelevant: "if only I knew what I have been saying. Bah, no need to worry, it can only have been one thing, the same as ever" (p. 335). Since the Unnamable never has anything new to say, it is doomed to repeat all the old things (that had not been worth saying, anyway), if only to emphasize the pointlessness of saying anything at all. The voice itself would just as soon be still, but it continues to feel the strain of those using it to get somewhere:

The fact is they no longer know where they've got to in their affair, where they've got me to, I never knew, I'm where I always was, wherever that is, and their affair, I don't know what is meant by that, some process no doubt, that I've got stuck in, or haven't yet come to, I've got nowhere, in their affair, that's what galls them, they want me there somewhere, anywhere, if only they'd stop committing reason, on them, on me, on the purpose to be achieved, and simply go on, with no illusion about having begun one day or ever being able to conclude, but it's too difficult, for one bereft of purpose, not to look forward to his end, and bereft of all reason to exist, back to a time he did not. Difficult too not to forget, in your thirst for something to do, in order to be done with it, and have that much less to do, that there is nothing to be done, nothing special to be done, nothing doable to be done. . . . no point in telling yourself stories, to pass the time, stories don't pass the time, nothing passes the time, that doesn't matter, that's how it is, you tell yourself stories, then any old thing, saying, No more stories from this day forth, and the stories go on, it's stories still, or it was never stories, always any old thing, for as long as you can remember, no, longer than that, any old thing, the same old thing, to pass the time, then, as time didn't pass, for no reason at all, in your thirst, trying to cease and never ceasing, seeking the cause, the cause of talking and never ceasing, finding the cause, losing it again, seeking no longer, seeking again, finding again, losing again, finding nothing, finding at last, losing again, talking without ceasing, thirstier than ever, seeking as usual, losing as usual, blathering away, wondering what it's all about, seeking what it can be you are seeking. . . . (P. 384–85)

This passage is representative not only of the story's progress in depicting the Unnamable's lack of progress, but also of the stylistic technique of hammering repetition, which renders theme by reenacting it: the circular structure of the novel, the infinite cessation that constitutes plot, and the frustrating futility of movement which originates and ends in the despairing vision underlying everything—all these fruitless cycles are represented in the style, so similar in effect at times to Faulkner's spiraling sentences, which helped to signify the hysteria of those characters running desperately from panic to peace, yet never leaving the panic behind.

As the stylistic embodiment of frantic movement, the passage seems to be quite satisfying, but the substance of the speech provokes some uncomfortable thoughts. The novelist here seems to have reached an absolute dead end, for while he has caught the cycle of the voice's activity, he has nothing new to add from the last time he had caught it, or the time before that. How many times must the reader be hurled along the narrative hoops in order to know what the process is like and be able to include it in his imaginative experience? Must the endless cycle be represented by endless cycles? Did we need a third act to *Waiting for*

Godot? If the story never changes, how many times must the reader read the same one before the experience seems worthless and wasteful? Once the *impression* of repetition—always a common technique for writers of chaos—*becomes* mere repetition, the reader's tedium is hardly compensated for by the knowledge that tedium is the main point of the story. Art need not reproduce all experience in order to provide us with illusions of it; the self-perpetuating dog song that opens the second act of *Waiting for Godot* really *could* have gone on forever, but not many of the audience would have been left by the second hour. We cannot insist that the novelist have something new to say (or even something new to see) with each novel, yet surely there is some alternative to hearing the same story spun out endlessly long after we have gotten the point of its pointlessness.

This remains a problem to consider, but for the moment, we can at least vindicate Beckett from having erred in his effects: the author here has achieved just the impression I believe he wanted. I discussed *Malone Dies* in terms of Camus's theory of absurd creation, and the basic processes working behind *The Unnamable* can also be better understood with some reference to Camus's notion of art's role in an absurd universe. The true work of absurdity, Camus says, "marks both the death of an experience and its multiplication. It is a . . . monotonous and passionate repetition of the themes already orchestrated by the world. . . ." The absurd creator is not interested in penetrating, analyzing, or interpreting appearances but only in working up fresh images to represent the multiplicity of experience. The Unnamable itself could be seen here as the absurd creator both in the act of inventing new images to describe experience and in its passionate (and monotonous) repetition of the struggle at the heart of its existence. Wanting only to find peace, it uses its imagination to retrace over and over its constant quest for solace in a dark world:

it's only natural, you want yourself, you want yourself in your own little corner, it's not love, not curiosity, it's because you're tired, you want to stop, travel no more, seek no more, lie no more, speak no more, close your eyes, but your own, in a word lay your hands on yourself, after that you'll make short work of it. (P. 400)

But it has already given us the image of those two huge, unlidded, bloodshot eyes staring vacantly into space, paralyzed in a state of petrifaction which permits no movement: no sidelong or upward or downward diversions, but only the slow rotation of the mind as it attempts to sift the veils of grayness floating in the vacuum.

The last phrases in the passage point to another of art's functions, and that is, to quote Camus again, "the sole chance of keeping his consciousness and of fixing its adventures. . . . All try their hands at miming, at repeating, and at re-creating the reality that is theirs." Art, then, becomes the only means for man to gain contact with himself, to set up a mirror which will reflect the reality he cannot capture without an image to look upon. "The fable must be of another," says the Unnamable, because "how can I recognize myself who never made my acquaintance?" (p. 398). The point is an important one: we can confront ourselves, *know* ourselves only through the imagination which makes a character out of us. It is true that whenever we think of ourselves, visualize ourselves doing something, it is not really ourselves we see, but an imaginative conception of ourselves—a figure moving in our minds who we take to be ourselves, whom we call ourselves. The purpose behind Beckett's writing, then, is to get a glimmer of the self—and this is not too terribly far from Conrad's objectives in *Lord Jim*. The effort begins as an attempt to distinguish the self from the incidentals which so often block accurate perception, yet that search must finally be abandoned when the full mystery of ourselves becomes impossible to work with. Still, art offers some compensation, even after we have grasped the futility of trying to pinpoint the core of our elusive existences: "you don't try any more, no need to try, it goes on by itself, it drags on by itself, from word to word, a labouring whirl, you are in it somewhere, everywhere . . ." (p. 402). It cannot be separated or even distinguished, perhaps, but somewhere inside all the whirl of activity, the self *is* captured long enough to be displayed to the self. This is Virginia Woolf's point, too, in *To the Lighthouse*, and her warning that "the vision must be perpetually remade" provides an adumbration for the repetitiveness that we find all through Beckett. Further, both Conrad's and Woolf's observation that truth cannot be scooped up from the instant that gives it form, but can be rendered and contemplated only within the re-creation of the moment itself, may justify to a good extent the amount of chaos involved in Beckett's presentation of his story. Imagination cannot mirror vision directly, but only the experience through which vision is finally, if always momentarily, cap-

tured. Because Beckett's vision is circular, so his form must be:
the end will always lead us right back to the beginning. The chaos
in *The Unnamable* thus becomes the artful rendering of the
chaos in life.

Nevertheless, Beckett's novel is certainly an emptier experience than any we have yet considered, and that leaves one question still to be answered. If the imagination cannot represent vision directly but must wrap it in the moment that gives it life,
why do we not have a satisfactory representation of reality here?
The philosophical truth of our lives may be designated through
veils of vague gray clouds, but that is hardly the atmosphere our
bodies live in. For Beckett, though, that *is* the essential reality of
our lives; the solipsistic gaze discerns nothing real beyond its self-
image, and so conceives itself through the imagination as a solitary form in the vacuum:

Even if there were things, a thing somewhere, a scrap of nature, to talk
about, you might be reconciled to having no one left, to being yourself
the talker, if only there were a thing somewhere, to talk about, even
though you couldn't see it, or know what it was, simply feel it there, with
you, you might have the courage not to go silent . . . if only there were a
thing, but there it is, there is not, they took away things when they
departed, they took away nature, there was never anyone, anyone but
me, anything but me, talking to me of me, impossible to stop, impossible
to go on, but I must go on, I'll go on, without anyone, without anything,
but me, but my voice, that is to say I'll stop I'll end, it's the end already,
short-lived, what is it, a little hole, you go down into it, into the silence,
it's worse than the noise, you listen, it's worse than talking, no, not worse,
no worse, you wait, in anguish, have they forgotten me, no, yes, no,
someone calls me, I crawl out again, what is it, a little hole, in the wilder-
ness. It's the end that is the worst, no, it's the beginning that is the worst,
then the middle, then the end, in the end it's the end that is the worst,
this voice that, I don't know, it's every second that is the worst, it's a
chronicle, the seconds pass, one after another, jerkily, no flow, they don't
pass, they arrive, bang, bang, they bang into you, bounce off, fall and
never move again, when you have nothing left to say you talk of time,
seconds of time, there are some people add them together to make a life,
I can't, each one is the first, no, the second, or the third, I'm three
seconds old . . . the seconds must be all alike and each one is infernal. . . .
And yet I have memories, I remember Worm. . . . It is I invented him,
him and so many others, and the places where they passed, the places
where they stayed, in order to speak, since I had to speak, without speaking of me, I couldn't speak of me. . . . (Pp. 394–96)

The Unnamable's solipsism explains the emptiness of the book: there is really nothing to talk about—no *thing*—and that is why everything is so abstract. This idea dictates Beckett's subject matter (or rather, *lack* of subject matter) as well as the novel's form, style, method, characterization, and atmosphere. The disembodied voice is an abstraction of the intellect but the only reality the imagination can find. Because nothing else has concrete existence, the imagination creates a visualization of its atmosphere, coloring nothingness gray. Characters, also members of the outside world, cannot possibly exist except as fragmented figments of the imagination, shadowy shells of forms, incomplete and inconstant, appearing, fading, reappearing, receding. Illusory, elusive, and dim, their occasional presence is felt, rather than seen, and this is true of inanimate objects as well. I have mentioned the methods of reduction, ellipsis, and repetition, the cyclical form, and the panting style—expressive of hysteria. Long sentences set up a spiraling effect; the one huge paragraph that constitutes the bulk of the book blocks out any sense of order, distinction of individual effect or identity. We could say that the unbroken paragraph keeps time moving on, unbroken, until it becomes the stylistic equivalent of infinity; while the short, choppy phrases, set off only by commas, are justified stylistically as expressive of the idea that "the seconds must be all alike and each one is infernal." The paradoxical texture of the style thus becomes a brilliant device for reflecting the vision of "finality without end," as Moran had called it in *Molloy:* each phrase is a crisis, just as every second is the worst; each phrase explodes with certainty, then clashes immediately with the next one, which contradicts it with equal certainty. "it's every second that is the worst, it's a chronicle, the seconds pass, one after another, jerkily, no flow, they don't pass, they arrive, bang, bang, they bang into you, bounce off, fall and never move again. . . ." Each phrase bangs into the next, bounces off the next, yet all are gradually assimilated into the sameness of that infinite paragraph, the terror of each crisis frozen onto the huge face of the iceberg, where the individual instant loses its identity and significance in the general mass of life which levels all experience and smears it into the chaos.

Every effect in this novel has, then, been carefully chosen and artfully achieved. Vision insinuates itself in every line, image, and movement. The novel must be called a masterpiece of solipsistic expression.

But impossible situations cannot be prolonged, unduly, the fact is well known, either they disperse, or else they turn out to be possible after all, it's only to be expected, not to mention other possibilities. (P. 361)

Beckett's novel, while it may seem skeletal, is actually broad enough to contain its own refutation. For brilliant as the novel is, it cannot sustain an impossible situation with intensity. Whether the entire situation eventually becomes quite possible, or whether one's mind simply dismisses the whole experience is, of course, a matter known only to the individual reader. For me, it goes on much too long; I grow groggy with it and finally dulled to it. Its masterful moments are many indeed, but their effect diminishes with constant repetition. Because the triology traces the gradual elimination of the self, the abstraction of *The Unnamable* seems justifiable to me, but since, too, this last stage is certainly the least interesting phase of the process, I cannot justify the length as easily. Still, it is not a matter of judging *The Unnamable*, which does seem to me a major accomplishment, but of considering the chaotic factors which account for so much of the book's effect, and the extent to which they manage to undermine the novel.

For this reason, *The Unnamable* represents a crucial point in our survey of the novel of chaos. While I have been able to justify any peculiarity as an intentional part of Beckett's purpose and even further proof of his artistic skill, so much of what has always constituted the fundamental life, nature, and workings of the novel has been lost or betrayed, that the experience of *The Unnamable* seems less one of chaos in the novel than of the novel in chaos. The vacuum always comes first here; Beckett chooses to be true to his vision even if he can do so only at the expense of his form. As we stumble around in the confusion, dullness, disorder, abstraction, and irritation (the one endless paragraph which blears both eyes and mind) of this novel, and note how much of ourselves remains outside of it (the sensory, emotional, and imaginative potential left untapped by the author), we realize that aesthetic attitudes have abdicated to philosophical ones. The more faithfully the vision is adhered to, it would seem, the emptier is the artistic experience it engenders. This is the point where the novel sinks into the grayness of its own vision and perhaps "goes under" for the third and final time.

8

The Soul's Haunted Cell

The Omnipotent Art of Jean Genet

He, who grown aged in this world of woe,
In deeds, not years, piercing the depths of
    life, ... he can tell
Why thought seeks refuge in lone caves, yet
    rife
With airy images, and shapes which dwell
Still unimpair'd, though old, in the soul's
haunted cell.

'Tis to create, and in creating live
A being more intense, that we endow
With form our fancy, gaining as we give
The life we image. . . .
                              —Lord Byron,
                                Childe Harold's Pilgrimage

I refer everything to my system. . . .
                              —Jean Genet,
                                Miracle of the Rose

*W*hile Beckett has concentrated on compressing the novel to delineate the lowest common denominator of human experience, Jean Genet has expanded it to allow full play to the imagination, which disregards that experience. The result is an exercise in freedom which releases art from any obligation to reality, consistency, or the natural expectations of the reader. Confined only by what the imagination can conceive, Genet's novels emphasize idiosyncratic experience—the very diversity which Beckett sought to erase. The void remains, but now it is treasured because it grants the writer freedom to fill it as he wishes. Working in his small, dark cell, Genet as author could easily resemble a character talking to himself in a Beckett novel (there is little difference between Genet dreaming and Malone dying, for example), but Genet's darkness, rather than threatening obliteration, nurtures creativity and engenders life. As Genet pours his images into the vacuum, his cell continues to expand until he has achieved a freedom unparalleled in the world outside. The prison finally becomes a metaphor for the novel itself, as confinement intensifies the imagination and fans it to a brilliance which mocks active, conventional, or singular life styles. Unity is uninteresting, convention is stifling, and activity is shallow, when multiplicity means freedom, invention nourishes awareness, and dreaming heightens our sense of life.

Genet quite naturally produces paradoxes, because the friction they generate sparks the emotional flame which is always his chief interest in creating. Thus, emotional reality is realized as external reality is ignored; beauty finds new energy working through ugliness, and the soul is revitalized as it struggles to transcend its sordid surroundings. The novelist's aim is to feed the fires of emotion, and reality is useful only as so much kindling. It is not surprising, then, that dream replaces reality as the subject of Genet's novels. After all, it is in the most inactive hours of our physical lives—while asleep—that we often seem to apprehend the deepest, truest parts of our existences, intuiting the emotional realities behind unfamiliar forms. "Dreaming is nursed in darkness,"[1] and the novel is nursed in dreams.

Kafka's works, too, are based on dreams, but we have seen in such a novel as *The Trial* that Kafka used the context of dream to suggest vision and represent his conception of chaos. Genet, however, is not concerned with communicating his vision of reality; for him, imagination is an end in itself—it creates because it chooses to, and what it expresses is subservient to the pure pleasure of creation. Whereas Kafka utilizes the world of dreams to convey the horror of a chaotic universe, Genet relishes dreams for the chaos they themselves contain and so makes them the object as well as the principal device of his novels. Because for Genet dream *is* reality, it not only dictates form, but *becomes* the

1. Jean Genet, *Miracle of the Rose*, trans. Bernard Frechtman (New York: Grove Press, 1967), p. 37. All future page references, cited in parentheses, are to this edition.

form of the novel rather than a means of representation. The dream elements in Kafka's novels are, finally, controlled by vision, while Genet's novels abdicate all control in order to flow into dream and elude form. An art rendering chaos through dream is quite different from one immersed in the chaos *of* dream, for once chaos functions as technique, as well as theme, the transition has been made from chaos in the novel to the novel in chaos.

The chief function of the imagination in Genet's works follows to some extent the Absurdist tradition of creating personae to reflect experience so that the mind may focus on the beauty and significance of its adventures. Genet himself becomes, then, the subject of his novels, and his imagination the means through which he is able to recall and relive his life. But Genet differs from the Absurdists in his purposeful distortion of the experience being re-created. If his imagination is not an accurate mirror, Genet values it for that very reason, for he is not concerned with *representing* his life so much as *transcending* it. Reality holds no fascination for him beyond what his imagination can do to enhance it. By ignoring the external world, Genet forsakes universals for the eccentric: he is both the subject and object of his art, creating new images of himself *for* himself. Subjectivity is therefore paramount, and Genet stresses his interest in the individual, the distinctive, and the egocentric over the common experience:

Each object in your world has a meaning different for me from the one it has for you. I refer everything to my system, in which things have an infernal signification, and even when I read a novel, the facts, without being distorted, lose the meaning which has been given them by the author and which they have for you, and take on another so as to enter smoothly the otherworldly universe in which I live. (P. 89)

The insistence on the individual interpretation is, of course, perfectly in accord with Genet's value system, which prizes the "real man"—he who lives apart from society, above conventional values, and whose every action expresses contempt for the ordinary world. Genet's attraction to the outlaw becomes ultimately his homage to imagination, for the outlaw's genius, courage, and independence are demonstrated through the creation of his own system; and that is just what Genet is able to attain through his imagination. As an antisocial artist, he performs the equivalent gesture of the murderer and gradually comes to embody the men he most admires.

Since his creation is an antisocial act, Genet's *Miracle of the Rose* necessarily scorns tradition. By writing solely for self-gratification, Genet reveals his contempt for the reader, and by turning the novel into a private system which need defer to no law outside of his own pleasure, he mocks the form he has chosen for self-expression. Yet Genet's contempt is abstract and therefore inoffensive; the defiant gesture pleases him even when his attitude is obviously gracious. This is typical of a man who admires just those gestures which do not come easily to him. As a result, Genet's gestures are often beautiful but usually false: he strikes a stance, assumes a pose, or asserts a position for effect; the real feeling hidden beneath is almost always the opposite of the one showing on the surface.

No matter how scornful he may sound, then, Genet *is* allowing us to enter his inner world, and he takes some pain to make it accessible to us. Once inside, it is hard for us to resist the show, for Genet's mind is a fascinating place, intriguing as an exotic bazaar, where a reader can see the handiwork of the imagination displayed, amid common surroundings, in all its colorful detail. Genet offers us the magic of alchemy, the excitement of a circus sideshow, the intensity of mystic vision. It is true that his is a totally private system permeated with criminals and characterized by eroticism, but the sensationalism of his material is transcended by the purity and dynamism of the unfettered imagination, which transforms freaks into saints, murderers into heroes, and orgiastic self-gratification into mystical fervor. Like William Blake's, Genet's imagination feeds on freedom, and heroism is determined by the amount of freedom one dares to seize. Just as Satan becomes Blake's idol, so the criminal becomes Genet's, for the rebel is he who demands emancipation from the forces seeking to subdue him. Once liberated from moral restraints, the imagination impresses its vision on a mundane world and transmutes it into a rich, personal experience. Genet uses his masturbatory fantasies as a metaphor for imagination being worked up to a frenzied peak of activity, then culminating not in the simple release of sperm, but in the transformation of sperm into pearls, doves, flowers, or whatever other form beauty decides to take. When it is all over, the masturbator-as-creator might well say, like Lily Briscoe in *To the Lighthouse,* "I have had my vision." Thus, by making his system accessible to us, Genet is treating the reader to much more than a simple exposé of his sexual dreams; he is performing feats of imaginative gymnastics whereby ejaculation becomes the ultimate aesthetic experience.

In *To the Lighthouse*, Virginia Woolf depicted the imagination in perpetual struggle with the reality it sought to control, but Genet's *Miracle of the Rose* demonstrates the freedom found after the battle has been given up. Reality no longer dictates the role of the imagination; imagination now dictates the role of reality. And the novel no longer renders chaos; instead, chaos renders the novel. *Miracle of the Rose* is Genet's attempt to make imagination omnipotent so that it can change reality at will to suit its own purposes. Truth is never at stake here because the author prefers his own world of wish fulfillment and is interested in the creative process only as an intensifier of the imaginative realm in which he prefers to live:

The wind to which I listen is more lulling than the one which moans in the real firs of a real park. . . . This autumn is more intense and insidious than real autumn, external autumn, for in order to enjoy it I must invent a detail or a sign every second and must linger over it. I create it every instant. (P. 146)

Like Lily Briscoe, Genet finds that "the vision must be perpetually remade," but his vision makes no pretense at having caught reality; it hopes to capture only the feeling that Genet wants to experience at a particular moment. The process is slow and deliberate as Genet selects the proper fantasy to embody his mood:

This is the luxury I allow myself. In the cell, gestures can be made with extreme slowness. You can stop in the middle of one. You are master of time and of your thinking. You are strong by dint of slowness. Each gesture is inflected in a flowing curve. You hesitate. You choose. That is what the luxury of cell life is composed of. But this slowness of gesture is a slowness that goes fast. It rushes. Eternity flows into the curve of a gesture. You possess your entire cell because you fill its space with your engrossed mind. (P. 183)

This is a god speaking. Alone in his cell, Genet creates a world to his own making and possesses eternity in a simple movement of his arm. Supreme master of time and space, he re-enacts the Creation according to his own will, and "it's all so real that I wonder whether it is real and whether the prison isn't a house of illusion" (p. 216). The world of the imagination becomes more real for Genet than the very place in which he is creating. Obviously, reality cannot intrude when fantasy blots it from the mind—and the result is complete autonomy for the imagination, which simply covers with images whatever it does not care to notice. Reality pales and recedes the moment the artist begins his work.

"Bulkaen is the finger of God; Harcamone is God, since he is in heaven (I am speaking of the heaven I create for myself and to which I am devoted body and soul)" (p. 111). With this, Genet wipes out all reference to any system but his own, and the reader is warned that his own conceptions of reality must be deposited outside the novel. Thus, as we read of the miracle of the rose, we are, I think, supposed to take it on the literal level, even though we may feel safer interpreting it as metaphor working on reality. As Harcamone crosses the courtyard, Genet has his vision:

I felt in all my veins that the miracle was under way. But the fervor of our admiration and the burden of saintliness which weighed on the chain that gripped his wrists—his hair had had time to grow and the curls had matted over his forehead with the cunning cruelty of the twists of the crown of thorns—caused the chain to be transformed before our scarcely astonished eyes into a garland of white flowers. (P. 15)

Of course this description will not fit into our framework of reality, and so we are tempted to explain it in terms of Genet's associations, which find a meaningful metaphor suggesting Christ's procession to Calvary. But such an interpretation opens Genet's system by referring it to a mythic superstructure. Imagination would thus control reality by adding a new dimension of meaning to mundane events. But Genet insists on the perfect independence of his imagination: it does not modify reality—it replaces it. Thus, after watching the above spectacle, Genet rushes over to Harcamone and with a pair of scissors cuts off the loveliest rose hanging from Harcamone's left wrist. Later, as the procession moves away from him, Genet's vision vanishes as the real world returns:

the chain that bound his hands no longer suggested a garland and was now only a steel chain. He disappeared from my sight, whisked away by the shadow and the bend of the corridor. I put the rose into the false pocket that was cut in my jacket. (P. 17)

At this point, the novel frees itself from reality: Genet actually deposits the rose in his pocket *after* the vision has faded! We can no longer see the rose as strictly a symbol when its literal reality remains after its symbolic function has been completed. We must assume that what we took to be metaphor was in fact independent of art's impact on the external world. Art has not deigned to work on reality but has simply replaced it with a different system that answers only to itself. Just as the false pocket in Genet's jacket serves the function of a real pocket, so the illusory world created by Genet's imagination is substituted for reality.

The absolute supremacy of the imagination in this book means that the reader cannot refer to any familiar context outside of his own dreams. There, of course, he knows intimately the ease with which logic slips away, cause and effect disappear, and experience floats on mysterious waves which rock us back and forth from the known to the unknown. If we surrender our will to pursue and impose meaning everywhere, we can recapture some of the wonder in life and live for a while with greater innocence and intensity. Genet wishes to flower us with images, but we must become the passive partner in our relationship to him. His world is not to be worked with, but to be experienced. Dreams recast our lives because the mind senses possibilities behind appearances and events which it wants to consider. Thus, Genet, while talking of Bulkaen, can say: "He refused me on the stairs, but I invent him more docile" (p. 88), and reality immediately expands to accommodate the mind's will. We can see, then, that when imagination and reality clash in Genet's world, no contest results because reality promptly yields to the stronger force. Furthermore, reality then submits to a reconditioning which validates the mind's new perspective. After inventing a beautiful love scene between Pierrot and himself, for example, Genet finds his attitude toward the real Pierrot transformed by what he has envisioned because "after crediting him with such a tender gesture, I cannot believe that he could have remained unfeeling toward me, for if I have imagined that gesture it is because something about Pierrot suggested the image, something about him told me he was capable of it . . ." (p. 116). Recalling that Genet's own most pugnacious gestures were almost always used to conceal his timidity, what can we conclude but that the world predicated by the imagination contains more reality than what we call reality itself?

The transforming powers of the imagination become, finally, the subject of *Miracle of the Rose,* and the book is permeated with metaphors of Genet's ability to convert ugliness into beauty.

Speaking of Botchako ("the biggest fucker in the jug"), Genet describes his grossness only to transcend it. The harshness of his voice is an irritant, yet refines itself through song into a source of beauty:

When he spoke, his voice was hoarse and hollow. It also had some acid scratches which were like cracks, like fissures, and, considering the beauty of his voice when he sang, I examined his speaking voice more attentively. I made the following discovery: the irritating hoarseness, forced by the singing, was transformed into a very sweet, velvety strain, and the fissures became the clearest notes. (Pp. 19–20)

The implication would be that the most loathsome aspects of life are the most suitable subjects for the artistic process of refinement, for it was Botchako himself "who revealed to me that beauty is the projection of ugliness and that by 'developing' certain monstrosities we obtain the purest ornaments" (p. 20). The huge amount of scatology in this novel can be justified, then, not only as presenting the writer with a greater challenge for testing his artistic powers but as suggesting a realm as pure in its way as the chaste form it is to become. Excrement is as untarnished by beauty as the rose is untarnished by ugliness. In order to create the sublime, one must experience the sordid, for it is in the contrast that each becomes defined and fully realized. Genet accustoms himself to excrement as preparation for discovering the divine, just as Christian poets such as Dante have traditionally put themselves into Hell before starting the ascent toward Heaven:

And perhaps I allowed myself to drift into this so readily because in that way I estrange myself from the world. I am carried along in that fall which, cutting by its very speed and verticality all threads that hold me to the world, plunges me into prison, into foulness, into dreaming and hell, and finally lands me in a garden of saintliness where roses bloom, roses whose beauty—as I shall know then—is composed of the rims of the petals, their folds, gashes, tips, spots, insect holes, blushes, and even their stems which are mossy with thorns. (P. 237)

The emotional counterpart of excrement would be the anguished suffering of the prisoners—those creatures of hell whose lives are immersed in the dank, odious, foul-smelling, bug-infested cells—and the moral counterpart would be the evil, cruelty, and criminality to which their energies have been directed. On all levels, though, the opposites are similar in purity: the rose and the excrement; heaven and hell; suffering and ecstasy; shame and glory; evil and saintliness. Working from his models of misery, Genet transforms them with his love into models of dignity and beauty. "It is essential that your gesture be beautiful," he says. Thus, "any gesture performed in suffering, wrought of suffering, born of suffering and danger, deserves respect, despite the contortions it brings to the face, despite the grotesque postures of the body. . . . Your pride must be able to undergo shame in order to attain glory" (p. 261). That glory is attained, finally, through Genet's vision, which sees the force and brutality of prison life imbued with love from within—that which exists in the personal relationships between the prisoners—and it is that love which lifts them from the dregs of reality up to the summit of divine purity. Through Genet's imagination, the prisoners are transformed into a hierarchy of angels leading Genet to God:

I was still astounded at the thought that each male had his own glorious male, that the world of force and manly beauty, loved in that way within itself, from link to link [formed] a garland of muscular and twisted or stiff and thorny flowers. Those pimps were always being women for someone stronger and handsomer than they. They were women less and less the further away they were from me, all the way to the very pure pimp who dominated them all, the one who lorded it over the galley, whose lovely penis, grave and distant, moved about the Colony in the form of a mason. Harcamone! (P. 262)

This "grave and distant" penis is Genet's idol, and if we can imagine him getting down on his knees to pay homage to his god, are we to call it an act of sex or an act of religion? Harcamone, as pimp, is the basest of creatures, but the qualities Genet attributes to him—"pure," "grave," "distant"—and the verbs used to describe his manner—"dominated," "lorded"—divest the passage of its sexual connotations and transmute it into a description of divine holiness. The mystic has transcended his surroundings by converting hell into heaven. Like Milton's Satan who also understood the transcendent powers of the imagination, Genet knows that "The mind is its own place, and in itself/ Can make a Heav'n of Hell, a Hell of Heav'n," but whereas Satan comes to see that "myself am Hell," Genet might easily say that he carries *heaven* within him.

But heaven would surely bore Genet; what he actually seems to treasure is the process of creating which intensifies existence. It is the imagination which enables him "to burn with a hard, gem-like flame," and this becomes the criterion by which he judges his life to be superior to those wasting away outside of

prison. By freezing and controlling time, art expands consciousness, and the imaginative world it renders to the mind excels the
real one because we know more intimately the moment we create. "Certain acts dazzle us and light up blurred surfaces," he
says, "if our eyes are sharp enough to see them in a flash, for the
beauty of a living thing can be grasped only fleetingly" (p. 8). It is
the blurred surfaces which Genet is determined to avoid, and
that is why he resists the dull lives generated by a society which
cherishes the kind of bland goodness dictated by convention. Genet values prison life just insofar as it enables him to escape the
enervating life outside. As soon as he notices elements of medioc-
rity entering within the prison walls, Genet, who had accustomed
himself to excrement with little trouble, finds the prison loathsome:

In short, we're tied to your life by too many strings. I think that my love
of prison is perhaps the subtle well-being of plunging into a life among
men whom my imagination and desire wish to be of rare moral beauty.
This well-being is only slightly attenuated by the fact that prisons lose
their hard glitter as they come to be frequented by honest people and as
pimps take on the qualities of solid citizens. In prison, when the sun that
streamed through the window scattered the cell, each of us became
more and more himself, lived his own life, and lived it so acutely that we
ached, for we were isolated and were made conscious of our imprisonment by the brilliance of the fete that dazzled the rest of the world, but
on rainy days it was otherwise and the cell was merely a shapeless, pre-
natal mass with a single soul in which the individual consciousness was
lost. (P. 135)

Loss of consciousness is to be dreaded above all things, and imagination is the vitalizing force in constant combat against the
mind's extinction. By stirring up those moments, events, and
faces which dazzle, imagination energizes consciousness until the
intensity of it is felt as our basic life force. Lying motionless in his
bed, Genet becomes infatuated with fantasizing Bulkaen's death
in different ways, each "elicited by the wretched disorder of his
face," and as he contemplates the imaginary contortions of his
lover's face, Genet's own life is heightened to the point where he
seems to be climbing out of his body:

though I lie motionless in bed, my chest swells, I breathe more quickly,
my lips are parted, my bust feels as if it were straining toward the tragedy which the boy experienced, the rhythm of my circulation quickens, I
live faster. I mean that all this seems to me to *be*, but I actually think that
I haven't moved and that it is rather the representation of myself, one of

my images which *I see*, confronted with the image of Bulkaen in his loftiest attitude.

Thus, Bulkaen had taken increasing possession of me. He had surged into me. . . . (P. 65)

The real Bulkaen could never have generated the kind of power Genet feels welling up inside him—Bulkaen's character was sweet, childlike, sincere, trusting, and mild, and his death, though violent, lacked majesty. He was really a rather common "tough." But the image Genet celebrates is quite a different Bulkaen, raised to heights of tragic passion, noble purpose, and regal demeanor. *This* is the Bulkaen that excites him, that enters him and expands him—and it is the pure product of the imagination. Working from a posture or gesture—let us say Bulkaen's mildly tortured expression as he begged Genet for a few more cigarettes or a new pair of pants—Genet builds on it, erasing the mundane, heightening the unique until he has created an agonized Christ pleading for love in a hostile world, a betrayed Caesar seeking to understand the new coldness in the eyes of Brutus, a horrified Agamemnon watching his wife coming toward him with a knife. . . . Once elevated to such a stature, the illusory Bulkaen can die in a way that will elicit pity and fear and induce catharsis from his creator. Through the imaginative process, Genet can create a new life which then begins to feed into his own, exciting his mind, energizing his spirit, and renewing his life by extending awareness.

The therapeutic benefits of imagination are by now obvious, and Genet never underestimates the rehabilitating potential of his art, which gives him a psychological advantage over his surroundings. The shining image produced by imagination rejuvenates his psyche and pulls him up from despair into the ecstatic realm of divine glory:

We know only the bleak, impossible grayness within us, and this grayness, which is even bleaker when shot through with a ray of sunlight, is the faces of the guards and the dismal severity of the objects. But it is so sweet—for then I can thumb my nose at the world of guards and judges, even at your world—when in its mists I see again the gleam of Harcamone's radiant image. . . . The murderer seemed to me more dazzling, which proves the delicacy of my feeling for Bulkaen. This love did not lure me to a nether region but, on the contrary, lifted me up and brightened my surroundings. I am using the very language with which mystics of all religions speak of their gods and mysteries. They arrive, as is said, in sun and lightning. It was thus that the condemned man appeared to my inner gaze, the vision being governed by my love for Bulkaen. (P. 118)

It seems fitting that Genet's language echoes the system traditionally providing spiritual comfort and relief, even if his salvation is signified by his ability to thumb his nose at all those below, including the reader. After all, his therapy had been for himself all along, not for us.

Indeed, the egocentricity of Genet's imagination is one of its most striking features, and it is this more than anything which turns his novels into a private experience. Using the novel as an intensely personal form of self-expression, Genet brings the form terribly close to autobiography, but his indulgence seems justified by the fact that he almost always uses his own life as metaphor for his exploration of more universal issues. The following passage is typical of many in which Genet begins talking about himself and the needs which drive him to recall his past, only to find himself arriving at a broader philosophical perspective:

Thus, my interest in adventure novels wanes in so far as I can no longer seriously imagine myself being the hero or being in his situation. I stopped plunging into those complications in which the slightest feat, criminal or otherwise, could be copied, carried over into life, utilized personally and lead me to wealth and glory. Thus, it was now extremely difficult for me to re-immerse myself in my dream-stories, stories fabricated by the disheartening play of solitude, but I found—and still find, despite my new plunge—more well-being in the true memories of my former life. Since my childhood is dead, in speaking of it I shall be speaking of something dead, but I shall do so in order to speak of the world of death, of the Kingdom of Darkness or Transparency. (P. 31)

Even so, it would be more appropriate for Genet to add the word, "my," in front of "Kingdom," for the line he casts out from himself will always follow a circular path until it returns to his own ego. The most obvious examples of this are the characters he creates as images to reflect himself. The novelist has traditionally used fictional characters in order to gain the artistic detachment necessary for creating an autonomous product. Objectification is the means through which the writer finds a common meeting ground with the reader. Genet scorns this concept: subjectivity remains the chief value in his life, just as he permits himself to be the main character of his novel. The vision emanates from him and returns to him; he is the one who profits most from his experience. Thus, as he decides to insert Divers as a character, he is

delighted at the immediate effect it has on him: "And so he gal-
loped in and took possession of the world, that is, of me. And he
dwelt within me. Henceforth, I enjoyed him as if I were pregnant
with him" (p. 79). By embodying the lives of his characters, Genet is able to use them for the enrichment of his own inner life.
Whereas the traditional novelist, even while throwing himself
into his characters, gave them an independent existence, Genet
throws his characters into himself, making them inseparable from
his own mind. If *Miracle of the Rose* does present us with more
characters than, say, one of Beckett's novels, those characters are
still only extensions of Genet's mind, which pulls all its created
images back to itself. Genet's imagination projects an image, and
the next step is completed when Genet swallows it (Malone, we
remember, set much the same goal for himself). By the end of the
book, all his creations are inside him, and his satiety implies that
the novel's purpose has been fulfilled.

Must we come to the conclusion, then, that the novel's objective is no more than its author's self-gratification? It would seem
so, because if we try to consider Genet's theme here, we find that
theme and purpose are one: by demonstrating the transcendent
powers of the imagination, *Miracle of the Rose* becomes the bible
for Genet's private religion—a system with its own gods (with
Bulkaen the Christ-like intermediary between Genet and Harcamone, his Lord), its own symbols (the sperm equivalent, perhaps,
to the wine of holy communion), its own concept of salvation (the
seaminess of prison life transformed through dream into the
Kingdom of Heaven). A book of miracles need owe nothing to
reality, and so Genet never feels impelled to justify his creation in
terms of the reader's logic. Rather than resist reality, he simply
ignores it, so that while a writer such as Conrad despairs of ever
knowing one's true motivations, and a writer such as Beckett
mocks our concern for finding the right causes to explain effects,
Genet simply inserts the cause he wishes to believe and lets it go
at that: "I didn't answer, but I lowered my head," he says at one
point, "and I would like the cause to have been an obscure sense
of shame at having a big shot other than this insolent tough" (p.
100). The one, real, objectively verifiable cause has become im-
material to Genet, so all conflict with chaos vanishes as reality
itself is dismissed as irrelevant.

If the imagination is unwilling to enter into contest with reality, the images it creates are for its own pleasure only, and there-

fore gratuitous to any philosophical purpose. Yet the very gratuitousness of his art defines it as a renderer of the Absurd, and this parallels Genet's devotion to the gratuitous crime—committed for no good reason or passion, but only for the purpose of making a gesture. "Harcamone's crimes," says Genet, "will appear to be foolish acts," yet that is exactly why he treasures them: the act itself is its own end, just as the imaginative process—the act of creating—becomes, too, a gesture, an attitude, a posture of defiance with no end beyond greater consciousness of the gesture (embodied in the image) made. Genet is not interested in accounting for Harcamone's criminality, for he is not a psychologist, but an artist: "I am a poet confronted with his crimes, and there is only one thing I can say: that those crimes gave off such a fragrance of roses that he will be scented with them, as will his memory and the memory of his stay here, until our waning days" (p. 47). Harcamone's crimes were beautiful just because they were unnecessary: the criminal had chosen to kill because in a spiritual vacuum, the question, Why not? deserves to be dealt with. Harcamone's murders are therefore acts of pure absurdity representing his willingness to accept the challenge of freedom which existentialism offers. Like those of Gide's Lafcadio and Camus's Meursault, Harcamone's crimes become an expression of freedom, which Genet values as creative acts of the will, similar to his own artistic creations.

Harcamone is a hero to Genet because most men cannot handle freedom—it drives them directly to despair. The ultimate value of Genet's art is also the book's theme: that one unable to bear freedom in reality can turn it to advantage in his imagination, thus gaining the solace he needs in order to transcend despondency. Faced with a life sentence in prison, Genet gradually comes to welcome the confinement he had earlier dreaded, and it is clear that he was saved by the discovery of art, which offered escape and fulfillment:

I once wanted to escape [prison]. Was it really because I was hopeless and unhappy? But the violence that quickens me when my hopelessness is too great would, at present, make me seek other means of flight. And I wonder whether a life sentence will not help me find them. . . . and it occurs to me, so that you may have a clearer understanding of my despair, to write that I was like the living leper who, with a taper in his hands, hears himself singing, behind his hood, the Office for the Dead, the Libera me. But hopelessness draws you out of yourself (I weigh my words). Mine was so deep that, in order for me to live (continuing to live being the important thing), my imagination first organized—and was first in doing so—a refuge for me in my very fall and created a very beautiful life for me. The imagination being rapid, this was done quickly. My imagination surrounded me with a host of adventures which were aimed perhaps at cushioning my encounter with the bottom of the precipice—for I thought it had a bottom, but hopelessness hasn't—and the deeper I fell, the faster my mind worked, accelerated by the speed of the fall. My tireless imagination kept weaving. It wove other adventures thick and fast. Finally it ran wild, excited by the violence, and a number of times I had the impression it was no longer the imagination but another and higher faculty, a salvatory faculty. All those splendid, invented adventures took on more and more a kind of consistency in the physical world. They belonged to the world of matter, though not here, but I felt they did exist somewhere. It was not I who lived them. They lived elsewhere and without me. This new and, as it were, eager faculty which sprang from but was higher than the imagination showed them to me, prepared them for me, organized them so that they were all ready to receive me. It would not have taken much for me to withdraw from the disastrous adventure that my body was living, to withdraw from my body (I was thus right in saying that hopelessness draws you out of yourself) and to project myself into those other consoling adventures which were unfolding parallel to poor mine. (Pp. 224–25)

This is at once Genet's theme and the function of his novel. He writes to save himself, and *Miracle of the Rose* is the story of his salvation.

Since imagination is the supreme value for Genet, it will determine, too, his other values. This is the only way of explaining the attraction prison holds for him. Like the monk who needs the privacy and silence of his cell in order to concentrate more fully on his God, Genet regards prison as the perfect atmosphere for the imagination to flourish and produce. By providing a peculiar combination of freedom and restraint, prison life caters to the imagination's need for the scope of license and the intensity of restriction. "As our life is without external hope, it turns its desires inward," says Genet (p. 109), and this becomes the primary requisite for an art growing out of continuous introspection. Again: "Prison was indeed the closed area, the confined, measured universe in which I ought to live permanently. It is the universe for which I am meant" (p. 33). By cutting off all other means of mental escape, prison intensifies the inner life and sharpens one's self-awareness. Speaking of his fellow prisoners,

Genet believes their brilliance to have been created by the solitary condition of their lives:

Living in so restricted a universe, they thus had the boldness to live in it as passionately as they lived in your world of freedom, and as a result of being contained in a narrower frame their lives became so intense, so hard, that anyone—journalists, wardens, inspectors—who so much as glanced at them was blinded by their brilliance. . . . the audacity to live (and to live with all one's might) within that world whose only outlet is death has the beauty of the great maledictions. . . . (P. 46)

Closed in on all sides, the prisoners' lives are concentrated, but the severe limitations on their external existences encourage a more active, vibrant, expansive inner life. "A man must dream a long time in order to act with grandeur, and dreaming is nursed in darkness" (p. 37), so prison, while it limits the life of the body, compensates by feeding the spirit the excess energy. Imagination becomes the benefactor of this new vitality and immediately begins to work up a fantasy life.

The ordinary prisoner, however, does not use his imaginative freedom productively but allows it to dissipate in the mundane. For such men, heaven remains as distant as it ever was for them outside:

Some men take pleasure in fantasies whose basic contents are not celestial delights. These are less radiant joys, the essence of which is evil. For these reveries are drownings and concealments, and we can conceal ourselves only in evil or, to be more exact, in sin. And what we see of just and honorable institutions at the surface of the earth is only the projection, necessarily transfigured, of these solitary, secret gratifications. (P. 37)

The base fantasists, then, are those who keep their dreams grounded in trivia instead of using them as a means to transcend the hopelessness of their lives. Their dreams, like those of the people outside, are built on the shallow precepts of short-term gratification; like useless daydreams, they consume time but do not nurture a new system on which to construct a higher form of life. Genet's superiority over the other inmates is in his awareness of the imaginative possibilities opened up by his environment: the combination of spiritual freedom and intensity, mental scope and concentration allows him to pursue a divine world in the darkness. Inspiration, revelation, and infinity grow out of the darkness and lead him to the breathtaking beauty that will deliver him unto God:

Abhorring the infinite, religions imprison us in a universe as limited as the universe of prison—but as unlimited, for our hope in it lights up perspectives just as sudden, reveals gardens just as fresh, characters just as monstrous, deserts, fountains; and our more ardent love, drawing greater richness from the heart, projects them on the thick walls; and this heart is sometimes explored so minutely that a secret chamber is breached and allows a ray to slip through, to alight on the door of a cell and to show God. (P. 47)

The prison thus becomes a metaphor for religion and, finally, for the novel itself, for all three are confining forms allowing paradoxically the apprehension of infinity. Each is a public system which can also accommodate the private system of the mystic; each offers its insights through revelations of beauty, and each can be used as the pathway to God.

If the novel is to be considered equivalent to prison in its ability to heighten and extend the scope of the imagination, then it must share with it also the intensification and concentration resulting from confinement. This would imply the author's tight control of his form through a rigid discipline of those components which expand the finite universe into a vision of infinity, multiplicity, and unlimited freedom. The novel should further illusion by cramping it into a corner where it can only turn inward.

To start with Genet's method of characterization, we can see that its extreme subjectivity distinguishes it from conventional techniques of endowing characters with sufficiently strong traits to insure their independence from the author so that they may stand on their own as representations of real people. Genet's method is just the opposite: as soon as he conceives his image of a character, he tries to shake him off solid ground and draw him into his own life. At times, this process seems almost cannibalistic, as if Genet wanted to swallow his characters whole, then digest them through dream. His pursuit of Divers is typical: "And I, having only the name Divers as a visible, prehensible asperity for grasping the invisible, shall contort it to make it enter mine, mingling the letters of both" (p. 80). Genet invents characters as means for grasping the invisible; his task, therefore, is not simply to find an image, but to embody it. His relationship to his characters is necessarily parasitic, because he, as the visionary, is the only one who counts; the others live only to the extent that they suggest the quality he needs in order to ascend to heaven—that highest level of the imagination where self-gratification is complete. What cannot be grasped can only be absorbed, so Genet invents characters in order to suck their vitality out of them. "I have the nerve to think that Bulkaen lived only so that I could write my book," says Genet (p. 19), though his egocentricity *is* mitigated by the fact that the Bulkaen he has created both for us and himself is quite different from the model who inspired the image. *That* Bulkaen is allowed his independent existence. Genet is not interested in the real Bulkaen, but only those qualities he evokes in Genet, which are then imposed onto the image Genet creates in the darkness. When the image has been perfected, Genet has his revelation, as the image shines with brilliant intensity, then burns itself out. Meanwhile, the creator has had his vision, has beheld the roses of paradise as the image entered him and breathed new life into his soul. This symbolic process of absorbing an ideal into one's own system is quite similar, really, to Christian communion.

Of course, the fictional creations of most novelists are imaginative reworkings of real people they have known, but Genet's relationship to his characters is exceptionally volatile and often confusing. While contemplating Bulkaen's projected death, for example, the author seems to sense his own fate bound up in that of his character:

I already knew he would lead me to death. I know now that this death will be beautiful. I mean that he was worthy of my dying for him and because of him. But may he lead me to it quickly. In any case, sooner or later it will be because of him. I shall die worn out or shattered. Even if, at the end of this book, Bulkaen proves to be contemptible because of his stupidity or vanity or some other ugly quality, the reader must not be surprised if, though aware of these qualities (since I reveal them), I persist in changing my life by following the star to which he points. . . .

He therefore had to die, after a life I can imagine only as bold and arrogant, slapping every pale face he came across. His death will be violent and mine will follow close on his. I feel that I'm wound up and heading for an end which will blow us to bits. (Pp. 18–19)

For Genet, Bulkaen's real life seems insignificant next to his creative force as a fictional image. By impressing its vision on Bulkaen's image, the imagination has transformed him into a star worth following to destruction. But why should the author's own death be intertwined with that of his character? An explosion seems imminent, yet the clash is not visible. Is it simply that Genet's feeling of an impending violence that will blow them both to bits is one he enjoys? Has he managed to achieve, through Bulkaen, that intensifying factor he wishes his life to be controlled by? It is hard to say exactly. It seems likely, though, that Genet is after the brilliance of the moment, and if the sense of violent death can make the moment burn with a hard intensity, then he will use it for that very purpose. Certainly, the omen planted so early in the book is far from substantiated by future events. Although Genet proclaims, "I want to possess Bulkaen," it is clear that Bulkaen offered no resistance to Genet's lust and also promised his fidelity to the older man. Yet Genet grows bored with the boy, and finally discards him after having siphoned off those qualities he needed:

The more I write about Bulkaen, the less attractive I find him. I have given life on paper to a paragon which I have adorned with all the beauties of my friend. I have stripped the flesh-and-blood Bulkaen whom I see emerging little by little from banality. I wonder whether he ever did possess all the charm that I discovered in him and that thrilled me so. Perhaps it was Bulkaen's role to be loved, and the ecstasy aroused by this love made it all the more possible for me to discover—thanks to language—the qualities of the ideal creature who is now fixed once and for all. The reader may ask whether I did not love Bulkaen precisely because I found these qualities in him *too*. I cannot answer.

I loved him less and less. . . . He no longer inspired me. I had got all I could from him—either for lack of means or because he himself had been emptied. By the play and tricks of language, he has helped me to portray a human being, to give him life and force. (Pp. 243–44)

The real-life Bulkaen possessed a beauty and sweetness which overwhelmed Genet at first, but when he got to know him well, Genet saw that what the flesh suggested was a nobility which Bulkaen himself never had. His criminality was petty, his mannerisms common, his values sentimental and shallow. Transformed by Genet's love, Bulkaen assumes a stature and force of personality which were never his. As Genet's love wears out, however, the magic wears off, and the image can no longer be used:

It is with words of love that I have recorded in this book his acts and gestures, all the attributes of his personality, which stands forth spiked with sharp angles. But as I no longer need, for the work of art, to seek within me—or to find there without seeking—the expressions that sublimated him. . . . I content myself with *seeing* him carry on without the help of magic words. I no longer name him. I have said all I have to say about him. The work flames and its model dies. . . . And now I feel only infinite pity for the poor birdie that can no longer fly because I have plucked all its feathers. (P. 244)

And so the artist who sensed his own violent destruction in the pursuit of his character has now sapped the vitality from his creation and put him out to pasture; his fear of the dynamic force represented by his image of Bulkaen has now turned into pity for "the poor birdie" whose beautiful feathers he has plucked for his own needs. Bulkaen turns back into the common creature he had always been, and Genet seeks a new object for his love. Nevertheless, Bulkaen has not been wasted: the intensity Genet has absorbed from him is now able to carry him to a higher rung in his imagination. For "although Bulkaen was not the fiery archangel, the archangel Harcamone, whose adventure transpired in Heaven, that is, in the highest region of myself," now becomes accessible to Genet, who needed the image of Bulkaen to lead him toward that of Harcamone. The effort involved in reaching Harcamone in order to capture him within his soul is a much greater challenge than Genet's previous attempt to imbibe Bulkaen, because Harcamone dwells in the loftiest regions of the imagination: "The expression 'in the highest region of myself' also means that I had to strain every fiber in order to see very high or very far within me, because I could barely make out the patterns, the diagrams inscribed there by the vibrations produced by Harcamone's human gestures, by his deeds on earth" (pp. 244–45). Bulkaen, then, has provided the means whereby he can be transcended: he, the visible lover, has enabled Genet to grasp the invisible Harcamone, just at Christ becomes the intermediary of flesh through which man can reach the purely spiritual God. Still, because God is the highest form of abstraction, the imagination must stretch itself into a position of torture before it can hope to gain access to the Heavenly Kingdom.

In discussing Harcamone's character, Genet makes it clear that the radiance he gave off was due less to his natural personality than to the situation which distilled his purest qualities: "he was as dull in free life as he was dazzling in prison" (p. 59). Comparing hardened convicts to actors who "in order to reach the highest pitch, require the freedom provided by the stage and by its fabulous lighting, or the situation, which is outside the physical world," Genet concludes that their "brilliance comes from the expression of their pure feelings. They have time to be tragic. . . . A man with a powerful personality is incapable of cunning or guile or of putting on an act" (p. 59). Art, then, extracts from the human personality its potentials for greatness and tragedy and then intensifies these qualities by confining the universe in which the character moves. Finally, by freezing time, art allows the potentials to develop into powerful illusions of reality. The result is a hero—a human being transformed through concentration and intensity into the quintessence of nobility.

Genet's method of creating images to worship is, therefore, equivalent to the means by which prison concentrates and intensifies one's imaginative life. Just as the imprisoned mind has no place to turn but inward, so Genet works on his human images by pulling them into his imagination, then pushing them deeper and deeper into his interior life until he can no longer distinguish the point where he leaves off and they begin. Genet creates characters in order to devour them into his own system; and when they have been successfully assimilated, the original models are discarded, while their images burn within him until the glow they give forth enables Genet to glimpse Heaven. While Beckett's Unnamable sought images by which he could slide down the hierarchy of man to reach the worm beneath, Genet seeks images by which he can ascend the hierarchy to reach the God above. We can see clearly here the contrast between a reductive system and an expansive one.

There are other ways, though, in which Genet has opened the novel to give it greater freedom. Given his primary values of subjectivity and omnipotence, it is not surprising that Genet exploits expressionistic techniques at will; what does make his use of them unusual is his incorporation of them into a realistic framework while refusing to apologize by turning them into metaphors. The result is a purposeful confusion of the worlds of reality and imagination which makes it impossible for the reader to become grounded in a consistent system. Just as the rose cut off from below Harcamone's left wrist retains its literal existence even after the rest of the garland has reverted to a steel chain, Genet frequently insists on the real-life consequences of his imaginative powers. Where does reverie end and reality begin? It becomes impossible to say as the author keeps us shifting from one world to the other with no signals to indicate where we are at a particular moment. Thus, when after trying to steal by the guards in order to pass Harcamone's cell, Genet is caught by one of them:

"What are you doing here?"
"You can see for yourself. I'm going by."
"You're going by? Where are you going? . . . And besides, I don't like your tone. Take your hands out of your belt."
I was on horseback. (P. 38)

Nothing has prepared us for this last line which Genet states as fact, and so the reader is at first almost tempted to take it literally. Of course, it soon becomes clear (Genet himself, in this instance, confesses it) that this "fact" is simply a metaphorical expression of the pose, stance, and gestures Genet had assumed while being reprimanded by the guard, but the suddenness with which Genet has carried us from physical reality to mental reality is still jolting enough to leave the reader unbalanced for a while. We could compare this technique to Kafka's, but Kafka's world is still consistent enough to provide a unified context within which the reader can gain a minimal security. Whereas Kafka's novels are supreme objectifications of the author's feelings, Genet's works do not offer an independent world which can be worked with without reference to its creator. Everything that happens in *Miracle of the Rose* happens because Genet wants it to, because it satisfies his need of the moment, not because the development of his novel has demanded it. And so it is with the continuous, effortless shifts from reality to dream: our minds flow into fantasy with incredible ease, whether or not we sanction their freedom, and Genet has simply reproduced this flux by interweaving, transposing, and blending the two worlds. The reader, as a result, can never adjust himself completely, because Genet throws the dream into reality and reality into dream. His expressionism, therefore, is used to make us aware that we had already slipped from one world to the other without having realized it.

If much of the book has a dreamlike quality, that is because Genet has used dream as a basic technique in presenting his real world. At one point, he sees himself as "a dream character who knows that he lives only in the darkest region of a being whose face he will not know when the dreamer is awake" (p. 34). Since he feels his truest existence as one immersed in dreams and generating his power *through* dreams, the worlds of reality and fantasy are inseparable, and his novel must therefore reflect the fusion of the two systems. Thus, *Miracle of the Rose* moves *by* dream as well as *through* dream: it is the momentum of dreams which propels the novel forward, the context of dreams which turns the concrete world of reality into a symbolic system, and the mirroring quality of dreams that suggests Genet's use of "the double." Just as reality feeds itself into dream as subject matter, so dream feeds back reality, transformed into a world of symbolic richness:

Dreams are peopled with characters, animals, plants, objects, which are symbols. Each is potent, and when the one who occasioned it substitutes for the symbol, he benefits from this mysterious power. The potency of the sign is the potency of the dream. . . . (P. 223)

Thus, the context of dream must be superimposed upon reality before the concrete world can be incorporated into the vision which provides it with power, import, and meaning. Furthermore, dream extends reality to include the ineffable and the infinite. The "mysterious power" with which it infuses its subjects is the power of a spell that cannot be broken with words or created with thought which is bound to language; one can apprehend the results of its magic but can never express directly its evocative powers. Finally, by transcending time, dreams enable us to grasp the infinite. Structuring his novel on the principle of dream, Genet distorts the reader's sense of time until he moves through the creator's world utterly disoriented. Time is slowed down for the reader in much the same way as it is for those prisoners with life sentences. We are shocked to learn toward the end of the book, for example, that Genet's entire acquaintance with Bulkaen lasted only twelve days—we would no doubt have guessed years. This distending of time can be seen, too, in Genet's description of the calendars made by those prisoners with finite sentences of, say, twenty years:

Over those twenty years they indulge in the most frightfully complicated mathematics. They multiply, divide, juggle the number of months, days, weeks, hours, minutes. They want to arrange those twenty years in every possible way, and it seems as if the twenty years were going to be extracted from the numbers in pure form. Their calculations will end only on the eve of their release, with the result that the twenty years will appear to have been necessary in order to know the combinations contained in twenty years, and the aim and justification of the imprisonment will be these calculations which, placed flat against the wall, look as if they were being slowly swallowed up in the darkness of the future and the past and, at the same time, seem to be shining with so unbearable a present brightness that this brightness is its own negation. (Pp. 58–59)

When time stops moving, even twenty years can give the illusion of infinity. But infinity can be captured equally as well in the reverie of a moment because the dream works outside of time and cannot, therefore, be bound by it, just as the gratuitous murderer dwells outside of the values common to other men, and so cannot be touched by them.

It is clear that the dream is crucial to Genet's vision, for it is only through capturing the dream that the vision can be apprehended. In his pursuit of dream, Genet is actually pursuing the ineffable, the infinite, and the double; he is trying to purify himself into a poet who intuits through his symbolical powers the world which lies beyond words. What he needs now is an image that will reflect his present world, but draw it into dream and therefore, beneath language and beyond time. This image he finds in Mettray, the prison where he lived out most of his childhood.

"My childhood was dead and with it died the poetic powers that had dwelt in me," Genet says early in the book. "I no longer hoped that prison would remain what it had long been, a fabulous world. One day, I suddenly realized from certain signs that it was losing its charms, which meant perhaps that I was being transformed, that my eyes were opening to the usual view of the world" (p. 25). Genet's sentiments here are so similar to William Wordsworth's in his "Ode on Intimations of Immortality Recollected in Early Childhood" that we may easily use the Romantic sensibility to explain Genet's reasoning. Like Wordsworth, Genet conceives of the poet as the inspired visionary who sees the Divine splendor that common men miss. Through his superior imagination, intuitive faculties, and powers of insight, the Romantic poet is able to transform the ordinary world into a shimmering image of divinity. As he ages, however, and becomes increasingly aware of his own mortality, he must work harder to recapture the joy and spontaneity of childhood. And so the poet, through conscious, willful use of the imagination, pursues the lost vision, the quintessentially poetic one—for it needed no words to apprehend the Divine, which the child carried inside him—of immortality embodied in innocence. The vision which is felt has no need for language and concepts which destroy the mystery of life through the intellect's attempt to analyze, comprehend, and master it. Dissection kills.

Mention of the word love between Bulkaen and me aged us. It made me realize that we were no longer at Mettray and that we were no longer playing. But at Mettray we obviously had more gusto, for the fact of not naming our feelings, out of shyness and ignorance, made it possible for us to be dominated by them. We submitted to them entirely. But when we knew their names, it was easy for us to speak of feelings that we could think we were experiencing when we had named them. (P. 83)

The sense of immortality is, then, ineffable; it is words which "age" us, throw us into the world of time and mortality. When Genet recalls Mettray, it comes back to him as a feeling that cannot be conveyed through language, and he wonders how he can ever communicate it to the reader:

But this feeling—or its reflection—flares up within me. I cannot make it last. If ever I do, *will you know* what Mettray was like? But I think it as hard to render as to convey *to you* what the odor of my mouth is to me. However, I shall tell you that the white banners, the cedars, the statue of the Holy Virgin in the wall of Family E were not commonplace things, the kind you can find anywhere. They were signs. In a poem, ordinary words are shifted around in such a way that their usual meaning is enriched by another: the poetic import. Each of the things, each of the objects that recur to my mind composed a poem. (Pp. 209–10)

Poetry here shares all the qualities of the dream: just as words, though unable to communicate deep feeling, can in the context of poetry, become meaningful as *suggestions* (rather than definitions) of feeling, so too can objects, when placed in the context of dream, assume symbolic power as signs, and thus be used to intimate the ineffable world where all profound feelings have their source and fulfillment.

It is Mettray, in fact, that Genet seems to be pursuing in his love for Bulkaen, for it is just after he has learned that Bulkaen too had spent most of his childhood at Mettray that Genet feels his friendship turning into love:

The love I had been damming up for several days broke through its reserve and flowed out in the form of great pleasure in finding a Mettray colonist in my division. The word pleasure isn't quite right. Neither is joy, nor the other synonyms, nor satisfaction, nor even felicity or delight. It was an extraordinary state since it was the fulfillment of what I had been desiring (though with a vague desire that remained obscure to me until the day of my encounter) for twenty years: to find in someone other than myself the memory of Mettray, as much perhaps in order to relive

Mettray as to continue it in my adult life by loving in accordance with the ways of the past. (P. 53)

From this point on, Mettray becomes for Genet what childhood had been for Wordsworth: the means through which memory can recapture the pure, religious ecstasy needed to transcend philosophical despair. But since success must be characterized by silence, however, Genet feels the conflict between the creation that can be made only with words (since he is writing a novel) and the mystical vision that lies *beyond* words. After one typically frustrating experience of trying to communicate to the reader what cannot be caught through language, Genet senses the inevitable failure of his form: "But all I have just said exists through words, whether flat or luminous. Will it be said that I'm singing? I am. I sing of Mettray, of our prisons and my hoodlums. . . . Your song has no object. You sing of the void. Words may conjure up for you the pirate I want to speak of. To me he remains invisible" (p. 90). Forced, though, to find an image for a face he himself cannot remember, Genet decides to use for a model a handsome German soldier, who purified himself by committing a pointless murder:

He will serve as a model for my description of that figurehead whose face and body have worn away, but if I start using this subterfuge to revive my galley, am I quite sure that all of Mettray will not be described according to models quite different from the reality and chosen, as chance would have it, from among my lovers? But what does it matter! If I restore such a limbo bit by bit, it is because I carried it scattered within me. It is because the Colony is contained in my loves, or else my only loves are those that can revive it. (Pp. 90–91)

Mettray must be reconstituted by the only means possible—that is, by the careful selection of images that keep Mettray alive for Genet. The images themselves may be arbitrary, just so long as they awaken the feelings or profound love which signifies Mettray's meaning for him.

In searching for his models, the author feels no obligation to reality, but only to his imagination: words, images, and settings are nothing more than the indirect means through which the novelist pursues and presents his vision. The vision is pure feeling, but objective correlatives must be found to project just the right tone, color, and mood. As indicated by the above passage, however, Genet's method will be fragmentary, because few feelings can be expressed entirely through a one-to-one relationship with a central image. Instead, multiple images will be used to connote a multifaceted experience. Snatches of objects, incidents, characters, and settings will be utilized—drained for their relevant import—and then discarded. We have already found that Genet's expressionism is particularly striking and effective because it appears as fact amid a scene of literal reality and so does not warn us of its immediate psychological intentions. A perfect example of this is when Genet, in speaking of Mettray, suddenly and inexplicably changes the prison into a galley ship. The terminology immediately shifts to that of navigation, and the roles of the prisoners are redefined in nautical terms:

I had become particularly friendly with the pilot (note how I speak of that galley on which, though I could have been the master, I accorded myself only the lowliest post, that of cabin boy, and sought the friendship of my mates. You'll say that I wanted to be a cabin boy in order to enjoy the love of the whole crew, but you ask why I didn't choose, by inventing some other story, of kidnaping or of boarding a boat, to be a fair captive). Perhaps I had vowed the pilot this friendship because of the melancholy, of the loneliness too, which never left him and so made me think he was gentler, more tender, more affectionate than the other sailors. For all the buccaneers were brutes. . . . I continued on board ship the life I had led at Mettray, but with even more cruelty, with such cruelty that I could thereby project my real life and perceive its "double," which too often was invisible. (P. 92)

Like the dream which reflects reality by rendering it in new terms enabling us to grasp it, the double holds great significance for Genet, because it aids him in pursuing the meaning of his reality. In the act of reflecting, the double clarifies ineffable reality and makes it possible for our minds to focus on it. Obviously, this is the same principle we have already seen at work in Genet's method of characterization, his use of language, and his choices of setting. In each case, his inner life is enriched as he comes to embody the model he has chosen to represent what he wants to capture in reality. This technique has repercussions in time, too, as Genet uses a model in the present to capture a love of the past (Bulkaen for Mettray, for example), one from the past to capture a love in the present (Divers for Bulkaen), or a love in the present to capture one in the future (Bulkaen for Harcamone). Therefore, just as Bulkaen in the present is used by Genet to grasp his past love for Mettray, so Mettray itself "blossomed curiously in the heavy shadow of Fontevrault" (p. 104). The result is a multiple vision in time and space which, by distilling all the elements of reality it can make use of, enables the imagination to live with greater consciousness in the present. It is really Genet's life at Fontevrault that is the subject of *Miracle of the Rose,* and so even the pursuit of Mettray is not an end in itself, but simply another means through which Genet hopes to come to terms with his present life. "Mettray," he says, ". . . dared the act of wanting to become Fontevrault" (p. 229). His former home is, in short, a double for the new prison he hates.

Genet's re-creation of Mettray helps him to grasp what it was about the Colony that made it such a powerful love experience for him. At one point, he identifies the prison with a woman, and sensing something significant, "I endowed the Colony with all these ridiculous and disturbing attributes of womankind, until there was established in my mind not the physical image of a woman but rather a soul-to-soul bond between us which exists only between mother and son and which my undeceivable soul recognized" (p. 230). Finally, the meaning of Mettray becomes clear as the mother metaphor begins to work. The mother is, after all, the origin of all feeling, the primary source of love, the ultimate symbol of comfort in a world of chaos. It is Mettray which forms the foundation of Genet's existence, Mettray which showed him the singular value of love in a life that would otherwise be unmitigated despair.

The closing lines of the novel would seem to indicate that Genet has accomplished all that an artist can hope for: "Have I told all there was to tell of this adventure? If I take leave of this book, I take leave of what can be related. The rest is ineffable. I say no more and walk barefoot" (p. 344). What can be said has been said, and the rest—so much more important—has been suggested through the indirect means which is the novel's only way of dealing with the reality it wishes to transcend. The man walking away from his novel is now a god: like Lily Briscoe, he has had his vision.

I have said that each component of the novel, as handled by Genet in *Miracle of the Rose,* works paradoxically, like prison, to create an impression of freedom confined. Dream, though, would seem to offer total liberation not only to the spirit, but also to the form. How can we find an organizational principle for that which lies beneath form and beyond words? If Genet were to take away the tension of reality, and make dream the sole impetus for the novel, he would never have been able to end it as he does; his form would have dissolved entirely in ineffable experience. Yet Genet must, at the same time, give us the *illusion* of dream to suggest imagination in its purest state, working itself up to Heaven. The author's solution is ingenious and unique: he controls and organizes his use of dream through the process of masturbation. Thus, in creating fantasies with no end beyond his own pleasure, he experiences freedom; yet that freedom is structured by and contained within the climax of orgasm.

The masturbation fantasy is, for Genet, an act of love, as well as the means through which he conceives and retains that love. From the beginning, the novel gets its impetus and purpose from the author's need to possess, purify, and focus on his love for Bulkaen:

> I arrived in the morning from a punishment cell where in order to enjoy by means of words the memory of Bulkaen, who had remained above, in order to caress him by caressing the words which are meant to recall him to himself by recalling him to me, I had begun the writing of this book on the white sheets with which I was supposed to make paper bags. (P. 43)

Again, the imagination is used as a mirror to reflect reality and capture one's own most elusive and significant experiences. By providing a free form for Genet's fantasies, masturbation becomes a useful way of projecting imagination onto reality in the form of wish fulfillment. Even if limited to sexual content, the fantasy can still suggest love, clarify relationships, and render vision. Genet's preoccupation with sex should not, I think, be interpreted solely as metaphor, but because his deepest feelings tend to manifest themselves in sexual terms, we can certainly be justified in considering sex here as a means as well as an end. Just as Harcamone's penis becomes Genet's image of God, so his other sexual attractions always have a spiritual or philosophical dimension. Ultimately, the worlds of fantasy and reality begin to fade into each other, until the symbols acquired from the "mysterious power" of dreams find their realistic equivalents and become embodied by the everyday world. I have already referred to the dream which turns Mettray into a galley ship, so it might be appropriate to use that sequence as an illustration of these points. Genet begins by defining his role as dreamer:

At night, I often stay awake. I am the sentinel at the gate of the sleep of others, whose master I am. I am the spirit that hovers above the shapeless mass of dream. The time I spend there pertains to the time that flows in the eyes of dogs or in the movements of any insect. We have almost ceased to be in the world. And if, to cap it all, rain is falling, then everything sinks, engulfed in the horror where only my galley remains afloat on those ponderous waves. On rainy nights, the storm-tossed ship rolled gunwale under. The thick squalls seriously disconcerted the males whom nothing frightened. . . . (Pp. 135–36)

Dreams freeze time and confound form, and Genet, who spends so much of his life in this world, that he sees himself as a "spirit," becomes a kind of Queen Mab, drifting in and out of dream with such ease and frequency that he cannot even distinguish the infinite world from the finite one. Hearing the rain outside (which I take to be real rain, actually falling), Genet immediately injects it into a reverie, without giving the slightest warning to the reader that he is now floating out of reality and into dream. As a result, the reader misses the transition (just as he can miss the movement of an insect by blinking), and so tumbles into the dream before knowing where he is. Suddenly the rain has become expressionistic rather than real, as the "storm-tossed ship" rolls over the waves, and Genet describes his shipmates' fear. Genet, who has just indentified himself as the master of dreams, now takes on the role of slave as the sequence develops. Finally, as we begin to orient ourselves to an expressionistic context, we realize that the shipmates are his fellow prisoners (whose "past crimes were purified by their being at last so close to God") and the ship itself, Mettray. Now the dream becomes increasingly erotic as Genet uses sexual fantasies to stimulate himself:

We went back and forth in the dark warm rain. Our naked torsos were gleaming. At times, without recognizing each other, men would embrace as they passed in the darkness and would then rush to do their job, with their muscles both excited and softened by that single caress. The most light-footed of the pirates swayed in the rigging, but I carried the lantern in the most tangled note of the maneuver, and it was at times a knot of rough love. The sea was roaring. I was sure that nothing could happen since I was with those who loved me. They were sure that nothing could harm them since the captain was there. And in my hammock I would fall asleep in his arms where I would continue making love despite the fatigue of the love in which I had just indulged. My life on the galley threaded its way into my daily life. One day I heard myself thinking: "Anger fills our sails." And it was enough for rebellious colonists to be called mutinous for the night's confusion to settle on my days. (P. 136)

The real rain has provided the setting for Genet's dream, and the real prison floats into it with all its relationships intact. Roles and terminology are adjusted to the new environment, but feelings and identities remain the same. Now projected as a double, the dream works through imagination for its own pleasure: eroticism builds along with wish fulfillment (as masturbation is indicated by the description of frequent back-and-forth movements of friction), and finally reaches a climax with Genet securely asleep in the arms of the Captain (the Harcamonian figure, whom Genet wants to serve) and yet continuing to make love to him. Orgasm. And then—again with no transition—we are back in reality, and Genet explains the influence of such a dream on his real life, until his reality itself is transformed by it (having caught the mysterious power of its symbolic counterpart) and the language of the dream carries over, too, until the two worlds become fused.

It is little wonder, then, that Genet will not permit his reader to become more securely oriented than he himself can be. Tossed from dream to reality, and then back again, we are forced into his world: Genet, whose complete subjectivity demands that everything in the external world be drawn into his inner life, has managed to consume the reader as well as his own created characters, for his awareness of an audience provides the added thrill of exhibitionism. It is only after the orgasm that the imagination stops working solely for its own gratification and attempts to build a vision from the objects and scenes it has been playing with. When Genet feels himself prompted to say, "Anger fills our sails," his intellect has by now gained sufficient control for him to recognize the dream as metaphor for reality, and that becomes, in turn, his method of dealing with real experience and interpreting the events in his life.

Genet wants more than this, however: he wishes not only to *know* his life, but to *transcend* it. Yet he insists on attaining the state of religious ecstasy not simply in spite of, but *through* his preoccupations with sex and crime. Since these are the most shocking and sensational aspects of his novel, the reader must overcome a good many of his own values and assumptions before he can make sense of Genet's system. Genet does help us, though, by planting some striking sexual metaphors throughout the novel in order to prepare us for the mystical state through which he finally achieves communion with Harcamone—that episode toward which his book has been building all along.

I have mentioned those erotic scenes which Genet creates strictly for his pleasure, but sexual images are also used to fashion some of the most pungent metaphors in the book. The psychological validity of these metaphors gives them political, social, and spiritual significance, even though their bluntness and brutality would seem at first to preclude such high-minded purpose. Thus:

I realize that I loved my Colony with my flesh just as, when it was reported that the Germans were preparing to leave, France realized, in losing the rigidity they had imposed on her, that she had loved them. She squeezed her buttocks. She begged the supplanter to remain inside her. "Stay a while," she cried. . . .

In my sadness, I feel such a need to go rampant that I could tear out my heart and throw it in your face. (P. 280)

The metaphor slams into us with such force that the line which follows seems a most accurate description of the way Genet is determined to work on us. Yet, as the shock dissolves, some truth seems to remain. Surely the relationship between conqueror and victim, master and subject, sadist and masochist is so terribly complex that it takes an unusual metaphor to suggest all the psychological intricacies involved. By portraying the enemy countries as lovers, Genet blasts us onto unfamiliar territory, where our old reflexes will no longer work to protect us, and we are almost ready to acknowledge a kind of sad beauty in a relationship where pleasure and grief commingle.

The thin line between sexuality and spirituality is depicted later on in the book in a fascinating sequence that brings together the beauty of sex and its strange mysticism in sordid surroundings. As Genet relates the prisoner Toscano's drowning and the attempt of his lover, Deloffre, to revive him, he creates what is for me the most moving scene in the novel:

Toscano swam out a way with Deloffre. He must have fallen into a hole. He disappeared in the water, and Deloffre brought him back in his arms, drowned. He put him down on the grass of the meadow. The entire family B was there, and we were some distance away from the head of the family. We were thunderstruck. Deloffre stretched Toscano on his stomach and sat astride him. He began his rhythmic pressures as advised by the subway poster. This poster is illustrated by a curious drawing: a young man straddling the back of another who is lying on his stomach. Did the memory of that picture (evoked by the necessity of the moment) arouse obscene thoughts in Deloffre . . . or was his posture itself sufficient? Or the proximity of death? The rhythmic pressure was at first desperate but big with hope, with mad hope. The despair subsided at the slightest hope. His movements grew slower, but though less rapid, they were extraordinarily vigorous, they seemed charged with a spiritual life. Naked in the green meadow, with the sun drying our bodies, we formed a circle of worried, anxious souls. . . . (P. 301)

Stunned and entranced, the prisoners look on, feeling unconsciously that they are witnessing a miracle:

Deloffre's gesture in that green grass was sacred. Nobody laughed.

Finally, there was a moment when he was completely shaken with little shudders: it was neither the wind drying the water on his shoulders, nor fear, nor shame, but pleasure. At the same time, he collapsed on the dead body. His grief was frightful and we realized that it would have taken a woman to calm him. (P. 302)

Psychologically the event makes sense. Deloffre's desperation is so great that it collides with passion. Since the act of trying to bring life back into Toscano is an act of love, there is no inconsistency when this turns into a literal act of love as well. At the point of orgasm, Deloffre's pleasure reaches its peak at the very instant his anguish becomes supreme. Pleasure and grief coincide, and their juxtaposition is so strange that the act assumes a mystical significance of shattering intensity. What seems at first to be sensational, obscene, and revolting is transcended into a metaphor of dazzling beauty and pathos. The multiplicity of Genet's vision is constantly manifested through paradox, and this metaphor becomes a powerful statement of the enigmatic density at the roots of profound feeling. It is through such metaphors as these that Genet prepares us for the culminative experience which completes the book.

In his attempt to reach a spiritual communion with Harcamone, Genet has used Bulkaen and Divers as models on which he hopes to raise himself toward his god. That god has attained his stature because he has taken on the great challenge life can offer: the fact of his own death. Death lurks around Harcamone until the two become intimate, and it is this intimacy with death along with Harcamone's fearlessness in confronting it that accounts for Genet's admiration and wonder. He will not be satisfied, therefore, until he has made contact with his god, experienced communion:

I therefore buried myself, as I have said, in the depths of the atmosphere created here by the secretly united presences of Harcamone and Divers. Harcamone lived in the twists and turns of a slow, complicated death that wound in and out of itself. Without saying anything expressly, Divers and I communed—by virtue of our haunted looks and gestures—in Harcamone's death. The extraordinary purity with which I endow Bulkaen, the living light, the moral rectitude with which I adorned him, had given my aspiration toward Harcamone, and the form of his destiny, the semblance of an ascension. I felt I was rising toward him, and this necessarily made me place him very high, radiant, in the very stance of Bulkaen waiting for me at the top of the stairs. But this interpretation was erroneous. (P. 311)

In aspiring toward Harcamone, Genet again demonstrates the subjectivity at the heart of his book, for what he wants is to become God! To aspire toward Harcamone does not mean that Genet wants to get to him so that he can shake his hand, but so that he may draw Harcamone into himself and thus acquire the attributes of God. And now Genet's emphasis on crime finally becomes clear: it is through crime (or by embodying those criminals who have committed the great crimes) that Genet will seek his salvation:

If customary saintliness consists in rising heavenward toward one's idol, it was quite natural, since the saintliness leading me to Harcamone was its exact opposite, that the exercises which were orienting me were of an order other than those which lead to heaven. I had to go to him by a path other than that of virtue. I did not seek access to brilliant crime. The abjection in which Divers remained—and the more intense abjection of our two united wills—drove us head downward in the direction away from heaven, into the darkness, and the thicker the darkness, the more sparkling—hence, the blacker—Harcamone would therefore be. I was happy about his agony, about Divers' treachery, and we were more and more capable of so ghastly an act as the murder of a little girl. The joy I feel when I am told of certain acts which the multitude calls infamy should not be confused with sadism. (P. 311)

Genet concludes that he loved Bulkaen for his ignominy, and perhaps this makes clear why he had said originally that Bulkaen was to be the cause of his own destruction. It seems now that Genet *desired* self-destruction because he saw it as the bottom rung in the darkness from which he could step toward Harcamone. All traditional values are reversed here as the author chooses his own unique system as a pathway to God and resolves to make it work. He is taking full advantage of his role as novelist to dictate his will upon his form, and he chooses a process so unusual that its success alone would validate his independence and omnipotence as creator; the novel's function as wish fulfillment, ego gratification, and self-therapy; and the powers of imagination to intensify and transcend its own gratuitous forms.

Genet succeeds: the final segment of *Miracle of the Rose* becomes entirely expressionistic as reverie and masturbatory fantasy fall into the freedom of ineffable dream. "Can the name reverie be given to the workings of my mind or of whatever faculty it was that enabled me to live in Harcamone, to live in Harcamone as we say to live in Spain" (p. 318)? It is not reverie, but the active will of the imagination that enables Genet to experience the revelation in which "Harcamone's cell appeared within me" (p. 319). Finally, Harcamone has been captured. Now Genet must make the murderer subservient to his own will, must make Harcamone's life indistinguishable from his own. Slowly, the author concentrates his powers, "strong in the knowledge that I was operating in accordance with the poetic powers. That entire exercise had been governed by what I am obliged to call the soul of Bulkaen" (p. 320). Gradually, Genet feels Harcamone bending to the poet's will, moving under his orders. The mystic is beginning to get control over his vision. When he awakes the next morning (and are we to assume, then, that he awakes from dream into reality?), "I was still holding between my teeth the stem of the rose which I had stolen from Harcamone and which my fervor preciously guarded. . . . I was tremendously excited at the thought of being the mystic betrothed of the murderer who had let me have the rose that had come directly from a supernatural garden" (p. 321). Do real roses grow in supernatural gardens? Genet forces us to assume that they do: the power of dream has now taken reality in its grasp and is manipulating it as it pleases. It is for dream now to determine what is real.

That night, Genet sleeps with Divers, and as Divers opens Genet's trousers to make love to him, Genet controls his vision at last. "The string snapped. I was leaving Harcamone. I was betraying Harcamone" (p. 322). Genet's joy is complete. He has now performed the counterpart of Divers' betrayal of Harcamone: he has extricated himself from the last remnants of a conventional value system. He has asserted his independence from even his god. He himself has replaced Harcamone as the omnipotent deity who need offer fidelity to no one. Whatever exists outside of himself counts for nothing: he is supreme, aloof, alone. His imagination is now the sole determinant of reality—it directs not only Harcamone, but the workings of the whole world. With the purity and power of dream, Genet's imagination finally breaks away from literal reality completely, and creates its own. Thus, as Harcamone prepares himself to slip out of prison,

His right hand moved away from the wall, grazed his fly, the cloth of which heaved like the surface of a sea shaken by a terrible inner storm, and then opened it. A bevy of more than a hundred doves pressed together in a rustle of wings, emerged, flew to the window, and entered the night, and it was not until morning that the youngsters who keep watch around the prison, lying in the moss behind the tree trunks, awoke in the dew with the dove of their dreams nestling in the hollow of their hands. (P. 323)

The doves are real; even those in the outside world can hold them in their hands. Reality is now discarded as imagination takes the novel in hand. "I no longer seek in reveries the satisfaction of my amorous desires, as on the galley," says Genet (p. 326), and it is obvious that his imaginative powers have become much more ambitious; they wish now to transform the sordid into the most elegant vision, whereby a legend can take hold and become a new religion:

It is not to be wondered at that the most wretched of human lives is related in words that are too beautiful. The magnificence of my tale springs naturally (as a result of my modesty too and of my shame at having been so unhappy) from the pitiable moments of my entire life. Just as the Golden Legend flowered from a banal sentence to torture pronounced two thousand years ago, just as Botchako's singsong voice blossomed into the velvet corollae of his rich, rippling voice, so my tale, which issues from my shame, becomes glorious and dazzles me. (Pp. 325–26)

It is no wonder, then, that Genet can turn farts into pearls: he is the new Christ, the Miracle Worker, and he stands at the apex of his own symbolical system. Christ could transform cripples into healthy men, bring the dead to life; Moses could part the Red Sea; Genet can open his fly and watch doves emerge, fart and watch pearls emerge, take a steel chain and turn it into a garland of roses. If such feats remind us more of a kiddie-matinee magician than a Savior, we must remember that all religious systems have seemed theatrical until they had gathered enough converts to be considered miraculous. Genet's religion is his art, imagination its God, freedom and beauty its commandments.

As Harcamone lies in his cell on the morning of his execution, he hears the door open, the men in black entering to take him, "but he also realized very quickly that, in order to die in his sleep, he must not disrupt or destroy the state of dreaming in which he was still entangled. He decided to maintain the dream" (p. 333). And he does. When he stands up to greet the men, he fills the entire universe, dwarfing the lawyer, judge, executioner, and chaplain into tiny bedbugs running up and down his body. Climbing up his fly, they enter Harcamone through the mouth and ears, then "moved forward a little along the edge of the lower lip and fell into the gulf. And then, almost as soon as they passed the gullet, they came to a lane of trees that descended in a gentle, almost voluptuous slope. All the foliage was very high and formed the sky of the landscape" (p. 335). The four men press forward through forests, over fences, past the remains of a country fair, until "they realized that they had unwittingly been following a succession of winding paths more complicated than those of a mine. There was no end to Harcamone's interior. It was more decked with black than a capital whose king has just been assassinated" (p. 335). Working their way to Harcamone's heart, the men hear its beat all around them but cannot locate it. Finally, they come upon an open area where "upright on a wooden block, stood a young drummer. . . . The drumsticks rose and fell sharply and neatly" (p. 337). The drummer is not surprising because the heartbeat Genet hears is no doubt that of Divers, whose body is wrapped around his own. More surprising, though, is the monstrous, dazzling rose which the men find inside the door of Harcamone's heart. They leap madly into the petals, "staggered by the splendor" (p. 337) until, dizzy, they lose their balance and "toppled into that deep gaze" (p. 338). Harcamone seems to have devoured the men who have come to murder him. He also seems to be dreaming!

But Harcamone's dream is generated through Genet's imagination—an imagination now entirely expressionistic and oriented toward perpetuating its own religion. The center of *Miracle of the Rose* is, finally, not Bulkaen, not even Harcamone, and only to a degree Genet himself. The main character is the author's imagination, which not only reflects experience, but determines experience. Reality is made to embody dream, but dream finally renders reality. If it can transform the sour world of prisons, the abject world of convicts into a world of dazzling beauty, what, then, can it not do? Nothing, of course.

And that does seem to be Genet's main point. Reality is sordid, dull, incomprehensible, and unknowable. But whereas chaos cannot be fought on the literal level, we can accommodate it with ease on any other level. Reality can therefore be dismissed as a matter of serious concern: it is totally at the mercy of our inventive faculties, which can transform it at will to satisfy our needs. Like the mind of Beckett's Murphy, Genet's novel is a place for the imagination to live for a while: it chooses a subject, then plays with it and works with it until it has discovered just the right way of looking at it for its own purposes. To bring imagination down to the world of reality where it can only confess its inability to find truth is useless activity. Instead, allow the imagination to soar, and let it take reality along for the ride. The roles of master and subject must be changed. Rather than bump against the chaos of our lives, let us unloose the natural chaos of the imagination and live *there*. That world may be no more meaningful, but it *can* be much more beautiful, and, in any case, we have made it for ourselves and can move out at any time.

9

The Contours of Chaos

The Noninterpretative Art of Robbe-Grillet

> The art of the novel . . . has fallen into such a
> state of stagnation—a lassitude acknowledged
> and discussed by the whole of critical opinion—
> that it is hard to imagine such an art can sur-
> vive for long without some radical change. To
> many, the solution seems simple enough: such
> a change being impossible, the art of the novel
> is dying. This is far from certain. History will
> reveal . . . whether the various fits and starts
> which have been recorded are signs of a death
> agony or of a rebirth.
>
> —Alain Robbe-Grillet,
> "A Future for the Novel"

*A*s a spokesman for the "New Novel," whose
convulsions signal for him the stirrings of new life rather than the
death pangs of an old one, Robbe-Grillet, in his collected essays
For a New Novel, attempts to orient the reader to a work which
seems to have no recognizable ancestry. Noting that "the stam-
mering newborn work will always be regarded as a monster,
even by those who find experiment fascinating,"[1] he feels impelled to explain the principles which brought this "monster"
into being. Monster? In what sense? Obviously, in every sense
whereby the reader evaluates its unfamiliar features: "a new

---

1. Alain Robbe-Grillet, *For a New Novel: Essays on Fiction*, trans. Richard Howard (New York: Grove Press, 1965), p. 17. All future page references, noted in
parentheses, are to this edition.

form will always seem more or less an absence of any form at all, since it is unconsciously judged by reference to the consecrated forms" (p. 17). It is, then, only in the light of our traditional expectations as readers that this New Novel's deformities seem to become glaring evidence of literary failure. After all: Where is plot? Where is character? What has happened to structure? To the richness of language? Where is the author's vision, his substance? Where is the author's reality? Where is *our* reality? Where is art, where is form, where is purpose? Are our emotional needs to be left unsatisfied? Our intellectual needs dismissed? Our anguish not to be depicted? Our lives and relationships not to be represented? Certainly, life itself seems less chaotic than this new novel.

And Robbe-Grillet would no doubt agree: our lives have familiar forms which we take for granted as part of that reality we always want to see more clearly. But until we discard this false sense of security and confess our ignorance of those forms which we assumed to have constituted our limited knowledge, we shall never make contact with the reality we feel to be hidden behind them. Reality is much closer to us than we suspect—and much less accessible. It is useless to sit on a sofa and contemplate the depths of our lives when the very sofa beneath us is as remote from our understanding as the shadows at the bottom of our minds. Of course, the sofa is familiar to us—we recognize its form, know its function, and feel secure in the standards by which we evaluate its beauty, comfort, and utility—but are these qualities embedded in the sofa or only in our own minds? And if we divest the sofa of all those attributes we have so arbitrarily assigned to it, it immediately becomes mysterious, alien, and inscrutable. Our search for reality might as well begin at the beginning, then: speculation on the sofa should precede metaphysics, for here is where our ignorance begins—in the familiar, the mundane, the concrete.

Does such a notion damage the novel, or does it instead open up exciting new possibilities for investigation? According to Robbe-Grillet, anything which jogs a stale form into new life must be seen as affirmative, expanding, and rejuvenating. True, we must be reeducated into this new form; we must adjust our expectations, enlarge our vision, train our intelligence to accommodate the unfamiliar. But to remain bound to traditional ways of seeing things is to remain blind when traditions have broken down and forms have become decadent. The New Novel is a necessity for rendering new experience, and what appears to be formlessness is only a new form which we have not yet been able to discern. "Each novelist, each novel must invent its own form. No recipe can replace this continual reflection. The book makes its own rules for itself, and for itself alone" (p. 12). Thus, the New Novel asserts its freedom, independence, and artistic validity.

In reviewing "several obsolete notions," Robbe-Grillet quickly dismisses as irrelevant all the familiar components of the traditional novel. While he considers them effective inventions for representing the reality their creators sought to express, he finds that they simply will not do for a writer who has a different reality to communicate. Traditional forms tend toward stabilization, unity, clarity:

All the technical elements of the narrative—systematic use of the past tense and the third person, unconditional adoption of chronological development, linear plots, regular trajectory of the passions, impulse of each episode toward a conclusion, etc.—everything tended to impose the image of a stable, coherent, continuous, unequivocal, entirely decipherable universe. Since the intelligibility of the world was not even questioned, to tell a story did not raise a problem. The style of the novel could be innocent. (P. 32)

Even if reality does not change, certainly man's concept of it does, and "if the reader sometimes has difficulty getting his bearings in the modern novel, it is in the same way that he sometimes loses them in the very world where he lives, when everything in the old structures and the old norms around him is giving way" (pp. 136–37). The novel, in short, is conditioned by vision, and since the vision of an artist living in the twentieth century shares little with that of his nineteenth-century counterpart, it is not surprising that his novels will require new techniques to render that new vision. For modern man, "the significations of the world around us are no more than partial, provisional, even contradictory, and always contested. . . . We no longer believe in the fixed significations, the ready-made meanings which afforded man the old divine order and subsequently the rationalist order of the nineteenth century, but we project onto man all our hopes: it is the forms man creates which can attach significations to the world" (p. 141). Chaos is, then, no longer a threat—it is a fact. What Melville feared, Robbe-Grillet confirms. Yet the despair so typical of such nineteenth-century skeptics as Melville and Conrad is somehow transcended in such contemporary figures as Genet and Robbe-Grillet, who assert that the lack of meaning in life only gives added impetus, importance, and freedom to man's search for his own meanings. Whereas Melville worries that man-made meanings are arbitrary and therefore futile, Robbe-Grillet finds freedom in futility and affirmation in the very arbitrariness of man's significations. Our minds are no longer dependent on reality; instead, they now *create* reality, and thereby determine their own meanings. *"Everything is constantly changing,"* says Robbe-Grillet, "and *there is always something new"* (p. 168)—but whereas Melville would have seen this truth as cause for anguish, Robbe-Grillet sees it as cause for hope. The world exists to be rediscovered, and the mind exists to invent new ways of discovering it. Once we stop expecting the world to speak to us and shelter us, to offer security and reassurance, provide meaning and comfort—then we feel freed to experience its multiplicity without torturing ourselves for having failed to find unity. If life is too chaotic to satisfy our need for meaning, then at least our imaginations can find permanent employment in presenting possiblities to consider. Robbe-Grillet finally differs from such writers as Melville, Conrad, Kafka, Faulkner, and Virginia Woolf in his ability to adjust to chaos with grace and ease. Indeed, his attitude is sometimes reminiscent of Beckett's Moran, who having found himself utterly "stupefied by the complexity" of his dancing bees, felt no sorrow, but simply "said *with rapture,* Here is something I can study all my life, and never understand" (my italics).

Still it would be wrong to equate Robbe-Grillet's resignation to chaos with a kind of philosophical masochism; it is not the chaos itself he relishes, but the rejuvenation of an art form which is willing to accommodate it. Because a new vision necessitates a new form to reflect it, the artist must liberate himself from outworn techniques which had themselves functioned as a means of seeing, exploring, and communicating reality—a reality, though, founded on different assumptions. Robbe-Grillet's vision is characterized by negation of order and the rationalist view that sought knowledge and found meaning through the structures made possible within that system. Order presumes stability, and stability allows for the creation of clearly defined opposites. But today's life, today's science are dissolving many of the categorical antinomies established by the rationalism of past centuries. It is natural that the novel, which, like every art, claims to precede systems of thought and not to follow them, should already be in the process of melting down the terms of other pairs of contraries: matter–form, objectivity–subjectivity, signification–absurdity, construction–destruction, memory–presence, imagination–reality, etc. (Pp. 166–67)

Until our minds learn to work in new ways, we must call Robbe-Grillet's system essentially chaotic: when what the imagination creates cannot be distinguished from what the eyes see; when an image from the past becomes hopelessly confused with one before us in the present; when the creative force includes its own destruction—then the world truly becomes an alien place for minds fueled by logic. And no less alien will appear at first the form which embodies this vision: Robbe-Grillet does not intend to compromise, and so his art will discard the concepts, values, and techniques of an outdated system.

There is, then, first a rejection of the analogical vocabulary and of traditional humanism, a rejection at the same time of the idea of tragedy, and of any other notion leading to the belief in a profound, and higher, nature of man or of things (and of the two together), a rejection, finally, of every pre-established order. (Pp. 72–73)

The traditional novel now disappears because it can no longer handle chaos without falsifying it. In its place the New Novel springs to life, destined to flounder in the chaos which created it and will destroy it. By reflecting its own negation, the novel in chaos can never transcend its vision, but must by definition be overcome by it.

"'I can't get it out of my mind: a book—what a presumption in one sense, but what an extraordinary wonder if it is spoiled in its broad outlines'" (p. 127). Quoting Robert Pinget, Robbe-Grillet finds his own ambitions expressed by the author of *Mahu or the Raw Material;* the work designed to self-destruct, dedicated to its own denial, and purified by its refusal to signify anything outside of itself, becomes the ultimate artistic experience. In discussing *Mahu,* Robbe-Grillet finds that every aspect of the book falls into chaos:

The characters of this *novel* belong neither to the realm of psychology nor to that of sociology, nor even to symbolism, still less to history or ethics; they are *pure creations* which derive only from the spirit of creation. Their existence, beyond a confused past of dreams and ineffable impressions, is merely a process without purpose, subject from sentence to sentence to the most extravagant mutations, at the mercy of the least thought passing through the mind, of the least word in the air, of the most fugitive suspicion. Yet they *make themselves*, but instead of each of them creating his own reality, it is an ensemble that is produced, a kind of living tissue each cell of which sprouts and shapes its neighbors; these characters continuously create each other, the world around them is merely a secretion—one could almost say the *waste product*—of their suppositions, of their lies, of their delirium. . . . The story, in this regard, can only turn in circles, unless it stops short, unashamedly turning back on itself; still elsewhere it branches off, divides into two or more parallel series which immediately react on each other, destroy each other, or unite in an unexpected synthesis. (P. 128)

An "unexpected" synthesis is closer to a collision, really, than to any concept of unification. If opposites do come together and merge for a moment or two, we can be sure that the embrace will last no longer than the instant it takes for the birth of a new antithesis. We will remember, too, that the New Novel does not so much unite opposites as melt them down until they become indistinguishable from each other.

What can we say, then, of the host of more or less episodic walk-ons, materializations of the thoughts of one or another protagonist, who appear and vanish, transform themselves, multiply, drop out and create in their turn new fictions which mingle with the story and soon turn against the reality from which they had emerged. (P. 129).

We can see here that the self-destructive impulse of the New Novel cannot be equated with the philosophical nihilism typifying the views of many of those writers discussed in the first section. While it is true that the traditionally chaotic novel utilized narrative techniques and symbolical devices that canceled out all clues to viable knowledge, the New Novel refuses to be conclusive, to lead us toward an ending of any sort. Instead, all negations push us farther out to sea, as new possibilities and perspectives are ignited from the ashes of those just destroyed. Just as an egg breaks to hatch a bird or a bomb detonates to release new forms of energy, so do the novel's forms self-destruct to expose new directions, new systems, new realities. This, of course, is a continuous process, and the one to which the New Novel is devoted. Even while each book creates its own laws for itself alone,

the movement of its style must often lead to jeopardizing them, breaking them, even exploding them. Far from respecting certain immutable forms, each new book tends to constitute the laws of its functioning at the same time that it produces their destruction. Once the work is completed, the writer's critical reflection will serve him further to gain a perspective in regard to it, immediately nourishing new explorations, a new departure. (P. 12)

The New Novel, then, does not try to take us anywhere; all lines opened up lead right back into itself. Like Genet, Robbe-Grillet is interested in creating a closed system that owes nothing to the world outside. No longer can the novel be "used" to resist chaos by functioning as philosophical leverage pushing it back; art *as* means is the first "obsolete" concept to be rejected by the New Novelist.

Robbe-Grillet's insistence that art be nonrepresentational stems less from his desire to purify form than from his conviction that representational systems have actually taken us away from reality by implying a false sense of intimacy between man and his world. By humanizing everything around himself, man has made all things simultaneously familiar and subservient—and art has served as principal intermediary, synthesizer, and controller. But humanization cannot lead to knowledge, for man merely reflects himself in everything he sees, thus growing farther and farther away from the essence and truth of external objects. Metaphor, therefore, corrupts all it touches, and every analogical system— no matter what particular philosophy it embodies—falsifies reality exactly to the extent it offers us any sense of knowledge, meaning, or security. In his essay on "Zeno's Sick Conscience," Robbe-Grillet admires the attitude that prompts Zeno to declare: "It was so clear that I no longer understood anything about it" (p. 93). Zeno, at least, is aware that clarity siphons off reality.

Looked at objectively, the world around us mocks meaning; nothing really signifies anything beyond itself, which means that it cannot relate to men's moral, philosophical, aesthetic, or psychological systems. In trying to make reality intelligible to the human mind, the traditional novelist "had thought to control it by assigning it a meaning, and the entire art of the novel, in particular, seemed dedicated to this enterprise."

But this was merely an illusory simplification; and far from becoming clearer and closer because of it, the world has only, little by little, lost all its life. Since it is chiefly in its presence that the world's reality resides, our task is now to create a literature which takes that presence into account.

The writer's traditional role consisted in excavating Nature, in burrowing deeper and deeper to reach some ever more intimate strata, in finally unearthing some fragment of a disconcerting secret. (P. 23)

Today, however, something is changing—"changing totally, definitively—in our relations with the universe," (p. 23) and it is the New Novelist who is willing to take that change into account by freeing the universe from man's mind and allowing it to assume once more its essential inscrutability. The New Novel will stop at appearances, will content itself with observing rather than excavating. This does not mean, though, that man's influence must diminish; to the contrary, man now becomes the sole benefactor of his quest for meaning. It is important only that he refuse to render unto reality what is his alone. If a cloud has the shape of a camel, he must simply realize that this resemblance is not an attribute of the cloud itself, but only of his own imagination. There is nothing wrong with finding meanings for ourselves; it is only when we *apply* them as intrinsic properties of the outside world that we become victims of our illusions.

Speaking of Joë Bousquet, Robbe-Grillet affirms his concept that "it is man himself who must 'give unity to the world and raise it to his own image.' " His only reservation is that Bousquet "has not specified that the operation will remain on the human scale and will have importance for man only, that it will not thereby attain to any essence of things, and that the creation, finally, to which we are invited will always have to be begun again, by ourselves and by those who come after us" (p. 109). It would seem, then, that man need only acknowledge his humility in order to pursue meanings in a valid way; once he has done that, there is really no end to what the imagination can create for itself:

It is then, as a matter of fact, that the *invention* of the world can assume its entire meaning—a permanent invention which, as we are told, belongs to artists but also to all men. In dreams, in memory, as in the sense of sight, our imagination is the organizing force of our life, of *our* world. Each man, in his turn, must reinvent the things around him. These are real things, clear, hard, and brilliant, of the real world. They refer to no other world. They are the sign of nothing but themselves. And the only contact man can make with them is to imagine them. (P. 109)

Like Genet, Robbe-Grillet believes that the imaginary world becomes somehow more real than the reality which inspires it. It is crucial, therefore, that the novel be nonrepresentational. "I do not transcribe," he says, "I construct," and here again, we find a strong parallel to Genet's conception of the artist as inventor of his own reality: "to make something out of nothing, something that would stand alone, without having to lean on anything external to the work; today this is the ambition of the novel as a whole" (p. 162).

Since art no longer intends to render reality or seek to penetrate it for meanings, the novel's function must be redefined. It is too easy, perhaps, to throw out the line, "Art for art's sake," and leave it at that, for such a principle predisposes us to a view of art's value as primarily aesthetic, and Robbe-Grillet does not seem very interested in art as beauty. Instead he seems to see the novel's purpose as an exploratory, interrogatory act leading to self-discovery. If we ask the novelist why he created a certain work, his answer, Robbe-Grillet insists, can be only "to try and find out why I wanted to write it" (p. 14). Art's function is discovered, then, in the very process of being created. Put another way, its function is its form, its process its product, its end itself.

What constitutes the novelist's strength is precisely that he invents, that he invents quite freely, without a model. The remarkable thing about modern fiction is that it asserts this characteristic quite deliberately, to such a degree that invention and imagination become, at the limit, the very subject of the book. (P. 32)

This is surely the kind of novel Flaubert envisioned when he asked for a creation so pure that it could refer to nothing outside itself. Imagination becomes its own subject as the work of art refines itself by eliminating all thematic matter. What is left is style—the creative process which does nothing but *be*.

Of course, too, since imagination is its own subject, it is also its own end; Robbe-Grillet is quite adamant on this point:

art cannot be reduced to the status of a means in the service of a cause which transcends it, even if this cause were the most deserving, the most exalting; the artist puts nothing above his work, and he soon comes to realize that he can create only *for nothing;* the least external directive paraly es him, the least concern for didacticism, or even for signification, is an insupportable constraint; whatever his attachment to his party or to generous ideas, the moment of creation can only bring him back to the problems of his art, and to them alone. (P. 37)

Art is to be divested of any philosophical value; it works only for itself. "It creates its own equilibrium and its own meaning. . . . the *necessity* a work of art acknowledges has nothing to do with utility. It is an internal necessity . . ." (p. 45). According to Robbe-Grillet, the true artist has nothing to say, but only a manner of speaking (p. 45). Autonomous and self-sufficient, the New Novel "is an exploration . . . but an exploration which itself creates its own significations, as it proceeds. Does reality have a meaning? The contemporary artist cannot answer this question: he knows nothing about it. All he can say is that this reality will perhaps have a meaning after he has existed, that is, once the work is brought to its conclusion" (p. 141). Finally: "the novel is not a tool at all. It is not conceived with a view to a task defined in advance. It does not serve to set forth, to translate things existing before it, outside it. It does not express, it explores, and what it explores is itself" (p. 160).

All of these statements somehow ring with conviction, but it is difficult to come to terms with them. Purity is one thing, but triviality another. The serious student of art would never ask for propaganda, but is it enough to have virtuosity spinning in a vacuum, chasing its own tail, and finally devouring itself as a grande finale? By utilizing the same means—language—by which we think, literature has always had greater potential than most of the arts to make a direct appeal to our minds; philosophical consequence has not been inconsistent with emotional impact or imaginative insights. By removing all these reference points from the realm of the novel, Robbe-Grillet seems to be closing more doors than he is opening. Is it not possible that the novel will refine itself right out of existence?

It is at this point, I think, that Robbe-Grillet's theory seems itself on the verge of self-destruction. Yet it survives—and in quite a legitimate way. The crucial fact to consider here is that for Robbe-Grillet, "Art is life," and the novel itself reality. To experience the New Novel is not to feel it as a representation of life, but as life *itself*—chaotic, enigmatic, inscrutable, intriguing, but above all, *there*. It moves without getting anywhere, it suggests without signifying, it sees without translating, and ends without concluding. Chaos is not rendered—it is *caught;* reality is not represented—it is *captured*. Life need not be reflected in the novel, for it is *lived* within the novel:

Art is life. Nothing, in art, is ever won *for good*. Art cannot exist without this permanent condition of being *put in question*. But the movement of these evolutions and revolutions constitutes its perpetual renaissance. (P. 159).

not only does each of us see in the world his own reality, but . . . the novel is precisely what creates it. The style of the novel does not seek to inform, as does the chronicle, the testimony offered in evidence, or the scientific report, it *constitutes* reality. It never knows what it is seeking, it is ignorant of what it has to say; it is invention, invention of the world and of man, constant invention and perpetual interrogation. (P. 161)

The New Novel offers us neither a way out of chaos nor a means for controlling it. It does not, in fact, even discuss chaos; it simply *is* chaos—and to read the novel is to be pushed into the experience of living in a world that has nothing to tell us and nothing to give us beyond the experience of having lived there. Yet while living there, we may be able to touch reality, for it is only in the imagination that such contact becomes possible.

Because the novel's reality must be self-contained, Robbe-Grillet insists that it be noninterpretative, as well as nonrepresentational. "A text both 'dense and irreducible,' so perfect that it does not seem 'to have been touched,' an object so perfect that it would obliterate our tracks" (p. 108) becomes the novelist's ideal. The novel has so often concerned itself with the theme of appearance vs. reality that even absurdist writers have automatically humanized the vacuum which causes their despair, turning nothingness itself into the truth behind appearances. But the New Novelist is interested only in the appearance itself, not in what it may be hiding:

not only do we no longer consider the world as our own, our private property, designed according to our needs and readily domesticated, but we no longer even believe in its "depth." While essentialist conceptions of man met their destruction, the notion of "condition" henceforth replacing that of "nature," the *surface* of things has ceased to be for us the mask of their heart, a sentiment that led to every kind of metaphysical transcendence.

Thus it is the entire literary language that must change, that is changing already. From day to day we witness the growing repugnance felt by people of greater awareness for words of a visceral, analogical, or incantatory character. On the other hand, the visual or descriptive adjective, the word that contents itself with measuring, locating, limiting, defining, indicates a difficult but most likely direction for a new art of the novel. (P. 24)

Robbe-Grillet finds the traditional novel to have been ruled by the Romantic sensibility—one that seeks meaning through penetration of forms. The writer read the world of nature and delivered its secrets to the reader in the form of a vision which embodied the novelist's view of reality. The New Novelist, however, is not interested in a reality "constantly situated elsewhere," but only in the one right in front of him "here and now." Divested of human value systems, the world's existence is reduced to its "concrete, solid, material presence; beyond what we see (what we preceive by our senses) there would henceforth be nothing" (p. 39). And if reality resides on the surface of things, the novel, as another form of reality, must also resist domestication by man's mind: "The work of art, like the world, is a living form: it *is*, it has no need of justification" (p. 43). Again, the novel no longer reflects reality within its own ordered sphere, but *becomes* a living part of reality. In his essay on Raymond Roussel, Robbe-Grillet considers some of the characteristics of the novel in chaos, and its main feature does seem to be its self-containment; there are no outside reference points at all:

everything is given as in movement, but frozen in the middle of that movement, immobilized by the representation which leaves in suspense all gestures, falls, conclusions, etc. eternalizing them in the imminence of their end and severing them from their meaning.

Empty enigmas, arrested time, signs which refuse to signify, giant enlargement of the tiny detail, narratives which come full circle: We are in a *flat and discontinuous* universe where each thing refers only to itself. A universe of fixity, of repetition, of absolute obviousness, which enchants and discourages the explorer. . . .

Obviousness, transparency preclude the existence of *higher worlds*, of any transcendence; yet, from this world before us we discover we can no longer escape. Everything is at a standstill, everything endlessly reproduces itself. . . . (Pp. 86–87)

If the traditional novel has served primarily as an interpreter of reality, we may well ask what the noninterpretative novel can do with the surfaces it chooses to treat. Obviously, they can be described, but is that all? Well, yes. And that might be enough, for it is not simply a matter of describing an object or scene once. Since the novel itself now lives in *our* world, it becomes subservient to time and space, and that means that no description can be static or definitive: At what moment, for example, and at what angle, should the novel describe a woman sitting on a sofa?—in the morning, evening, afternoon of this week, last week, tomorrow? From our view of her across the room, at the window, behind a portal, from the stairway, etc.? In the "flat, discontinuous" world of the New Novel, life unreels itself in repetitious, meaningless patterns that many readers cannot help but recognize as their own realities.

Because the novel's familiar components—so familiar, indeed, that they seem to be organic parts of the form itself—have developed in accordance with the novel's interpretative function, the noninterpretative novel must make radical alterations in its use of those elements carried over from the old form. Some must, of course, disappear altogether (symbolism, for example, would have to be abandoned immediately by the New Novelist), while others are readapted toward the New Novel's concerns. The reader must therefore be reoriented to the techniques used by the novelist in noninterpretative fiction.

Description of scenes and objects might well seem the most easily disposable element in the traditional novel, yet it becomes the central technique of the New Novel—though only, we must add, after its role and purpose have been redefined. Robbe-Grillet compares the "old" use of description to a picture frame, while description in the New Novel becomes the picture itself:

This is because the place and the role of description have changed completely. While the preoccupations of a descriptive order were invading the entire novel, they were at the same time losing their traditional meaning. . . . Description once served to situate the chief contours of a setting, then to cast light on some of its particularly revealing elements; it no longer mentions anything except insignificant objects, or objects which it is concerned to make so. It once claimed to reproduce a pre-existing reality; it now asserts its creative function. Finally, it once made us see things, now it seems to destroy them, as if its intention to discuss them aimed only at blurring their contours, at making them incomprehensible, at causing them to disappear altogether. (P. 147)

Description, in short, is no longer used to project a setting, but simply to set creative energy in motion. It starts from nothing, ends in nothing, and blurs rather than clarifies the object it describes. Robbe-Grillet details its process in this way:

It is not rare . . . to encounter a description that starts from nothing; it does not afford, first of all, a general view, it seems to derive from a tiny fragment without importance—what most resembles a *point*—starting from which it invents lines, planes, an architecture; and such description particularly seems to be inventing its object when it suddenly contradicts, repeats, corrects itself, bifurcates, etc. Yet we begin to glimpse something, and we suppose that this something will now become clearer.

But the lines of the drawing accumulate, grow heavier, cancel one another out, shift, so that the image is jeopardized as it is created. A few paragraphs more and, when the description comes to an end, we realize that it has left nothing behind it; it has instituted a double movement of creation and destruction which, moreover, we also find in the book on all levels and in particular in its total structure. . . . (P. 148)

It is the cinematic rather than literary image which Robbe-Grillet wants to create in his novels because the former object is never frozen but, curled up in time, rolls along in continuous flux from one frame or second to the next. As a result, it can never be captured or clarified, steadied or controlled. To walk around a statue, for example, is to set it in perpetual motion as each angle reveals new contours and hides others, heightens one element and throws another into relief. Every step we take toward it provides a new perspective—we might say, a new object. The artist tries continually to still the object in what finally amounts to an obsession, but no matter how exact his description is, the object manages to elude his attempt to freeze it:

The concern for precision which sometimes borders on the delirious (those notions so nonvisual as "right" and "left," those calculations, those measurements, those geometric points of reference) does not manage to keep the world from moving even in its most material aspects, and even at the heart of its apparent immobility. It is no longer here a question of time passing, since gestures paradoxically are on the contrary shown only frozen in the moment. It is matter itself which is both solid and unstable, both present and imagined, alien to man and constantly being invented in man's mind. The entire interest of the descriptive pages— that is, man's place in these pages—is therefore no longer in the thing described, but in the very movement of the description. (P. 148).

Description as process—the creative process in man's mind which renders reality to him second by second—rather than substance: this is Robbe-Grillet's concern. And because description destroys what it describes, keeps us from "seeing what it was showing" (p. 151), it is consistent with the author's ambition to create an art with self-destruction built into it. Whereas the traditional novelist's description was evaluated in terms of his ability to project an illusion of reality with such vividness that we could believe in that description *as* reality, the New Novelist is too fond of illusion to want to convince us of its reality. Instead he wants to create illusions of an illusory character, so to speak; by *re*inventing his subject continuously, he reminds us each moment that he has been inventing all along. The process is what lives, and it is what lives that counts. A snapshot, on the other hand, is dead just because it has stolen its subject from time.

Time, slinking like a caterpillar, overlaps itself, heaping forward, now collapsing its crawling accordion body; as it humps up, tightly tense before distending, its front and rear parts gravitate toward the center—and past and future seem to converge in the present. Here the moment includes all its minutes; then, the tension breaks, the body relaxes, and the caterpillar moves on, forwards and backwards. It is this double movement of time which fascinates Robbe-Grillet: by using up the life it engenders, it satisfies his requirement for a self-devouring creative force built into the novel's structure. "Why seek to reconstruct the time of clocks in a narrative which is concerned only with human time?" he asks. "Is it not wiser to think of our own memory, which is *never* chronological?" (p. 139). The past tense cannot exist in the world of the imagination, for images called up by the mind live in a state of perpetual presence. My mind may invent an image to focus on—let's say a snowy night—then later reflect on it, recall it, dream about it. And at some time during all this mental activity, I may well look outside my window and see a *real* snowy night. But is there really any mental difference between the actual experience and my projections or memories of it? In all cases, the scene exists as a living, immediate presence in my mind; the memory does not see it as the middle of a long line representing everything I have known in the past, and the imagination does not see it at a certain point along the line of possible future experiences. To call up the image means to be faced with it directly, just as our dreams provide no outside reference points, but hold the incident in front of us for as long as the vision lasts. Now if we think of this snowy evening as a scene from *In the Labyrinth,* we can see that no version of that scene can seem to have preceded another chronologically: each time the scene is reinvented, it lives in the present, here and now, as Robbe-Grillet would say. Is one rendition dream, another delirium, another memory, another actual, another a future projection? The question is irrelevant and impossible to answer, for the author is concerned with "private mental structures" of time (p. 152), which create their own chronologies, then break down the pattern and begin again.

Discussing his film *Last Year at Marienbad,* Robbe-Grillet reminds us that the mind's perpetual reconstruction of reality is best represented by the cinematic technique which compresses time into a continuous present:

The universe in which the entire film occurs is, characteristically, that of a perpetual present which makes all recourse to memory impossible. This is a world without a past, a world which is self-sufficient at every moment and which obliterates itself as it proceeds. This man, this woman began existing only when they appear on the screen the first time; before that they are nothing; and once the projection is over, they are again nothing. Their existence lasts only as long as the film lasts. There can be no reality outside the images we see, the words we hear.

Thus the duration of the modern work is in no way a summary, a condensed version, of a more extended and more "real" duration which would be that of the anecdote, of the narrated story. There is, on the contrary, an absolute identity between the two durations. . . . This love story we were being told as a thing of the past was in fact actually happening before our eyes, here and now. For of course an *elsewhere* is no more possible than a *formerly*. (Pp. 152–53)

It is quite logical for Robbe-Grillet to equate time with space here, for both planes—when represented by linear movement—provides a safety valve of distance which enables any number of images to coexist. By confining himself to the present, though, the New Novelist forces each recurring image to be superimposed upon the preceding one, thereby obliterating it. Thus, the new creation destroys what it replaces, and is itself doomed to destruction by the relentless surge of time which manufactures an endless sequence of "present" moments.

This is really the way we live in dreams, as each successive image absorbs us completely and we confront the incident directly before us without placing it in a linear temporal context. In his essay on Joë Bousquet, Robbe-Grillet mentions the affinity of his art to the world of dreams, but while he values the force and presence inherent in the reality rendered by dreams, he also insists that the illusion be controlled on a conscious level:

It would be too easy if it were enough to close our eyes in order to discover the real contours of our life. The necessary disjunction is less easy to provoke, and doubtless we can do so more effectively by not falling asleep. As we suspected, this *waking dream* could simply be *art*, of which sleep, it is true, affords fragments on occasion but which only a conscious activity permits us to assemble and unite. (P. 102)

Art, therefore, is dream prodded onto higher levels of consciousness, where it can be made subject to the creator's will. The artist assembles his fragments and pushes the dream on, directing its focus if not its outcome, and forcing it to repeat the process of re-creating until. . . .

Until when? Since the New Novel utilizes no plot, and since it is structured on a cyclical pattern of creation–destruction, re-creation, at what point does the writer consider his novel finished? Robbe-Grillet does not deal with this matter, though perhaps we can assume that the end is reached when the author finally understands what made him write the novel, or when he feels he has exhausted his subject by interrogating it to his satisfaction. That point, nonetheless, would probably have to be called arbitrary—unless we assume that the novel has reached its natural ending when it finds itself back at the beginning.

Still, it is essential that one arrive nowhere. Traditional novelists have always used plots to take us somewhere, but Robbe-Grillet wants no part of a work that knows its direction in advance. Scoffing at the idea of a prefabricated story running smoothly to its "realistic" (that is, believable) conclusion, while suggesting a much longer duration of which the novel is only a small, if typical, part, Robbe Grillet insists that "to tell a story has become strictly impossible" (p. 33). Not that there is anything wrong with stories themselves:

The books of Proust and Faulkner are, in fact, crammed with stories; but in the former, they dissolve in order to be recomposed to the advantage of a mental architecture of time; whereas, in the latter, the development of themes and their many associations overwhelms all chronology to the point of seeming to bury again, to drown in the course of the novel what the narrative has just revealed. Even in Beckett, there is no lack of events, but these are constantly in the process of contesting themselves, jeopardizing themselves, destroying themselves, so that the same sentence may contain an observation and its immediate negation. In short, it is not the anecdote that is lacking, it is only its character of certainty, its tranquillity, its innocence. (P. 53)

The story, then, must have no independent existence from its style. Stories, as events, are legitimate subject matter for the novelist, but carefully contrived plots have no place in an interrogative fiction. Story as subject, subject as style, style as self-exploration, self-exploration as self-destruction, self-destruction as creative regeneration leading to self-discovery—this is the process that replaces plot in the New Novel, and it is a process which proclaims, above all, its own artifice.

Yet it also proclaims its own limitations: the work of art is to exist for its own sake alone, not as a means toward some higher level of meaning. To eliminate such possibilities, Robbe-Grillet wants his language to restrict, rather than encourage the suggestive power of words. "Formal description," he says, "is above all a limitation: when it says 'parallelipiped,' it knows it achieves no Beyond, but at the same time it cuts short any possibility of seeking one" (p. 72). In a noninterpretative work, words must be carefully guarded against, for they are rich in implication, which almost always leads to interpretation. In his desire to deflate language in order to keep the novel self-contained, Robbe-Grillet alienates himself from all the other writers we have discussed. Only Beckett shows a similar need to clamp down an art which always seems to express more than he wants it to. Beckett, however, would like to eliminate language entirely, whereas Robbe-Grillet only wants it to stop *signifying* a transcendent level. In this way, though, he does have much in common with Beckett's Watt, who needed to know an object well enough to conceive it, so that he could then dismiss it from his mind. Robbe-Grillet, too, wants to *place* the object clearly in his mind just so that he may then proceed to destroy it. The object must be described—which is the act of invention—but not humanized; and language, therefore, must be stripped of suggestion, all its poetic properties removed, its analogical value obliterated.

If language and plot—two of the most basic ingredients in the traditional novel—have lost their status in the New Novel, consider the consequences for man himself, who, as character, has always been the novel's primary concern. While Robbe-Grillet insists that "the novel of characters belongs entirely to the past," to a period "which marked the apogee of the individual" (p. 28), he takes strong exception to those who criticize his novels for having emptied man right out of fiction. His point seems to be that his creations all take place inside man, and are therefore humanized and totally conditioned by his character's mind, vision, and imagination. It is true, he admits, that he refuses to create the kind of character who must have a name, heredity, and a "character" which molds his face, reflects his past, dictates his actions, "makes him react to each event in a determined fashion," and "permits the reader to judge him, to love him, to hate him." He distrusts the traditional presentation of a character "who must be unique and at the same time must rise to the level of a category," who "must have enough individuality to remain irreplaceable, and enough generality to become universal" (pp. 27–28). Instead, "a new kind of narrator is born" in the New Novel: "no longer a man who describes the things he sees, but at the same time a man who invents the things around him and who sees the things he invents" (pp. 162–63). But this narrator could hardly be said to replace the traditional character, who *does* seem to have vanished altogether from Robbe-Grillet's novels (except as an appearance himself, an object to be described); rather, the mind of this new narrator, by becoming the center of the novel, the consciousness through which events are filtered, replaces the author himself, who has decided that the artist can no longer play God. I have said before that the traditional artist found characters necessary to objectify his vision of reality, but Robbe-Grillet is not interested in achieving the objectivity so deeply valued by artists who wish to make a general statement on man and his universe:

It is God alone who can claim to be objective. While in our books, on the contrary, it is a *man* who sees, who feels, who imagines, a man located in space and time, conditioned by his passions, a man like you and me. And the book reports nothing but his experience, limited and uncertain as it is. It is a man here, now, who is his own narrator, finally. (P. 139)

Such a character need not have a strong or even decipherable identity, because "a man like you and me" is nothing more than a hollow form in which we place ourselves. All distance between the author, his creation, and the reader disappears as the three move together, then merge into the single mind through which the experience is flowing. "The only important 'character' is the spectator," says Robbe-Grillet; "*in his mind* unfolds the whole story, which is precisely *imagined* by him" (p. 153). While this method is to a degree reminiscent of Genet's technique of imbibing all experience, Genet, as narrator, would never have equated his own mind and imagination with those of the reader. In the world *he* creates, he is God, whereas Robbe-Grillet makes no distinction between the mind which conceives, the one which *per*ceives, and the one which *re*ceives. Again, the novel in chaos abandons all order, identity, classification.

The narrative, then, becomes the center of the New Novel, embodying as it does the experience itself, the style which renders it and is inseparable from it, and the mind or sensibility which creates it. And it is within the narrative, too, that time, space, and description perform their paradoxical movements, perpetually going forward and backward, simultaneously creating and destroying one another:

in the modern narrative, time seems to be cut off from its temporality. It no longer passes. It no longer completes anything. . . . Here space destroys time, and time sabotages space. Description makes no headway, contradicts itself, turns in circles. Moment denies continuity. . . .

Now, if temporality gratifies expectation, instantaneity disappoints it; just as spatial discontinuity dissolves the trap of the anecdote. (P. 155)

Applying these techniques to *Jealousy*, Robbe-Grillet explains why his handling of the narrative in that book was bred out of necessity, rather than perversity; because he had to structure the experience through a narrative which was its only reality, he could not order events chronologically, but only in the chaotic way by which the mind itself receives impressions:

The narrative was . . . made in such a way that any attempt to reconstruct an external chronology would lead, sooner or later, to a series of contradictions, hence to an impasse . . . precisely because there existed for me no possible order outside of that of the book. The latter was not a narrative mingled with a simple anecodote external to itself, but again the very unfolding of a story which had no other reality than that of the narrative, an occurrence which functioned nowhere else except in the mind of the invisible narrator, in other words of the writer, and of the reader. (P. 154)

How can the reader of *Tristram Shandy* resist such an explanation? For in that book, too, the narrator's mind becomes the subject—it is the *opinions* of Tristram that determine the narrative structure, *his* mind which both creates and justifies the confusion. But the last few lines of the above passage move Robbe-Grillet's narrator closer to the mysterious voice in Beckett's *Unnamable:* the narrator is invisible, inseparable from the author, and indistinguishable from the reader. He is, in short, a pure abstraction which we cannot identify, and our relationship to him is unclear throughout. The chaos in Sterne's narrative was steadied and controlled by the "certainty" present in the other components, but the chaos in Robbe-Grillet's narrative is not stabilized by anything outside it. We drift with it from one impasse to another, but there is nothing to hold onto along the way. The result is an inconclusive experience which relates to nothing but itself.

What *are* the compensations of chaos, then? Obviously, Robbe-Grillet is not interested in giving us a "slice" of reality to chew, or a puzzle to solve, or a system to transcend chaos. Robbe-Grillet offers us another kind of participation which only the New Novel can achieve:

These descriptions whose movement destroys all confidence in the things described, these heroes without naturalness as without identity, this present which constantly invents itself, as though in the course of the very writing, which repeats, doubles, modifies, denies itself, without ever accumulating in order to constitute a past—hence a "story," a "history" in the traditional sense of the word—all this can only invite the reader (or the spectator) to another mode of participation than the one to which he was accustomed. If he is sometimes led to condemn the works of his time, that is, those which most directly address him, if he even complains of being deliberately abandoned, held off, disdained by the authors, this is solely because he persists in seeking a kind of communication which has long since ceased to be the one which is proposed to him.

For, far from neglecting him, the author today proclaims his absolute need of the reader's cooperation, an active, conscious, *creative* assistance. What he asks of him is no longer to receive ready-made a world completed, full, closed upon itself, but on the contrary to participate in a creation, to invent in his turn the work—and the world—and thus to learn to invent his own life. (Pp. 155–56)

Is Robbe-Grillet's art intended primarily as an exercise manual for our own minds which must be retrained before they can work with reality in this new way? Robbe-Grillet does seem to see the novel as a kind of calisthenics for the reader's imagination, something thrown its way to keep it limbered up until the reader is ready to send his own life through the imagination and there grasp a bit of his particular reality. It seems to me a nice thing for the author to want to do, but I wonder to what extent a reader can apply whatever he has gained from Robbe-Grillet's novels to his own reality—a reality where, like it or not, one does feel identities rather strongly (no matter how many ambiguities are involved) and knows that the people he loves are much closer to traditional fictional characters than to objects. What, for example, is the *here and now* of a beloved person in one's life? We do not live in a world of statues; other people do seem real to us as more than appearances. I recognize little of my own reality in Robbe-Grillet's novels and would certainly question the practical applications of his theory: that reading the New Novel will help me invent my own life.

But that, of course, is not necessarily important. At its best, the New Novel does provide us with a new way of seeing things, and beyond that, it intrigues one, absorbs one, and in a strange way seems a profound, fascinatingly elusive, and fulfilling experience. It generates chaos, yet captures and sustains it with oftentimes brilliant virtuosity and imaginative excitement. It is its own private experience, self-contained and, again, at its best, beautifully rounded-off, aesthetically pleasing. By creating a world intact, complete, yet unending in the mind that receives it, it justifies itself.

> The scene would have to be re-invented from beginning to end, starting with two or three elementary details. . . .
>
> —*The Voyeur*

The novels of Jean Genet could have been produced only by a man who sees himself as a god—one who exercises consummate control over his universe, rendering all things meaningful, referring all things to a private system, determining the transcendent reality of objects which would otherwise be trivial images having nothing to tell us. Mettray is a construction of stone and bars, silent and remote. Man's mind calls it a prison, and the walls immediately become part of our property; then the artist calls it a mother figure, and presto!—the walls are penetrated, the stones yield to our imaginative power, and the building is transformed into a vital presence signifying the source of all love. Behind the walls was lurking a mother, and all it took was human insight to make the discovery and deliver the truth.

Robbe-Grillet would be appalled. Look where interpretation has gotten us: we have humanized a stack of stones, given it maternal identity, and made it part of our knowledge. Knowing that appearances are deceptive, we transcend them, work our way into their hidden realities, and emerge with a truth that has simply to be inserted into a philosophical system for it to reflect our notion of reality. But are appearances truly deceptive? Can a stone wall really want to deceive? Does it have a will, a mind, a motive? Does its silence indicate that it is keeping something from us? Or does its silence really mean nothing? Ah, yes: nothing. The wall is indifferent to us, it has nothing whatever to tell us; how perfectly it signifies this absurd, alien universe!

No, Robbe-Grillet would insist; instead, how perfectly it *fails* to signify anything at all beyond itself—and from this vision, the New Novel is born: determined to produce a work of man, not God; to view the universe as what it appears to be and go no further; to divest objects of their customary intimacy and return them to the world of the inanimate.

The New Novel is noninterpretative—it does not try to make things signify. It has no intention of approaching reality for philosophical enlightenment, or of using the imagination for transcendent purposes. It does not use plot to order experience; it does not use symbolism to make meaning mandatory; it does not use character to make man decipherable; it does not use metaphor to make incident analogical; it does not use structure to render experience conclusive. Assuming that reality is inscrutable and human objectivity unattainable, yet asserting that man can grasp reality by inventing it in his imagination, the New Novel follows the form of its own creative process, making its style its subject, its contours its reality and experience, its end self-discovery, and its means self-destruction.

Our difficulty in deciphering *The Voyeur* begins with the title: Who is the voyeur, and what, in fact, has *any* voyeur to do with the story? So long as we regard the incidents of the book *as* a story, our answers will be irrelevant and almost certainly arbitrary. The critics have already had their fling at the possibilities, and one can, naturally, take his choice, but it seems clear to me that the author's title labels a *process*, not a story, and that the voyeur is the author, the narrator, and the reader, through whose minds the events are flowing. All three are outsiders looking in, trying to contact reality by inventing it: three imaginations working in unison to see, to learn what has happened, to get at the truth.

When Mathias removes from his wallet the newspaper article detailing the death that we assume to be the major incident of the novel, the narrator dismisses its validity as a documentation of what has taken place:

The article did not have much of importance to say. It was no longer than a minor news item. In fact a good half of it merely traced the secondary circumstances of the discovery of the body; since the entire conclusion of the article was devoted to commentaries on the direction the police expected their investigations to take, very little space remained for the description of the body itself and none at all for any discussion of the kind of violence to which the victim had been subjected. Adjectives such as "horrible," "unspeakable," and "odious" were of no use in these matters. Vague laments over the girl's tragic fate were scarcely more helpful. As for the veiled formulas used to describe the manner of her death, all belonged to the conventional language of the press for this category of news and referred, at best, to generalities. It was evident that the copy writers used the same terms on each similar occasion, without attempting to furnish the slightest piece of real information in a particular case, concerning which they were probably in complete ignorance themselves. The scene would have to be re-invented from beginning to end, starting with two or three elementary details, like the age of the victim or the color of her hair.[2]

And that, of course, is what this novel does: working with a few concrete details, the imagination reinvents reality, almost creating a complete story but always coming to an impasse, snag, or contradiction along the way which destroys it; then, returning to the same details, the imagination goes to work again, creating another sequence of events until these too become negated, at which point it is replaced with yet another sequence, and so on. There is no single story, finally—only the process of *creating* a story—that forms the substance of the book. The traditional novel would surely have handled all this quite differently—very much like the newspaper account, in fact—but such a presentation is suspect in a reality that can never be interpreted, but only reinvented. With no "real information" ever possible, one must work with what one has—which are appearances. And so we look at these appearances over and over again, placing them in new contexts, reconstructing their roles, realigning them in our angle of vision until . . . we stop. There is no voyeur in the novel, but there *are* voyeurs *to* the novel, watching, investigating, and speculating, always from a distance and never seeing enough to feel satisfied.

We do, of course, *see* things, but since we cannot establish their significance or import, we simply bump against them as appearances, finally knowing them in no other way. Each appearance is a dead end; we feel the *force* of its presence without ever knowing the meaning behind its existence. And this is true of

2. Alain Robbe-Grillet, *The Voyeur*, trans. Richard Howard (New York: Grove Press, 1966) pp. 61–62. All future page references, cited in parentheses, are to this edition.

people, as well as objects; the recurring image of a girl or woman staring at or through or beyond Mathias, for example, is as indecipherable as anything inanimate:

Her features were frozen in the very expression they had assumed when she first saw him—as though unexpectedly recorded on a photographic plate. This immobility, far from making it easier to read her countenance, merely rendered each attempt at interpretation more uncertain: although the face, judging from appearances, expressed some intention—a very banal intention that seemed indentifiable at first glance—it ceaselessly avoided every reference by which Mathias attempted to capture its meaning. He was not even altogether certain whether she was looking at him. . . . (P. 30)

It is indeed as if we were looking at a photograph, but the longer we stare, the more elusive becomes the abstracted gaze frozen onto the features in front of us. Because the photograph exists outside of time, it renders the familiar strange, the most intimate acquaintance remote. Just as we can look at our own faces in a mirror until the reflection takes on a life of its own and we see ourselves with such detachment that we no longer feel the face gazing back at us to be our own, so too we can stare at a picture of the person we know best in the world until the face becomes that of a stranger, and we wonder who it was we had thought to have known so well. Time moves too quickly for us to have such doubts often, but there are always those moments that fall outside of time and disorient us completely: our most common experiences become suddenly mysterious, inscrutable, and seemingly alien even from we who have lived them. It is a matter of abstraction: we can repeat the most familiar word over and over until it loses its existence *as* word and settles into a meaningless sound pattern. Robbe-Grillet's world works in just this way: appearances lose their depth, their meaning, their familiarity, and become abstract forms of compelling impact which, however, have nothing to tell us.

Reason will not help us at all. When paying for the bicycle he has rented, Mathias has only to consider the price for a second to realize that all thinking is useless: "In consideration of the bicycle's newness, on the one hand, and its irregular operation on the other, it was difficult to say whether this was cheap or expensive" (p. 145). Mathias stops right there, and it is just as well that he does, for when he does become obsessed with the *why* of any situation, his reason always takes him just far enough to feel totally frustrated and baffled. Reality simply cannot be explained, and Robbe-Grillet would therefore prefer that we accept our position of complete ignorance in all humility. Whereas Beckett's characters fight the world with their minds, always losing, Robbe-Grillet's narrators rarely engage in open warfare; instead, at the first sign of impasse, they signify their surrender by simply yielding the ground lost, and immediately resorting to a new reinvention of reality. The many fresh starts attest to the mind's failure to come up with workable solutions.

It is just the mind's inadequacy, however, that frees the imagination to reconstruct reality as it wishes. Mathias realizes that the imagination can exploit the mind's impotence in a world where "appearances were more important than anything else" (p. 22). In attempting to sell his watches on the island, he knows that "today especially, success would be a matter of imagination. . . . People don't remember . . . things; he would manufacture childhoods for them leading straight to the purchase of a wrist watch" (pp. 22–23). Yet Mathias himself gets caught in the same trap he has set up for his customers when the man he assumes to be named Jean Robin recognizes him and recalls their childhood together. Mathias now searches *his* memory for affirmation of their former friendship, but he makes no headway at all, for he has perhaps forgotten the one important thing to remember in Robbe-Grillet's world: that life is not lived anywhere but in the imagination, which makes even the past subject to constant change. By projecting an event into the past, the imagination *makes* it exist as a memory in the present. The past, then, can be opened up at will to include new matter, for the imagination automatically verifies whatever it can conceptualize.

This is what the reader must realize also, before he can understand the kind of experience being opened up for him in this book. Since the subject of *The Voyeur* is the creative process which sets it in motion, sustains it, and then destroys it, the style is the appearance taken by the imagination, and its contours constitute our experience of its reality. Structured by the two countermovements of creation and destruction which come together to cancel out all knowledge, the narrative depicts the imagination's struggle with its material as it breaks down, picks itself up again, selects a new point of departure, takes off, sputters, and breaks down. When Mathias first sees the photograph of Jacqueline, for example, he is struck by her resemblance to Violet, then thinks of her as Violet. Impressed by her beauty, he compliments the mother on her child, only to hear the mother respond

unsmilingly of the girl's "magic power," and [she] assured him that "not so long ago she would have been burned as a witch for less."

At the foot of the pine tree the dry grass began to blaze, as well as the hem of the cotton dress. Violet twisted at the waist and flung back her hair, opening her mouth. Finally, however, Mathias succeeded in taking his leave. (P. 70)

There is no distinction made here between literal and imaginative reality. On the basis of the image brought forth by the mother, the imagination takes over immediately, building on suggestion until it has reinvented the picture to accommodate the new fragment of reality it has obtained. Mathias leaves with that reality embedded in his mind—Violet-as-Jacqueline-as-witch being burnt at the stake—but when he tries to recapture it a little later in the restaurant, his imagination seems to break down: "the shiny metal frame, the photograph, the . . . the photograph showing the photograph, the photograph, the photograph, the photograph . . ." (p. 98). The former reality is no longer working, so Mathias will have to start over again.

Robbe-Grillet says in *For a New Novel* that it is the reader himself who ultimately creates the story he is reading. Perhaps, then, we can link some details together and put our own imaginations to work: Mathias has killed Jacqueline because he identifies her with the Violet of his childhood; he never recounts the murder directly because he himself is estranged from it. Having seen the image of Jacqueline victimized at the stake, he puts that expression on her face in reality as he approaches to kill her. His mind has obviously blotted out the central incident—which obliterates it for the reader as well—because he was really quite divorced from it. Well, maybe so, maybe not: our own minds must spin in confusion, endlessly speculating but never knowing.

One of the watches Mathias sells signifies the hours "by tiny, complicated designs of interlaced knots rather than by numbers. Originally, perhaps, the artist had been inspired by the shapes of the twelve numbers; so little of them remained, however, that it was virtually impossible to tell the time—without a close examination, in any case" (pp. 104–5). This is exactly the kind of novel Robbe-Grillet has designed for us. The details are there, but the imagination has used them as inspiration for its own workings until the original details are almost impossible to discern. We need the imagination to convert these "knots" back into their original numbers, or it will be impossible for us to tell the time. Imagination transforms, confuses, and weakens our perceptions, but it alone can lead us back to the reality we want to rediscover.

Yet we can never get close enough to the truth here. When Mathias meets the girl he had encountered the day before at the house of Jean Robin, she upsets one of his earlier assumptions by referring to his former "friend" as Pierre, rather than Jean. Then she goes on:

> "He said you told me. . . . He said he had heard you."
> "Heard what?"
> "What you told me."
> "And what did I tell you?"
> "I don't know." (P. 155)

Where do we go from here? Obviously, the imagination will have to recast everything until it has finally obliterated all its own tracks.

And so *The Voyeur* succeeds in leading us nowhere but back into itself, where we continue to struggle for the sequence of events which has eluded the author and his main character, as well as ourselves. Only Julian seems to feel in control of the story which has never gotten told, but his motives and actions are so puzzling that we are afraid to rely on him completely. Besides, he too deals only with the level of appearances; he cannot tell us *why* the murder has taken place. Finally, all the evidence he so dramatically draws out of his pocket—the cord, some gumdrop wrappers, a cigarette butt—really proves nothing at all; they are just so many appearances, details, objects which *seem* terribly significant and suggestive, yet which reveal in themselves nothing of consequence. It is only our imagination that provides a context which renders them meaningful, and this same imagination can easily build up a whole new context that will make Julian look terribly suspicious, perhaps, and Mathias quite innocent. Whatever the imagination can create, it can also destroy—in fact, both extremes seem to be part of the same process.

The real story, therefore, exists only as so many fragments in our imaginations, but surely that is exactly where Robbe-Grillet wanted the pieces to fall—and if they never do come together satisfactorily . . . well, neither do our own lives, but that does not make them less real; it is, in fact, the only reality we have.

Jealousy operates on much the same assumptions as *The Voyeur*: again, reality is inexplicable—offering only fragments which leave everything in doubt; again, we are confined to the level of appearances which intrigue and perplex without yielding the slightest bit of meaning; again, reason fails because life is too complicated to be deciphered by logic; again, all experience remains inconclusive. But whereas the stylistic pattern of *The Voyeur* seems to unravel as so many attempts to bridge the one enormous chasm in the middle of the narrative, the crater-like texture of *Jealousy* directs us along a more concentric route. While technique is similar, contour is quite different in the two books, and since in the New Novel, shape *is* experience, the difference is really more a matter of form than plot. If *Jealousy* does seem a more subtle and mature work, that is perhaps because it captivates, resists, and eludes us much more completely than *The Voyeur*. Here, we cannot even determine what the situation *is*, much less assess its significance. Time, too, is much more active, rippling over the static scene as yesterday flickers into tomorrow, and events which seem to be taking place in the present are suddenly referred to as a part of the past or future. It is all most confusing, yet compelling, too: each scene almost begs to be reassembled, interpreted, understood. . . .

But of course it cannot be: the author guarantees our failure and has taken pains to insure it. In the narrator's criticism of the newspaper article (reporting the murder) Mathias extracts from his wallet in *The Voyeur*, the basic point seems to be that our subjectivity blinds us to the true nature of reality, and this explains why Robbe-Grillet feels impelled to reconstruct literal reality in such a way that it becomes newly alien and inscrutable. This process can be detected in every aspect of *Jealousy*, but the characteristic common to each is the noninterpretative spirit which signifies the artist acting as man rather than God. Because the narrator refuses to provide the security of even minimal knowledge, even the simplest "facts" fall outside our range of comprehension. There is, for example, the sound of animals (crying? whimpering? howling? barking? No—that would imply *knowing* the meaning of the sounds) heard in the distance from the veranda:

There are probably different kinds of animals. Still, all these cries are alike; not that their common characteristic is easy to decide, but rather their common lack of characteristics; they do not seem to be cries of fright, or pain, or intimidation, or even love. They sound like mechanical cries, uttered without perceptible motive, expressing nothing, indicating only the existence, the position, and the receptive movements of each animal, whose trajectory through the night they punctuate.[3]

By his refusal to interpret, attribute motives to, or in any way domesticate the unknown, Robbe-Grillet makes it impossible for us to "control" the sounds of the night by identifying them as expressive of some feeling we can understand. Instead, he keeps the sounds remote by describing them as nothing more *than* sounds breaking through the stillness. As long as we cannot bring our minds to bear on the outside world, we must remain strangers to it.

This should not imply, however, that the human world is any less mysterious. Robbe-Grillet presents his characters at such a distance from us that they become no more than shapes moving about. "A . . .'s silhouette, outlined in horizontal strips against the blind of her bedroom window, has now disappeared," says the narrator (p. 55), and it is a typical perspective from which the reader views the action. The reader is often forced to look up at A . . . from a few stories below, to look down at her from a great height, to see her in alternate slices from the other side of a venetian blind, or simply to view her from so far away that she becomes indistinguishable from any other concentrated form of mass. We watch her shadow, or the top part of her body leaning out a window, or her legs emerging from an automobile, but we are never *with* her (the way we are with Mrs. Ramsay, for example, in *To the Lighthouse*), never close enough to make out her features and identify her clearly. We seem hardly to be in the same story with her, but must simply observe her from the periphery of the scene. When she walks, the sounds of her footsteps echo hollowness because we experience her as an object rather than as a human presence.

Nor is our physical detachment compensated for by psychological intimacy. As the narrator describes A . . . sitting in a chair, he makes it impossible for us to determine what she is doing;

3. Alain Robbe-Grillet, *Two Novels by Robbe-Grillet: Jealousy* and *In the Labyrinth*, trans. Richard Howard (New York: Grove Press, 1965), pp. 49–50. All future page references, cited in parentheses, are to this edition.

instead, we are made to feel as if we were sitting in a theater directly behind a lady with a huge hat, and no matter how often we keep changing our position, switching from one side of the hat to the other, we are never able to get all the action into our line of vision:

A . . . is sitting at the little work table against the wall. . . . She leans forward over some long and painstaking task: mending an extremely fine stocking, polishing her nails, a tiny pencil drawing. . . . But A . . . never draws; to mend a run in her stocking she would have moved nearer the daylight; if she needed a table to do her nails on, she would not have chosen this one. (Pp. 55–56)

What *is* she doing, then? The narrator is not holding anything back; he would obviously like to help us if he could, but his vision is as limited as ours—or rather, he *sees* but does not interpret, thereby breaking the line that would have brought her into our minds as a conventional character.

And if Franck could only *talk* a little louder! We hear his muffled tones, and can *almost* make out what he is saying—but no, the words are not clear enough: "Franck's voice has uttered an exclamation: 'Hey there! That's much too much!' or else: 'Stop! That's much too much!' or, 'Ten times too much,' 'Half again too much,' etc." (pp. 56–57). Another time, "his sentence ends in 'take apart' or 'take a part' or 'break apart,' 'break a heart,' 'heart of darkness,' or something of the kind" (p. 126). Something of the kind, indeed! We are never able to know Franck well enough to guess which of the alternatives would most likely have been the right one, and the narrator himself has no more knowledge than the most distant observer. He refuses, in fact, even to make guesses—to speculate on which of the possibilities seems most probable. Robbe-Grillet prevents us from making subjective judgments that would block out the true nature of reality by replacing it with what we would interpret reality to be. And since of course we can interpret only within the range of our own experiences, we would be automatically limiting reality to a human meaning. This inclination, says Robbe-Grille, leads only to facile analogies rather than to any real knowledge. So the artist teaches us humility by turning down the role of God we want to assign him. His viewpoint is subjective because it is confined to the narrator's perspective and sensibility, but it is also objective in its determination to supply no information beyond what one can know to exist by his senses alone. Our ignorance starts right here on the surface of life, so that is where the search for knowledge must begin.

But not yet. Our vision has become so distorted by the mental attitudes we include as a natural part of perception that we cannot even see *appearances* for what they are. The first step, then, must be to regain our innocence so that we can see only what is there, rather than those attributes we project onto the images before us. This process entails stripping language of humanizing (and therefore falsifying) metaphors, divorcing objects from their familiar functions, and accepting the limitations of our minds.

Robbe-Grillet's language is divested of all the poetic richness that typified Genet's; it simply transmits verifiable information. An example:

She takes a few steps into the room, goes over to the heavy chest and opens its top drawer. She shifts the papers in the right-hand side of the drawer, leans over and, in order to see the rear of the drawer better, pulls it a little further out of the chest. After looking a little longer, she straightens up and remains motionless, elbows close to her body, forearms bent and hidden by the upper part of her body—probably holding a sheet of paper between her hands. (P. 41)

This is the flat language of stage directions—those messages conveyed to the reader before the play proper begins, and expendable enough to be replaced by action during an actual performance. Such messages, in short, are not considered a part of the playwright's art; they are superfluous to his imaginative rendering of reality. For Robbe-Grillet, however, such language is art in its purest form, distilled of all artificial, "poetic" ingredients. Take another example:

Furthermore, instead of being rectangular like the one above it, this patch is trapezoidal; for the stream bank that constitutes its lower edge is not perpendicular to its two sides—running up the slope—which are parallel to each other. The row on the right has no more than thirteen banana trees instead of twenty-three.

And finally, the lower edge of this patch is not straight, since the little stream is not: a slight bulge narrows the patch toward the middle of its width. The central row, which should have eighteen trees, if it were to be a true trapezoid, has, in fact, only sixteen.

In the second row, starting from the far left, there would be twenty-two trees (because of the alternate arrangement) in the case of a rectangular patch. There would also be twenty-two for a patch that was precisely trapezoidal, the reduction being scarcely noticeable. (P. 51)

One almost expects the next sentence to read: "Now solve for X!"
The language is familiar to anyone who has ever attacked a mathematics problem. But can we call a geometry hypothesis art? This
is a shaky question. I would suspect, though, that the passage
would have to be placed back in context before an answer would
be possible, and even then it might become a matter of individual
taste. But surely, Robbe-Grillet's language is a legitimate and in-
tricate expression of his means of approaching reality. Whereas
the language of geometry attempts to render the abstract concrete, Robbe-Grillet uses it to estrange us from what we would
see otherwise as a standard description. By drawing his scene like
an architectural blueprint or geometric design, he has abstracted
the concrete, thereby making it impossible for us simply to "picture" the scene. Another writer might well have suggested the
scene by splashing a bit of poetic color into his language, which
would have enabled us to have conceptualized it immediately—
oh, yes: a field of banana trees. But Robbe-Grillet has not settled
for that; instead, he has forced us to reinvent the scene detail by
detail, row by row of trees (as each row of trees files through our
imaginations, impressing itself individually and then collectively
as design and geometric pattern). His language, then, while not
"artistic" in the conventional sense, finally does deserve to be
called that because it is a purposeful part of his expression of
reality *as he wants us to know it.* It is not a matter of being cold
or analytical but of finding a precise means of communicating his
intentions. The reader cannot get beyond the *appearance* of
those trees—he sees them as just what they are, nothing more
(such as a beautiful pastoral setting, an exotic atmosphere, or
what have you). He cannot use any preconceptions in coming to
terms with the scene as Robbe-Grillet has presented it to him.

And the same is true of Robbe-Grillet's description of familiar
objects. Again, the language is bare, but here it is used to present
familiar things in a way that renders them alien and us innocent.
What scene, for example, could be more familiar than a person
sitting at the dinner table, eating a piece of fowl?

She begins meticulously cutting up the bird on her plate. Despite the
smallness of the object, she takes apart the limbs, as if she were performing an anatomical demonstration, cuts up the body at the joints, detaches
the flesh from the skeleton with the point of her knife while holding the
pieces down with her fork, without forcing, without ever having to re-

peat the same gesture, without even seeming to be accomplishing a difficult or unaccustomed task. . . . (P. 70)

Of course the task does not "seem" difficult: we eat quite frequently and learn very early how to manipulate utensils. But is this really what we do while we eat? This simple process which we all undergo several times a day seems suddenly mysterious. And no wonder. The more commonplace an event is, the more dulled we become to it; we no longer see it with any objectivity. But once we break through the pattern of familiarity, how strange many of our actions seem. Yes, eating a piece of meat *is* very much like dissecting an animal in a laboratory; taking a shower is very similar to scrubbing a sink. To observe someone brushing his teeth, eating corn-on-the-cob, cracking a nutshell, putting a record on the stereo, drinking a glass of milk, driving a car, settling into a chair, getting in and out of clothes, tying a shoelace or tie, shuffling a deck of cards, writing, typing, playing a cello—ad infinitum—is to realize the strangeness of our lives. A . . . sits at her vanity, brushing her hair:

The brush descends the length of the loose hair with a faint noise something between the sound of a breath and a crackle. No sooner had it reached the bottom than it quickly rises again toward the head, where the whole surface of its bristles sinks in before gliding down over the black mass again. The brush is a bone-colored oval whose short handle disappears almost entirely in the hand firmly gripping it. (P. 66)

Like this shapeless darkness, the silky hair flows between the curving fingers. It falls free, thickens, pushes its tentacles in all directions, coiling over itself in an increasingly complex skein whose convolutions continue to let the fingers pass through it with the same indifference, with the same facility.

With the same facility, the hair lets itself be unknotted, falls over the shoulder in a docile tide while the brush moves smoothly from top to bottom, from top to bottom, from top to bottom. . . . (P. 117)

The lustrous black curls fall free to the shoulders. The flood of heavy locks with reddish highlights trembles at the slightest movement the head makes. The head must be shaken with tiny movements, imperceptible in themselves, but amplified by the mass of hair, creating gleaming, quickly vanishing eddies, whose sudden intensity is reawakened in unlooked-for convulsions a little lower . . . lower still . . . and a last spasm much lower. (Pp. 98–99)

Suddenly the brush becomes an alien object as it seems to move of its own accord. This is the kind of "innocent" description we might get from someone who has never seen a brush before and does not understand its function; the observer does not seem to realize that the brush's movements are controlled by the woman's hands, which are in turn controlled by her will. The hair itself seems to have a mysterious existence quite detached from its owner, as it falls into different patterns around the head and shoulders. We familiarize ourselves with most objects by means of their functions, and as soon as we divorce the two, all meaning and "depth" drain out of the object, leaving only a certain form which we can know only by its description. Thus,

the razor blade is a flat, polished rectangle, its short sides rounded, and pierced with three holes in a line. The central hole is circular; the two others, one on each side, reproduce precisely—on a much smaller scale—the general shape of the blade, that is, a rectangle with its short sides rounded. (P. 98)

Such a description makes us realize how rarely we ever *look* at a razor blade *as* a shape; we simply *use* it without seeing it.

At the center of the novel is a scene utterly divested of people: when A . . . and Franck go into town, the narrator—identified only as a roving consciousness—stays behind in the empty, silent house. Such scenes, devoid of all human influence, would seem at first to hold no interest for the observer, yet they do exist with a life of their own: the refrigerator keeps running, the clocks tick, a window shade flaps in the breeze. As the husband–narrator presents the scene, it begins to have an eerie effect quite apart from what we eventually surmise to be his frenzied sensibility; even though he describes nothing that we would call unusual—the furniture does not jump around, the trees do not strike up a chorus of "It's a Long Way to Tipperary"—a large black spot left behind by the car seems almost ominous as it appears to move slowly with a life of its own:

This is a little oil which has dripped out of the motor, always in the same place.

It is easy to make this spot disappear, thanks to the flaws in the rough glass of the window: the blackened surface has merely to be brought into proximity with one of the flaws of the windowpane, by successive experiments.

The spot begins by growing larger, one of its sides bulging to form a rounded protuberance, itself larger than the initial object. But a few fractions of an inch farther, this bulge is transformed into a series of tiny concentric crescents which diminish until they are only lines, while the other side of the spot shrinks, leaving behind it a stalk-shaped appendage which bulges in its turn for a second; then suddenly everything disappears. (Pp. 95–96)

Looked at in this way (from behind the flaws of the rough glass), the spot of oil is divested of all familiarity and can no longer be included among the things we presume to know. Our perception of it as pure flowing form abstracted from its everyday identity as "oil" provides it with new meanings and enriches its potential for the imagination.

This scene without people (except, of course, for the consciousness perceiving it) forms an interesting contrast to a similar situation in the second section of *To the Lighthouse:* while both authors focus on an uninhabited house, Virginia Woolf continues to see objects in the same way. Chairs, bureaus, and beds are described as familiar inanimate pieces of furniture, while it is time, rain, and darkness that "live" in the house. Or do they really live? We are tempted to say so just because they have been described metaphorically—which means that they soon take on human attributes. Thus, the dark "devours" all the furniture in the room. But Robbe-Grillet's darkness would not devour anything; it might move in such a way as to cover up a table, for example, but it would not be seen as *eating* that table. Virginia Woolf's novel is about people, so it is not surprising that objects are imbued with human qualities; but Robbe-Grillet's novel is finally *about* objects—even when it is dealing with people—so an anthropomorphic perspective has no place here. That is why the reader's own perspective must be altered: he is asked to see things in a new way that will force him to confront reality on different terms. To do this, the author must find the means to render the commonplace uncommon—and Robbe-Grillet has achieved this by rendering all objects strange, and people themselves as remote from our understanding as robots.

We must remember, however, that Robbe-Grillet does not expect to capture reality—he does not even believe this possible—but only to reinvent it in his imagination and then in ours. As in *The Voyeur,* we are forced to contemplate a scene again and again, running it through our imaginations like a film running through a projector. We must, of course, stop often to rethread, and whenever we do, the novelist makes a new adjustment in time so that when the scene next unreels, we see it from a different temporal perspective. Robbe-Grillet uses time much more radically here than he did in *The Voyeur:* even while the one scene seems always to be standing still, it is kept revolving in time, perpetually renewing itself.

> "We'll be leaving early," Franck says.
> "What do you mean—early?"
> "Six o'clock, if you can make it."
> "Too early for you?"
> "Oh no." She laughs. Then, after a pause, "in fact it'll be fun." They sip their drinks.
> "If all goes well," Franck says, "we'll be in town by ten and have an hour or two before lunch."
> "Yes, of course. I'd prefer that too," A . . . says.
> They sip their drinks. (P. 74)

There follows a conversation about the book they have both been reading, and then when that subject has been exhausted (a matter of a couple of paragraphs),

> They sip their drinks. In the three glasses, the ice cubes have now altogether disappeared. Franck inspects the gold liquid remaining in the bottom of his glass. He turns it to one side, then the other, amusing himself by detaching the little bubbles clinging to the sides.
> "Still," he says, "it started out well." He turns toward A . . . for her support: "We left on schedule and were driving along without any trouble. It wasn't even ten o'clock when we reached town." (P. 75)

There is absolutely no transition here: the trip to town which had been referred to as a future event a few paragraphs before is suddenly cited as having already taken place during the course of what we had assumed all along to be the same conversation (although there is always the possibility, too, that the last version occurs in the same present, but as an imaginative reinvention of the future *as* past. A . . . and Franck would then be projecting their premeditated alibis into the future as explanations for the past which has not yet occured). And this is typical of how Robbe-Grillet keeps time rotating within the novel so that the reader can never get oriented to the sequence of events. Thus, the author achieves his goal set forth in *For a New Novel* of incorporating a paradoxical movement of time in his work; in one sense, time seems to be standing still, while in another, it is in constant motion. The reader, as a result, is pushed onto a track of concentric circles, always coming back to the same scene, but sometimes sloping gradually onto it, other times swooping suddenly into it. At one time we may enter at the middle, watch the scene end and then overlap; another time, we meet it at the end and leave it at the middle (though the next time around may well put us into a different temporal perspective); another time, we may watch it run through from beginning to end. It must be emphasized, however, that we never know whether we are seeing the beginning, middle, or end of the action, because we really have no sense of the totality of that action. Since there is no story, we can hardly be expected to know just where the beginning or end *is* or, for that matter, which parts of the action exist totally outside of time as imaginative reworkings of the basic situation. All we have are fragments fed into *our* imaginations, which we must use as we can.

The contrast between the traditional novel and New Novel is too obvious to be made much of, but by including a traditional novel as a topic of conversation *within* the New Novel, Robbe-Grillet encourages some reflection on the different standards, attitudes, and implications engendered by the two forms. As Franck and A . . . sit on the veranda, they discuss the book both of them have now finished: "their remarks can therefore refer to the book as a whole; that is, both to the outcome and to the earlier episodes . . . to which this outcome gives a new significance, or to which it adds a complementary meaning" (p. 74). A book structured on cumulative effect leading to a meaning consistent with earlier events sounds very much like a traditional novel, rather than one which has abdicated all attempts at meaning; and therefore the conventional mode of a clear sequence of events (which we would call plot) leading to a climax which heightens impact and induces meaning, is indicated in the discussion. Because the New Novel works to destroy whatever clarity it has created, it could not possibly be described in this way. Also, because it is not analogical, the reader could not refer it to another system which A . . . and Franck seem to do almost immediately:

They have never made the slightest judgment as to the novel's value, speaking instead of the scenes, events, and characters as if they were real: a place they might remember (located in Africa, moreover), people they might have known, or whose adventures someone might have told them. Their discussions have never touched on the verisimilitude, the coherence, or the quality of the narrative. On the other hand, they frequently blame the heroes for certain acts or characteristics, as they would in the case of mutual friends.

They also sometimes deplore the coincidences of the plot, saying that
"things don't happen that way," and then they construct a different
probable outcome starting from a new supposition, "if it weren't for
that." Other possibilities are offered, during the course of the book,
which lead to different endings. The variations are extremely numerous;
the variations of these, still more so. They seem to enjoy multiplying
these choices, exchanging smiles, carried away by their enthusiasm,
probably a little intoxicated by this proliferation. . . .

"But that's it, he was just unlucky enough to have come home earlier
that day, and no one could have guessed he would."

Thus Franck sweeps away in a single gesture all the suppositions they
had just constructed together. It's no use making up contrary possibilities, since things are the way they are; reality stays the same. (Pp. 74–75)

Frank's and A . . .'s reaction to the novel is totally subjective and
analogical. What they enjoy is the feeling of "life" engendered by
the novel, which enables them to "relate" "scenes, events, and
characters" from the novel to their own lives. Their only standard
for evaluating the book seems to be not its style or verisimilitude,
but the extent to which the plot sounds probable. Is it amenable
to our sense of logic? Is it reasonable? Is it, in short, "realistic"?
They find their greatest pleasure in talking not about the book
itself, but the story it might have depicted *if* any one thing had
happened instead of what actually *did* happen. Their discussion,
in short, takes the form of the *New* Novel, which demonstrates
Robbe-Grillet's assertion that the New Novel *is* life, unlike the
traditional novel which substitutes a reasonable representation of
life for the thing itself. Franck finally does dismiss the proliferation of possibilities because "it's no use making up contrary possibilities, since things are the way they are: reality stays the same."
But Robbe-Grillet would disagree: reality can *never* stay the
same, since it exists only in our imaginations which discover it just
through the speculation of contrary possibilities. Franck's statement that "he was just unlucky enough to have come home earlier that day, and no one could have guessed he would" suggests a
parallel between his own reality and events in the novel. Is the
"he" the jealous husband–narrator in whose mind this scene
keeps taking place? Well, it is a possibility—and if we invent it, it
can become a reality. At any rate, nothing is very clear here:
fragments can be put together in so many different ways.

Immediately after Franck and A . . . have had the above discussion, they return to the subject of their trip into town. Now, however, the trip is mentioned as a thing of the past—though it often

seems to be a *projection* of the future into the past. The two supposed lovers seem to be making up excuses, inventing different possibilities, and playing with alternatives—just as they had done a minute before in their discussion of the novel—in order to create a story that will explain the length of their trip to those they will have to account to. Is this, then, a parallel to the story they are reading, or is that "novel" the traditional novel's treatment of their *own* affair, just as their discussions of the novel and the real-life event of their trip *is* the New Novel *we*'re reading? The possibilities are endless, the climax is absent, the truth has never been uncovered. But the New Novelist is not interested in such goals. "Reality" can be re-created at will, then just as soon destroyed; truth itself is out of the question entirely, and the only verisimilitude of importance is that of style and form—those very qualities ignored by A . . . and Franck *in* their discussion but represented by Robbe-Grillet's presentation *of* that discussion to the reader.

As A . . . sits in her room at one point in the novel (which could be the beginning, middle, or end of the story—it is impossible to tell), she hears the singing of one of the workers driving a truck up to the veranda. His song is a native tune "with incomprehensible words, or even without words," and "because of the peculiar nature of this kind of melody [one which flows easily from one note to another, but breaks off suddenly], it is difficult to determine if the song is interrupted for some fortuitous reason—in relation, for instance, to the manual work. . . . Similarly, when it begins again, it is just as sudden, as abrupt, starting on notes which hardly seem to constitute a beginning, or a reprise." As the narrator continues to describe the unconventionality of the tune, it soon becomes clear that it is the New Novel, too, whose progress is being depicted:

At other places, however, something seems about to end; everything indicates this: a gradual cadence, tranquillity regained, the feeling that nothing remains to be said; but after the note which should be the last comes another one, without the least break in continuity, with the same ease, then another, and others following, and the hearer supposes himself transported into the heart of the poem . . . when at that point everything stops without warning. (p. 83)

A . . . is writing as she listens to the song, and the parallel becomes unavoidable:

It is doubtless the same poem continuing. If the themes sometimes blur, they only recur somewhat later, all the more clearly, virtually identical. Yet these repetitions, these tiny variations, halts, regressions, can give rise to modifications—though barely perceptible—eventually moving quite far from the point of departure. (P. 84)

Even while Robbe-Grillet has insisted that we refrain from any analogical associations in his novels, the temptation here is too great: the movement of the poem, its techniques and form, provide an exact correlation to the aims of the New Novel. In both song and novel, form is reality and the whole purpose behind the creation. To discover the form is to know the work. To get into the work means watching lines blur, finding a melodic rhythm and then losing it, thinking all along that one is getting nowhere only to discover that he has traveled quite a distance after all. It is to feel finality in each new recasting of the scene, yet to be pushed by each final note into another, until finally, one sees the feeling of finality itself as the continuous pattern behind the work (as it was all through Beckett's novels), when: poof, it does stop; it has been ended. The poem in this passage does seem to "refer" to something else, then—but what else is it truly referring to, after all, but itself? All roads within the work only lead us back *to* the work, so perhaps we can justify our analogy in this way.

And what are our obligations as readers of this book—if it is not to judge its fidelity to life, the "reality" of its characters, the validity of its structure, etc.? The author implies that we do nothing but keep the action running through our minds. Reinvent and reinvent. How? By the process of contrary possibilities, each taking us in new directions which seem to lead us back always to the same starting point, but which do ultimately get us somewhere. If the method is not clear by now, Robbe-Grillet spells it out for us in what could be his equivalent of "How to Write a Novel." Once again, the novel which A . . . and Franck have read is the topic of conversation. What is the book about?

Psychological complications aside, it is a standard narrative of colonial life in Africa, with a description of a tornado, a native revolt, and incidents at the club. A . . . and Franck discuss it animatedly. . . .

The main character of the book is a customs official. This character is not an official but a high-ranking employee of an old commercial company. This company's business is going badly, rapidly turning shady. This company's business is going extremely well. The chief character—one learns—is dishonest. He is honest, he is trying to reestablish a situation compromised by his predecessor, who died in an automobile accident.

But he had no predecessor, for the company was only recently formed; and it was not an accident. Besides, it happens to be a ship (a big white ship) and not a car at all. (P. 137)

Apparently, the reader is to go to work and invent his own novel. Certainly, all the possibilities are there: contradictions which constantly cancel one another out yet which never manage to erase everything, but lead instead to a whole new set of possibilities. The result, once again, is a series of fragments to be churned up by the imagination, and then redistributed through time, space, and action. The fragments are the author's, but the story, ultimately, is the reader's.

In the Labyrinth seems to me indisputably Robbe-Grillet's greatest achievement. It becomes the supreme justification for the New Novel by pointing to its potential as a stirring artistic accomplishment indicative of nothing but itself, yet embodying within itself an experience so dramatic, intense, and absorbing that the New Novel suddenly seems capable of the emotional force common to the most memorable works of traditional fiction. The most "human" of Robbe-Grillet's novels, it sacrifices nothing to his theory, yet seizes that theory from the realm of intellectual puzzles and casts it into the deepest levels of our psyches. Here theory is refined into consummate expression of a reality created in our imaginations, struggled with in our minds, and suffered from within our souls.

In his short preface to the book, Robbe-Grillet warns the reader "to see in it only the objects, actions, words, and events which are described, without attempting to give them either more or less meaning than in his own life, or his own death."[4] The reader, then, is asked to remain within his own system as he determines the novel's meaning; but at the same time, the reference to our own lives and deaths leaves latitude for a broad spectrum of thoughts and feelings. We are free to intuit more than we can comprehend, just as we can feel the weight of death on our lives without being able to understand it. Robbe-Grillet's Labyrinth, while characterized by concreteness, evokes powerful responses

4. Alain Robbe-Grillet, *Two Novels by Robbe-Grillet: Jealousy* and *In the Labyrinth*, trans. Richard Howard (New York: Grove Press, 1965), p. 140. All future page references, cited in parentheses, are to this edition.

which, if they remain ineffable, may be for that very reason all the more profound.

From the first sentence—"I am alone here now, under cover"—the reader is dislocated, yet at the same time safe. "Here" could refer to the imagination itself, but since Robbe-Grillet has cautioned us against such analogical thinking, we can do as well by saying simply that "here" can be anywhere—wherever the mind can take refuge from the outside world. And since reality exists only in the imagination, its particular features are always arbitrary: the concrete details of reality are whatever the imagination wants them to be:

Outside it is raining, outside you walk through the rain with your head down, shielding your eyes with one hand while you stare ahead nevertheless, a few yards ahead, at a few yards of wet asphalt; outside it is cold, the wind blows between the bare black branches; the wind blows through the leaves, rocking whole boughs, rocking them, rocking, their shadows swaying across the white roughcast walls. Outside the sun is shining, there is no tree, no bush to cast a shadow, and you walk under the sun shielding your eyes with one hand while you stare ahead, only a few yards in front of you, at a few yards of dusty asphalt where the wind makes patterns of parallel lines, forks, and spirals. (P. 141)

And so the arbitrariness of art is admitted from the beginning: the reality art chooses to work with can be anything. Why, then, confine oneself to a representational fiction when the supremacy of fiction lies in its very ability to fabricate its own forms? The above passage is reminiscent of Robbe-Grillet's mock-treatment of the traditional novel in the last passage quoted from *Jealousy:* as each idea contradicts the preceding one, we are led out of the conventional novel and into the New Novel, which gets its impetus not from reality itself, but from the possibilities engendered by that reality in the higher life of the imagination.

"Inside," meanwhile, the artist is assembling his materials before beginning his act of creation. This strikes me as similar to the avant-garde production of a play which leaves the curtain open as the audience arrives, and sets up its props while they watch, thereby accomplishing two things: (1) the assertion of imagination's independence from reality (by breaking down the basic assumption of representational art, which seeks to establish an illusion of reality); and (2) the dissolution of any clear demarcation between the real world and its imaginative equivalent (by blurring the line where one ends and the other begins). Contemplating the dust on the table—and, later, the pattern on the wallpaper—the artist changes his scene again, so that now it is snowing outside. Snow seems the most satisfying atmosphere because it also embodies the silence of the room in which the author is reinventing the world: "No noise, even muffled, ever penetrates the walls of the room, no vibration, no breath of air, and in the silence tiny particles descend slowly, scarcely visible in the lamplight, descend gently, vertically, always at the same speed, and the fine gray dust lies in a uniform layer on the floor, on the bedspread, on the furniture" (p. 142). This room is literal reality, and the imagination is roaming around in it, seeking the proper forms through which it can reinvent that reality in order to know it more intimately. The narrator looks at the wallpaper, and his imagination immediately takes over:

As for the wallpaper itself, the innumerable tiny spots which constitute its pattern look no more like a torch than a flower, a human figure, a dagger, a street light, or anything. The wallpaper merely looks as if silent feathers were falling in regular lines at a uniform rate, so slowly that their movement is scarcely noticeable, and it is difficult to decide whether their direction is up or down, like particles suspended in motionless water, tiny bubbles in a gaseous liquid, snowflakes, dust. (P. 184)

In the Labyrinth could have been about the torch or flower or dagger or whatever other image the narrator had associated with the tiny spots in the wallpaper's pattern (earlier he had referred to them as little gray insects). The final (which need never be final) decision is arbitrary, but in this case, it happens to be the image of snow that seems most satisfying—tying in, as it does, with the sight of dust falling and fallen, with the silence permeating the room, etc.—and becomes, therefore, the central image around which the rest of the story will be created. And for construction materials, the room supplies other objects as well:

The picture framed in varnished wood, the striped wallpaper, the fireplace with its heap of ashes, the table with its lamp and its glass ashtray, the heavy red curtains, the large day bed covered with the same red velvety material, and finally the chest with its three drawers and its cracked marble top, the brown package on top of it, and above that the picture, and the vertical lines of little gray insects rising to the ceiling. (P. 149)

As each object is reinvented, it assumes a reality far more dynamic and insistently "present" than its former reality outside the imagination. The brown package, for example, is one of the most ordinary, unexciting objects in the room. It has no inherent interest at all, and is furthermore so commonplace that we recognize it immediately and quickly pass it by. By re-creating it as a principal prop in his story, however, Robbe-Grillet forces us to become almost fixated upon it, and the longer we attend to it, the more mysterious and singular it becomes. Its existence is now too important for us to bypass as though we were familiar with it. It *almost* becomes symbolic, and yet it symbolizes nothing beyond itself. As in *Jealousy*—but in a much more subtle and sophisticated way—Robbe-Grillet has divested the ordinary of its familiar associations and functions, thereby compelling us to confront reality from a new perspective; and again, it is the imagination which has heightened our sense of reality. The picture, too, is significant, for it supplies all the characters for the story, and continues to sift through our imagination until its primary reality is *there*, rather than in the "real" world of the room. Of course, though, no matter how important each object becomes for us, the book is not ultimately about any of them—it is about reality and imagination. And because other objects could have served as well, we know that the story itself is less important than its style. The story, in short, can be only "about" itself.

In *For a New Novel*, Robbe-Grillet has said that his descriptions never serve simply to provide a setting for the action, but rather, constitute in themselves one of the principal actions of the novel. Thus, while it is true that the objects in *Labyrinth* are used to set up scenes in which they then play an important role, their real significance is not as props, but as process: the way the narrator uses them to create reality and then destroy what they have just created. Each time an object is assigned a different role in the action, that role erases its previous one. If the lamp in the room becomes a lamppost outside in the snowy street, or if the sound of a motorcycle suddenly translates itself into the sound of rapid gunfire, such transformation, by indicating the ease with which imagination is recasting reality, forces us to focus on the perpetual process of creation and destruction by which we conceive reality; the object itself is used less to describe a scene, therefore, than to help us through the imaginative process.

Since the minds of the narrator and reader are to converge as we pick up the process and make it our own, we share the novelist's torment in struggling with his story. Unlike *The Voyeur* and *Jealousy*, the tension between creative and destructive impulses here has emotional effects and consequences quite similar to the agonies and frustrations of the narrator–artist in *Malone Dies*. The deeper the narrator's involvement with his story, the deeper becomes our involvement with the story *and* with him, and *In the Labyrinth* abounds with illustrations of the artist wrestling with his material—trying to figure out motivations, arrange sequences of action, define the quest both for his character and himself. As the novel knits and unknits itself in the imagination, the precariousness of artistic invention settles into a kind of emotional fear and pity for the reader—and it is this emotional involvement, I think, which justifies most convincingly Robbe-Grillet's assertion in *For a New Novel* that it is the reader himself who actually invents the experience of reality he finds in the novel.

When the narrator remarks, in his description of a man whose sudden appearance has shaken the soldier, that the shoes "probably have rubber soles, for there has been no sound of steps down the hallway" (p.195), we feel some genuine relief at the author's success at having found an explanation for what seemed to be an utterly inexplicable appearance. Or again, when the military jacket and cap of this man are described as lacking all identifying insignia, but that "the difference is so evident" between "small areas of new material softer and brighter than the faded surrounding areas dirtied by long wear" that "there can be no doubt about the shape of the missing insignia" (p. 195), we know that the artist has regained control because his description here parallels that of the table in the room, whose dusty surface is interrupted by clear areas indicating the size and shape of the object which had once been there. In both cases, the author is able to identify by their formal outlines and *know* the objects that are absent from his vision. This knowledge must be called progress for him, while the parallel itself reveals another sort of progress, which establishes the contour of the work. If the missing insignia are identified by the same means as the objects which have left their trace on the table, then there is a law operating within the work that perpetuates its movement. Remember that each description is to engender not only its own destruction, but a new creation to replace itself. The process always leads us back to the beginning (just as the insignia information leads us right back to the first scene of the novel), until we assume that we have gotten nowhere. Yet, as the narrator of *Jealousy* has told us concerning the poem sung by the truck driver: "these repetitions, these tiny

variations, halts, regressions, can give rise to modifications—
though barely perceptible—eventually moving quite far from the
point of departure" (p. 84).

The regressions, certainly, are obvious enough. At one point,
the soldier, exhausted from his traveling, follows the tracks of the
boy who had been leading him to the street where he could finally deposit the package into the hands of the right person.

Now the tracks stop suddenly in front of a door just like the others, but
not completely closed. The stoop is very narrow and can be crossed in
one stride without setting foot on it. The light at the other end of the
hallway is on; the ticking sounds like an alarm clock. At the far end of the
hallway is a rather narrow staircase rising in short flights, separated by
small square landings, turning at right angles. . . . At the top is the closed
room where the gray film of dust gradually settles on the table and on
the small objects on top of it, on the mantelpiece, on the marble top of
the chest, on the day bed, on the waxed floor where the felt slippers . . .
The tracks continue, regular and straight, across the fresh snow. (P. 207)

We seem really to be closing in on our goal when we suddenly
realize where the boy's tracks have led us: right back to the place
from which our search had started. The narrator himself seems to
realize this only as he proceeds with the description and finds it
all so familiar. When he realizes where he is, he inserts an ellipsis
and, in one spontaneous and magnificent gesture of heroic defiance, simply turns away from the room, changes completely the
earlier fact which led him back here, and picks up the story
again—this time with the boy's tracks *continuing* (rather than
disappearing), "regular and straight" across the snow. It is a brilliant maneuver and an admirable escape, but the problem, so
nicely evaded here, is never really solved satisfactorily. Always
we find ourselves returning to the original scene, wondering
where to place it, how to activate it, when to use it so that it will
help lead us to the end. The answers are never forthcoming, but
the questions hold us as we participate in the creation of the
novel and, with each dead-end, come to know its form *as* a labyrinth.

The scene depicted in the picture, "The Defeat of Reichen-
fels," is even more central to the story's development, but while
it operates as a continuous source of inspiration, its proper location in and meaning to the narrative seem always to elude the
author. "It is probably here that the scene occurs," he says in a
typical passage: "the silent gathering which steps back in every

direction around him, the soldier finally remaining alone in the center of a huge circle of pale faces. . . . But this scene leads to nothing" (p. 246). Again, the creative process leads to its own destruction as the scene appears, blurs, rubs itself out, reappears, builds, destructs, and springs to (another form of) life again later on. The picture haunts us, but the scene's proper place and meaning elude us—and this becomes a constant pattern throughout the work.

Even when a scene has found its proper place in the narrative and the author feels satisfied with it, he is apt to find trouble in the transition between that scene and the one it leads him to next. He has, for example, built up a nice scene in which the woman and the lame man (her husband? a deserter? an impostor?) argue over whether the boy should be allowed to go out in order to lead the soldier to the street they presume he is looking for. The narrator has the next scene worked out: the boy *is* finally permitted to go, and this gets the story moving again, as the soldier and his guide leave the house, and . . . but wait, this will not do. Why has the woman changed her mind and given the boy permission to leave the house? "Has the woman finally given in? Yet the soldier has not noticed that she has given her consent, in his presence, for the child to go out. Had this scene taken place out of his sight? But where and when? Or was her consent not being considered?" (p. 191). So one small snag necessitates another recasting, results in the breakdown of a sequence that really seemed to be working. We remember that Malone had the same trouble: a dark spot would grow even as he tried to continue in spite of it, until it finally enveloped everything and cast the entire scene into darkness, from which Malone had to work desperately to rescue it.

Like Malone, too, the narrator of *In the Labyrinth* is subject to making false starts as he tries to push the narrative on, lift it off the ground; he stumbles with it, gets it going again, stumbles, and pushes on until he finally achieves enough momentum to move forward again. The important thing is not to consider defeat, even as everything seems to be breaking down:

The soldier . . . notices at this moment that the door is ajar: door, hallway, door, vestibule, door, then finally a lighted room, and a table with an empty glass with a circle of dark-red liquid still at the bottom, and a lame man leaning on his crutch, bending forward in a precarious balance. No. Door ajar. Hallway. Staircase. Woman running from floor to floor up the

spiral staircase, her grey apron billowing about her. Door. And finally a
lighted room: bed, chest, fireplace, table with a lamp on its left corner,
and the lampshade casting a white circle on the ceiling. No. Above the
chest is a print framed in black wood . . . No. No. No.
    The door is not ajar. . . . (P. 194)

The door is such a small detail, yet the narrator cannot get on
until he has gotten it right; each detail must fit or the whole scene
falls apart. In this case, the problem of the door left ajar becomes
a major snag, and the next scene resists development until it has
been taken care of. By including his failures in this way, the author keeps us conscious of the fact that the reader is *not* to consider the work an illusion of reality but rather the imagination's
attempt to create its own reality subject to no laws but its own.
The material is not to be evaluated by any standard other than
what pleases the imagination inventing it.
    Given the frequent breakdowns in the narrative, it may seem
odd to note that these too are arbitrary, since there are other
times when the narrator slips out of a tight spot with perfect ease.
When the soldier is in the barrack's hospital, for example, he gets
up to try to find an escape only to realize a bit later that he has
left his package on the bed. Returning to the bed, he finds it
gone—a fact which promises to lead us into a radical turn of plot.
Has the box been stolen? Removed by the doctors for his benefit?
Is it possible that it never existed at all? The soldier is stunned by
the box's disappearance:

he turns the bolster over as if it were necessary to convince himself
further of the fact, turns the bolster over twice more; finally, he straightens up, no longer knowing what to do, but there are no longer blankets
on the mattress either. And three beds farther along the soldier recognizes some blankets bundled into a ball on an empty mattress. He has
simply gone to the wrong bed. (P. 209)

This seems rather an easy way out for a creator who has simply changed his mind. How easily he has eliminated the endless
complications he seemed to be getting himself into. This artist
wants to remind us of his self-sufficiency, his dictatorial control.
The imagination's supremacy over reality (rather than obligation to it) is largely accounted for by its absolute power in creating the laws it cares to live by. If the reader wants to cry, "Foul
play! Coincidence! Unbelievable! Unrealistic!" he simply shows
that he is playing with the wrong set of rules. Verisimilitude to
the outside world is an irrelevent criterion to such a work as this

which has its own reality to be faithful to. The artist's integrity can be measured only in terms of the art itself.

This novel, in fact, includes its own explication—even though it is inconclusive. As the story starts drawing to an end, the narrator becomes more compulsive about justifying the events he has recorded. He finds several different sets of motives, all of which, by providing new interpretations, supply a different plot. It is not surprising, of course, that each new possibility obliterates the preceding one, as the narrator (who has mysteriously thrown himself back into the story by having witnessed the dead soldier on "my" last visit) continues to interrogate his story. He considers possible plots that might provide cohesive frameworks within which character and action could unite:

> The woman who has taken care of the wounded soldier has obtained no information from him as to his comrade who died before he did. Toward the end he talked a good deal, but he had already forgotten most things that had happened recently; besides, he was delirious most of the time. The woman declares that he was already sick before he was wounded, that he had fever, and that he sometimes behaved like a sleepwalker. Her son, a serious-looking boy of about ten, had already encountered him in the street, perhaps even several times, if it is actually the same boy each time, as is likely despite slight contradictions. His role is significant since he is the one who, by his heedlessness, has provoked the actions of the occupants of the side car, but his many appearances are not all decisive to the same degree. The lame man, on the other hand, plays virtually no part at all. His presence in the morning at the Rue Bouvet military offices (transformed into a barracks or hospitalization center) has nothing surprising about it, given the ease with which he maneuvers when no one is there to observe his means of locomotion. Besides, the soldier does not seem to have paid much attention to his remarks. The bartender, for his part, is problematical or insignificant. He does not say a word, does not make a move; this heavyset bald man might also be a spy or an informer, the nature of his reflections is impossible to determine. (Pp. 269–70)

As the narrator works with his material, trying to discover his plot and the significance of his characters, he finds that each plot possibility clears up some of the dark spots left by the preceding one but creates new shadowy areas that will have to be dealt with by the creation of yet another plot. The imaginative process must be perpetual, then—just as the vision for Lily Briscoe had to be perpetually remade. In the above passage, many seemingly inexplicable incidents are accounted for, but then the problem focuses on the lame man who suddenly becomes irrelevant to the action. His very irrelevance, however, makes him that much more mystifying—to the point, indeed, where our attention becomes riveted on him, and we cannot consider as complete the explanation that renders him superfluous. And yet, as soon as we recast the story to give him a significant function, we find that the shadow now slips over the boy or the woman or whomever, thus leaving us with new areas of darkness which will have to be resolved by yet another reinvention. And the process can work in reverse, too: the bartender has been paid no special notice throughout the narrative, yet the novelist now begins to wonder if this seemingly minor character might not be the key figure in the whole drama. So again we can reinvent the action to give the bartender his due—knowing in advance, however, that once he becomes the major character, one of the other characters will lose his function, some of the principal incidents will again resist explanation, and we will be right back where we started. In its attempt to discover itself, the story is set into perpetual motion, which insures the constant activity of our imaginations.

This seems to be Robbe-Grillet's method throughout: the narrative moves in spasms of progression and regression, creation and negation, successes and failures. The imagination pounces on a scene and directs it to a dead end, where it sputters, flounders, recuperates, and finally escapes. As in *Jealousy*, the reader is pushed back from the action so that he has the sense of a vision so cloudy that he must constantly squint to get the scene into focus, and strain his ears to hear what the characters are saying. "His words are so faint that they disintegrate before he has actually spoken them; afterwards he even doubts whether he has actually pronounced them at all" (p. 216). "At times he speaks so low that the soldier has trouble hearing him. . . . The end of his sentence is inaudible" (p. 217). Such passages are common throughout, and emphasize the sense of silence that the narrator has prescribed in the first scene. As the spoken word evaporates, we wonder at first if we have heard it correctly, and then whether it was ever really uttered at all. Thus, like the other aspects of the work, speech—through the very process which brings it into being—annihilates itself, having served only to emphasize the silence of the void which remains.

This silence adds to the dreamlike quality of *In the Labyrinth*, which is one of its chief characteristics. Time, for example, is compressed into a continuous drifting present tense which forces us to confront the novel as a "here and now" presence by cutting off the past and future as possible escape passages. The narrative is every second in the midst of *being;* we can neither control it by time nor escape it *through* time. We are caught in the present from beginning to end—which means, of course, that we cannot possibly distinguish beginning or end, since both are defined only through time. In such a suspended world, it is not surprising that speech drifts into the air and disappears immediately. As soon as the words are uttered, they sink into the remote past (all past must be remote), and our minds cannot recall what the ears no longer hear. As soon as the present becomes past, then, that past is obliterated, just as in our dreams we live in a perpetual present, never able to gain the detachment or perspective needed for interpretation.

Surely, too, it is the dreamlike atmosphere of *In the Labyrinth* that accounts for a good deal of its emotional impact. Whereas *The Voyeur* and *Jealousy* put us through the intellectual process of reinventing reality, the characters and episodes being re-worked were suggestive of little beyond themselves. *In the Labyrinth,* however, is full of dreamlike situations which the reader can identify with emotionally. When the soldier meets the man with the umbrella who *may* be the man to whom he should deliver the package, he tries simultaneously to put forth sufficient information for the man to identify *him* as the proper agent, while trying to hold back as much information as possible in case this man is *not* the right one. Of course, he simply blunders on, unable to stop the more he realizes he *should* stop. Caught between saying too much or not enough, "the soldier had to choose between two solutions: to speak more openly or else to beat an immediate retreat. But he had not had time to choose one course or the other, and he had persisted in both directions at once, which further risked discouraging his interlocutor if he were, in spite of everything, etc. . ." (p. 229). The passage carries strong echoes of Kafka's world, where we somehow recognize the situation and apprehend it emotionally. We know the *feeling,* even if we cannot remember a particular incident which embodied or provoked it. So, too, when the boy, standing by the soldier's bed, asks with the directness so typical of innocence: "Are you going to die here?" (p. 257), the very bluntness of his question seems characteristic of our dreams; it sounds, or rather *feels* familiar.

It may be true, finally, that the entire narrative itself has been a dream—the product of the soldier's delirium moments before his death. As the soldier lies in bed, "the sheets pulled up to his chin, half listening to a confused story the same young woman with pale eyes is telling him," her words merge with his own memories—or were they rather hallucinations?

Then come scenes still less distinct—still more inaccurate, too, probably—violent although generally silent. They take place in vaguer, less characterized, more impersonal areas; a staircase recurs several times; someone is going down it rapidly, holding onto the railing, taking several steps at the same time, almost flying from one landing to the next, while the soldier, in order not to be knocked over, is obliged to step back into a corner. Then he goes more calmly down the stairs himself, and at the end of the long hallway he finds the snow-covered street again; and at the end of the street he finds the busy cafe again. . . . (Pp. 260–61)

He continues to relive variations of the episodes which have constituted the narrative up to this point, and we begin to wonder which of the variations preceded his present delirious state. Since no one alternative seems any more valid than another, and since there is no clear line separating past from present, all renditions coalesce in a single dimension of time and space, hindering any attempt to make meaningful distinctions. Yet the mystery of it all intrigues and compels us in a way made possible only by some relation to our own lives. Something very deep inside us is touched, some response is set off that we can identify only as a sense of reality located, known, and guarded in the most remote regions of our psyches. And to recognize it is to live it all over again, so that we are reliving something in our own experiences as we observe the soldier's experience.

Reality, we ultimately conclude, *is* mystery—and the deeper we feel such a truth, the less we can explain it. Like the soldier, we feel we need just a little more time to bring our vague intuitions to fruition, to capture the truth we know to be there just as we feel it eluding us. The dying soldier stares at the ceiling and, as he traces its contours, seems to be on the verge of some revelation:

his eyes no longer able to remain lowered so long, his gaze is obliged to move up the length of the red curtains to the ceiling and the hair-thin, somewhat sinuous crack whose shape also has something distinct and complicated about it which it would be necessary to follow with application from one turn to the next, with its curves, vacillations, uncertainties, sudden changes of directions, inflections, continuations, slight regressions, but it would take more time, a little time, a few minutes, a few seconds, and it is already, now, too late. (P. 266)

Reality, then, is infinitely mysterious; one keeps trying to trace its contours, to get it inside one's mind long enough to grasp it and hold it there. But since each delineation necessitates another, and each successive one effaces the last, we can conclude only that the awareness of life's mystery, its elusiveness, its cryptic suggestiveness constitutes our closest contact with reality.

After the soldier's death, the narrator reconsiders the basic elements of his story in order to find a consistent set of explanations that would justify all the characters and events within a unified plot line. I have already discussed his failure here: like Moran's observation of his dancing bees, the novelist's study of his novel leads to a process of interrogating which produces only endless speculation. And so the author ends by returning to the beginning, knowing now that one can do nothing more than constantly retrace the contours of a reality which will always evade him:

Outside it is raining. Outside you walk through the rain with your head down, shielding your eyes with one hand while you stare ahead, a few yards ahead, at a few yards of wet asphalt. The rain does not get in here, nor the snow nor the wind; and the only dust that dulls the gleaming horizontal surfaces, the polished wood of the table. . . . (P. 271)

The circle is complete, but the story is not finished—it will be traced again, *known* again—perhaps as something different this time—in the world of the imagination. Again, the author begins by describing.

But the image grows blurred by trying to distinguish the outlines, as in the case of the inordinately delicate pattern of the wallpaper and the indeterminate edges of the gleaming paths made in the dust by the felt slippers, and beyond the door, the dark vestibule where the umbrella is leaning against the coat rack, then, once past the entrance door, the series of long hallways, the spiral staircase, the door to the building with its stone stoop, and the whole city behind me. (Pp. 271–72)

The last phrase implies that the mystery of the story the author has not been able to decipher is typical of all reality, but the fact that the city is now *behind* him suggests that he has gotten through the labyrinth after all, and come out on the other side. What has he learned from the experience of having wandered through the labyrinth? He has learned its shape, has felt its contours, has known its reality through the process of having invented it. His work is completed, for although the story can go on indefinitely, he has touched its reality. One cannot "know" reality; he can only experience it—and that experience has been achieved.

One more conclusion may be inserted here: since mystery is, finally, the quintessence of reality, the art which renders this mystery is itself reality—not a reproduction or reflection or "slice" of the real world, but a self-contained, autonomous life. In *For a New Novel*, Robbe-Grillet has said that the novel is not to be used as a tool to express the outside world; the New Novel "does not express, it explores, and what it explores is itself." I have tried to demonstrate the New Novel's independence, and yet it is true that *In the Labyrinth* is so highly evocative that we are in danger of relating it to the reality we live in, rather than the one we invent. Granted that the distinction is not always clear, I think it would be a mistake to persist in thinking that this book's power originates from our associations which relate it to the real world. Consider, for example, the scene (pp. 234–40) in which the soldier is chased by the men on the motorcycle, shot and wounded and thrown into unconsciousness. It is really a very powerful scene for me—intriguing and highly suggestive, yet suggestive of nothing beyond itself. We identify with the soldier, recognize the dreamlike anxiety, frustration, and struggle of being hunted down by hostile forces. Yet the power is not in the representational aspects of a dream, but in the world of art and the imagination. We do not need to create an allegory in order to feel the scene unleash its power within us; neither do we have to refer it to any experience outside of itself. The scene—as does the work as a whole—creates its own intensity, its own dynamism, its own life, its own reality. The novel includes its own generator, and the currents we feel throbbing through our systems are being charged not from the world, but from the work.

In the Labyrinth seems to me not only Robbe-Grillet's finest work, but a truly original and memorable one as well. More than any of his books, it becomes a haunting emotional experience as well as an intellectual challenge. The author has thrown his novel into chaos in order to create the impression of chaos more precisely than any conventionally structured novel could have done, but he has not forgotten the reader's need to contemplate a reality in art that will at least match his own in richness of texture, depth of feeling, and scope of humanity. The soldier, the woman, the boy, the bartender, the waitress, the lame man are little more than images, appearances, objects without depth or individuality; yet each one remains in the mind—not as representative of but at least with the same *force* as people we have met in our own lives, dreams, and nightmares. The restaurant, the snow-covered street, the streetlamp, the hallways, the staircases, the winding routes which constitute the form and appearance of the particular labyrinth through which Robbe-Grillet has directed us—all are commonplace objects, yet each fastens itself onto our minds— not, again, as representative of but with the same clarity and conviction that constitute the role (though not the function) of objects in our lives. Robbe-Grillet's triumph here is not a theoretical one; it is an artistic one. The novel appeals to and remains in the imagination not because it expresses a theory, but because it is truly strong enough to express itself.

10

"Confusion Hath Fuck His Masterpiece"

The Random Art of William S. Burroughs

What I want to do is to learn to see more of
what's out there, to look outside, to achieve as
far as possible a complete awareness of surroundings. Beckett wants to go inward. First he
was in a bottle and now he is in the mud. I am
aimed in the other direction: outward.
                              —William S. Burroughs

In order to propel himself outward, William
Burroughs has severed all lines securing the novel to its own aesthetic system, and as the novel floats out into reality, chaos infiltrates to the point where art and accident often become indistinguishable. When asked in a 1965 *Paris Review* interview whether
he composed on the typewriter, Burroughs replied: "I use typewriter and I use scissors,"[1] and only five years later, this answer
was modified to include tape recorders, film, and any other media which can reflect chaos with maximum immediacy and minimal artistic control. Willingly yielding up aesthetic authority,
Burroughs welcomes any method—whether more or less sophisticated than scissors—that will allow chaos to interfere in the very
creation of conscious art. The result is a new kind of novel, which

1. *Writers at Work: The Paris Review Interviews,* ed. George Plimpton (New
York: Viking Press, 1967), p. 170. All future references to this interview conduct-
ed by Conrad Knickerbocker are to this edition and will be cited in parentheses.

lives in chaos and utilizes art solely as a selective device for splicing reality into a new context of associative patterns. The novel born from this process bears little resemblance to traditional concepts of art or reality, and the experience engendered is private, shocking, sometimes effective and exciting, often inaccessible, and even more often dull. Its existence calls into question all the conventional assumptions of art, while its frequent failures call the questions themselves into question. Although Burroughs proposes to liberate the reader from the traditional confines of the novel, the freedom he offers, ironically enough, tends more than anything else to arouse nostalgia for the form he has destroyed.

In the *Paris Review* interview, Burroughs agrees that he is interested in "bypassing the conscious, rational apparatus to which most writers direct their efforts," and adds that his fiction is deliberately addressed to the area of dreams, which he defines as a "certain juxtaposition of word and image" (p. 149). "In other words," he says, "I've been interested in precisely how word and image get around on very, very complex association lines." But Burroughs' interest in words, like Beckett's, is requisite only to the possibilities of destroying them: he hopes to expand consciousness by eliminating "nonbody experience" (p. 150).

I think that words are an around-the-world, ox-cart way of doing things, awkward instruments, and they will be laid aside eventually, probably sooner that we think. Most serious writers refuse to make themselves available to the things that technology is doing. I've never been able to understand this sort of fear. (P. 153)

Citing the cutup method originated by Brion Gysin (an American expatriate poet, painter, and personal friend), Burroughs praises it as an exciting way of discovering new connections between images and, consequently, expanding one's range of vision. "Any narrative passage or any passage, say, of poetic images is subject to any number of variations, all of which may be interesting and valid in their own right" (p. 155). Defining cutup as a juxtaposition of what's happening outside and what you're thinking of while it's happening, Burroughs values the method's potential to break down the Aristotelian construct—the whole either–or proposition—which he calls "one of the great shackles of Western civilization" (pp. 156–57). Whereas logic presumes our imbibing experience on a one-dimensional plane, the way we actually experience reality is, he insists, quite different: our minds are often out of touch with our senses, and what we take in through the senses is always conditioned by where our minds happen to be at the time. Now take a solitary image and watch its meaning squirm, its significance expand and deflate, as the mind, already occupied with a battery of other images, tries to assimilate it. If the association can be revelatory of a new truth found in the juxtaposition of the images inside commingling with those outside, all the writer has to do is produce new arbitrary associations to force the reader to perceive reality in a new way. Consider our familiar associations with carnivals: fun, gaiety, shallow but enjoyable activity. Now place a soundtrack of screams onto the images of the carnival, and its reality is immediately transformed into a startling image of hell. The roller coaster becomes a ride of horror, the ferris wheel a spinning device of pure torture, the converging crowds an image of panic, fear, terrifying closeness. Once the traditional associative pattern has been broken, our image of reality undergoes a radical change which puts us in touch with the multifaceted planes constituting experience as we live it, and quite unlike the way the novel has traditionally presented it to us. Admitting that the fiction he creates dismisses the straight plot, the declarative sentence, or any other component confined to a single level of meaning, Burroughs claims that new techniques, such as cutup, "will involve much more of the total capacity of the observer. It enriches the whole aesthetic experience, extends it" (p. 157).

If, however, the novel's impact is to be extended, how far can it go before the aesthetic experience becomes indistinguishable from our living experience? The quintessence of art has always been its conscious selection and control of materials drawn from life. The cutup technique is, on the other hand, based on random juxtaposition, and is valued only to the extent that its results could not have been predicated in advance by the author. Wary of conventional control systems, the author is now eager to surrender control of his material in order to expand his and the reader's vision. Put another way: Burroughs works to *discover* his material, his new visions of reality, rather than to objectify a preconception. "I think there's going to be more and more merging of art and science," he says (p. 158), and it is indeed difficult in his works to separate the two—not simply because the random artist uses methods of modern technology to express his sense of reality, but because the expression itself is closer to the scientist's careful blending of components within a test tube than to the artist's organic invention. Burroughs insists that his product *is* an artistic one, though—even if it does come from machines—since *he*, after all, must choose the control group of words, sentences, or images which are then arbitrarily (but, he insists, aesthetically) rearranged. It takes a conscious mind to feed the computer, and the artist is apparently similar to a programmer who knows that the machine can produce variations only from the material he has fed it. Still, any literary purist will likely feel uneasy about Burroughs' interest "in extending newspaper and magazine formats to so-called literary material" (p. 164), and our discomfort grows when he compares literature to advertising, on the basis that both "are concerned with the precise manipulation of word and image" (p. 167). Not only the integrity of the novel seems at stake here but its very identity as a work of art distinct from other facets of our culture. While the novel may well be enriched by techniques adopted from other media, its chief value must remain in the realm of art, rather than in any psychological, social, economic, or political domain, if it is to retain its identity as an aesthetic form.

It is hard to say just what Burroughs wants the novel to *do*. In a more recent interview,[2] he says that the novel form is outmoded, and one wonders if Burroughs should not consider discarding it altogether. "We may look forward," he says, "to a future in which people do not read at all or read only illustrated books and magazines or some abbreviated form of reading matter. To compete with television and photo magazines, writers will have to develop more precise techniques producing the same effect on the reader as lurid action photo" (p. 39). It would seem, then, that the novel need not be replaced by other media if it can absorb their techniques and effects to produce an equivalent impact on the reader. Here is where cutup becomes useful: Burroughs regards this technique as the means toward discovering the role of language in our emotional lives. Words create images which in turn produce associative patterns controlling both our thought processes and our nervous systems. This nervous system forms the foundation of our lives because it is here that reality makes its impression upon us, and here too that we respond to it. Bur-

2. Daniel Odier, "Journey Through Time-Space: An Interview with William S. Burroughs," *Evergreen Review*, XIII, 67 (June 1969), 39–41, 78–89. All future references to this interview will be cited in parentheses.

roughs hopes that "the extension of cutup techniques will lead to more precise verbal experiments . . . giving a whole new dimension to writing. These techniques can show the writer what words are and put him in tactile communication with his medium. This, in turn, could lead to a precise science of words and show how certain word-combinations produce certain effects on the human nervous system" (p. 39). The emphasis here is on the writer rather than the reader, which suggests that the cutup technique is for the benefit of the artist, putting him more deeply in touch with the materials (words, in this case) he uses to create. "The writer does not yet know what words are," says Burroughs. "He deals only with abstractions from the source points of words" (p. 39). We can infer, then, that cutup does not in itself constitute an artistic method, but is rather a means whereby the novelist can break through his own "word image" barrier in order to discover new associations which can then be passed on to the reader. But Burroughs is inconsistent on this point, for he does seem at times to consider the discovery itself the end, rather than the beginning of the artistic process. When asked about his experience with both the foldin and cutup techniques, Burroughs insists that "when you make cutups you do not get simply random juxtapositions of words," but "that they do mean something, and often that these meanings refer to some future event" (p. 39). Now this would be more a mystical goal than an artistic one; and at other times, Burroughs seems interested exclusively in the political and psychological possibilities of the novel. Unlike Robbe-Grillet, who tries to isolate art so that it contains its own reality and refers only to itself, Burroughs appears to define art as a process used to evoke psychological revelations leading to political insights which can ultimately improve the quality of our lives. Of course art may have a social purpose and still be distinct from advertising; what counts is the artist's handling of his material, the degree to which his art molds language into powerful expressions of experience and emotion. Above all, while art may always be used as a means to push products or propaganda, the novel, as art formalized into vision, must regard fidelity to aesthetic criteria as its ultimate goal.

Burroughs does agree that the artist must be fully conscious and responsible even when working with material he himself does not always understand, but his concept of the artist remains ambiguous:

The selection and arrangement of materials is quite conscious, but there is a random factor by which I obtain the material I use, then select and work it over into an acceptable form. . . . you control what you put *into* your montages; you don't fully control what comes out. That is, I select a page to cut up and I have control over what I put in. I simply fit what comes out of the cutups back into a narrative structure. . . . the cutups will give you new materials, but they won't tell you what to do with it. (Pp. 40–41)

Again, cutup precedes art; it does not replace it. Cutup provides the material, but the artist controls the creation. Burroughs, however, is difficult to pin down here: the above statements seem contradictory to me. There is quite a difference between the writer who intends to "select and work" his material "over into an acceptable form" and the one who "simply fits what comes out of the cutups back into a narrative structure." While the former sounds like an artist, the latter does sound more like a computer programmer, translating digital codes back into comprehensible language; atom think orange harry becomes Harry thinks orange atoms. Of course, one *could* choose to do it in a variety of other ways—Orange Harry thinks atoms; Orange thinks Harry an atom; Atom thinks Harry an orange; Think orange, atom Harry!, etc.— and perhaps it is the artist's instinct which selects the best alternative, just as the art of a collage is in the arrangement, balance, and rhythm created by that particular juxtaposition of material. But we can talk about alternatives only when more than one exists, while the author who says he "simply fits what comes out of the cutups back into narrative structure" implies that his arrangements are arbitrary, and that any one is likely to be as good as another. Later in the interview, however, Burroughs modifies his conception of narrative structure until it becomes clear that his choices are many indeed. Asked whether his experiments might conflict with clarity, he replies:

When people speak of clarity in writing they generally mean plot, continuity, beginning, middle, and end, adherence to a "logical" sequence. But things don't happen in logical sequence and people don't think in logical sequence. Any writer who hopes to approximate what actually occurs in the mind and body of his characters cannot confine himself to such an arbitrary structure as logical sequence. Joyce was accused of being unintelligible and he was presenting only one level of cerebral events: conscious subvocal speech. I think it is possible to create multi-level events and characters that a reader could comprehend with his entire organic being. (P. 78)

The artist, then, must find the most effective sequence to break down the control system locking us into limited conceptions of time and space. But while cutups enable the author to penetrate the limited boundaries of the familiar, the new system emerging must be accommodated to the reader, made accessible through the writer's control. In this interview, Burroughs repudiates his previous assertion that he is no more than a recorder who does not pretend to impose story, plot, or continuity onto the materials resulting from cutup: "When I said that [in the Atrophied Preface to *Naked Lunch*] I was perhaps going a bit far," he now admits. "One tries not to impose story, plot, or continuity artificially, but you do have to compose the materials; you can't just dump down a jumble of notes and thoughts and considerations and expect people to read it" (p. 85). Burroughs, therefore, does acknowledge the role of art in turning "non-literary materials" into powerful expressions of the new systems cutups make possible. "Great art," he says, "is a shattering, blinding, liberating experience," but he admits that this experience is not in the experiment itself. "I've done writing that I thought was interesting, experimentally, but simply not readable," he says (p. 89), thus confessing that experiment is the raw material only. It is art, finally, which fashions an experience sufficiently vital to gain access to the reader's nervous system.

The artist's first responsibility is to break down the reader's sense of familiarity with the world which has dulled his responses and perception. The reader must be shocked out of mental and emotional ruts in order to regain the innocence necessary to apprehend new systems. Burroughs is quite similar to Robbe-Grillet in his desire to awaken our senses by divesting the world of the intimacy created by old systems. The ability to see what is in front of us must be the first step toward freedom from the "image-prison" which holds most of us in bondage.

But this is an ability which very few people have, and fewer and fewer as time passes. For one thing, because of the absolute barrage of images to which we are subjected, we become blunted, . . . if you're absolutely bombarded with images from passing trucks and cars and television and newspapers, you become blunted, and this makes a permanent haze in front of your eyes; you can't see anything. (P. 78)

There are certain formulas, word-locks, which will lock up a whole civilization for a thousand years. Another thing is Aristotle's *is* of identity: this *is* a chair. Now, whatever it may be, it's not a chair, it's not the word "chair," it's not the label "chair." The idea that the label is the thing leads to all sorts of verbal arguments; when you're just dealing with labels, you think you're dealing with objects. (P. 86)

While Robbe-Grillet seems most concerned with deflating philosophical systems, Burroughs is more involved with tearing down sociopolitical systems. Yet both share the desire to see the world in new terms, to sharpen our perception of reality by destroying outmoded and inadequate approaches to it.

Burroughs see the primary value of the montage technique as a "message of resistance" to break down "the principal instruments of control which are word and image, and, to some extent, to nullify them" (p. 78). Tape recorder and cinematic techniques are especially useful here because they can make "holes" in reality, which the artist can then enlarge at will. Burroughs cites an interesting example of this:

Take a talking picture of you walking out in the morning to buy cigarettes and the paper. Run it back; you remember everything that happened—there it is on screen and muttering off the sound track. . . . Now, I can make you remember something that didn't happen by splicing it in. A truck passed just then; there it is on the screen, spliced in for you to remember. Always need a peg to hang it on. Well, I plant a truck passed just then, and what's so strange about that? Nothing, except it didn't pass just then; it passed a year ago, and what more logical than said truck hitting a woman on a Paris corner three years later? "I wonder if the old cow died or not," he said dazedly as the medics led him away. You see what I mean? Once you have a truck on set with Larry the Lorry at the wheel, down Canal Street with no brakes, blood and tennis shoes all over the street, a limp foot dangles, or, say I splice in a little daffer asks you for the time it happens, funny I didn't remember till now. Well, once that little man who wasn't there is there on set he might well whip out a stilleto and assassinate the French Consul once the hole in reality is made. . . . (Pp. 78–79)

Like Alice stepping through the looking glass, the reader is asked to push himself through this hole into a different reality, structured on new associative mental and emotional patterns. Depending on how open he is to new experience and how agile he is at moving out of his own frame of reference, the reader can expand his awareness and learn to move about more freely in time and space (p. 79). We may recall that this was exactly Robbe-Grillet's goal—to help the reader invent his own life by exploiting fully the imagination's freedom. That may explain why the above passage is so strikingly reminiscent of Mathias' reinvention of his own past in *The Voyeur*.

Still, even the most willing reader is apt to have a hard time breaking into a new system by means of the old medium. Like Beckett, Burroughs seeks silence but must resort to words as his sole means of reaching the wordless state. And like Robbe-Grillet who, faced with the limitations of words on the printed page, tries to drain them of emotional value in order to achieve cinematic effect, Burroughs also seeks the spontaneity of the cinematic image as an escape from the discursiveness of verbal language. But the novel *is* created with words, communicates itself through words; like all other art forms, it is restricted by the materials which bring it into existence. Burroughs realizes this:

Of course you can do all sorts of things on tape recorders which can't be done anywhere else—effects of simultaneity, echoes, speedups, slowdowns, playing three tracks at once, and so forth. There are all sorts of things you can do on a tape recorder that cannot possibly be indicated on a printed page. The concept of simultaneity cannot be indicated on a printed page except very crudely, through the use of columns, and even so, the reader must follow one column down. We're used to reading from left to right and then back, and this conditioning is not very easy to break down. (P. 40)

One wonders then why Burroughs does not simply give up writing novels and begin making films. If the system itself is outmoded, then why retain the idiom through which it has expressed itself and gained control? Burroughs, however, does think the novel can be expanded to include new experiences resulting from new systems: by applying what he has learned from his experiments in foldin, cutup, and splicing techniques, he expects to revolutionize conventional writing. He appears here as a reformer rather than an anarchist.

Like Robbe-Grillet, Burroughs shows respect for his form in the very act of trying to gnaw away at its traditional assets in order to refashion it to meet the very different and unique demands of contemporary experience. Rather than ignoring the novel as an obsolete form, both writers attempt to rejuvenate and extend it so that it can continue to express a vision of reality—even if that vision is by now totally devoted to chaos, and form totally shattered by it.

Burroughs' novels are so chaotic that life itself seems calm and ordered by comparison. Structure and plot simply do not exist; characters are flat, interchangeable, and strangely unimportant; the narrative thrashes about with no apparent direction or coherence, and words scatter like so many jig-saw-puzzle pieces thrown into the air. Each book is a montage of startling images, fragmented episodes, scraps of dialogue, patches of exposition, and cultural echoes ranging from Renaissance drama to modern poetry, from Christian and Eastern myth to Madison Avenue jargon. The language itself is a pastiche from the media of journalism, film, literature, Holy Scriptures, textbooks. Burroughs seems to have cast the novel out like a net to catch whatever debris it can drag in from the outside world, and the result is a circus of confusion: laughs, thrills, horrors—you name it, it's all there. Images zoom by, explode, writhe, choke, puke themselves up into new combinations. Subtle satire merges with outrageous burlesque; low comedy mixes with the most sordid reality; the worlds of business, science, and entertainment become indistinguishable. Everything gushes together in a dizzying experience that revolts, amuses, shocks, and confuses the disoriented reader. Even familiar images, adjectives, styles, and references cannot be worked with in a conventional manner, since the random juxtaposition which places them in strange contexts somehow distorts their reality into a grotesque reflection of the sort that greets us in fun-house mirrors, nightmares, and drug fantasies. The reader, in short, can never feel comfortable, and his insecurity works for the author, who forces him into a position of openness to new ways of viewing which lead to experiencing new layers of feeling.

Neither Robbe-Grillet nor Genet feels obligated to restrict the novel to a representation of literal reality, yet both do insist that the novel at least contain its own system as a separate entity to replace the real world. Burroughs, however, forces his novels to spill out of any frames—even their own—which might confine them to a single system. Material from one novel is likely to appear intact in another novel—and such material ranges from phrases to whole chapters. Interestingly enough, though, the novels do seem to vary in quality and impact, and this suggests that an examination of Burroughs' four most important novels may help to determine where and why his techniques are most successful. While some of his effects seem to enlarge the novel's capacity to communicate multilevel experience, others seem only to bore and desensitize the reader, thus closing off more possibilities than are opened. By allowing himself maximum freedom, Burroughs opens the doors to chaos so widely that he invites at the same time admiration for artistic courage and condemnation for artistic irresponsibility. The line, I think, is almost always a thin one, and no two readers are likely to take the same position, but nevertheless, judgments should be made if we are to assess his contribution to the novel's future.

> "And what do you conclude from that?"
> "Conclude? Nothing whatever. Just a passing observation."
> —*Naked Lunch*

In one of the zanier conversations from *Naked Lunch*, Dr. Benway tells of his experiments with homosexual and heterosexual patients: he finds that the homosexuals manifested strong undercurrents of heterosexuality while the heterosexuals manifested equally strong undercurrents of homosexuality. The result "makes the brain reel, don't it?"[3] But when the narrator asks what Benway has concluded from these facts, the doctor refuses to conclude anything; he is simply interested in the observation. Benway's ability to withhold judgment would make him the ideal reader for a writer like Burroughs, who says in the last chapter of the book that "*Naked Lunch* is a blueprint, a How-To Book. . . ."

How-To extend levels of experience by opening the door at the end of a long hall. . . . Doors that only open in *Silence.* . . . *Naked Lunch* demands Silence from the Reader. Otherwise he is taking his own pulse. . . . (P. 224)

Such a statement comes as a consolation to the reader who has already read this far without being able to make much sense of the experiences to which the book has subjected him; now he discovers that all the noise of the book was intended primarily to drown out his own rabid thinking and thus to intimidate him into the silence requisite for expanding awareness. Like the Zen master who has his disciple repeat a word or phrase until, divested of all meaning, the sound ushers in a meditative state beyond

---

3. William S. Burroughs, *Naked Lunch* (New York: Grove Press, 1966), p. 36. All future page references, cited in parentheses, are to this edition.

speech, Burroughs may be leading his reader into the same non-verbal area by inundating him with a barrage of grotesque images and incidents which defy systematic interpretation.

The reader, then, is to submit to the chaotic conditions imposed by the novel: "So instead of yelling 'Where Am I?' cool it and look around and you will find out approximately. . . . You were not there for *The Beginning*. You will not be there for *The End*. . . . Your knowledge of what is going on can only be superficial and relative . . ." (p. 220). All of us are thrown into life long after it has started, and leave it before it ends. Therefore, why impose false frames on existence, use the novel to suggest a self-contained experience when life itself always eludes such systems?

You can cut into *Naked Lunch* at any intersection point. . . . I have written many prefaces. They atrophy and amputate spontaneous like the little toe amputates in a West African disease confined to the Negro race and the passing blonde shows her brass ankle as a manicured toe bounces across the club terrace, retrieved and laid at her feet by her Afghan Hound. . . . (P. 224)

And so all structure is discarded: one can pick up the novel and start his reading anywhere, then go forward, backward or jump around at will—it makes no difference where you get on or where you get off. Like the above passage which begins with a rather simple point, then adds an unnecessary but intriguing simile, then builds on the simile until it reaches absurd and hilarious proportions, the book itself offers free license to the imagination. It is not a question of stopping when one has made his point, for there is really no point to be made; the novel is set up to break down any rational approach to it, any logical system which attempts to reduce a multilevel experience directed toward our central nervous systems (one that "a reader could comprehend with his entire organic being") to a one-dimensional experience aimed at the intellect. There is no logical beginning or end to a book drifting in chaos.

The Atrophied Preface which ends *Naked Lunch* is really quite a concession for an author who disdains the reader's desire for security, yet at the same time cannot resist satisfying that need. By orienting the reader to the purposeful absence of orientation within the novel, Burroughs confesses to some extent his own insecurity in the fear that the reader will not understand his purpose in writing the novel as he did:

Why all this waste paper getting The People from one place to another? Perhaps to spare The Reader stress of sudden space shifts and keep him Gentle? And so a ticket is bought, a taxi called, a plane boarded. We are allowed a glimpse into the warm peach-lined cave as She (the airline hostess, of course) leans over us to murmur of chewing gum, dramamine, even nembutal.

I am not American Express. . . . If one of my people is seen in New York walking around in citizen clothes and next sentence Timbuktu putting down lad talk on a gazelle-eyed youth, we may assume that he (the party non-resident of Timbuktu) transported himself there by the usual methods of communication. (P. 218)

Thus Burroughs justifies his frantic movements through time and space. The imagination can take short cuts; it does not have to be coddled and led around on a leash by the novelist. But if we compare Burroughs' tone here to that of Laurence Sterne in similar passages, we can see that Burroughs is in danger of underestimating his reader and indulging himself. There is no humor here, no apparent good will which would prevent the reader's becoming offended. Burroughs' comments are just too serious, grim, reminiscent of the propagandist.

Still, if the tone is somewhat patronizing, Burroughs, by his willingness to furnish explanations making the book more accessible, does show concern for the reader getting lost in the words. Words, he says, must be destroyed, for they are so many labels closing off the real richness of experience: "Gentle Reader, The Word will leap on you with leopard man iron claws, it will cut off fingers and toes like an opportunist land crab, it will hang you and catch your jissom like a scrutable bushmaster . . ." (p. 230). Words lock us into closed systems where we can never contact the reality of a multifaceted world. The solution is to demolish the efficacy of the word by exploding it into powerful, soundless images. And this is what Burroughs has tried to do:

The Word is divided into units which be all in one piece and should be so taken, but the pieces can be had in any order being tied up back and forth, in and out, fore and aft like an innaresting sex arrangement. This book spill off the page in all directions, kaleidoscope of vistas, medley of tunes and street noises, farts and riot yipes and the slamming steel shutters of commerce, screams of pain and pathos and screams plain pathic, copulating cats and outraged squawk of the displaced bull head, prophetic mutterings of brujo in nutmeg trances, snapping necks and screaming mandrakes, sign of orgasm, heroin silent as dawn in the thirsty cells, Radio Cairo screaming like a berserk tobacco auction, and flutes of Ramadan fanning the sick junky like a gentle lush worker in the grey subway dawn feeling with delicate fingers for the green folding crackle. . . .

Gentle reader, we see God through our assholes in the flash bulb of orgasm. . . . Through these orifices transmute your body. . . . The way OUT is the way IN. . . . (P. 229)

This passage is not only a perfect description of the book, but another illustration as well of the way Burroughs builds an idea beyond recognition. Images are piled on top of one another, certain words (such as "scream") jump in repeatedly as if trying to find their right context—and the result is a passage which gathers momentum as it gushes out, drawing in so many diverse images that the individual word gets lost in the impact created by the juxtaposition. The effect is cinematic, as the imagination receives a series of images which the mind does not have time to cope with. Only sense impressions have meaning and validity for Burroughs as the means to push the reader through "these orifices" (here signified by the asshole) where the way out becomes the way in.

Like any prescription for mysticism, however, what provides the source of revelation for one man may remain sheer nonsense to another. Random techniques such as the cutup can sometimes provide astonishing effects, and occasionally even produce a revelation. That in itself, though, is really no more than what poets have been doing for quite some time, or what Genet (whom Burroughs calls a writer in the classical tradition) has attempted by placing an object or image in a "dream" or unfamiliar context, where it takes on fresh, poetic meaning and can often assume symbolic power. By leaving the context to chance, however, Burroughs hopes to surprise himself as well as the reader, for he is seeking to break through traditional modes of perception. From his interviews, we can assume that he has included within the novels themselves only those experiments which he felt to be successful. Thus, a passage such as the following (which I presume to be cutup) should have some impact on the reader:

Give me two cunts and a prick of steel and keep your dirty finger out of my sugar bum what you think I am a purple-assed reception already fugitive from Gibralter? Male and female castrated he them. Who can't distinguish between the sexes? I'll cut your throat you white mother fucker. Come out in the open like my grandchild and meet thy unborn mother in dubious battle. Confusion hath fuck his masterpiece. I have cut the janitor's throat quite by mistake of identity, he being such a horrible fuck like the old man. And in the coal bin all cocks are alike. (P. 40)

I must admit that the phrase "thy unborn mother" becomes quite provocative for me and that there are whole phrases and sentences I can relate together, as well as a basic theme (the Oedipus complex) of the passage which I can identify; but a succession of such dense passages soon becomes dull and unrewarding. Finally, it seems to me that most of the positive effects of Burroughs' techniques (and there are many) are not nearly that radical—not, at least, since the publication of "The Waste Land"—and that these effects would be more consistent if the author were to *take* control rather than surrender it. Of course, that would mean the author's imposition of *his* vision on experience, and Burroughs does want to avoid that. His random techniques do seem to be the most legitimate way to render chaos, but once accident overwhelms and replaces conscious creation, the result is as suggestive but as meaningless as life itself. When art abdicates its control, it also relinquishes its value. Even the daily newspaper can often provide shocking, humorous, or ironic impressions by the accidental juxtaposition in space of two or more different articles, intended to have no relation to each other. Or we may turn the radio band from one station to another, thereby often picking up startling or intriguing juxtapositions in time. Or we may watch the television with the sound turned off, or better yet, place two television sets side by side, each one tuned to different channels—and the two programs will often seem to be commenting on each other as we discover unexpected and interesting relationships between them. This is true, also, of the tape-recorder experiments performed by Brion Gysin and continued by Burroughs. But all these experiments have in my own experience provided interest and amusement only at isolated moments amid long stretches of boredom. Although I think *Naked Lunch* does sustain interest through most of its parts, the obvious danger for Burroughs is the tendency of random techniques to sacrifice cumulative effect for the impact of an instant.

Many of Burroughs' most startling and successful juxtapositions, in fact, are not apparently the result of cutup, but of the author's purposeful use of surprise tactics to throw us off the track of his point just long enough for him to develop another situation which unexpectedly becomes analogous to the one he had seemed to be departing from. This technique is very similar to Sterne's digressive method in *Tristram Shandy* and is what Burroughs may be referring to in his Atrophied Preface when, after recalling the feeling of finding himself in an unfamiliar place and wondering if he has not somehow opened the wrong door, he says: "I decide to play it cool and maybe I will get the orientation before the Owner shows" (p. 220). He explicitly asks for the same patience from the reader, and the reader who plays along is more often than not rewarded. One of the most stunning achievements of this type is Burroughs' handling of the apparently pointless tale of the talking asshole. This is a masterpiece of the "tall story" genre: outrageous and uproarious. Doc Benway tells of a man who worked for a carnival and created a novelty act around his ability to make his asshole talk:

"After a while the ass started talking on its own. He would go in without anything prepared and his ass would ad-lib and toss the gags back at him every time.

"Then it developed sort of teeth-like little raspy incurving hooks and started eating. He thought this was cute at first and built an act around it, but the asshole would eat its way through his pants and start talking on the street, shouting out it wanted equal rights. It would get drunk, too, and have crying jags nobody loved it and it wanted to be kissed same as any other mouth. Finally it talked all the time day and night, you could hear him for blocks screaming at it to shut up, and beating it with his fist, and sticking candles up it, but nothing did any good and the asshole said to him: 'It's you who will shut up in the end. Not me. Because we don't need you around here any more. I can talk and eat *and* shit.' " (Pp. 132–33)

The story does not stop here: Burroughs continues to build upon it, stressing the fact that the one thing the asshole never could do on its own was see—it did not have eyes. This leads Benway into a discussion of sex in America, and the basic rottenness of American life which slips through the censors but manifests itself everywhere, growing into

some degenerate cancerous life-form. . . . Some would be entirely made of penis-like erectile tissue, others viscera barely covered over with skin, clusters of 3 and 4 eyes together, criss-cross of mouth and assholes, human parts shaken around and poured out any way they fell.

"The end result of complete cellular representation is cancer. Democracy is cancerous, and bureaus are its cancer. A bureau takes root anywhere in the state, turns malignant like the Narcotic Bureau, and grows and grows, always reproducing more of its kind, until it chokes the host if not controlled or excised. Bureaus cannot live without a host, being true parasitic organisms. (A cooperative on the other hand *can* live without the state. That is the road to follow. The building up of independent units to meet needs of the people who participate in the functioning of the unit. A bureau operates on opposite principle of *inventing needs* to justify its existence.) Bureaucracy is wrong as a cancer, a turning away from the human evolutionary direction of infinite potentials and differentiation and independent spontaneous action, to the complete parasitism of a virus.

"(It is thought that the virus is a degeneration from more complex life form. It may at one time have been capable of independent life. Now has fallen to the borderline between living and dead matter. It can exhibit living qualities only in a host, by using the life of another—the renunciation of life itself, a falling towards inorganic, inflexible machine, towards dead matter.)

"Bureaus die when the structure of the state collapses. They are as helpless and unfit for independent existence as a displaced tapeworm, or a virus that has killed the host.

"In Timbucktu I once saw an Arab boy who could play a flute with his ass, and the fairies told me he was really an individual in bed. He could play a tune up and down the organ hitting the most erogenously sensitive spots, which are different on everyone, of course. Every lover had his special theme song which was perfect for him and rose to his climax. The boy was a great artist when it came to improving new combines and special climaxes, some of them notes in the unknown, tie-ups of seeming discords that would suddenly break through each other and crash together with a stunning, hot sweet impact." (Pp. 133–35)

The last anecdote is amusing, yet there is absolutely no transition into it; its inclusion is abrupt and seems totally incoherent—a perfect example of the chaotic narrative in this book. The paragraphs preceding it are straightforwardly scientific and might well have come directly from a textbook; they certainly play no part in preparing us for the anecdote of the Arab boy. But if we go back to the beginning and start putting together the various parts, we find that the narrative has worked in exactly the same way Sterne used his to relate the sash incident in *Tristram Shandy*. Now the story of the talking asshole becomes a pointed one, directed toward a political statement of the evils of a democratic system. The talking asshole becomes an allegorical equivalent of bureaucracies that feed off their host, creating their own needs which finally render the host helpless and unhappy. The biological explanation that follows adds a scientific level of meaning, as talking asshole equals bureaucracy equals virus feeding on living tissues. Meanwhile, immersed in parentheses, the author includes a statement on cooperatives which, because they allow independent units to fulfill the needs of their participants, are much the preferable type of government. Now we may go back to the author's previous description of the cancerous tissues created by democracies, and we see that some are "entirely made of penis-like erectile tissue, others viscera barely covered over with skin, clusters of 3 and 4 eyes together, criss-cross of mouth and assholes," and we have picked up two important associations: the image of the talking asshole, and the image of the eyes on a flute. The first relates, as has been said, to a bureaucratic system while the second relates to the anecdote of the Arab boy who played the flute with his ass. This then falls in line with the "penis-like erectile tissue" which becomes the penises of the boy's lovers to whom he is able to provide such pleasure. The boy's greatest virtue lies in his being "really an individual in bed," and his greatness as an artist is due to his ability to suit each penis with its own special song (since "the most erogenuously sensitive spots . . . are different on everyone"), providing "tie-ups of seeming discords" that would result in a magnificent orgasm. And now we suddenly see that the boy's activities are analogous to the "building up of independent units to meet needs of the people" existing in a cooperative state. Whereas the democratic state crushes the individual (host) by insisting that its own needs be satisfied first, the cooperative unit values the individuality of all its participants and fulfills *their* needs.

Burroughs, then, *does* have a vision (in this case, a political one) to impose on his material, even though he has denied it. And the subtlety of his method here can hardly be a result of accidental juxtaposition. On the contrary, his intention of jolting us into political awareness by means of a shocking sexual metaphor is quite similar to Genet's exploitation of the sensationalism of sex to make a political statement more forceful and dramatic (as in his allegorical representation of the relationship between Germany and France during the war, which he depicts as an act of physical love, with France spreading the cheeks of its buttocks to receive the penis of Germany). The analogy works remarkably well, not simply because it is shocking and unexpected but because it all *works out* as a result of Burroughs' careful, conscious handling. What seemed at first a series of incoherent, unrelated, and chaotic passages turns out to be a highly unified sequence, projecting different facets and manifestations of the same idea. In this way, the writer throws his thoughts to us on many levels at once, thereby breaking through the usual one-dimensional response of our intellects. The mental idea is embodied emotionally (through the shock value of sex) so that it will jar us not just in our minds, but deep down in our central nervous system as well. One may of course argue that great art has always done this—and that is true—but to do Burroughs justice, he would probably say that modern life has dulled us emotionally to the point where very few traditional artistic experiences can have much impact. Shock treatments are necessary to awaken us from our numbed existences, and the deeper the shock penetrates, the more of ourselves will spring back to responsive life.

In *Miracle of the Rose*, Genet uses prison life as a powerful metaphor for an existence of pure despair, and Burroughs sees the life of a junky as a suitable metaphor for a political system that dominates and degrades the individual. Again, while sex and sordidness are used to communicate vision, they are not themselves the real subject of either novel. *Naked Lunch* is no more an exposé of the junkies' world than *Miracle of the Rose* is an exposé of criminal or prison life. It is, rather, an exposé of all modern life, but patterned on the junk scene as a recurring image of such devastating emotional impact that the reader will be repulsed by what is ultimately his own "normal" life. Abstractions will not work: we need to be shocked into awareness of what our own lives in this society have become, and Burroughs has found the metaphor to break through our apathy.

Like Genet, Burroughs also uses *his* world (that of the addict) as a metaphor for Hell, the lowest level of human abjection and degradation. The world of the junky is situated in cheap, filthy hotel rooms in the most hideously run-down sections of the city; here he agonizes over the difficulty of making a connection, is tormented with excruciating pain when the narcotic wears off, and finally settles into a stupor when the long-awaited needle finds its way into his vein. The junky's life is painful, unproductive, uneventful; yet even the horror of it is lost on the victim himself, who is oblivious of his surroundings and conscious of nothing but his physical need to ease the pain of his body. As his mind decays and his body rots, the junky becomes so much carrion to be devoured by the buzzards streaming out of the sewers of the contaminated city.

Buzzards swimming out of sewers? Insects, bats, and purple-assed baboons stalking the city streets? Is this the world of the junky or the delirium of dreams? It is of course the latter, for whereas the repellent atmosphere of prison needed only to be realistically presented for Genet to use it symbolically as Hell, Burroughs' detailing of the junk scene is far more grisly than any realistic account could render it. Again, while Genet distorted prison life by reflecting it through his imagination, where it was transcended into something divine and beautiful, Burroughs distorts *his* reality—also through the imagination—into something demonic and loathsome. Genet's world is transformed through Romanticism, while Burroughs' is transformed through surrealism.

Burroughs has said that his fiction is deliberately addressed to the area of dreams, and this is no doubt why surrealistic effects run rampant throughout the book. In almost every case that I can think of, the surrealistic detail adds horror and hideousness to what is already seamy material; as a result, our repugnance is heightened to such an extreme that we either recoil or laugh. In short, we are forced to *react,* and strongly, to release the emotion created by intense shock. Depressing as the addict's connection is, for example, it is rendered almost intolerable when the pusher, probing futilely for a vein, says: "Now I sometimes have to slip my penis under his left eyelid" (p. 67). Or when the Oblique Addict, lacking a connection, is described in terms that sever him from his own bones, which suffer such agony that they assume a separate identity:

Tensions build up, pure energy without emotional content finally tears through the body throwing him about like a man in contact with high tension wires. If his charge connection is cut off cold, the Oblique Addict falls into such violent electric convulsions that his bones shake loose, and he dies with the skeleton straining to climb out of his unendurable flesh and run in a straight line to the nearest cemetery. (P. 68)

It is a stunning image, and one that the reader finds as difficult to shake off as a bad dream. Again, the sordid life of a cheap whore becomes repulsive in a whole new way as she is depicted staggering out "through dust and shit and litter of dead kittens, carrying bales of aborted foetuses, broken condoms, bloody Kotex, shit wrapped in bright color comics" (p. 75). Or consider the ancient rites of sacrifice as

Aztec priests strip blue feather robe from the Naked Youth. They
bend him back over a limestone altar, fit a crystal skull over his head,
securing the two hemispheres back and front with crystal screws. A wa-
terfall pours over the skull snapping the boy's neck. He ejaculate in a
rainbow against the rising sun.

Sharp protein odor of semen fills the air. The guests run hands over
twitching boys, suck their cocks, hang on their backs like vampires.

Naked lifeguards carry in iron-lungs full of paralyzed youths.

Blind boys grope out of huge pies, deteriorated schizophrenics pop
from a rubber cunt, boys with horrible skin diseases rise from a black
pond (sluggish fish nibble yellow turds on the surface). (P. 80)

It is not enough that the cannibalistic aspects of sex are indicated
by the image of vampires, but the helplessness of their victims
becomes unendurably grotesque and odious when they are depicted as paralyzed youths in iron-lungs. While the idea itself is
upsetting, the images make it almost physically nauseating. All
this applies to the Blue Movie sequence, too, where we hardly
expect at first to be so shocked that the scene's eroticism will
nauseate rather than titillate. Yet what stomach can withstand
the description of Mary's love play, after having cut down Johnny
from the noose?

She bites away Johnny's lips and nose and sucks out his eyes with a pop.
. . . She tears off great hunks of cheek. . . . Now she lunches on his prick. . .
. Mark walks over to her and she looks up from Johnny's half-eaten geni-
tals, her face covered with blood, eyes phosphorescent. (P. 97)

If only she were not enjoying it so much! At any rate, the image is
unforgettable because it hits us right in that central nervous system Burroughs is always aiming at, like a well-directed punch in
the stomach. The alert reader of *Naked Lunch* is indeed treated
to a surrealistic feast, but the effect is rather like that of Thyestes'
learning of the contents of his meal. Our gorges rise right along
with our intellects and emotions.

At other times, however, the distasteful description evokes
laughter rather than revulsion, probably because the exaggera-
tion of reality is so incredible that we simply cannot take it seriously enough to feel threatened by it. The talking asshole is a case
in point, but the book abounds with great comic passages based
on the same kind of shock effect that typified the repugnant ones.
The difference between black horror and black humor is difficult
to pin down, but some of the funniest episodes here involve an
uncharacteristically bland acceptance of the most outrageous and

chaotic situations. Thus, a male hustler shows no surprise at an event that astonishes us, but rather, simply loses patience with it:

MALE HUSTLER: "What a boy hasta put up with in this business. Gawd! The propositions I get you wouldn't believe it. . . .

"I am fucking this citizen so I think, 'A straight John at last'; but he comes to a climax and turns himself into some kinda awful crab. . . . I told him, 'Jack, I don't hafta stand still for such a routine like this. . . . You can take that business to Walgreen's.' " (P. 125)

The character's inability to share our surprise at such drastic happenings—but instead to retain his preoccupation with his original point—is similar to Walter Shandy's reaction to his son's death. Whereas the reader here is taken aback by a man's sudden and inexplicable transformation into a crab, the speaker takes it quite as a matter of course, and it does not for a second distract him from the point of his own self-righteousness. The situation is so ludicrous that the reader can only laugh.

Again, Burroughs' depictions of what goes on in a hospital operating room are appalling but overdone to the point of pure farce, so that even the most sickening images become ridiculous enough to provoke laughter:

Dr. Benway washes the suction cup by swishing it around in the toilet bowl. . . .

DR. BENWAY: " . . . Did I ever tell you about the time I performed an appendectomy with a rusty sardine can? And once I was caught short without instrument one and removed a uterine tumor with my teeth."

"Did any of you ever see Dr. Tetrazzini perform? I say perform advisedly because his operations were performances. He would start by throwing a scalpel across the room into the patient and then make his entrance like a ballet dancer. His speed was incredible: 'I don't give them time to die,' he would say. Tumors put him in a frenzy of rage. 'Fucking undisciplined cells!' he would snarl, advancing on the tumor like a knife-fighter."

The anesthetist takes advantage of the confusion to pry a large gold filling from the patient's mouth. . . . (Pp. 60–61)

All this is mad, funny, shocking, and sickening at once; and there is an uncomfortably close relationship between these seemingly incongruous reactions. Although the anesthetist's greed is really too disgusting to be humorous, the almost vaudevillian spirit of the whole scene does mitigate our response somewhat; and except for the odiousness of the specific descriptions, Dr. Benway—as the self-righteous, self-made, pioneer-spirited man—and Dr. Tetrazzini—as the artist–hero foolishly determined to fight off the inevitable ugliness and horror of human life—could well have come straight out of Dickens. Because they are caricatures, they lack the kind of consciousness that makes *us* cringe at the foulness of their activities, yet we are somehow able to laugh at them because no matter how cynical the attitude that produced them, their utter outlandishness is so far beyond our concept of how people react to and in reality that we can afford to find them funny.

Still, we may hate ourselves for laughing, because the events here are completely degrading and inconsistent with any notion we may have of the dignity of human life. But the validity of the satire finally does justify Burroughs' savage treatment of the human species. Like Swift's, his contempt results from idealism, and finds expression in the most debased aspects of life. Beckett, too, examines man as so much *flesh*—diseased, rotting, and stinking—who obeys before anything else, his need to piss, fart, shit, masturbate, and copulate. The ugliest facets of our existences are the most common; what, truly, could be more obscene than cancer, which simply humiliates our bodies before destroying them? Death, disease, blood, shit, urine, and the like lurk on every page of *Naked Lunch* because they are finally what matter most in the process of living and dying. In fact, the images which Burroughs feeds his reader resemble a dinner at the *Chez Robert:*

> Robert's brother Paul emerges from retirement in a local nut house and takes over the restaurant to dispense something he calls the "Transcendental Cuisine." . . . Imperceptibly the quality of the food declines until he is serving literal garbage, the clients being too intimidated by the reputation of *Chez Robert* to protest.

Sample Menu:

The Clear Camel Piss Soup with boiled Earth Worms

—————

The Filet of Sun-Ripened Sting Ray
basted with Eau de Cologne and garnished with nettles

—————

The After-Birth Suprême de Boeuf,
cooked in drained crank case oil,

> served with a piquant sauce of rotten
> egg yolks and crushed bed bugs
>
> ---
>
> The Limburger Cheese sugar cured in diabetic urine
> doused in Canned Heat Flamboyant. . . . (P. 149)

Burroughs is obviously having fun here with any attempt on man's part to presume that his sophistication places him above the animal species. No matter how elaborate the menu, we are always eating garbage really: slabs of flesh from dead bodies, bathed in blood disguised as juice or gravy, usually constitutes the main dish, along with piles of peas or mounds of potatoes, soup, cake, coke, coffee—throw it all down and the stomach churns it, the intestines assimilate it, the bowels convert it, and the next day, there it all is again as feces, unless we throw it up first as vomit. Burroughs will not let us forget that being human is a rather unpleasant business, and truthfully, I doubt that he would be able to shock us as much if we had not forgotten it in the first place.

Because they both see man as a pathetic victim of forces he cannot reason with or understand, Burroughs shares with Beckett a tendency to laugh at the ridiculous odds against man. One can feel only so much fury before it all becomes funny; misery heaped on misery finally becomes so outrageous that it seems comic rather than tragic. The life of Leif the Unlucky, for example, could easily have come from *Watt:*

Leif the Unlucky was a tall, thin Norwegian, with a patch over one eye, his face congealed in a permanent, ingratiating smirk. Behind him lay an epic saga of unsuccessful enterprises. He had failed at raising frogs, chinchilla, Siamese fighting fish, rami and culture pearls. He had attempted, variously and without success, to promote a Love Bird Two-in-a Coffin Cemetery, to corner the condom market during the rubber shortage, to run a mail order whore house, to issue penicillin as a patent medicine. He had followed disastrous betting systems in the casinos of Europe and the race tracks of the U.S. His reverses in business were matched by the incredible mischances of his personal life. His front teeth had been stomped out by bestial American sailors in Brooklyn. Vultures had eaten out an eye when he drank a pint of paregoric and passed out in a Panama City park. He had been trapped between floors in an elevator for five days with an oil-burning junk habit and sustained an attack of D.T.'s while stowing away in a foot locker. Then there was the time he collapsed with strangulated intestines, perforated ulcers and peritonitis in Cairo and the hospital was so crowded they bedded him in the latrine, and the Greek surgeon goofed and sewed up a live monkey in him, and he was gang-fucked by the Arab attendants, and one of the orderlies stole the penicillin substituting Saniflush; and the time he got clap in his ass and a self-righteous English doctor cured him with an enema of hot sulphuric acid, and the German practitioner of Technological Medicine who removed his appendix with a rusty can opener and a pair of tin snips (he considered the germ theory "a nonsense"). Flushed with success he then began snipping and cutting out everything in sight: "The human body is filled up vit unnecessitated parts. You can get by vit one kidney. Vy have two? Yes dot is a kidney. . . . The inside parts should not be so close in together crowded. They need lebensraum like the Vaterland." (Pp. 181–82)

The excessiveness here is similar to pure slapstick, but again the difference is in the accumulation of *loathsome* details, the mixture of humor and horror through which Burroughs mocks man's frail position in a universe that continually abuses him. The shock value of such passages works to jolt the reader out of his familiar "control system" to which he has been dulled and to force him to react violently, thereby extending his awareness and (because his emotions are also involved) his experience.

And what *does* the reader experience through *Naked Lunch?* Above all, a dizzying trip through time and space in the form of random images and episodes which explode all around him, juxtaposing in new combinations aspects of his life and society that he must see as intolerable. In the guise of a gigantic carnival, modern civilization is out on display, and Burroughs takes us on all the rides: the spiritual dimension of modern life is so much hocus-pocus; political systems are all parasitic, inefficient, and inhumane; social and personal relationships are sadistic, manipulative, and exploitive. In each case, Burroughs uses metaphor, analogy, and allegory to attack a decadent system. Religion, for example, is quickly reduced to carny-quackery:

"Christ?" sneers the vicious, fruity old Saint applying pancake from an alabaster bowl. . . . "That cheap ham! You think I'd demean myself to commit a miracle? . . . That one should have stood in carny. . . .

" 'Step right up, Marquesses and Marks, and bring the little Marks too. Good for young and old, man and beast. . . . The one and only legit *Son of Man* will cure a young boy's clap with one hand—by contact alone, folks—create marijuana with the other, whilst walking on water and squirting wine out his ass. . . . Now keep your distance, folks, you is subject to be irradiated by the sheer charge of this character.'

"And I knew him when, dearie. . . . I recall we was doing an Impersonation Act—very high class too—in Sodom, and that is one cheap town. . .

Strictly from hunger. . . . Well, this citizen, this Fucking Philistine

wandered in from Podunk Baal or some place, called me a fuckin fruit right on the floor. And I said to him: 'Three thousand years in show business and I always keep my nose clean. Besides I don't hafta take any shit off any uncircumcised cocksucker.' . . .
    "*Buddha?* A notorious metabolic junky. . . . Makes his own you dig. . . .

    "And all them junkies sitting around in the lotus posture spitting on the ground and waiting for The Man.
    "So Buddha says: "I don't hafta take this sound. I'll by God metabolize my own junk.'
    " 'Man, you can't do that. The Revenooers will swarm all over you!'
    " 'Over me they won't swarm. I gotta gimmick, see? I'm a fuckin Holy Man as of right now.'
    " 'Jeez, boss, what an angle.'

    " 'Clear the cave for action. I'm gonna metabolize a speed ball and make with the Fire Sermon.'
    "*Mohammed?* Are you kidding? He was dreamed up by the Mecca Chamber of Commerce. An Egyptian ad man on the skids from the sauce write the continuity.

    "Leave what Confucius say stand with Little Audrey and the shaggy dogs. . . ." (Pp. 113–15)

In this conglomeration of language and images from the worlds of Damon Runyon, the Bible, Madison Avenue, show business, and carnivals, we can see Burroughs' determination to inject nonliterary material into literature. Since each world works as an independent control system, using language to form images which manipulate the thinking of the people, a fiction that confines itself to its own tradition is necessarily parochial and old-fashioned. Modern man lives in a multimedia world, assaulted on all sides, through all senses, by all interests until he has become so numbed that he is little more than a mechanism responding obediently to the Pavlovian experimenters working to exploit him.
    The junky becomes the supreme metaphor for a society utterly deadened—intellectually, psychologically, politically, and sensorily—to the forces working to undermine it; and Burroughs makes it clear that *all* systems disposed to control word and image associations in our minds finally control our emotions too, and are therefore detrimental to living organisms:

You see control can never be a means to any practical end. . . . It can never be a means to anything but more control. . . . Like junk . . . (P. 164)

Artist will confuse sending with creation. They will camp around screeching "A new medium" until their rating drops off. . . . Philosophers will bat around the ends and means hassle not knowing *that sending can never be a means to anything but more sending, Like Junk.* Try using junk as a means to something else. . . .

The sender is not a human individual. . . . It is The Human Virus. (All viruses are deteriorated cells leading a parasitic existence. . . . They have specific affinity for the Mother Cell; thus deteriorated liver cells seek the home place of hepatitis, etc. So every species has a Master Virus: Deteriorated Image of that species.) (P. 168)

The artist himself, then, must give up his role as "sender" of image control systems; his is no worthier than the others since it helps only to block the receiver's awareness. The artist of the cutup, on the other hand, purposely surrenders his own control system to the accident of arbitrary juxtapositions which arrange materials independently of his own mind (thus achieving willfully the amnesiac state Burroughs refers to when he says in his Introduction: "I have no precise memory of writing the notes which have now been published under the title *Naked Lunch*," p. xxxvii.) Finally freed from his own associative limitations, the artist of the random method frees the reader too, thereby promoting new perspectives, new insights, and new sensory experiences.

To an extent, *Naked Lunch* certainly succeeds in breaking down traditional associative patterns, yet the ironic (though perhaps predictable) result is that we eventually adapt to the new pattern and are just as restricted to it as we were to all the others. After all the farts have faded, after the scatology has lost its shock value, after the sexual perversions have lost their punch, etc., we ultimately settle down to a vicious but hardly unprecedented satire of American life. Politically, the country has gone to the (for dogs, substitute) baboons:

There is a Senate and a Congress who carry on endless sessions discussing garbage disposal and outhouse inspection, the only two questions over which they have jurisdiction. For a brief period in the mid-nineteenth century, they had been allowed to control the dept. of Baboon Maintenance but this privilege had been withdrawn owing to absenteeism in the Senate.

The post of President is always forced on some particularly noxious and unpopular citizen. To be elected President is the greatest misfortune and disgrace. . . . (P. 183)

That the political system represented here is that of a mythical island does not, of course, disorient us in the slightest. Burroughs is following in the convention of such satirists as Swift, who have simply moved their country to foreign shores in order to attack it. The writer who can unreel such a line as "The Old Court House is located in the town of Pigeon Hole outside the urban zone" (p. 170) shows an obvious penchant for allegory, but Burroughs is enormously successful too at a satire based on realistic speech and settings. His devastating attack on the South, for example, is the result of a deadly accurate eye and ear:

" 'You know that yaller girl used to work in Marylou's Hair Straightening and Skin Bleach Parlor over in Nigga town.'
" 'Getting that dark chicken meat, Arch? Gettin' that coon pone?'
" 'Gettin' it steady, Doc. Gettin' it steady. Well, feller say duty is goosing me. Gotta get·back to the old crank case.'
" 'I'll bet she needs a grease job worst way.'
" 'Doc, she sure is a dry hole. . . .' " (P. 174)

"They burned that ol' nigger over in Cunt Lick. Nigger had the aftosa and it left him stone blind. . . . So this white girl down from Texarkana screeches out:
" 'Roy, that ol' nigger is looking at me so nasty. Land's sake I feel just dirty all over.'
" 'Now, Sweet Thing, don't you fret yourself. Me an' the boys will burn him.'
" 'Do it slow, Honey Face. Do it slow. He's give me a sick headache.'
"So they burned the nigger and that ol' boy took his wife and went back up to Texarkana without paying for the gasoline and old Whispering Lou runs the service station couldn't talk about nothing else all Fall: "These city fellers come down here and burn a nigger and don't even settle up for the gasoline.' " (Pp. 175–76)

Certainly such material is not accidental, nor does its creator seem to be a revolutionary novelist—Faulkner's novels are filled with similar passages of broad satire. Ironically, the most brilliant effects in *Naked Lunch* are not usually those that smash our traditional word-image associations, but those that communicate *through* them.

Still, no matter how many conventional techniques it contains, *Naked Lunch* is unique in its encompassing so many diverse effects in a single work. Time and space are opened up in a way that enables the novel to breathe more freely; lurching through chaos, the novel no longer stops to organize what it sees into a consistent, unified vision but is instead content to consider the diversity of experience and pour it through the reader's senses with a barrage of images so striking that they stick in his mind and filter down through his nervous system. As Camus has said, art multiplies what it cannot unify—and all we have ever asked of the novel is that it bring us into touch with the world so that our minds and emotions can work with it.

In A. J.'s blue movie, Mark has been fucking Johnny, and as he reaches orgasm, Johnny's body quivers while the liquid enters him:

A train roar through him whistle blowing . . . boat whistle, foghorn, sky rocket burst over oily lagoons . . . penny arcade open into a maze of dirty pictures . . . ceremonial cannon boom in the harbor . . . a scream shoots down a white hospital corridor . . . out along a wide dusty street between palm trees, whistles out across the desert like a bullet (vulture wings husk in the dry air), a thousand boys come at once in outhouses, bleak public school toilets, attics, basements, treehouses, Ferris wheels, deserted houses, limestone caves, rowboats, garages, barns, rubbly windy city outskirts behind mud walls (smell of dried excrement) . . . black dust blowing over lean copper bodies . . . ragged pants dropped to cracked bleeding bare feet. . . . (place where vultures fight over fish heads) . . . by jungle lagoons, vicious fish snap at white sperm floating on black water, sand flies bite the copper ass, howler monkeys like wind in the trees (a land of great brown rivers where whole trees float, bright colored snakes in the branches, pensive lemurs watch the shore with sad eyes), a red plane traces arabesques in blue substance of sky, a rattlesnake strike, a cobra rear, spread, spit white venom pearl and opal chips fall in a slow silent rain through air clear as glycerine. Time jump like a broken typewriter, the boys are old men, young hips quivering and twitching in boy-spasms go slack and flabby, draped over an outhouse seat, a park bench, a stone wall in Spanish sunlight, a sagging furnished room bed (outside red brick slum in clear winter sunlight). . . . (Pp. 93–94)

The passage goes on and on for several more pages before returning to Mark and Johnny, and by the time we return to the two boys, we have been tossed around in time and space with such velocity that we are left too breathless and exhausted to reconstruct the journey in any coherent way. Yet the experience has been lived, the scenes have been taken in, and our vision has been extended by the adventure. Burroughs pushes the reader through a cyclone of images and events, and as reality and dream become indistinguishable, as the novel embodies elements of other media, and as language begins to transmit new associative signals, we feel the literary form expanding to the dimensions of life itself. If the experience is inconclusive, if the novel seems inseparable from the chaos caught within it, then we might console ourselves with the thought that art has always sought new directions from which to approach reality, and perhaps it was inevitable that it would eventually try them all at once.

> But I guess I'm talking too much about private things
> —*The Soft Machine*

> In the beginning was the word and the word was bullshit
> —*The Ticket That Exploded*

> Now   fast—Now slow—slower—Stop—Shut off
> —No more—My writing arm is paralyzed—
> —*Nova Express*

Burroughs' increasing disrespect for his reader, his form, and the language which creates and communicates becomes more apparent with each novel, and the novels themselves become duller, more private, more indulgent, and less impressive. What seemed shocking in *Naked Lunch* becomes repetitious in *The Soft Machine,* and alternately annoying and uninteresting in *Nova Express* and *The Ticket That Exploded.* What was innovative and exciting in *Naked Lunch* becomes stale and tiresome in the succeeding novels. And finally, while the creator of *Naked Lunch* seems original and challenging in his refusal to orient the reader to his chaotic work, the creator of the other novels seem simply self-indulgent and irresponsible. As his earlier preoccupations settle into propaganda, his experiments into formulas, and his intensity into petulance, Burroughs has less and less to offer both the reader and the novel. As his theories become more explicit, they become less powerful; as his methods become more obvious, they become less effective; and as his books become more chaotic, they become, also, more parochial.

What has gone wrong here? For one thing, Burroughs has used up his reader's patience by repeating concepts, effects, and even whole sections that he had already delivered in *Naked Lunch.* For another, he has estranged himself from the reader by permitting his novels to be overridden by the theories behind them; he has fallen into the very trap against which he cautioned us—that of sending the message rather than creating the experience. Finally, as an artist of chaos, he has surrendered so much of his control over his material that the reader, faced with real rather than apparent chaos, simply cannot function, and so has no alternative but to shrug off the whole confrontation as an unnecessary and unproductive experience. This is not to say that Burroughs' later books are devoid of many stunning effects, but only that they seem to me increasingly isolated. Certainly, none of these novels has the richness or power of *Naked Lunch*, and none impresses as a whole.

The Soft Machine, like *Naked Lunch*, contains a good many startling images, but here they are quite obviously the result of cutup methods. By using a limited number of control words and phrases, and juxtaposing them arbitrarily until a variety of combinations has been accumulated, Burroughs puts into the novel itself those techniques which he had implied in interviews were primarily for his own revelation, and preceded the actual act of creation. Now he is either unwilling or unable to select from all the alternatives the one he considers most interesting and valuable; instead, he throws them all in:

I draped myself over his body laughing. His shorts dissolved in rectal mucus and carbolic soap. Summer dawn smells from a vacant lot.[4]

Made it five times under the shower that day soapy bubbles of egg flesh seismic tremors split by fissure spurts of Jissom. . . . (P. 10)

I drape myself over him from the pool hall. Draped myself over his cafeteria and his shorts dissolved in strata of subways . . . and all house flesh. . . . (P. 11)

in that grey smell of rectal mucus. . . . night cafeterias and junky room dawn smells. Three hours from Lexington made it five times. . . . soapy egg flesh. . . . (P. 12)

Freight boat smell of rectal mucus went down off England with all dawn smell of distant fingers. . . . About this time I went to your Consul. He gave me a Mexican after his death. . . . Five times of dust we made it . . . with soap bubbles of withdrawal. . . .

Looking at dirty pictures casual as a ceiling fan short-timing the dawn we made it in the corn smell of rectal mucus and carbolic soap. . . . (P. 14)

4. William Burroughs, *The Soft Machine* (New York: Grove Press, 1967), p. 10. All future page references, cited in parentheses, are to this edition.

There are some nice effects here, but one tires quickly of the game as the senses become blurred and the mind numbed. Still, even these passages seem preferable to others in which syntax, along with coherence, breaks down completely. What remains is so much gibberish, no matter how noble Burroughs' intentions:

I was the blood jumped out his mouth, nose receding flesh to finish. Across the room huddled by clothes shivering grey flannel suits under terminal drugstore. So I am a public agent and the whole through a light pink instruction from street. I winked at the commuters. "Conversation I snap out of queers," I sniffed warningly, "It's a spot up on my back cases." Queers supporting the floor like the three monkeys. "Grope movies and Turkish our own," I said warmly and walked exempt narcotic. Cool boys chase each other with the first one of the day. To a Turkish Bath and surprised you bloody nance. Soapy towel glove hit him in the lungs and eyes spattered: Ping! And walked into the gaberdine topcoats. Five minutes to that broken fruit. (P. 33)

"Much you using young fellow?"
"I can smell them fucking all the junk bottles and scripts." In any case bloody grass. . . . See a young man snafu his and strangled him like rot do something for you in the blood. Jumped cure and stay off to finish. Grey flannel suit under all public agents of the bus from street. Grope movie and walked in on the wrong room warmly. Exempt light and lungs. And eyes spattered night clerk and threw a piece of coats. . . . I hate sloughed him with the iron room life script. Maybe I can cantelope. Them I had to check you. Promise me to take out his mouth, nose receding flesh. (P. 34)

His face got an erection and turned purple. . . .

His eyes got an erection and turned the effluvia and became addicts of vacant lot. (P. 35)

Isn't this fun? Burroughs has given us a do-it-yourself novel: here are the pieces; you put it together. The artist of the cutup has become a cutup artist. First cut up, then fold in, splice together, and just follow the simple directions. . . .

Such prose does indeed break through traditional word-image associations, but where does it get us? Maybe I can cantaloupe; maybe not. The sentence is amusing, but hardly extends our awareness. If a face can get an erection, then certainly eyes can too, but is it worth our time to consider such possibilities?

You will die there a screwdriver through the head. The thought like looking at me over steak and explain it all like that stay right there. She was also a Reichian analyst. Disappear more or less remain in acceptable form to you the face. (P. 74)

What *is* a reader to do with such a jig-saw-puzzle passage? If we attempt ingeniously to read coherence into it, we are simply resorting to traditional control systems, which is just the habit Burroughs wants to break us of. So finally, we give up all attempts to *read* the novel and simply gaze at the words. For a writer who has promised to expand our awareness, Burroughs seems much more successful at turning us into retarded readers, staring dumbly at blocks of print while—except for a few striking combinations which amuse, evoke, or disgust—nothing at all is happening in our minds or emotions. The reader is put into a trance.

One wants to be fair to Burroughs, and certainly the reader who works hard may find some scattered rewards which he feels justifies the chaos. But if the author is intent on keeping his own mind out of the goings-on here, then *we* might as well make up our *own* list of images and play with *them*. It might be interesting and valuable to discover just what combinations we draw up for ourselves; our own free-association games might well provide some revelations for us. But someone else's choices can have little meaning—unless, of course, they are the conscious choices of an artist whose superior imagination can take us farther into the experience of language and living than we could manage to get by ourselves. By abdicating his role of leader, Burroughs may be asserting humility or arrogance; it is hard to tell which. At any rate, the result is not a novel, but the raw materials for one that the reader may put together for himself. This means, of course, that the novel must be a personal and different experience for every reader, a fact which renders critical evaluation meaningless. Whereas the novel traditionally has tried to universalize experience, Burroughs seems intent on personalizing it. That is, in fact, his message for the reader: resist all control systems and storm the reality studio where your life is being programmed by the parasitic exploiters (in this case, the media) who, by sending images through the soft machine inside your head, are controlling your mental associative patterns, and ultimately your body, your soul, your life.

We cannot really identify the narrator of *The Soft Machine*, but although he takes different forms, he does seem to be a resistance leader. He himself storms the reality studio by taking a job in the Trak News Agency ("We don't report the news—We write it"). While the supervisor sees him as executive timber, the narrator recognizes the company's political intentions: "I sus [sic] it is the Mayan Caper with an IBM machine . . ." (p. 152). (The Mayan caper obviously refers to one of Burroughs' obsessions: the Mayan calendar which enabled the priests of that civilization—who formed two per cent of the population—to control an entire society through manipulation of symbols and ritual.) The narrator takes revenge on his employers by sabotaging their system:

We fold writers of all time in together and record radio programs, movie sound tracks, TV and juke box songs all the words of the world stirring around in a cement mixer and pour in the resistance message "Calling partisans of all nation—Cut word lines—Shift linguals—Free doorways— Vibrate 'tourists'—Word falling—Photo falling—Break through in Grey Room." (P. 153)

Uranian Willy ("the Heavy Metal Kid, also known as Willy the Rat") seems to have the same plan:

"This is war to extermination—Fight cell by cell through bodies and mind screens of the earth—Souls rotten from the Orgasm Drug—Flesh shuddering from the Ovens—Prisoners of the earth, come out—Storm the studio."

His plan called for total exposure—Wise up all the marks everywhere Show them the rigged wheel—Storm the Reality Studio and retake the universe. . . . (P. 155)

The proliferation of short phrases patched together with dashes makes both passages sound as if they came directly out of comic books. The novel itself has the atmosphere of science fiction, but the lack of characterization, structure, and subtlety makes it read less like a novel than a script for a Superman serial.

But of course *The Soft Machine* does more than simply trace the fight of the good-guy liberators against the evil oppressors of mankind; rather, it demonstrates a system—that of language and image in literature—being broken down before our very glazed eyes:

Spectators scream through the track—The electronic brain shivers in blue and pink and chlorophyll orgasms spitting out money printed on rolls of toilet paper, condoms full of ice cream, Kotex hamburgers— . . . grey luminous flakes falling softly on Ewyork, Onolulu, Aris, Ome, Oston— . . . (P. 164)

The image of Kotex hamburgers certainly breaks down traditional associative patterns, and chlorophyll orgasms definitely adds something new to sex, yet neither has the striking impact of a typical image from Genet; the shock alone is not enough to produce new ways of conceiving familiar objects. And what is the reasoning behind leaving off the first letters of such famous cities as New York, Honolulu, Paris, Rome, and Boston? Has the foldin method simply cut off the first letters? While Burroughs' random techniques seem quite legitimate as a means for the novelist to make new connections, their appearance in the novel itself can be justified only so far as the reader can be expected to share in the revelation. Men have never lacked the means to blow up existing institutions; few things are as easy as finding explosive devices. But rubble and debris are no compensation for an outmoded system; the artist must accept the responsibility of rebuilding new structures to provide new insights. Destruction is always exciting—and *The Soft Machine* does generate some startling effects—but creation is infinitely more valuable. Burroughs has succeeded in his mission to storm the reality studio, but he has failed to make that mission seem worthwhile.

The Ticket That Exploded, is another thesis novel (with the same thesis) which includes its own book of exercises for the reader to help himself break out of the control system which lives his life for him. Although Burroughs called *Naked Lunch* a "How To . . ." book, the description seems more appropriate for *The Ticket That Exploded*, which in its make up and intentions resembles other nonfiction books of this type: How to Attain Satori in Twenty-Seven Easy Steps (With Illustrations); How to Stay Trim and Fit; How to Impress Your Peers, etc. Again, Burroughs' motives seem noble, while the novel itself seems unenlightening and tedious. Again he promises to promote awareness while the novel itself only dulls it. A new raid on the reality studio has yielded approximately the same results: the theory remains more exciting than the work it has engendered.

Like Beckett, Burroughs sees salvation in silence: words have smothered our lives, and must be eliminated from the system before health becomes possible.

The "Other Half" is the word. The "Other Half" is an organism. Word is an organism. The presence of the "Other Half" a separate organism attached to your nervous system on an air line of words can now be demonstrated experimentally. . . the symbiotic basis. From symbiosis to parasitism is a short step. The word is now a virus. . . . The word may once have been a healthy neural cell. It is now a parasitic organism that invades and damages the central nervous system. Modern man has lost the option of silence. Try halting your sub-vocal speech. Try to achieve even ten seconds of inner silence. You will encounter a resisting organism that *forces you to talk*.[5]

The point is a good one: one continues to talk even when there is no longer anything to say (which is the chief problem of most of Beckett's characters). The word has lost its import, its impact having been blunted by all the media relentlessly abusing language for purposes of politics, profit, deception, etc. Since, furthermore, language is our tool for thought, which enables us to conceptualize, both our thinking and perception have lost their sharpness. As a result, reality has receded from us, and we have lost touch with our own lives. Robbe-Grillet has, of course, said the same thing, and he, too, has founded a new artistic theory on his assumption; but whereas Robbe-Grillet's concerns seems primarily aesthetic, Burroughs' are obviously psychological, social, and political. For example:

Anyone who keeps his bloody eyes open doesn't need a Harly St. psychiatrist to tell him that destructive elements enter into so-called normal sex relations: the desire to dominate, to kill, to take over and eat the partner . . . these impulses are normally held in check by counter-impulses . . . what the virus puts out of action is the *regulatory centers in the nervous system*. . . . (P. 20)

The reality of our sexual feelings has receded beneath the familiar associations with love, which blot out the true complexity of a significant part of our lives and psyches. This is why we are shocked and appalled by the graphic, sadistic sex scenes in Burroughs' novels: we can no longer recognize or identify with the instincts that words have kept buried inside us.

The realization that something as familiar to you as the movement of your intestines the sound of your breathing the beating of your heart is also alien and hostile does make one feel a bit insecure at first. Remember that you can separate yourself from the "Other Half" from the word. The word is spliced in with the sound of your intestines and breathing with the beating of your heart. The first step is to record the sounds of your body and start splicing them in yourself. Splice in your body sounds

5. William S. Burroughs, *The Ticket That Exploded* (New York: Grove Press, 1968), p. 49. All future page references, cited in parentheses, are to this edition.

with the body sounds of your best friend and see how familiar he gets. Splice your body sounds in with air hammers. Blast jolt vibrate the "Other Half" right out into the street. Splice your body sounds in with anybody or anything. . . . *Communication must become total and conscious before we can stop it.* (Pp. 50–51)

Burroughs here offers us a way out of words that seems more practical than the attempts of Beckett and Robbe-Grillet, yet less successful artistically. Burroughs himself may be similar to the District Supervisor he mentions who "was contemplating the risky expedient of a 'miracle' and the miracle he contemplated was *silence*. Few things are worse than a 'miracle' that doesn't come off" (p. 51). The reason for his failure is clear: all the passages I've quoted from the book are didactic, direct addresses to the reader—hardly fictional embodiments of Burroughs' ideas just because they appear in a "fictional" work. The author now seems to have turned into a hard-core, hard-sell huckster, always hawking the same idea and trying to hammer it into our heads by sheer force rather than by the subtleties of artistic propaganda, which can at least make its appeal on a deep level. As author, Burroughs is failing more and more to present his readers with a valid artistic experience. As pauses for ideological messages (even ones professing anti-ideological sentiments) become increasingly frequent, the show itself seems thinner and weaker for the intrusions. Eventually, we may well feel inclined to turn off *all* the voices as so many irritants, so much distraction. Silence *is* a miracle, perhaps, but you can't sell it—you must *produce* it!

Still, if Burroughs fails to pull the reader beneath words to a deeper, more conscious level of awareness (and this, of course, is a matter of opinion), he does prescribe some remarkably ingenious exercises to help get us there on our own. Sex, for example, can be experienced silently by keeping ourselves moving so fast that we cannot possibly have time to *think* about what we are doing:

The point of these exercises is to maintain a state of total alertness during sexual excitement—Try simple exercises first like jacking off while balancing a chair—Driving full-speed on dangerous road—Flying plane—Performing precision operations at the same time like target shooting—So you can maintain alertness in the sex act and not be taken by the sex agents of the enemy who move to soften you up with sentimentality and sexual frustration to buy ersatz goo of their copy planet— (Pp. 75–76)

Other examples follow, but the point has been made. Is Burroughs serious? Probably not—and yet why not? His examples are extreme and amusing, but the basic idea behind them is valid and important: a desensitized society must be reawakened to life; cells must once again become *living* tissue, and man's acts of love must become acts of intense, spontaneous feeling rather than word-induced gestures, image-controlled responses, etc. When communication finally becomes total and conscious, then words will no longer be necessary and can drop off into extinction.

"What is word?"—Why do you talk to yourself all the time?—Are you talking to yourself?—Isn't there someone or something else there when you talk? Put your sex images on a film screen talking to you while you jack-off—Just about the same as the so-called "real thing" isn't it?—Why hasn't it been tried? And what is word and to whom is it addressed?— Word evokes image does it not?—Try it—Put an image track on screen and accompany it with any sound track—Now play the sound track back alone and watch the image track fill in—So? What is word?—Maya— Maya—Illusion—Rub out the word and the image track goes with it— Can you have the image without color?—Ask yourself these questions and take the necessary steps to find the answer: "What is sex? What is word? What is color?"—Color is trapped in word—Image is trapped in word—Do you need words?—Try some other method of communication, like color flashes—a Morse code of color flashes—or odors or music or tactile sensations—Anything can represent words and letters and association blocks—Go and try it and see what happens—science pure science—And what is love?—Who do you love?—If I had a talking picture of you would I need you? Try it— (P. 145)

The implication here is that words have become substitutes for real experience; we no longer know how to touch things directly and so would probably be unable to feel the difference between the presence of someone we love, and a talking image of that person. We need to recapture a state of innocent silence before and beyond words: "Now learn to sit back and *watch*—fifty a hundred thousand years if necessary until you know all the rules and combos penalties and angles—When you can see all the cards then move in and take it all—Learn to *watch* and you *will* see all the cards—" (p. 159). And of course Burroughs has written his book in such a way that the reader can do nothing but remain passive, *watching* without thinking as the images rush by him. We are induced into a state of innocence where words can no longer be depended upon to provide us with a sense of knowledge.

Politically, words have had their most devastating impact as men and nations use language to oppose one another, which "manipulated on a global scale feeds back nuclear warfare . . ." (p. 55). But the problem is not to be confused with semantics; it goes much deeper than that. Words have taken control of our lives to the extent that we have allowed them to do our living for us. The result is a generation of zombies, dulled even to the fact that their own deaths have already taken place:

When your image is dead you become virus and must obey virus orders. . . . Life without flesh *is* the ovens. Only way we can get out of Hell is through our image in the living. Remember the ovens? It is not only the heat. Remember the lack of "emotion's oxygen" the lack of what you breathe, the lack of everything that would ever make you want to live or breathe? Well like you say any image repeated loses charge and that loss is the lack that makes this Hell and keeps us *here*. Where we are *is* Hell. . . .

And like all viruses the past prerecords your "future." Remember the picture of hepatitis is prerecorded two weeks before the opening scene when virus negatives have developed in the mirror and you notice your eyes are a little yellower than usual—So the image past molds your future imposing repetition as the past accumulates and all actions are prerecorded and doped out and there is no life left in the present sucked dry by a walking corpse muttering through empty courtyards under film skies of Marrakesh. (Pp. 188–89)

Words, then, have become for Burroughs the chief villains of our lives, feeding off our cells like tapeworms until all substance has been eaten away and we are left as empty as ghosts. The struggle against control systems, which seemed little more than a science-fiction plot in *The Soft Machine*, here becomes *the* significant theme for the modern writer. Burroughs has now justified his chaos as a vital liberating force by which the novelist can lead humanity out of its Hell and into the world of the living. His experiments thus become crucial channels through which the reader can escape an existence that belongs in the grave.

Where to begin? Again, the reality studio must be stormed:

I mean what kind of show is it after everything has been sucked out? You want to sit for all eternity watching the yellow movie of hepatitis and the blue movie of junk? We know every line and they never change. They will change less and less. Let there be light in the darkrooms. Only solution is total exposure. (P. 193)

When Burroughs says, "Let there be light," he means to signify a new creation of the universe—one that will generate new life.

Oddly enough, the old system can be erased only by the same means—repetition—by which we became conditioned to it.

You know about the Logos group? . . . claim to have reduced human behavior to a predictable science controlled by the appropriate word combos. They have a system of therapy they call "clearing." You "run" traumatic material which they call "engrams" until it loses emotional connotation through repetition and is then refiled as neutral memory. When all the "engrams" have been run and deactivated the subject becomes a "clear" . . . It would seem that a technique a tool is good or bad according to who uses it and for what purposes. (Pp. 20–21)

In the *Evergreen Review* interview, Burroughs spends a good deal of time discussing the E Meter, a machine designed and patented by L. Ron Hubbard, the founder of Scientology, for the express purpose of eliminating traumatic tension from the patient's central nervous system. The E meter achieves this by running the trauma-inducing image over and over until it fails to make any impact on the mind. It seems ironic that Burroughs, who blames science and machines for much of the word distortion and image manipulation that has deadened our life instincts, can put his faith for recovery in yet another machine and another science that works to control men's minds. But his ability to do so is quite admirable, I think; he is not scared off by hackneyed *Brave New World* images of a society controlled by machines (and think of how we have all been conditioned to respond to *that* image!), but retains the objectivity to see that science can be used to help the man it has desensitized and that machines can work for our benefit as well as for our destruction. The difference, after all, is enormous between the man who manipulates the machine, and the man who is manipulated *by* the machine. So just as words can dull us to life, the purposeful repetition of them can dull us to *them* until we no longer respond automatically and mechanically to the signals they generate. At this point their power fails, and we are freed from their tyranny—freed to experience life directly again. This would be the principle behind Burroughs' constant repetition of a set of control words in different contexts. The result is to render them meaningless—an effect which the reader automatically rebels against, unaware that the author is doing this purposely for his own good.

I stopped at a newsstand on Shaftesbury Avenue and bought a copy of *Encounter* contemplating under Eros the feat of prose abstracted to a point where no image track occurs.

(The concomitance or rather juxtaposition with this relentlessly successful though diagrammatic schemata by sexualizing syntactically delinquent analogous metaphor.) (P. 27)

What reads like gibberish is, then, really a prose abstracted to release the reader from the standard image track which has caused him to substitute words for life. When language loses its connotative value and is reduced to mere sound, the reader is liberated from the virus choking him out of existence. The "sexualized" metaphor is language energized into physical experience, and the reader who resists this effort to save him (by reacting only with shock to Burroughs' style) proves only how far his disease has advanced.

Language, then, must be used systematically to destroy itself. Beckett's characters have, of course, already tried this and failed. But Burroughs is far more hopeful than any of Beckett's characters because he has discovered a way of freeing both himself and the reader from the stale image track by which words rejuvenate rather than self-destruct. Cutup and foldin methods are good for the beginner, but once past these, he is now ready for the more sophisticated devices that modern technology has made possible. The tape recorder may yet be our savior if we will only stop talking to ourselves and begin talking to *it:*

Get it out of your head and into the machines. Stop talking stop arguing. Let the machines talk and argue. A tape recorder is an externalized section of the human nervous system. You can find out more about the nervous system and gain more control over your reaction by using a tape recorder than you could find out sitting twenty years in the lotus posture. (P.163)

Once the recorder has received your words, you are ready to begin in earnest. Simply splice in the words of others. How many others? As many as you can get hold of: "Splice yourself in with newscasters, prime ministers, presidents. Why stop there? Why stop anywhere? Everybody splice himself in with everybody else. Communication must be made total, only way to stop it" (p. 166). We can now see the new artistic theory underlying Burroughs' novels, and if the experimentation produces a radically new experience, then we must be willing to adjust to a new concept: the novel now becomes the equivalent of a tape recorder in which the author has spliced together words from a large number of arbitrary sources. If we find it almost impossible to identify the narrator of *The Ticket That Exploded*, for example, that may well be because there is no narrator but only a collection of various voices constantly merging with one another until the babble becomes indistinct and finally resembles silence itself.

As if to illustrate this concept of multispeakers, Burroughs concludes this novel with a closing message by Brion Gysin, whom he always credits with having introduced him to cutup and tape-recorder techniques. Gysin's chapter is really a repetition of material already supplied by Burroughs on the uses of the tape recorder for purposes of breaking down old image tracks:

you can learn to do these things record a sentence and speed it up now try imitating your accelerated voice play a sentence backwards and learn to unsay what you just said . . . such exercises bring you a liberation from old association locks . . . take any text speed it up slow it down run it backwards inch it and you will hear words that were not in the original recording new words made by the machine different people will scan out different words of course but some of the words are quite clearly there anyone can hear them words which were not in the original tape but which are in many cases relevant to the original text as if the words themselves had been interrogated and forced to reveal their hidden meanings it is interesting to record these words words literally made by the machine itself you can carry this experiment further. . . . (P. 206)

any number can play
yes any number can play anyone with a tape recorder controlling the sound track can influence and create events the tape recorder experiments here will show you how. . . . (P. 207)

you will learn to give the cues you will learn to plant events and concepts after analyzing recorded conversations you will learn to steer a conversation where you want it to go the physiological liberation achieved as word lines of controlled association are cut will make you more efficient in reaching your objectives whatever you do you will do it better. . . . (P. 208)

the use of irrelevant response will be found effective in breaking obsessional association tracks all association tracks are obsessional

listen to your present time tapes and you will begin to see who you are and what you are doing here mix yesterday in with today and hear tomorrow your future rising out of old recordings you are a programmed tape recorder set to record and play back

who programs you (P. 213)

What Gysin seems to be saying is that each person should be a novelist, creating his own life, controlling his own destiny, writing his own texts for past, present, and future. The tape recorder is no longer material for party games.

Unfortunately, though, Gysin's obsession with the tape recorder begins to sound increasingly like the mad scientist who wants to rule the world. It is difficult to believe that the Machine as God will not lead ultimately to a more mechanized life than the one he is trying to lead us away from. Although Burroughs is deeply indebted to Gysin for his own theories, he seems much more aware of a different set of consequences that might follow from such extended use of machines. In one section of *The Ticket That Exploded,* he seems to be building to the same kind of fervor we have traced in Gysin's chapter, but Burroughs ends by satirizing his own obsession:

So record the whole war with its battles and sieges, victories and defeats, monumental fuck-ups and corny songs—Lovers exchange tapes—You understand nobody has to be there at all—So why ask questions and why answer?—Why give orders and why make speeches?—Why not leave your tape with her tape and dispense with sexual contact?—And then?—Since no one is there to listen, why keep running the tape?—Why not shut the whole machine off and go home? Exactly what i intend to do Turn all my tapes over to Rewrite and go home— (P. 168)

This would seem to be the ultimate abdication of the artist who has finally set all his machines in motion until they take over so completely that he finds himself no longer needed to tend the shop. The tape recorder sounds very similar here to the talking asshole in *Naked Lunch* which finally devours its owner. All the machines are humming away in the empty laboratory, but the artist is nowhere to be found, and the reader is left on his own to create his own entertainment.

Certainly there are some interesting things here:

orgasms of memory fingers—(P. 107)

(Sound of liquid typewriters plopping into gelatine)—(P. 21)

Naked dream (P. 65)

Naked good-bye (P. 66)

Naked ghost people—(P. 67)

Naked brain (P. 67)

Some striking images, some weird word combinations (all to destroy the word, "naked"? Add to the list Naked Candy from *The Soft Machine* and *Naked Lunch*, and we have surely broken through any old image tracks set up by *that* word!) and an awful lot of preaching in between. Maybe *we* had better go home, too.

Nova Express includes much of the material from Burroughs' other novels, and by now the junk and virus metaphors have become as stale as our old associations of "naked" with "bodies." Burroughs here is still trying to explode familiar connotations of words in order to create new life; he is still trying to dissociate words from images as a means toward reaching silence; and he still spends most of his time explaining his approach rather than making it work for us. We have seen that Robbe-Grillet often used the language of instruction in order to divest his words of metaphorical connotations, but in Burroughs' novels, the language of instruction is actually used for purposes of instruction, and the result seems increasingly to resemble a tract much more than a novel. Whereas Robbe-Grillet was content to address the reader directly about his artistic theories in a collection of nonfiction essays, then let his art speak for itself in separate books of fiction, Burroughs insists on throwing theory and practice together with the result that his novels have no life of their own but seem to contain by chance whatever is found between the covers.

"The enemy exists where no life is,"[6] says Burroughs, and so *Nova Express* becomes another attempt to expose the enemy for us—the word, the image, the junk, the virus which eats away at our tissues and sends us into a state of mental stupor where we are blinded to the possibilities of our lives.

As we have seen image *is* junk. . . . There is no true or real "reality"— "Reality" is simply a more or less constant scanning pattern—The scanning pattern we accept as "reality" has been imposed by the controlling power on this planet. . . . (Pp. 51–52)

Clearly, we must take a cure for the junk habit that is restricting our sense of reality, and Burroughs continues to find hope in the equivalent of apomorphine—the resistant drug that enabled him to break his own junk habit:

6. William S. Burroughs, *Nova Express* (New York: Grove Press, 1965), p. 14. All future references to this edition will be noted in parentheses.

"Yes—Apomorphine combats parasite invasion by stimulating the regulatory centers to normalize metabolism—A powerful variation of this drug could de-activate all verbal units and blanket the earth in silence, disconnecting the entire heat syndrome." (P. 40)

There does come a time when the reader himself would indeed enjoy a bit of silence, but Burroughs' constant banter seems only to intrude on our senses, keeping the quiet away. Finally, we come to the conclusion that great—and conscious—fiction may itself induce the highest, purest, most appropriate form of silence. The work of art that arrests us seems to freeze our own thoughts and keep us suspended in a timeless, spaceless world where our minds are quiet and watchful as our senses take in new experience. Burroughs' novels *rant*—they *will* not keep quiet— whereas those of Robbe-Grillet and Genet create a hushed feeling which is really the result of concentration. The novelist that doth protest too much stands at the door of his creation, keeping us out. There is no room for *us* at the still center of the novel's world.

Burroughs' theories are fascinating, and his experiments often exciting, but there is such a rush of sensations, such a conglomeration of diverse effects that we are distracted, rather than liberated, in his later novels. Only *Naked Lunch* seems somehow to remain vivid in the memory as an experience that has engrossed us sufficiently to cut out the outside noise of the world which confuses us. True, it contains as much chaos as life itself, but it also creates, ultimately, its own system which justifies and compensates for the confusion it forces us to submit to. Ironically, too, it is most effective because its effects have been most controlled by the artist. Theories and techniques may be interesting, but they can never count for much until they are embodied as vital experience; and it is the novel which has so often given life to ideas by using the art of fiction to humanize, formalize, or intensify them into emotional realities. Burroughs finally fails the reader not because his experiments are too radical for us to adjust to, but because most of his novels do not offer us *enough* to adjust to. Life slips in and out of his works, but is rarely held there long enough for the novel to begin breathing its own life. And for the reader, that is all that ever really matters.

Part III
Conclusion

11

Some Conclusions: The Damage Done

i. Some Conclusions

*E*mma Bovary's world is dull and common-place, yet the reader's impression of her surroundings is extremely different from her own because *our* vision has been infused with and conditioned by an imaginative force which transforms the most trivial objects into forms of stunning beauty and fascination. Here is a typical description from the book: "Daylight was fading. The muslin sash deepened the twilight; and the gilt barometer had just caught a ray of sun and was blazing in the mirror between the lacy edges of the coral."[1] While Emma might dream of exotic settings in which her romantic dreams would be fulfilled, she would never see the barometer in her own room as the reader has been made to see it. If she did, she would not have to leave the provinces, for what Flaubert has shown us is the imagination's power to convert whatever it touches. By depicting the barometer as reflected in the mirror at the exact instant it has caught a ray of sun, Flaubert turns this mundane, unexciting object into a dazzling image of beauty, mystery, and brilliance. And once the imagination has perceived the barometer in this new and striking way, reality itself (in this case, our standard, conven-

1. Gustave Flaubert, *Madame Bovary*, trans. Francis Steegmuller (New York: Random House, 1957), p. 175.

tional conceptions of barometers) must be modified to include the imaginative insight. Probably the greatest irony of the book is Justin's idealization of Emma herself, but the irony is also the main point: the imagination's superiority to a reality which it renders pliable to its own purposes. The character most out of touch with reality in the book is not Emma, but Homais, who lives in a flat world untouched by the imagination.

Although *Madame Bovary* is a conventional novel, the theory behind it points to the most characteristic quality of the modern experimental novel. Flaubert himself envisioned a work of "pure" art—one which refined its style to the point where it could dispense with all subject matter and be concerned solely with itself. This does indeed seem to be what the experimental work has done, and the result is a new conception of the novel which seems at first chaotic because it has shifted the old relationship between art and reality. The latter is no longer seen as a constant and verifiable experience, but rather, one that can be altered at will. Imagination, finally, *becomes* reality.

While we have seen that Beckett, Genet, Robbe-Grillet, and Burroughs tend to lead us in very different directions, we can still find some striking similarities among them, and the most significant is surely an increasing emphasis on the imagination at the expense of an urgent concern with reality. Whereas the traditional novel was devoted to a representational portrayal of the world from which it attempted to siphon off meaning, the experimental novel—working on an assumption of chaos which grants life no meaning at all—has become a nonrepresentational experience operating within its own closed system, where it has freed itself from obligations to reality, morality, philosophy, and psychology. As a result, we must put aside many of our traditional expectations for a form that renders increasingly private experience on the theory that the only reality that matters is the one perceived by and transmuted through the imagination.

Also common to the four experimentalists we have discussed is a fascination with dream. Kafka has, of course, prepared the way for a novel immersed in the subconscious world, but the novelists we have discussed are less concerned with using dream to express vision than to demonstrate the absolute freedom of the imagination. Dream liberates the imagination in time and space and also allows for a highly personal symbolic system. Finally, the dream experience is valued for its gratuitousness: while the mind is at rest, the imagination can play with images, sensations, and experiences which the mind has received but has proven unable to work with. The experimental novel often requires, therefore, that we suspend our rational powers before entering the work and, once inside, content ourselves (as we do in dreams) with observing, responding to, and absorbing experience, rather than trying to make sense of it by reasoning or unifying our impressions into useful knowledge. Since true knowledge is impossible to attain, we must be willing to suspend our rational faculties and respond instead with our *own* imaginations.

Another idea shared by these writers is the inadequacy of language in describing ineffable experience. Beyond this, however, is an even more serious problem: the tendency of language to falsify the reality it attempts to convey. While Robbe-Grillet finds a solution in stripping language of its connotative quality, and Genet is able to regenerate language's ability to communicate by immersing it in the context of dreams, Beckett and Burroughs are sufficiently disenchanted to want to annihilate it altogether. In a work which holds silence to be the greatest value, *all* language acts as so much interference to the novelist's goal. Certainly, this must be the oddest problem of the works we have discussed here. There is something terribly pathetic about an art struggling against its own medium, and I cannot see how such a rebellion could prove productive. In one of the most eloquent passages from *Madame Bovary*, Flaubert, too, despairs of language's inadequacy, yet his lament is a traditional one:

the truth is that fullness of soul can sometimes overflow in utter vapidity of language, for none of us can ever express the exact measure of his needs or his thoughts or his sorrows; and human speech is like a cracked kettle on which we tap crude rhythms for bears to dance to, while we long to make music that will melt the stars. (Pp. 215–16)

Just as Coleridge's *Dejection* ode is a great poem about the poet's loss of his creative powers, many writers (such as Conrad and Woolf) have recognized the futility of trying to express the ineffable even while doing it so brilliantly. Words, it is true, cannot express our profoundest feelings, but they *can* evoke an emotional equivalent that comes as close as human beings really need to in order to understand one another. Flaubert's statement itself is a paradox, for he has found a metaphor to suggest language's inadequacy that asserts implicitly language's victory. Genet and

Robbe-Grillet have met the challenge of their medium's deficiency by seeking new ways to rejuvenate it, while Beckett and Burroughs seem uninterested in constructive solutions—only silence will satisfy them. While one can sympathize with their attitude, one must also recognize its absurdity. A work built by language must respect it to the extent of being willing to work with it in new ways; otherwise, the result is a literary masochism which can solve the problem only by destroying itself.

Self-destruction: this is another concern of all the experimentalists we have mentioned. Once the artist feels he has nothing worthwhile to say about human experience, yet still finds himself writing about it, he concludes that his art is gratuitous and so takes steps to insure its destruction. Related to this is the author's self-consciousness, a result of his refusal to provide an illusion which the reader might want to take for reality. These writers insist that the reader recognize the artifice of art, and appreciate *it* rather than any accidental applications to reality (though Burroughs is at times an exception to this new rule). The value of art lies in its illusion itself, not in the illusion's references to outside systems. The novelist's self-consciousness as artist leads to a gratuitous art form, and art can prove its gratuitousness only by its willingness to destroy what it has created, thereby emphasizing the creative process itself as the primary value of the work, rather than any end—such as meaning—that might have resulted from it. Art works for self-revelation, not for revelation of reality.

Finally, all four writers are obsessed with chaos or, at least, some aspect or consequence of a chaotic world. Traditional novelists searched for and found meaning to life, and the authors discussed in the first section searched for meaning, but found none. Nevertheless, their novels depicted the tension of their struggle with a hostile reality. But the quest is behind us now: these avant-garde novelists have no interest in conducting the search for meaning. It is, in fact, just because they have accepted chaos as a basic, indisputable fact of life that their novels have had to make radical departures from a tradition which unified the experiences of living. When unification has become impossible, the artist who still has a need to do *something* with the experiences which define life, must, simply, find new things to do with them. Beckett, Genet, Robbe-Grillet, and Burroughs have all done just that.

ii. The Damage Done

As the experimental novel becomes increasingly unfamiliar to us *as* novel, we can recognize the consequences of chaotic vision on the form's traditional components. It might be worthwhile, therefore, to consider those components which have been ignored or reconceived by the experimental novelist. While some seem easily dispensable, others are so basic to the form that we may indeed wonder whether a drastic redefinition is necessary before we can distinguish the modificiations from the mutations. Those components which *seemed* dispensable were, to be sure, very quickly dispensed with by the writers mentioned in the first section as having been instrumental at finding ways to incorporate chaos into the novel. But the following—all of which have been tampered with by those authors who have thrown the novel into chaos—would seem crucial to the novel's very identity, and their distortion or disappearance presents serious problems for the novel's survival.

Since anything that happens must happen *somewhere, setting* would seem to be a natural part of the novel's life, yet it is obvious that for writers such as Beckett and Burroughs, our traditional idea of setting must be extended to include a vacuum and a Reality Studio, both of which have lost their place in time and space. Perhaps we should redefine setting to mean context rather than location, for the novel submerged in dream will not provide coherent transitions as it drifts around on temporal and spatial planes; and the novel drowning in the deepest layers of the subconscious will not offer much of a view (although Beckett *is* willing to mix a little gray into his darkness). The novel based on accident certainly cannot be expected to stay very long in *any* place—not even long enough, in most cases, to bother describing the change in atmosphere. We can expect setting to become increasingly neglected by the experimental writers.

Point of view has been played with freely even by traditional novelists, but the experimentalists have done some very strange things indeed. We can read an entire novel by Beckett, Burroughs, or Robbe-Grillet without having the slightest idea of the speaker's identity. Even when the point of view is consistent, restricted, and significant—as it is in Robbe-Grillet, for example—its identity often remains indefinite. Apparently, we must accustom ourselves to a speaker or mind which is not only Unnamable, but also invisible. This requires a much greater adjustment on our part than the lack of setting, but perhaps it is not surprising that a work which calls everything into question must break down every source of stability and security that would help us feel some control over the experience encountered. Point of view may well become increasingly complex and indistinct as a new relativistic concept of the novel continues to rebel against the traditional one moored to a single dimension. Cubism, as the delineation of multiperspectives on a single plane, is likely to be used increasingly as a major literary–philosophical technique.

Metaphor, too, seems to be disappearing rapidly. Whereas The Trial and Lord Jim are both metaphors for the inexplicable and elusive aspects of our lives, in a work such as *The Unnamable*, the metaphor *itself* is inconclusive and elusive. Robbe-Grillet, of course, refuses to let metaphor even enter his work, and Burroughs, intent on breaking down control systems, seems also to want to minimize its influence and effect (even though *Naked Lunch* is built on metaphorical foundations, one surmises that Burroughs would now repudiate his earlier methods). The result for the reader is increasing confusion in an experience that seems flatter, emptier, and duller once the richness of metaphorical expression has been siphoned off. Because metaphor leads to meaning, we can expect to see its importance diminish in a novel which tends to make much of its absence. The loss here is enormous for the reader's mind, emotions, and aesthetic sensibility; but the experimentalists seem so insistent on doing away with it that metaphor is apt to become less conspicuous, less meaningful, and generally more abused (by being inserted only so that we can watch it break down) as the novel continues to sink deeper into chaos.

It is astounding, really, that *language* itself is fighting for its life in the new chaotic novel, yet the writers' obsession with silence threatens the very medium of their form, and the attempt in Burroughs and Robbe-Grillet to rid language of its emotional connotations threatens to alienate the reader who wants to have his emotions fed rather than starved to death by the novel. So long as the novel exists, it simply cannot do without language, but it is obvious that language will continue to suffer at the hands of these artists seeking to degrade, destroy, or constrict it until all "poetry" has been shaken out. Actually, writers have always had to remold their language to render it capable of new expression,

so novelists such as Robbe-Grillet and Genet are very likely opening up new possibilities as they tear down language's traditional
role of rendering experience articulate. But as the subject matter
of experimental writers becomes increasingly ineffable and as
language is seen to limit by preconditioning our very ability to
perceive reality, the novelist's disdain for it is likely to continue.
We can prepare ourselves for more radical transmutations in language as the chaotic novel persists in trying to elude the tools
created to shape order and precision. A language that clarifies is
apt very soon to seem something from the remote past.

    Plot already seems so. The novel that tells a story has by now
become quaint. Since story unifies experience, it is anathema for
the novelist of chaos, and according to Robbe-Grillet, is gone forever. Plot, he insists, presupposes a world of rational order, a view
of life predicated on convictions of stability. Twentieth-century
man occupies a world so different, however, that the very concept of a plotted story becomes absurdly inappropriate for the
contemporary work. Certainly, the later novels of Beckett and
Burroughs would affirm this. Yet I doubt that story will continue
to have no part in the novel's future development. Aside from
the fact that its disappearance has left a hole in the experimental
novel and reduced it, in most cases, to a terribly tedious and
disappointing experience, the story seems to me still a valid literary format—even for a chaotic novel—because it most resembles
the structure of men's lives. It is not simply that stories excite our
emotions (as children, we are entranced by them, and even the
most sophisticated never seem really to outgrow them) but they
also offer more stimulus for the imagination than any vacuum.
Our own lives probably provide the most grist for the imagination, and they do so quite often *as* stories: we wonder how and
whether certain aspects of our lives will be resolved, and even if
we do not expect resolution, we continue to speculate on the
various forms chaos might take. Actually, chaos itself is often a
story—a story of the moment, hidden by time; a story without
perspective, detachment, or temporal distance (the difference
between a nightmare and reality is that the latter context allows
us time to adjust to the most hideous events, whereas the world
of dream keeps us locked into a state of perpetual presence so
that horror is never mollified through the passage of time). Finally, the history of man—his life—embodies both types of stories:
we exist from moment to moment, but we also exist from day to

day, year to year, decade to decade. The impression of chaos, then, may be in reality simply a story from a different perspective; we sit on top of an event, or inside it as it unravels—but even if the shapes are changing from one instant to another; even if, at moments, they are not even recognizable *as* shapes, the very fact of their flux implies that a story is going on. When Shakespeare has Touchstone say:

> 'Tis but an hour ago since it was nine;
> And after one hour more 'twill be eleven;
> And so, from hour to hour, we ripe and ripe,
> And then, from hour to hour, we rot and rot;
> And thereby hangs a tale.
>   —*As You Like It*, II, vii, 25–28

he knew the tale could place any time, at nine *or* eleven, or from nine *to* eleven. Either way, our lives do become a series of stories, which may be fragmentary, inconclusive, or completely chaotic, but which definitely embody as many episodes and experiences as those who lived out their lives before the twentieth century. The carefully plotted, beautifully contrived story will not reappear while the chaotic novel holds its ground, but *some* form of story might well return. If it does not, the novel is likely to expire from sheer inertia.

As experience dissolves, man himself disappears from the novel. In what may well be the single greatest blow to the form, the experimental novelist has removed *character* from the fiction that always seemed to be built around him. Beckett has by now pretty much eliminated character from his work, and while Robbe-Grillet and Burroughs have a few people appear, they are always flat and unimportant to the novels' impact. Robbe-Grillet uses his characters as so many objects, and Burroughs, resorting to caricature, provides his people with no depth or recognizable reality. Truthfully, it is almost impossible to imagine the survival of the novel without characters. Readers do not want textbooks or tracts to intensify the experience of living; they want works with human beings moving around inside them, even if they must be as broken-down as Molloy and Malone. One needs to recognize life in the novel, and the fiction that eliminates characters usually eliminates life at the same time. Man may be seen in new ways (as fragmented, inscrutable, elusive, monstrous, or whatever), but he must be *seen* if the experimental novel is to have any life span at all. Robbe-Grillet has argued that because his works emanate from and are restricted to the consciousness of man, they are therefore as fully human as those in more traditional works. His point is an important one but not entirely convincing. Even the reader who agrees with the necessity for a new concept of the novel is apt to *miss* the character who is recognizably human—that is, a creature with depth. *In the Labyrinth* does seem to offer a solution for the human-oriented reader of the New Novel by suggesting emotional depth in characters who remain nevertheless beyond our understanding. The soldier is still a very different sort of character from, say, Lord Jim, but his presence does satisfy our need to find in the novel an experience we can relate to in some way. The novel devoid of character can make little impact on us, and so will cease to be read.

A novelist without purpose seems almost unthinkable, yet we have only to read Robbe-Grillet to see that *theme*, as controlling idea, has lost its traditional value in the gratuitous novel. As the intellect's influence wanes in the experimental novel and as art becomes increasingly concerned with itself, theme will no doubt sink deeper and deeper into the texture of the work until it becomes indistinguishable from the imaginative process which had previously been used to explore the vital issues of living. Now that the imagination seems satisfied with expressing nothing more than its own freedom, the novel will probably continue to liberate itself from the necessity of *saying* anything. Beckett's recent title, *Stories and Texts for Nothing,* may well be indicative of this new direction.

The novel can probably survive the loss of theme, but it may not be able to surmount the loss of *vision:* an attitude toward the universe that determines, shapes, and controls the artist's use of particular techniques to make his sense of life accessible to the reader. In Beckett's work, for example, we can trace a vision becoming progressively more private and parochial. Whereas the conventional novel tended to see man's suffering as ennobling, Beckett has always seen it as pathetic, degrading, disgusting, and humiliating. But the chaos of his later works seems to result from the loss of any value system whatever, as all meaning evaporates in a parched, dried-out world. Impairment of vision here does not mean necessarily that the writer *sees* less but that he appears to *feel* less about what he sees; we miss an overriding attitude that condemns or approves of what is being depicted. Without an attitudinal frame of reference, we can draw no clear conclusions from what the novel has enabled us to experience.

Traditionally vision has communicated itself to the reader through particular people and experiences whose *universality* made them accessible to us. Certainly, the most irritating quality of many experimental writers is their lack of universality and wholeness. They tend to fasten their attention on one facet of existence (such as dream, disorientation, or the workings of the imagination), then to extend their investigation at the exclusion of other aspects of experience. To detach one element is to lose the sense of the whole, its resemblance to a reality we can all recognize. The result, many times, is a freak world composed entirely of those "unreal" moments when meaning drains away (similar to Camus's example of watching a man in a phone booth whose existence, in an instant of absurdity, becomes suddenly unfathomable). The idea is certainly valid, but it must be placed in its context before it can be made applicable, recognizable, convincing, and forceful. Is it the context of a dream? Then that dream must be rendered for us with full artistic integrity. When I dream of myself, I know who that self is, and my dream becomes powerfully symbolic only to others who know me, too, as the product of specific experiences and impressions. That no one can ever know anyone or anything *really* is irrelevant, because in practical terms the world is still accessible to us; both people and feelings do impress us with a force and identity that make them real. Camus, aware as anyone of the impenetrability of existence, still asserts its familiarity:

It is probably true that a man remains forever unknown to us and that there is in him something irreducible that escapes us. But *practically* I know men and recognize them by their behavior, by the totality of their deeds, by the consequences caused in life by their presence. Likewise, all those irrational feelings which offer no purchase to analysis. I can define them *practically*, by gathering together the sum of their consequences in the domain of the intelligence, by seizing and noting all their aspects, by outlining their universe. (*The Myth of Sisyphus*, p. 9)

Because they focus on that instant when the familiar becomes strange, the conveyance of vision by many contemporary writers depends on their ability to capture and hold that instant when reality seems unreal. But the universe must be outlined for us; we must be allowed to see the man in the phone booth before we can understand the feelings evoked by the experience. Similarly, the line must be drawn between sanity and insanity. We all embody elements of the insane person, but these elements are only a part of us. Once they are detached from the full context of our lives, we become totally private individuals, and at that point, no communication is possible, no common experience is recognized, and literature has no reason to exist as genuine probing of the human experience. Unless the experimental writer becomes more willing to universalize his private vision by providing a fully-drawn context which makes it accessible to us, the novel will alienate the reader more and more until it will cease to matter, if not *mean*, as vital experience. The work that scorns communication through forms which render vision is doomed to suffocate within its own closed system.

In *The Myth of Sisyphus,* Camus points to the primary problem for the modern novelist by wondering whether the absurd work of fiction can keep its integrity when the form itself tempts explanations, interpretations, and conclusions. The answer comes back from the experimental novelists as a resounding "No!" which in turn justifies their abdication of *structure,* the one component most closely tied up with the novel's identity *as* novel. While artists have always broken conventions, they have usually been careful to replace them or, at least, not to break any more conventions than the form could bear without becoming indistinguishable from other experience. The novelists discussed in the first section of this study did set limits to their freedom, but the antiformalist creators of the experimental novel have tried to defeat the very form in which they are working. The result is less often exhilarating and liberating than it is merely frustrating and self-negating. The artist's destruction of his form can lead only to a dead end because fiction *is* form: form structuring, controlling, managing feeling. Take the form away, and you may have something very worthwhile, but you will not have the novel and the particular experience it can offer. Once structure has been removed from the novel, the result is simply a different form, rather than an enlargement or extension of the original. So art is false to life—of course it is, but that is why it exists *in addition to* life. Art can deliver a certain kind of experience which will be relevant to life, which may imitate life, contain truths applicable to life, or simply appeal by way of beauty and power to something deep within us. But it never promises us life itself!

In drama, for example, the actors are never supposed to break character—they act as though no one were watching them—but that is the form. Take it away, throw the actors into the audience's laps, have them "be themselves," and you might end up with a very interesting, exciting, inherently dramatic experience, but it will not be the experience of art—it will be the experience of life. The soul of art is its indirectness. A painting of a wolf will not lunge out and bite you, nor will a written description of one, a musical imitation of one, etc. You can experience profound feelings such as fear, horror, or repugnance, but within a circle of certain safety—the killers in *Lear* will not get to you; their threat is on quite another level. If they *could* get to you, the resulting experience would be Hitler's concentration camps, war, or whatever: you would have *life*, in short, not art—which might be legitimate, except that you cannot *learn* too much (or even have time to know your feelings) while you are right in the middle of grappling with a bear. It takes distance, safety, reflection, perspective, *indirect* participation to reach general conclusions from the particular experience. A person in pain is too much involved with *that* to reflect on its human meaning, relevance, or universal applications. I remember once touring a national park with a group of companions who had been chattering continually as we marveled at the beauty of the setting. At one point, we had to climb a very steep hill, and suddenly we all became silent as each person was isolated in his own discomfort—that struggle of the breath, the effort of pushing upward against gravity, the burden and exhaustion of our bodies. Only when we had reached the top of the hill and I had caught my own breath did I see the analogy to the ultimate isolation of each individual trapped inside his suffering—knowing others were suffering in the same way yet still unable to share the experience with them. Only then did it *become* an experience.

The implication for the novel is clear. A form created and developed to embody our lives in an experience that life by itself does not offer can be opened up only so far before it swims out into the chaos it had previously been able to render a part of our conscious existence. By formalizing experience, art brings us closer to it and enables us to assimilate the deepest realities of our lives. Divested of form, art *becomes* (rather than *represents*) chaos, and so can offer us nothing more than the confused impressions of a life continuously fought with but never apprehended through our imaginations. By diving directly into reality, the truly formless novel actually pushes it farther away from us.

12

Toward
A New Theory

I've done writing that I thought was interesting, experimentally, but simply not readable.
—William S. Burroughs

What, then, do you want from me?
—An anonymous modern reader

I remember taking weekly trips to the library
as a child, and feeling each time the importance of my role as
selector of the next week's literary material. Completely innocent of the difference between Thomas Mann and Edna Ferber, I
felt the weight of decision-making in a world without definite
standards. I finally did choose the Edna Ferber book because it
had the nicer cover, and I also liked the feel of its pages better,
the way the book fit into my hands, etc. As I grew older, though,
my tastes naturally became more sophisticated: I developed the
typical adolescent aversion to "description" and looked, instead,
for the books with the most dialogue—these would be easier to
read—and those with the fewest pages. Already burdened by recognition of my limited life span, I suddenly wanted to read as
many books as quickly as possible. Joseph Conrad was anathema
to me; J. D. Salinger was beloved. Even a beautiful cover combined with soft, yellowing pages (my favorite) would never have
tempted me to sign out *Lord Jim.*

By the time I was a college student, I had become enough of a
snob to never make the mistake of mentioning my former love
for Edna Ferber without a good amount of self-mockery. George
Eliot, on the other hand, *was* respectable, and I doted on her. I

recall very vividly the feeling of genuine sadness as I got down to the last pages of *Adam Bede, The Mill on the Floss,* and *Middlemarch;* I did not want these novels to end. I enjoyed them the way I enjoyed ice-cream cones, pizza, and popcorn, and I was always quite unhappy to note the experience consuming itself as the cone got smaller, the pizza colder, the popcorn bag emptier, and the pages fewer. I was, in short, engrossed in the books—often almost spellbound by the characters and stories. My own life seemed thin and limited by comparison, and I came to the novel for intensity of experience which my life was not supplying in sufficient doses. One summer, I had a very dull job which did, however, permit time for reading; I remember the books I read that summer as seeming far more real to me than anything that was happening around me. I walked among office workers but lived among the Brothers Karamozav, Lady Chatterley and her lover, Tom Jones, Madame Bovary, Meursault, Ahab, Pip, Gatsby, and the like. My emotions fed out to these characters much more than to any of the real people surrounding me, and I appreciated the novel as a means to knowing and feeling my inner life more deeply.

I never did outgrow this emotional attachment to novels, but eventually, I found an intellectual need asserting itself, too: I now reread *Crime and Punishment* for its ideas as well as its excitement, and began to gravitate toward such writers as Mann, Gide, Conrad, James, Joyce, Camus, Kafka, Woolf, and others who dealt with the subjects that were becoming the most significant themes of my mental life. I wanted to explore how brilliant thinkers had tried to resolve ideas of life, death, time, art, and suffering. It was now the philosophical spirit of the novel that I most respected, and a book that settled for reaching my emotions while bypassing by mind seemed to debase the art of the novel.

The last stage of my lifelong intimacy with the novel was an aesthetic one: finally fascinated by the form itself from the standpoint of the artist and critic, I considered my earlier approaches to the novel parochial and "amateurish." One must read the novel as a student of literature—with detachment, objectivity, and intellectual insight. It was with this attitude that I first came to the experimental novel.

And suddenly I realized that I rarely "enjoyed" reading novels anymore. I worked hard at them until they became so much work. I would "appreciate" a book without really caring for it.

And I almost never felt any sadness, but only relief, as I got closer to the conclusion. The novel was no longer the dynamic experience it had once been for me: it did not grasp, compel, absorb me. I was reading the contemporary works that should have been the most relevant to my existence, but reading began more and more to seem tedious activity. Anyway, everybody prefers the cinema nowadays, and the novel seems less and less crucial to a sensitive person's life.

It is not just me, of course. Something has changed in our world, and because the contemporary novel is merely reflecting that change, it tends to alienate us. Anyone truly concerned with the novel's future wants it to go on, modifying itself as necessary to represent and generate new kinds of experiences. At the same time, though, most of us are probably afraid of terribly radical changes, because they tend to dispense with just those features of the novel that we most prized. As a result, it becomes extremely difficult to evaluate modern experimentalists who have transformed the traditional novel beyond recognition. To be closed to what they are doing may mean obscuring for ourselves an important step in the novel's evolutionary process, yet to accept every experiment means to surrender those critical standards used for the traditional novel.

The matter cannot be resolved here, but I have cited my own experiences with the novel in order to raise again the question on which any critical theory must be founded—i.e., what do we expect from the novel? What do we want it to do? And right away, I think we have the right to demand that the novel be readable, engrossing, accessible, enjoyable. Let it be new, let it be different, but let it be worth reading. And what books are worth reading? Any which justify themselves as legitimate experiences which somehow supplement our own living. A legitimate experience I would call any which we do not consider a waste of time. And a waste of time is time spent needlessly—in repetition of what has already been experienced. Thus, it would be a waste of time for art to re-create our lives so exactly that we can no longer distinguish between them. The novel must offer something more, something less, or something different—it should not just offer more of the same.

And it should be interesting not only as a theory, but again, as an experience. More than anything I would like a contemporary novel that flouts as many of the old standards as it likes, one that seems radically different from the traditional novel of plot, character, setting, structure, etc.—one, in short, that has almost nothing in common with the works of George Eliot—yet one which will make me feel the same sadness as I get close to the ending, and realize that there is so little left of the experience providing such pleasure. An experiment must be evaluated by its results, and unless the product is a novel that seems vital, absorbing, and powerful, then the experiment should be considered a failure.

There are a good many recent critics who have started calling for a new approach to literary criticism—one that responds in a human way to the work under consideration. I applaud such an approach and see it as crucial to significant criticism. Of course we are obligated to be sensible about all this: to understand what the author is trying to do before we judge his success or failure; we don't want to rebel against the unfamiliar just because it makes us feel uncomfortable. But neither must we, on the other hand, be so impressed with the theory behind a difficult work that we forget to consider whether its difficulty is justifiable. In all the criticism I've read on *The Unnamable* and *How It Is*, for example, I did not come across one critic who called these works unreadable. I have a great deal of respect for Beckett, and even for a work such as *The Unnamable*, but I must say the book gave me almost no pleasure. Even after one understands what Beckett is trying to do, and even if one happens to feel affinity for his view of life, he cannot necessarily forgive the writer who blurs his eyes and mind and causes his spirit to sag with one intolerably long paragraph, full of repetitious effects. Theoretically, I sympathize with the fragmented vision that produced *How It Is*, but I find the novel itself infuriatingly inaccessible, private, and tedious. My own life is too short to be bothered with a novel which offers so little pleasure, yet demands such fatiguing mental labor. How much patience, really, must we have with a writer so obsessed with achieving silence that he regards language as his prime enemy? Or Robbe-Grillet: his critics recount the characteristics of his works, explain the reasoning behind his theories, but never mention the tedium of reading most of his books.

With the increased emphasis placed on subjectivity by almost all avant-garde writers, it seems odd that contemporary criticism has resorted almost exclusively to highly objective, analytical responses to their works. But an Aristotelian approach is really inappropriate for discussions of avant-garde fiction; Coleridge is much closer to the contemporary sensibility and expression. The Romantics were, after all, thoroughly committed to many of the principles (such as imagination, subjectivity, individuality, enthusiasm, emotion, free thought, and free form) most cherished by contemporary experimental novelists. Earlier in this century, T. S. Eliot changed our tastes and rescued us from the excesses of Romanticism, but the classical sensibility, however well suited to the modern writers, seems terribly awkward when applied to contemporary ones. While many experimentalists are determined to shock us out of our traditions, much of contemporary criticism provides a purely analytical perspective that would hardly indicate how much has gone awry. Perhaps we are now due for another shift in critical sensibility to bring us more into line with the radically different kind of fiction being produced in our post-modern age.

I do think we must begin to respond in more human terms to works which challenge not only our intellects, but also our moral systems, humanistic assumptions, and psychological needs. In our search for standards to distinguish the important experiment from the sophomoric one, we must be willing to consult the recesses of our own feelings and experiences, for it is at this psychic level that all great works of art ultimately register their impact. With his emphatic insistence on subjectivity, the contemporary creator gives the critic not only the freedom but the responsibility to do just that. Put another way, the responsible reader of today must be also a freer one.

Let us consider some of the possibilities opened up by the contemporary novelists I have discussed—typical of those willing to confront the huge amount of chaos in our lives, and courageous enough to seek a new form to express it. Beckett is the originator and probably still the master of the reductive novel. But where is he taking it (and us)? *The Unnamable* and *How It Is* flatten the form so successfully that there is almost nothing left for the reader to experience: drained of character, plot, metaphor, setting, coherence, and (in the case of *How It Is*) the very structure of the language, the novel has deflated itself more and more until it does seem just about empty. The process of ellipses promises ultimately to eliminate the novel out of existence. I see no future for the kind of novel Beckett is writing, and his last two works would indicate that the present itself is almost used up. *Molloy* and *Ma-*

lone Dies still have human elements, events, and language that communicates—even if it communicates confusion. But Malone's death seems so far to have marked the death of character in Beckett's novels—character, that is, as recognizable human beings—and having sacrificed so much already, the novel cannot withstand this final loss. It becomes hollow, flat, and repetitive. All experience and sensations become indistinguishable, and only a little babble is left to show the last remaining signs of life. But they are not life signs any more; they are the signs of existence only—consciousness is in a coma, and it's just a matter of a few more breaths now before annihilation is complete and the body can be formally pronounced dead. Beckett is a great novelist on the basis of his own novels that do live, but his course, if followed, will yield no more novelists at all. He is driving his form to extinction.

Burroughs has already done this. By surrendering authorial authority (yet overextending authorial intrusion), he has surrendered his claim for our attention. *Naked Lunch* is a brilliant chaotic novel—shocking, offensive, revolting, but also genuinely original, hilariously comic, intense, and compelling. Most of the confusion is purposeful and ultimately very effective. The experience for the reader is startling, but unique, powerful, and memorable. His other novels, however, can be dismissed as a kind of nonexperience for most readers. *Naked Lunch* was no accident, but *Nova Express* is. The art of accident is, I think, still a legitimate theory and promising new technique, but accident itself is not art. An image such as "Kotex hamburger" is surprising but not edifying, and as soon as such phrases lose their surprise (let's say, after Kotex hot dog, Kotex sundae, etc.), their value evaporates. Burroughs' imagination is fertile enough to supply far more striking, significant, and consistently memorable images than those he discovers by chance. And when the aim of his cutup method is not to shock, but simply to dull us into silence, the experience becomes totally unproductive. Great artists have always been able to knock us out of conventional control systems by their ability to see more deeply into things and to formalize what they see into phrases, poems, and novels that rejuvenate the language we exhaust daily into powerful expressions that penetrate our emotional lives and settle deep into our psychic memories. Silence itself is not a worthy goal unless it enables us to expand our feeling, thinking, and perception. "The deepest feeling always shows itself in silence," says Marianne Moore, and her poem is a testament to the experience which enthralls, stuns, awes us. Great art has always done this: the reader who has just put down *King Lear, The Sound and the Fury, The Sun Also Rises,* or *Paradise Lost* knows a profound, inner silence that the reader of *The Soft Machine* will never get close to. The great work of art induces silence by *reducing* us to silence, because our hushed minds need it in order to absorb an overwhelming experience. *That* silence is a productive one, whereas the silence that Burroughs offers is one of apathy, boredom, and intimidation. Anyone who has ever been inspired knows the silence of total concentration, and the novel at its best can produce this silence by inspiring the awe that necessitates it. After the sea has closed over Ahab, the reader of *Moby-Dick* can *feel* the quiet inside him. Burroughs fails, I think, because instead of producing works that will render us inarticulate, he produces inarticulate works. Still, I think his theories and techniques can offer something for the novel's future in an increasingly technological world. Once his techniques are brought under the artist's control, once the novelist is willing to accept the responsibility of reshaping his random discoveries into the ordered realm of art, he may well present us with a novel that will shock us into silence in a totally new way.

The noninterpretative novel conceived by Robbe-Grillet is also more exciting in theory than in practice, but a work such as *In the Labyrinth* proves its possibilities for a truly new and significant literary experience. *La Maison de Rendezvous* seems to me a step backward for Robbe-Grillet, for although it contains the immensely evocative powers of all his novels, it matters less as a human experience than as an intellectual one. Like *Jealousy* and *The Voyeur,* it intrigues us, but does not *touch* us deeply. These three novels are interesting as experiments, but somehow not fulfilling as experience. *In the Labyrinth,* however, is brilliantly successful as *both* experiment and experience; while *expressing* nothing but itself, it manages somehow to *evoke* much more. Life filters through the novel in an elusive yet powerful way that moves something deep within us—perhaps our sense that some reality has been caught, some aspect of what it means to be alive, to search, to suffer, and to remain always ignorant of the meaning of the experience, even while we feel its impact. Both as theorist and as practitioner, Robbe-Grillet has something new and valuable to offer in the development of the novel.

Genet has something valuable to offer too: himself. The sheer force and magnetism of his personality is almost enough in itself to extend our experience, but as an artist, too, he has much to contribute. By expanding the novel to embody the will of an omnipotent imagination, he has revolutionized methods of characterization, narrative, and symbolism. *Miracle of the Rose* is an imaginative feat of a new kind, and *Our Lady of the Flowers* is for me even more successful as a vital novel built from fragments distilled through the imagination and transformed into new ways of dealing with experience. The raw materials offered by life are important only to the degree that they suggest their own enrichment through the imaginative process which assigns them whatever role, value, and dream-reality it pleases; then proceeds to shape, purify, and intensify them into meaningful metaphors and symbols which assert the imagination's supremacy over reality. Genet loosens and alters the novel's form considerably, but only so that he can twist it to his own purposes. The important point, however, is that he provides a richness of texture and context through art that forces his vision to become ours. As long as we are in his novel, we are in his power, and that means that we see the world through an imagination that enriches, intensifies, and finally transcends it. Genet uses all the traditional features of the novel—character, episode, structure, setting, and language—but each is manipulated in a new way to render the reality of the author's inner life. At a time when the novel is forced to meet the challenge of new perspectives on reality or become hopelessly obsolete, Genet offers the form the freedom it needs in order to describe life in new ways.

Sterne, Melville, Conrad, Faulkner, Woolf, and Kafka all took the novel to the brink of chaos because it was only at that precipice that they could command the view they wanted their readers to see with them. Chaos was a frightening reality of life for all of them, and a work which failed to include it for consideration simply could not express their impression of the world. As artists, they were faced with the dilemma of presenting a vision through the components of a form which almost by definition defied chaotic vision. Each writer, then, found his own solution to overcome the form's natural resistance to inconclusive experience, yet each showed respect for the form's tradition by working within its system to extend the kind of experience it could project. And as each succeeded, the novel became increasingly sophisticated, versatile, and malleable. The ease with which it seemed able to accommodate new versions of philosophical, psychological, and emotional realities appeared to insure its continual growth as a literary form flexible enough to delineate a life that seemed increasingly meaningless.

And then suddenly the funeral arrangements were being made, the eulogies prepared, the form assigned to oblivion. The post-World-War II world sensed chaos as its deepest reality as every assumption which had previously provided meaning in life was challenged and fell. Camus' sense of absurdity seemed the most accurate description of a world that had become newly alienated from man. The attempt to unify experience was now seen to falsify experience; all reality was lost the instant artifice conquered it. It was no longer enough to modify the novel's form, for form itself blocked reality out and sealed meaning in. Life suddenly became more mysterious than it had ever seemed before, and only a fragmented art could render its chaos adequately. Aristotle had said that art was immune from reality; it could create an *impression* of ugliness, chaos, or mystery without becoming itself loathsome, formless and inscrutable. But can it? The contemporary novelist tends to think not. Certainly, one *can* represent chaos within a tightly structured form—but is the chaos thereby represented really the same kind that we live with and despair about? Of course not, since even the likes of Sterne, Melville, Conrad, Faulkner, Woolf, and Kafka had found meaningful forms to embody their sense of meaninglessness. The form itself falsified the vision; art and chaos are incompatible: the validity of the one negates the force of the other. It was hard to see how the novel could survive as an effective conveyor of life's absurdity.

Those who have loved the novel for having brought us into closer contact with reality must now embrace a new kind of novel if we expect it to contain a new vision of reality. (And the vision *is* new: Melville and Conrad may have contemplated nihilism, but man and morality were still whole organisms definable *as* men and as issues. Virginia Woolf saw the complexities of character, but she *did* see characters as people—human beings who lived and communicated their suffering. Faulkner and Kafka saw life as indecipherable, but it *did* have a setting; it *was* real and recognizable.) We must adjust to a novel without characters that resemble "real" people, without plots that resemble sections of our lives, without descriptions that resemble our own environments, without language that furthers thought and articulates our conscious and subconscious life.

This study has been very restrictive in its survey of those contemporary novelists experimenting with their form in order to preserve it as an expression of reality, but I have tried to represent what I think are the four most significant and extreme directions taken by avant-garde authors. Each writer has his following, each direction has its ramifications, each disciple has his own peculiarities. But essentially, most of the experimentalists are rooted in one of these traditions:

The *reductive* artist is squeezing the life out of the novel to get it down to the essentials of existence. He presents us with the world as vacuum, and the novel's success is evaluated to the degree that it has managed to empty itself out.

The *noninterpretative novel* insists that we acknowledge our ignorance of what life and reality are so that we can investigate them more objectively. We begin humbly enough by confronting appearances *as* appearances, trying to see them more clearly rather than trying to see *through* them more ingeniously. This means stripping language of its tendency to humanize what is not human to make us feel more secure in a world where nothing can be known but only imagined.

The *omnipotent novel* infuses language with even more richness and suggestiveness than previously characterized it in order to make the deeper world of dream accessible to us. It is the individual vision fed by the omnipotent imagination that is most valued here, for to find the means of expressing the deepest realities of oneself is the closest one can come to knowing reality. Furthermore, this reality is not the objective one most of us think we live in—*that* world is trivial—but the subjective one fed by our imaginations, which transform the world into whatever we wish it to be. Man, finally, creates the reality in which he lives.

The *random novel* tries to project experience onto many levels at once so that it can reproduce the way the human mind and nervous system actually take reality *in*. It seeks to assault us through multimedia techniques in order to jar us out of apathy, security, and conventionality. Above all, the random artist (who does not necessarily have to take us to the dead end that Burroughs has brought us to) wants to leave himself and his form *open;* he believes he can catch more of reality in his net if he resists hunting it down himself. He does not want to be predisposed to a reality he does not know. He is sick of the traditional egocentricity of the artist who writes to express himself and *his* version of reality. The random artist wants objectivity, and that means finding ways, first of all, to resist his own subjectivity. Accident is the answer: one surrenders artistic control in order to render reality more completely and more objectively, to give reality a chance to emerge, rather than to push it out with our egos (which know nothing, anyway). And finally, the random artist is least willing to make concessions to chaos; he would rather make concessions to art. Reality *is* chaotic, and can be expressed only *by* chaos, not within a form simply providing an *illusion* of chaos. Illusions falsify and thus misrepresent the real world.

Each type of artist tends to emphasize certain techniques and underplay or ignore others, but speaking generally, we can say that the reductive artist tends toward solipsism and phenomenology; the omnipotent novelist to expressionistic and surrealistic devices (to express the all-important inner life); the noninterpretative writer to cinematic means of representing time and space in constant flux; and the random author to multimedia effects, surrealism, and the grotesque. There is, of course, a good deal of overlapping, and there are many exceptions, but these techniques are almost indigenous to the particular conception of the novel characterizing each type.

What conclusions can we come to about the novels that have emerged from these four approaches to readapt the form to modern specifications? The results are so uneven that any attempt to make final judgments would be foolish. I have already given my opinions on the particular merits and disadvantages of each type of novel, but taken together, I would like to make one final observation. Although it is obvious that the novel need no longer present us with a realistic equivalent of life, it must, if it is to have any impact at all, provide us with an *emotional* equivalent. The novel must continue to offer an experience that justifies the time we take to read it by enlisting our emotions, as well as our intellects and aesthetic sensibilities. If life is truly chaotic, then the novel may not have anything more to *tell* us, but it can still make us *feel*, and that has always been its greatest asset. Yet there are very few experimental writers who are turning out memorable novels. Instead, the writer tends to be so tied down by his theory for the novel's regeneration that he loses sight of why the novel should be regenerated in the first place. In many cases, the result is a successful experiment and an unsuccessful novel. The contemporary novelist must remember that in a world where logic, meaning, and stability seem to be drifting farther and farther away from our control, our ability to feel deeply can still keep us human. The need to feel gets stronger the more our need to know is thwarted, and so when chaos has been totally accepted and there is nothing left to be said, the novel can still speak eloquently by communicating its chaos with compassion. Ever after we have denounced it as chaotic, we still want to know life more intimately and feel it more deeply, meaningless though it may be. So long as the novel feeds us life, we will feed back feeling—and as long as we continue to feel, the novel must hold a very special place in our lives.